THE INFINITE STORY

THE PAST AND PRESENT OF THE RĀMĀYAṆAS IN HINDI

THE INFINITE STORY

THE PAST AND PRESENT OF THE RĀMĀYAṆAS IN HINDI

Danuta Stasik

MANOHAR
2009

Published with the financial support of the Faculty of Oriental Studies,
University of Warsaw, Poland

First published 2009

ISBN 978–81–7304–815–9

Published by
Ajay Kumar Jain *for*
Manohar Publishers & Distributors
4753/23 Ansari Road, Daryaganj
New Delhi 110 002

Printed at
Salasar Imaging Systems
New Delhi 110 035

FOR KUNWAR NARAIN

CONTENTS

PREFACE

This book has grown out of years of study on the Rāmāyaṇa tradition in Hindi that over this period materialized in the form of different research papers and articles[1] as well as in my book *Opowieść o prawym królu*, published in Polish,[2] which is the fullest exposition of the results of my enquiries into the Rāmāyaṇa subject to date. *The Infinite Story* owes a great deal to *Opowieść o prawym królu* particularly with regard to its basic approach and chief conclusions. However, it also includes new materials that have brought about new views and findings. In that sense, the present study is both a sum of my previous research and its sequel.

The main goals of this work are twofold. Firstly, it seeks to analyse the development of the Rāmāyaṇa tradition in Hindi literature from the perspective of its most important achievements against their historical background and socio-cultural context. Secondly, it attempts to examine the relationship between the story, i.e. Rāmkathā, as told by different authors, and Rām, the protagonist of the Rāmāyaṇa, who functions as a cultural hero and serves as a model of right behaviour for others and at the same time appears to be one of the most important factors in the continuing popularity of the tradition.

The focus of this analysis is, in principle, on the most important – either because of their place in the annals of Hindi literature or their innovative approach to the story and/or its form, etc. – full versions of Rāmkathā that are self-contained wholes and have appeared in print. This does not mean, however, that the works devoted to single episodes or forming a part of a larger whole have been ignored completely; they are referred to whenever they make a meaningful contribution to the development of the tradition. Nevertheless, works by different authors belonging to different periods that have remained in manuscript form have not been an object of my investigation. Although I have

[1] For the details of these works published in English and Polish see Bibliography at the end of this book; they are also referred to in notes appended to individual chapters, whenever they form their part.

[2] Danuta Stasik, *Opowieść o prawym królu. Tradycja Ramajany w literaturze hindi* (The Story of the Righteous King. The Rāmāyaṇa Tradition in Hindi Literature), Warszawa: Wydawnictwo Akademickie Dialog, 2000.

no doubt that a detailed analysis of such manuscripts can yield interesting results, nevertheless, it goes far beyond the scope of this study.

This book opens with an Introduction that outlines the diversity of the Rāmāyaṇa tradition in India, beginning with the first-known *Rāmāyaṇa* ascribed to the sage Vālmīki. It discusses later developments in Sanskrit and vernacular literatures, as exemplified by their best achievements originating from Hindu, Buddhist and Jaina contexts. It also considers the implications of all these works for the unfolding of the tradition in Hindi. In its closing portion, it gives an overview of the growth of the cult of Rām in north India. Special attention is paid to Bhakti that has shaped the countenance of the religious life in north India and has found a splendid expression in the *magnum opus* of Tulsīdās, the sixteenth-century *Rāmcaritmānas.*

The main core of this study is divided into two interrelated parts.

Part One, 'The Story and Its Authors', consists of six chapters that are devoted to the examination of the most representative Rāmkathās in the entire history of Hindi literature, which have been selected according to the already discussed criteria. This investigation becomes especially challenging with reference to tellings written by modern authors in which case the problem of their attitude to the myth of Rām, and to myth in general, becomes of great importance. In regard to this question, I have chosen to refer to Eleazar Meletinsky's findings put forward in his book *Poėtika mifa*.

Part Two, 'The Protagonist of the Story', is comprised of three chapters and concentrates on the image of Rām present in Hindi literature. This analysis is based on three works that emerge from the survey carried out in Part One as the most interesting and typical of their times. Firstly, I am concerned with the image of Rām in the *Rāmcaritmānas.* Secondly, I deal with the character of the protagonist of Maithilīśaraṇ Gupta's *Sāket* considered to be the best example of Hindi literature at the time of the national movement with regard to different retellings of Rāmkathā and, thirdly, the figure of Rām from Bhagvān Siṁh's novel *Apne apne Rām*, the most discussed – in Hindi literary circles – of contemporary Rāmkathās. In my analysis, I view Rām not only as a literary figure but also as a cultural hero, one who shows others how to lead a proper life. I believe that such an approach based on literary sources may contribute much to our understanding of the significance of Rām in north Indian culture.

At the end, I have provided Appendices with a summary of the story and a glossary of the names in Tulsīdās's *Rāmcaritmānas*.

* * *

Throughout these years, this work has gathered a lot of debt often difficult to acknowledge fully as help of different kinds came from various sources. However, there are several individuals to whom I owe much more than words can covey.

First of all, I would like to thank Kunwar Narain, to whom I have dedicated this book, for introducing me to Ayodhya, as well as to his wife, Bharati, and their son, Apurva. Over the years, they have provided me with family like support that can never be overestimated. I am also much obliged to Bimlendra Mohan Pratap Mishra of Ayodhya and his family for making my work in Ayodhya an enjoyable and unforgettable experience. My heartfelt thanks also go to Jacek Woźniak who read the entire manuscript and to Eric Baker for correcting my English.

The last credit goes to Staszek and Michalina, as well as to other loved ones, without whom no work would seem meaningful.

Notes on Transliteration

This study contains many words from Hindi but also from Sanskrit and, to a lesser extent, from other Indian languages. In general, they have been written following the rules common among scholars dealing with these languages. However, it should be stressed that because I have used materials that belong to different linguistic epochs and regions, I have not hesitated to alternate between the spellings of words typical of Sanskrit and of different forms of Hindi[3] in order to match them to their relevant context.

Thus, when dealing with Sanskrit literature, I have adapted the spelling 'Rāma' (as well as Śiva or *puruṣottama*, etc.), while

[3] The main difference between them is that in most cases the final (and in some cases also medial) 'a' in (modern) Hindi becomes mute; cf. e.g. S. *nirguṇa* and H. *nirguṇ*.

in the case of Hindi and in the modern context – 'Rām' (as well as Śiv or *puruṣottam,* etc.). However, in order not to multiply forms, I have decided to give preference to the non-italicized form 'Rāmāyaṇa' throughout the book, wherever I mean the Rāmāyaṇa tradition and refer to no particular title. Its italicized form has been used in the titles of particular Sanskrit works, e.g. 'the *Rāmāyaṇa* of Vālmīki', while in Hindi titles it has additionally dropped the final 'a', becoming thus *Rāmāyaṇ*.[4]

Some Indian words have become common in English and I have rendered them in their anglicized spellings, e.g. 'Brahmin', the same in the case of geographical names and all Indian words that have appeared in the passages translated by me from Hindi into English (the transliterations of the originals have been given for the reader's convenience in the footnotes). Thus, 'Rām' or 'Śiv' used in the analysis may appear next to 'Ram' and 'Shiv' in the English translation.

The use of capital letters in the transliterated titles of original works has been restricted to the first word and personal names, with the only exception of the name 'Rām(a)'; in the transliterated passages no capital letters have been used at all.

As a rule, I have italicized Indian terms (but not the names of individuals – imaginary and real) used in the English text of the analysis with the exception of those that I have used more frequently.

DANUTA STASIK

Warsaw, February 2009

---

[4] The form *Rāmāyan* is also occasionally encountered due to the alternation between the retroflex 'ṇ' and the dental 'n' typical of some Hindi dialects.

INTRODUCTION

Multiple Streams of the Rāmāyaṇa Tradition

INTRODUCTORY REMARKS

The story of Rāma's life and deeds has been popular in India for over two millennia. Its earliest known literary form, the great Sanskrit epic *Rāmāyaṇa,* is traditionally ascribed to the sage Vālmīki. The poem, whose protagonist epitomized kingly virtues, functioned as a kind of morality tale. The set of human, moral and aesthetic values contained in the *Rāmāyaṇa* has never disappeared from the cultural scene of India, which is graphically corroborated by the plethora of writing forming a diverse tradition crossing the boundaries of different regions, languages and religions. Looking at the growth of the tradition, one may be puzzled, realizing that well into the modern period there are no translations in the strict sense of the word – the story lived in the form of many tellings, closer to or more distant from one another. This feature also seems to testify to the oral provenance of both the poem and of the tradition in which it has its origin.

The story as told in Vālmīki's *Rāmāyaṇa* is connected with the Hindu tradition but it proved attractive for the Buddhist and the Jaina traditions and with time it also travelled far outside India to Central, South-East and East Asia.

In a discussion of the Rāmāyaṇa tradition one should not lose sight of its principal character. In this context, an observation made by Frank Whaling in his study on the rise of the religious significance of Rāma[1] is worth recalling here. He notes that until quite recent times both Western and Indian scholars dealing with Indian literature and religion have devoted much more attention to Kṛṣṇa than to Rāma. Commenting on the opinion of Sukumari Bhattacharji: 'The Viṣṇu-concept reaches its culmination in Kṛṣṇa

---

[1] Frank Whaling, *The Rise of the Religious Significance of Rama,* Delhi: Motilal Banarsidass, 1980.

because, as Kṛṣṇa, his anthropomorphism is most complete, full-blooded and hence most convincing and emotionally satisfying',[2] he aptly concludes that 'This idea that Kṛṣṇa has greater importance and significance than Rāma in Indian Religion is not argued, it is rather taken for granted as a self-evident fact'.[3] Bhattacharji's opinion seems to touch upon the most important cause of interest in Kṛṣṇa who fascinates scholars with his vigour, passion and ambivalence. But does it mean that he was more convincing (and more convincing to whom?) than other avatāras of Viṣṇu and especially that of Rāma? A positive answer to this question seems to negate or ignore the centuries of the growth of the Rāmāyaṇa tradition and the actual meaning that its leading character has had for generations of people both as man and God or just as the divine king. Of no less importance is the fact that millions of people in contemporary north India not only greet others with the name of Rāma, treating it as a synonym of the word 'God', but they also try to survive hard times invoking his name or, like Gandhi, depart from this world with it on their lips (*He Rām!*), being then seen off by the mourning party with the words *Rām nām satya hai!* (Rām's/God's name is truth). One could multiply such examples but explaining the reason why it is so I should point to the fact that Rāma, unlike Kṛṣṇa and partly also other gods, is not only the destroyer of Evil and the saviour god. He also commonly functions as a paragon of humanity, an embodiment of eternal human longing for righteousness and the order of things. Undoubtedly, he is a culture hero and that is why the story of his life allows Hindus to interpret their social reality. Being firmly rooted in their religious life, it directly relates to social practice and is an important factor forming Hindu social (and political) consciousness. Daniel H.H. Ingalls very rightly notes this, writing about a major neglect in the studies on Rāma. He stresses the role Rāma played in Hinduism and points out that 'in his Indian homeland his role was such that if we in the west would understand Indian religion, or Indian culture as a whole,

---

[2] Sukumari Bhattacharji, *Indian Theogony: A Comparative Study of Indian Mythology from the Vedas to the Purāṇas,* [London]: Cambridge University Press, 1970 and Whaling, *The Rise,* p. 1.

[3] Ibid.

we must try to grasp what Rāma meant to his worshippers'.[4] Therefore, just as there is no Rāmāyaṇa without Rāma, no thorough research of the Rāmāyaṇa tradition should neglect its hero.

THE BEGINNINGS: VĀLMĪKI'S *RĀMĀYAṆA*

The *Rāmāyaṇa*, along with the *Mahābhārata*,[5] is one of two famous Sanskrit epics. In its extant form it consists of seven books: *Bālakāṇḍa* (Childhood Book), *Ayodhyakāṇḍa* (Ayodhya Book), *Araṇyakāṇḍa* (Forest Book), *Kiṣkiṇḍhākāṇḍa* (Kishkindha Book), *Sundarakāṇḍa* (Beautiful Book), *Yuddhakāṇḍa* (War Book) and *Uttarakāṇḍa* (Later Book). As has already been mentioned, its authorship is traditionally ascribed to the legendary sage Vālmīki, although the text of the poem, as its analysis has proved, came into being over a period of several centuries, in all probability between the fifth century BC and the third century AD, and it was also written down then (perhaps about the first century AD).[6] The first and the last books are considered to be the latest additions to the poem.[7]

---

[4] Ibid., p. IX.

[5] The period of the formation of the text of the *Mahābharata* is traditionally given as the fourth century BC to the fourth century AD; M. Winternitz, *A History of Indian Literature*, vol. 1, Calcutta: University of Calcutta, 1927, p. 475; cf. J.L. Brockington, *The Sanskrit Epics*, Leiden: E.J. Brill, 1998, pp. 26–7.

[6] *Rāma the Steadfast: An Early Form of the Rāmāyaṇa*, tr. John Brockington and Mary Brockington, London: Penguin, 2006, p. XXII.

[7] For the earliest recoverable text of the poem see ibid. For more on the development of the poem see J.L. Brockington, *Righteous Rāma: The Evolution of an Epic*, Delhi: Oxford University Press, 1985, pp. 1, 329–46; cf. idem, *The Sanskrit Epics*, p. 348 and Robert P. Goldman, 'Introduction', in idem, general ed., *The Rāmāyaṇa of Vālmīki. An Epic of Ancient India*, vol. 1, tr. Robert P. Goldman, Princeton: Princeton University Press, 1984, pp. 22–3. For a *résumé* of the story in the critical edition see Brockington, *Righteous Rāma*, pp. 1–8 and Goldman, 'Introduction', pp. 3–13. For a summary of the story as told in the major Hindi telling, the *Rāmcaritmānas* by Tulsīdās, see Appendix 1 in the present study.

Due to some differences among different manuscripts of the poem, scholars usually speak of two recensions of the *Rāmāyaṇa* – the southern and the northern recensions.[8] Because versions of the manuscripts of the northern recension are less homogeneous than the versions of the southern recension, the northern recension is further divided into two sub-recensions, i.e. the north-eastern and the north-western.[9] Although discussions on the differences among the recensions have not been conclusive, scholars seem to concur with the opinion that the text of the northern recension is linguistically, and especially lexically, simpler; it also shows a tendency to gloss it. This seems to indicate that the southern recension contains the more archaic form of the *Rāmāyaṇa*.[10]

Even the earliest scholars of the *Rāmāyaṇa* have no doubts about its oral provenance.[11] Its beginnings, as well as the beginnings of the *Mahābhārata*, are related to, among other things, courtly charioteers acting as bards and counsellors (*sūta*), and to other compositions praising heroes (*gāthānārāśaṃsī*). Shorter forms most probably merged into longer structures focusing on an exceptional hero or an important event. It also seems that an important role in spreading the text of the epic was played by itinerant singers called *kuśīlavas*.[12]

---

[8] *The Vālmīki Rāmāyaṇa, Critically Edited for the First Time*, ed. G.H. Bhatt and U.P. Shah, Baroda: Oriental Institute, 1960–75, vol. 1, pp. XXIX–XXX and vol. 3, p. XXIII.

[9] Also see *The Vālmīki Rāmāyaṇa*, vol. 1, pp. XXIX–XXX and vol. 3, pp. XXIII, XXV. Cf. Brockington, *Righteous Rāma*, p. 8 and Goldman, 'Introduction', p. 5. Also see Hermann Jacobi, *Das Rāmāyaṇa*, Bonn: Verlag von Friedrich Cohen, 1893; Hans Wirtz, *Die westliche Rezension des Rāmāyaṇa*, Bonn: Universitäts-Buchdruckerei von Carl Georgi, 1894 and Camille Bulcke/Kāmil Bulke, *Rāmkathā: utpatti aur vikās*, 6th rev. edn, Prayāg: Hindī Pariṣad, 1999.

[10] Sheldon I. Pollock, 'The Rāmāyaṇa Text and the Critical Edition', in Goldman, *The Rāmāyaṇa of Vālmīki*, vol. 1, p. 83. Cf. Leendert A. van Daalen, 'Remarks on the Princeton Translation of Vālmīki Rāmāyaṇa, esp. on vol. III by Sh.I. Pollock', *Indologica Taurinensia*, vols 19–20, 1993–4, pp. 79–92.

[11] Jacobi, *Das Rāmāyaṇa*, pp. 8ff.

[12] An eponym from the names of the sons of Rāma, Kuśa and Lava, who are considered the first public performers of the *Rāmāyaṇa*. Winternitz, *A History of Indian Literature*, vol. 1, pp. 311–16; Eugeniusz

CHARACTER OF THE POEM AND ITS HERO

Scholars have also been concerned with the character of the poem, pondering mainly upon a question whether it is an epic or a religious text. To resolve this problem unequivocally seems very difficult and, from the point of view of the tradition maybe even pointless, because over the centuries many elements of different provenance – courtly, folk, mythic, poetic, didactic, religious – have been amalgamated in the *Rāmāyaṇa*, most probably thus determining the pervasive influence of the story.[13] What is more, at the latest stage of the formation of the text from around the eleventh century, parallel to the development of the cult of Rāma and blossoming of Vaishnava schools of theology and especially that of Rāmānuja,[14] commentators tirelessly attempted to verify the poem's cohesion from the standpoint of Vaishnava doctrine, as a result imposing on it its theological character, especially apparent in the latest additions to the poem, i.e. in the first and the last books. In this context, a very significant point made by R. Goldman is of much interest. He observes that the exceptional popularity of the poem cannot be explained as a function of its religious significance[15] and suggests just the opposite, namely that it was its immense popularity that from an early date attracted first sectarian bards and later Vaishnava theologians as well as

---

Słuszkiewicz, *Przyczynki do badań nad dziejami redakcyj Rāmāyaṇy*, Kraków: Polska Akademia Umiejętności, 1938, pp. 3ff.; Goldman, 'Introduction', pp. 29–32; Brockington, *Righteous Rāma*, p. 9; idem, *The Sanskrit Epics*, pp. 22–3, 27 and P.A. Grincer, *Drevneindijskij ėpos: Genezis i tipologija*, Moskva: Nauka, 1974, pp. 17–21, 25–6.

[13] Goldman, 'Introduction', vol. 1, p. 49.

[14] Rāmānuja, the traditional dating of whom is 1017 to 1137, played a crucial role in spreading Bhakti devotion in India; thanks to the philosophy of qualified monism (*viśiṣṭādvaita*) preached by him, Bhakti achieved a high philosophical standing and was finally recognized by the orthodox. For more on Rāmānuja and *viśiṣṭādvaita* see John Braisted Carman, *The Theology of Rāmānuja: An Essay in Interreligious Understanding*, New Haven: Yale University Press, 1974; Arvind Sharma, *Viśiṣṭādvaita Vedānta: A Study*, Delhi: Heritage, 1978 and C.J. Bartley, *The Theology of Rāmānuja: Realism and Religion*, London: RoutledgeCurzon, 2002.

[15] Goldman, 'Introduction', p. 47.

poets who were devotees of Rāma.[16] J. Brockington also stresses that Vālmīki's *Rāmāyaṇa* is not only not a Vishnuite poem but not a religious poem at all.[17] Referring to H. Jacobi's opinion,[18] he says that Rāma's transformation into Viṣṇu is a result of a long process. He makes an apt observation that 'the religious pattern of the core of the text is decidedly more archaic than has generally been recognized so far',[19] referring, among other things, to frequent comparisons of Rāma with Indra.[20] R. Goldman observes that the deification of Rāma belongs to the latest stage of the development of the poem[21] and, somewhat peripherally to his main argument, he alludes to the opinion of W. Ruben who, referring to the internal textual evidence, points out that over the centuries the text of the poem developed in an astonishingly consistent and coherent way. Ruben notes that although in the five middle books there is a number of later interpolations, they are not of a Vishnuite character and keep silent on the identity of Rāma and Viṣṇu.[22] According to him, this silence does not necessarily indicate a late provenience of such identification but may suggest that Books 2 to 6 consciously refrain from referring to it.[23] However, R. Goldman finds Ruben's argument implausible because 'it would seem to imply some unspoken but uniformly observed agreement among generations of *Rāmāyaṇa* scribes and reciters'.[24] An entirely different interpretation is proposed by Sheldon Pollock[25] who is of the opinion that such an 'agreement', and by no means 'unspoken', was a fact. He is inclined to see it as

---

[16] Ibid.

[17] Brockington, *Righteous Rāma*, p. 13.

[18] Jacobi, *Das Rāmāyaṇa*, p. 65.

[19] Brockington, *Righteous Rāma*, p. 194.

[20] Ibid., pp. 218–21 and Whaling, *The Rise*, pp. 76–81.

[21] Goldman, 'Introduction', pp. 43, 45.

[22] Ibid., pp. 43–4, n. 82.

[23] Walter Ruben, *Studien zur Textgeschichte des Rāmāyaṇa*, Stutgart: W. Kohlhammer, 1936, p. 63.

[24] *The Rāmāyaṇa of Vālmīki*, vol. 1, p. 43, n. 82.

[25] Sheldon Pollock, 'The Divine King in the Indian Epic', *Journal of the American Oriental Society*, vol. 104, no. 3, 1984, pp. 505–28 and idem, 'Introduction', in Goldman, *The Rāmāyaṇa of Vālmīki*, vol. 3, 1991, pp. 15–54. For a comment on Pollock's opinion see Brockington, *The Sanskrit Epics*, p. 467.

'a function of the literary, mythological, and in fact theological sensitivity of artists participating (...) authentically in a work of art of their own culture'[26] and as a convenient tool to understanding the problem of the divinity of Rāma. Unlike many other Indologists, he poses a very important question: why was it perfectly easy to remodel a 'heroic epic' in accordance with later theological doctrine without any trace of opposition?[27] He also draws attention to the fact that the more than a century-long discussion on the divinity of Rāma is based on an ethnocentric approach to the concept of divinity. Instead, he proposes a thesis of the motif of the divine king that according to him belongs to the earliest strata of the epic.[28] According to him: 'The king is functionally a god because like a god he saves and protects; he is existentially and ontologically a god because he incorporates the divine essence'.[29] With time, this concept was influenced, on the one hand, by the association of Viṣṇu with the earthly king, and on the other hand, by the development of the doctrine of the avatāras in Vaishnava theological circles.[30] No matter what stand is accepted in regard to Rāma's divinity,[31] its influence on the

---

[26] Pollock, 'Introduction', vol. 3, p. 18, n. 26.

[27] Ibid, pp. 18–19; cf. idem, 'The Divine King', pp. 507–8.

[28] Pollock, 'Introduction', vol. 3, p. 43 and idem, 'The Divine King', p. 524. For the complete argument see ibid., pp. 15–54 and ibid., pp. 505–28. For different opinions see Indira V. Peterson, 'The Rāmāyaṇa of Vālmīki: An Epic of Ancient India', *Religious Studies Review*, vol. 12, no. 2, 1986, pp. 97–102 (esp. pp. 100–1); van Daalen, 'Remarks on the Princeton Translation', pp. 86–9; Brockington, *The Sanskrit Epics*, pp. 467–8 and idem, 'The Rāmāyaṇa of Vālmīki: An Epic of Ancient India. Vol. III', *Orientalistische Literaturzeitung*, vol. 87, no. 6, 1992, p. 575.

[29] Pollock, 'Introduction', vol. 3, p. 47. Also see Jan Gonda, *Ancient Indian Kingship from the Religious Point of View*, Leiden: E.J. Brill, 1969 (1st published 1966), pp. 24–33, 47–54 and J.C. Heesterman, 'The Conundrum of the King's Authority', in J.F. Richards, ed., *Kingship and Authority in South Asia*, Delhi: Oxford University Press, 1998 (1st published 1978), p. 15.

[30] Pollock, 'Introduction', vol. 3, pp. 52–3 and idem, 'The Divine King', pp. 526–7.

[31] For a short review of different opinions on this question, see Brockington, *The Sanskrit Epics*, pp. 466–8. It is worth noting here that for contemporary Hindus there is no contradiction between the human and

development of the poem is a fact. The presence of a theological component, especially in its later strata, added to the belief in the soteriological character of the *Rāmāyaṇa* originating from the extraordinary power the story of Rāma's deeds. The fact that it was available to all classes of Hindu society (*varṇa*)[32] is also very significant, especially from the point of view of the later development of the tradition.[33]

A FEW REMARKS ON THE POPULARITY OF THE RĀMĀYAṆA

The phenomenal popularity of the Rāmāyaṇa makes its presence pronounced on all levels of Indian life, both in the past and in the present. All, irrespective of age, education and social status, know the story and its leading characters and the story itself has been continually reinterpreted and remodelled to accommodate different outlooks. However, the problem of its unprecedented popularity is commonly taken for granted and, as a result, the reasons for this have, up to now, not been researched in a complex and systematic way.[34] Of course, there have been many more or less convincing propositions but made incidentally, peripheral

---

the divine nature of Rām that in principle is an inseparable whole though one aspect or the other can at one time prevail, and at other times one of them can be 'entirely forgotten'. Cf. Whaling, *The Rise*, p. 75.

[32] *paṭhandvijo vāgṛṣabhatvamīyāt syātkṣatriyo bhūmipatitvamīyāt; vaṇigjanaḥ paṇyaphalatvamīyājjanaśca śūdro'pi mahattvamīyāt*; 1.1.79.

[33] Goldman, 'Introduction', p. 44.

[34] One of the exceptions with regard to Rāma is Frank Whaling's work: idem, *The Rise*. For more on the diversity of the Rāmāyaṇa see Bulke, *Rāmkathā*, pp. 36–78, 117–226; Brockington, *Righteous Rāma*, pp. 226–306; Paula Richman, ed., *Many Rāmāyaṇas: The Diversity of a Narrative Tradition in South Asia*, Delhi: Oxford University Press, 1991; Paula Richman, ed., *Questioning Rāmāyaṇas: A South Asian Tradition*, Delhi: Oxford University Press, 2003 and K.S. Singh and Birendranath Datta, eds, *Rama-katha in Tribal and Folk Traditions of India*, Calcutta: Seagull Books, 1993. A lot of, in part odd but paradoxically thanks to this, very interesting material is included in a 'Rām encyclopaedia'; see Bhagavatīprasād Siṁh, ed., *Śrī Rām viśvakoś*, vol. 1, Vārāṇasī: Siddhārtha Prakāśan, 1992, pp. 411–688. (It was planned to be in twelve volumes but to my knowledge the project was stopped for different reasons, one of them being the death of its general editor, Bhagavatīprasād Siṁh.)

to some other arguments. Most commonly, and no doubt in accordance with the mainstream of the tradition, Rāma was apprehended as the ideal of a son, a brother and a husband, the embodiment of righteousness – 'the best among men' (*puruṣottama*). However, it is much less commonly stressed that he is the ideal of a ruler, although his just rule (*rāmarājya*), which is often mentioned and discussed, is an obvious proof of it and as such has become an essential element of the north Indian ethos.[35]

Referring to Rāma as the ideal, his emotional and moral superiority over the common man is usually stressed. Tranquillity and his non-conditional respect for the rules of dharma[36] characterize him in almost all situations. Thus, his behaviour is not typical of epic heroes,[37] especially if one considers his placid acceptance of the fourteen-year exile and the abandoning of his wife after unjust allegations put forward by his subjects.[38] These moments are important not only because of the plot of the epic. They also underline the character of Rāma who in the name of upholding dharma relinquishes his right to the throne of Ayodhya and suppresses his emotions. In the first place, he does

---

[35] For n its place in the political life of north India see Philip Lutgendorf, *The Life of a Text: Performing the* Rāmcaritmānas *of Tulsidas*, 1st Indian edn, Delhi: Oxford University Press, 1994, pp. 371–92 (the chapter 'The Politics of Rāmraj').

[36] The word 'dharma' has many meanings and in modern Indian usage the word 'religion' is its most common equivalent. However, in the traditional context two interrelated complex meanings are the most important: 1. the order of all things established on the strength of the divine, natural and man-made laws; 2. righteousness understood as the right conduct in conformity with this order. Cf. Monier Monier-Williams, *A Sanskrit-English Dictionary*, new enl. and improved edn, Delhi: Motilal Banarsidass, 2002 (1st published 1899), p. 510. In this context, J. Brockington's apt observation is very significant. He notes that in so far as the *Mahābhārata* seeks an answer to the question about the nature of dharma and determines problems with its application to given situations, the *Rāmāyaṇa* confirms its fundamental meaning for any right deed. J.L. Brockington, 'The Rāmāyaṇa through the Centuries', *Utkal Historical Research Journal*, vol. 5, 1994, pp. 79–80.

[37] Goldman 'Introduction', pp. 49–50.

[38] Ibid., pp. 49–59. For the analysis of Rāma's conduct, especially in Book 2, see Pollock, 'Introduction', vol. 2, pp. 64–73.

it so that his father's word is not broken, as according to Indian tradition a king has to keep to his word. In the second place, although he loves Sītā, as king he cannot have his subjects have any doubts about him (like in the first instance he is involved in this situation through family ties) and has to send Sītā away. In both cases he is true to the Indian concept of *puruṣārtha*s (lit. 'goal of man') based on the idea of a prescribed conduct in the three spheres of life, i.e. in the sphere of dharma, i.e. righteousness, *artha,* i.e. worldly activity and material gain, and *kāma,* i.e. the sphere of emotions/passions (also sexual desires). Fulfilment in these three spheres is a precondition of attaining the highest goal – *mokṣa,* i.e. the release from the chain of rebirths. Thus, Rāma subdues his emotions (*kāma*) and renounces his rights to the throne (*artha*) as dharma ranks the highest in the hierarchy.[39] Moreover, because his behaviour conforms to the concept of *puruṣārtha*s in every respect, he has won the great esteem of generations of Indians.

As observed by some scholars,[40] the *Rāmāyaṇa* tries to minimize or even eliminate conflict from the family of Raghu. Of course, conflict is essential in an epic but it is not triggered off by a member of the family. Instead, it begins as a result of the intrigue of a servant, Mantharā, and in the ensuing events, the members of the family do not also come into conflict. The conflict is outside the Raghu family and is directed against Rāvana and his family of demons.[41]

At the same time, there is no lack of tension in the *Rāmāyaṇa* nor is its plot static. Such an effect, as noted by R. Goldman, results from the 'use of the technique of creating a series of closely associated but clearly differentiated composite character sets'[42] that are referred to as the 'composite hero'.[43] The most elaborate of

[39] Cf. Veena Das, 'Kāma in the Scheme of Puruṣārthas: the Story of Rāma', *Contributions to Indian Sociology* (n.s.), vol. 15, no. 1–2, 1981, pp. 183–203.

[40] Goldman, 'Introduction', p. 53; cf. Brockington, *The Sanskrit Epics,* p. 464.

[41] Goldman, ibid.

[42] Ibid., p. 54.

[43] For more on the epic's composite hero see Robert P. Goldman, 'Rāmaḥ Sahalakṣmaṇaḥ: Psychological and Literary Aspects of the

these sets is the group made up of the four sons of Daśaratha. It is further subdivided into two subsets, the one made up of Rāma and Lakṣmaṇa and the second – of Bharata and Śatrughna.[44] This technique permits the portrayal of the ambivalence of human nature 'while keeping the central characters largely free from inner struggle'.[45] This observation is very important for the understanding of the emotionality of the *Rāmāyaṇa* characters as well as the emotional background of many episodes of the story undertaken by later authors.

According to R. Goldman, thanks to careful dealing with the characters, the *Rāmāyaṇa* authors 'achieved a delicate balance in the characterization of Rāma'. Thanks to this, among other things, 'he is the most important, if not the most extreme, example of traditional India's ideal man', his behaviour serving as a model for generations of Indians.[46] At the same time, the story of his life helps Hindus to reassert their cultural identity as Hindus[47] and this feature also reveals itself in many tellings; with the most important of which I will deal further in this study.

As has already been mentioned, the story with time has been continually reworked and remodelled to suit the changing tastes and outlooks, and at times such recasting meant contesting the Rāmāyaṇa.[48] How right in this context seems the opinion of the late A.K. Ramanujan: 'The Rāma story has become almost a second language of the whole culture area, a shared core of names, characters, incidents, and motifs, with a narrative language in which Text 1 can say one thing and Text 2 something else, even the exact opposite. Vālmīki's Hindu and Vimalasūri's Jaina texts in India (...) are (...) symbolic translations of each other'.[49] Keeping

---

Composite Hero of Vālmīki's Rāmāyaṇa', *Journal of Indian Philosophy,* vol. 8, 1980, pp. 149–89.

[44] Goldman, 'Introduction', p. 54.

[45] Ibid., p. 54.

[46] Ibid., p. 58.

[47] Sudhir Kakar, *The Inner World: A Psycho-analytic Study of Childhood and Society in India,* 2nd edn, Delhi: Oxford University Press, 1988, pp. 63–4. Cf. Goldman, 'Introduction', p. 59.

[48] For more on this see Richman, *Questioning Rāmāyaṇas.*

[49] A.K. Ramanujan, 'Three Hundred *Rāmāyaṇas:* Five Examples and Three Thoughts on Translation', in Richman, *Many Rāmāyaṇas,* p. 45. For

track of the Rāmāyaṇa wanderings through India and far outside it, one cannot deny such a judgement.

The Development of the Tradition in India

Sanskrit

The mutual relation between two epics, the *Rāmāyaṇa* and the *Mahābhārata,* has for long been of interest to scholars, especially because with the latter both the story and the name of its author are known. The longest and the best-known passage devoted to the deeds of Rāma in the *Mahābhārata* is contained in the *Rāmopākhyāna,* agreeing in the main course of events with the *Rāmāyaṇa.*[50] Many scholars, among them a Polish specialist in the Rāmāyaṇa, Eugeniusz Słuszkiewicz,[51] pointed out the similarity or even identity of a number of fragments in both works. It was also suggested that the *Rāmopākhyāna* may have been a source of the *Rāmāyaṇa*[52] but the fact that its many fragments are incomprehensible without prior knowledge of the *Rāmāyaṇa* indicates that it draws on the Vālmīki.[53] In view of the fact that the date of the *Rāmopākhyāna* is estimated around the first century AD,[54] it is in itself a very convincing proof of the early popularity of the story.

Sanskrit literature abounds in different tellings and compositions that in one way or the other draw on the Rāmāyaṇa

---

more on the culture-making potential of the Rāmāyaṇa tradition see Richman, ibid.

[50] Edward Washburn Hopkins, 'Allusions to the Rama Story in the Mahābhārata', *Journal of the American Oriental Society,* vol. 50, no. 2, 1930, pp. 85–103; J.L. Brockington, 'Sanskrit Epic Tradition I: Epic and Epitome (*Rāmāyaṇa* and *Rāmopākhyāna*)', *Indologica Taurinensia,* vol. 6, 1978, pp. 79–111; idem, *Righteous Rāma,* pp. 226–32; idem, *The Sanskrit Epics,* esp. pp. 473–83 and Bulke, *Rāmkathā,* pp. 50–3.

[51] Słuszkiewicz, *Przyczynki,* pp. 13–32.

[52] E.g. Albrecht Weber, *Über das Rāmāyaṇa,* Berlin: F.R. Dümmler, 1870, pp. 34–8.

[53] Jacobi, *Das Rāmāyaṇa,* pp. 70–6; Brockington, *Righteous Rāma,* pp. 226–8 and idem, *The Sanskrit Epics,* pp. 475, 477. Cf. Słuszkiewicz, *Przyczynki,* pp. 33–8, 119 and Bulke, *Rāmkathā,* pp. 40–3.

[54] Cf. Brockington, *The Sanskrit Epics,* p. 477.

tradition. According to C. Bulcke, from the point of view of originality, dramas are especially noteworthy and tellings in a poetic form are closer to Vālmīki.[55]

Among the dramas, the earliest are two works of Bhāsa, perhaps of the third century AD,[56] the *Pratimānāṭaka* and *Abhiṣekanāṭaka*. The later Bhavabhūti's *Mahāvīracarita* and *Uttararāmacarita* of the early eighth century AD,[57] Murāri's *Anargharāghava* of the ninth or tenth century AD, based on the *Mahāvīracarita*,[58] and Jayadeva's *Prasannarāghava* of the early thirteenth century are also important.[59] The last two works are of special interest in the context of later developments in the tradition of Rāmkathā as some of their solutions were employed by Hindi authors, namely the *Prasannarāghava* is one of the sources of Tulsīdās and the *Uttararāmacarita* is the source of Keśavdās.[60] Of much importance in this context is also the *Hanumannāṭaka*, or *Mahānāṭaka*, a drama of narrative character[61] that was one of the sources of Tulsīdās.

As far as the poems are concerned, one can refer to the famous *Raghuvaṃśa* by Kālidāsa, of the fourth or fifth century, which deals not only with the life of Rāma but of his lineage as well,[62] Kumāradāsa's *Jānakīharaṇa*, probably of the seventh

---

[55] Bulke, *Rāmkathā*, pp. 149, 158.

[56] Brockington, *Righteous Rāma*, p. 242. Cf. A.K. Warder, *Indian Kāvya Literature*, 2nd edn, vol. 2, Delhi: Motilal Banarsidass, 1990, p. 264.

[57] Brockington, *Righteous Rāma*, p. 246; idem, *Sanskrit Epics*, p. 488 and Bulke, *Rāmkathā*, p. 160.

[58] Brockington, *Righteous Rāma*, pp. 246–8 and Bulke, *Rāmkathā*, pp. 160, 162.

[59] Ibid., p. 250 and ibid., pp. 166–7.

[60] For more on these authors see Chapters Two and Three respectively.

[61] Its fourteen-act version the *Hanumannāṭaka*, edited by Dāmodar Miśra, is considered to be older; a shorter ten-act version, the *Mahānāṭaka*, edited by Madhusūdana, originates from Bengal. The earliest strata of its text, of probably around the tenth century, expanded at least till the thirteenth century. Bulke, *Rāmkathā*, pp. 162–3; Brockington, *Righteous Rāma*, p. 249 and idem, *Sanskrit Epics*, p. 490.

[62] See e.g. Brockington, *Righteous Rāma*, p. 243; Siegfried Lienhard, *A History of Classical Poetry: Sanskrit-Pali-Prakrit*, Wiesbaden: Otto Harrassowitz, 1984, pp. 115, 171–5 and A.K. Warder, *Indian Kāvya Literature*, 2nd edn, vol. 3, Delhi: Motilal Banarsidass, 1990, pp. 123, 130–1.

century AD,[63] the *Rāvaṇavadha* of Bhaṭṭi, probably of the sixth or early seventh century AD, also known after the name of its author as the *Bhaṭṭikāvya*,[64] or the *Rāmāyaṇamañjarī* and the *Daśāvatāracarita* by a Kashmiri poet Kṣemendra of the eleventh century.[65] The last of these poems, depicting the avatāra of Rāma, stands out for its original treatment of the story in which the main point of reference is not Rāma but his opponent, Rāvaṇa.[66]

Rāma has also found his place in Puranic literature, a rich and a very important source of our knowledge about Hindu mythology. Nevertheless, although some Purāṇas include the story of his life they are not Rāmāyaṇas in the true sense of the word because they neither focus on the story nor on Rāma. However, they provide valuable evidence of the growth of the tradition and the cult of Rāma and one should not forget that Purāṇas were an important factor in their development. Looking at the profuse Puranic literature, one may feel puzzled at the fact that there is no single text dedicated to Rāma. Maybe the underlying cause of such a situation is the Rāmāyaṇa tradition itself with its numerous tellings in the past and present that no need arose to devote a separate Purāṇa to its protagonist?[67]

The story as well as the references to it are succinct and short in most Purāṇas, especially when one considers the earlier of them, such as the *Matsya purāṇa*,[68] the *Viṣṇu purāṇa*,[69] the *Vāyu*

---

[63] See V. Raghavan, 'Introduction', in Kumāradāsa, *Jānakīharaṇa: Study, Critical Text and English Translation of Cantos XVI–XX*, ed. and tr. C.R. Swaminathan, Delhi: Motilal Banarsidass, 1977, pp. VI–VII; Lienhard, *A History of Classical Poetry*, pp. 197–8 and A.K. Warder, *Indian Kāvya Literature*, 2nd edn, vol. 4, Delhi: Motilal Banarsidass, 1994, pp. 254–66.

[64] Brockington, *Righteous Rāma*, pp. 244–5; idem, *The Sanskrit Epics*, p. 487; Bulke, *Rāmkathā*, pp. 150–1 and Lienhard, *A History*, p. 180.

[65] Brockington, *Righteous Rāma*, p. 249 and Bulke, *Rāmkathā*, p. 152.

[66] Bulke, ibid.

[67] Cf. Ludo Rocher, *The Purāṇas*, Wiesbaden: Otto Harrassowitz, 1986, p. 34.

[68] Probably of the third to fourth century AD and not later than the sixth century AD; ibid., p. 199.

[69] Probably of the fourth or fifth century AD; ibid, p. 249 and Bulke, *Rāmkathā*, p. 123.

purāṇa[70] or the *Agni purāṇa*.[71] Though they have much in common with Vālmīki's version they also contain new elements. Especially in the later Purāṇas, Rāma is portrayed as an avatāra of Viṣṇu (complete or partial) and many of these presentations are imbued with the spirit of Bhakti, e.g. in the *Padma purāṇa*[72] or the *Bhāgavata purāṇa,* which is essentially devoted to Kṛṣṇa.[73] In this context, the *Kūrma purāṇa*[74] is also worth mentioning, as it contains an interesting combination of Shivaite and Ramaite beliefs. It modifies the episode of the seizing of Sītā in a significant way. Sītā, a virtuous wife, guesses the intention of Rāvaṇa and before he kidnaps her, she prays to the god of fire, Agni. Agni creates an illusory Sītā (Māyā-Sītā), very important in many later tellings of the Rāmāyaṇa, who is captured by the demon while the real Sītā dwells in fire. This motif is further recast in different ways in the *Brahmavaivarta purāṇa,* the *Devībhāgavata purāṇa* and the *Adhyātma rāmāyaṇa* thanks to which it has become particularly popular.[75]

The *Adhyātma rāmāyaṇa* allows one to enter yet another realm of the Rāmāyaṇa tradition – the domain of the texts that have a decidedly philosophical and/or theological orientation. They began to appear around the beginning of the second millennium AD parallel to the development of the cult of Rāma. Because of their teachings, they are very important for the understanding of the essence of this cult as they also played a prominent role in shaping the way of perceiving God (Rāma) and exerted an immense influence on the later Ramaite literature. Their

---

[70] Probably of the fourth or fifth century AD and later than the *Viṣṇu purāṇa;* Rocher, *The Purāṇas,* p. 245; Bulke, ibid. and Brockington, *Righteous Rāma,* p. 234.

[71] Dated as eighth or ninth century AD, includes much later material; cf. Rocher, *The Purāṇas,* pp. 136–7; Bulke, ibid. and Brockington, *Righteous Rāma,* p. 239.

[72] Because of its heterogenic character and two different recensions, it is very difficult to date; dates vary from the twelfth to fifteenth century. Cf. Rocher, *The Purāṇas,* pp. 206–14 and Bulke, *Rāmkathā,* pp. 126–7.

[73] Mostly dated as ninth to tenth century; Rocher, *The Purāṇas,* pp. 147–8; Bulke, *Rāmkathā,* p. 123 and Brockington, *Righteous Rāma,* p. 240.

[74] Dated as seventh or early eighth century AD; Rocher, *The Purāṇas,* p. 186 and Bulke, ibid.

[75] Bulke, *Rāmkathā,* pp. 123, 361–3 and Brockington, *Righteous Rāma,* p. 237.

emergence, as rightly pointed out by Revd F. Tokarz,[76] can be related to the fact that the *Rāmāyaṇa*, unlike the *Mahābhārata*, does not abound with philosophical teachings. Therefore, philosophically oriented *Rāmāyaṇa*s appeared to make up for that deficiency, perceived as especially acute with the emergence of Ramaite sects. All these texts, apart from their philosophical and theological teachings, are characterized by their narrative character. This very feature distinguishes them from the Upaniṣads composed around that time in Ramaite circles.[77]

One of the earliest and the most important texts of this type is the *Yogavāsiṣṭha rāmāyaṇa*, dated between 1100 and 1250 AD[78] and traditionally ascribed to Vālmīki.[79] This work, in the form of a dialogue, contains teachings given to Rāma by Vasiṣṭha, based on Advaitavedānta and Yoga. Although the focus of this work is *mokṣa*, i.e. the release from the cycle of births, the story of Rāma also found its place in it, especially the events from the Childhood Book. The appearance of the crow Bhuśuṇḍi who figures so prominently in the structure of Tulsīdās's *Rāmcaritmānas* is its most important feature from the point of view of later developments of the tradition.[80]

The *Adhyātma rāmāyaṇa* is traditionally believed to be a part of the *Brahmāṇḍa purāṇa*[81] but in practice it functions independently

---

[76] Franciszek Tokarz, *Z filozofii indyjskiej. Kwestie wybrane*, 2nd edn, part 1, Lublin: Towarzystwo Naukowe KUL, 1990, pp. 76–7.

[77] Brockington, *Righteous Rāma*, pp. 250–1.

[78] Also known as the *Ārṣarāmāyaṇa*, the *Mahārāmāyaṇa* or the *Mokṣopāyarāmāyaṇa*. Cf. G.V. Tagare, 'Introduction', in *The Yogavāsiṣṭha of Vālmīki*, ed. Vasudeva Laxmana Sharma Pansikar, Delhi: Motilal Banarsidass, 1984 (1st published 1918), pp. II, IX; G. Mainkar, *The Vāsiṣṭha Rāmāyaṇa: A Study*, Delhi: Meharchand Lachhmandas: 1977, pp. 170–86 and Helmuth von Glasenapp, 'Zwei philosophische Rāmāyaṇas', *Abhandlungen der Geistes- und Sozialwissenschaftlichen Klasse* (Akademie der Wissenschaften und der Literatur in Mainz), 1951, no. 6, pp. 432–8.

[79] See Tagare, 'Introduction', p. VII and Jan Gonda, *Medieval Religious Literature in Sanskrit*, Wiesbaden: Otto Harrassowitz, 1977, p. 37.

[80] For more see *The Yogavāsiṣṭha of Vālmīki*; Brockington, *Righteous Rāma*, pp. 251–2 and Bulke, *Rāmkathā*, p. 132.

[81] For more on the lack of textual grounds for such a contention see Vijayśrī, *Adhyātma rāmāyaṇa: ek vivecanātmak adhayan*, Dillī: Alaṅkār Prakāśan, 1979, pp. 22–7.

and is probably the most important work of this type.[82] The textual evidence indicates that it is one of the earliest texts composed by someone who was not only a worshipper of Rāma but also belonged to a community of his devotees.[83] However, its date is uncertain, and different proposals ranging from the fourteenth to mid-sixteenth centuries have been put forward and sometimes it is ascribed to Rāmānanda.[84] This work, although divided traditionally into seven books, has a non-traditional form, for a Rāmāyaṇa, of a dialogue between Śiva and Pārvatī, indicating Tantric influences.[85] Such a structure, i.e. the structure of a dialogue, or more precisely of four dialogues among which the dialogue between Śiva and Pārvatī figures prominently, was adopted by Tulsīdās in his *Rāmcaritmānas*.[86]

Rāma of the *Adhyātma rāmāyaṇa* is an avatāra of Viṣṇu but in fact he is Absolute (*Brahman*) both in its nonmanifest form, 'without qualities' (*nirguṇa*), and its manifest form, 'with qualities' (*saguṇa*). A particular emphasis is placed on the importance of Rāma's name which with time has become an essential feature of Rāmbhakti that is so typical of the *Rāmcaritmānas*. The *Adhyātma rāmāyaṇa* also introduced a new or modified treatment of certain episodes employed by later authors (among others by Tulsīdās). One of the most important of them is the elaboration of the motif of illusory Sītā (Māyā-Sītā) known to the *Kūrma purāṇa*, as has already been mentioned.

The *Adhyātma rāmāyaṇa*, despite its Advaitavedānta outlook, exerted an important influence on the forming of Ramaite Bhakti.

---

[82] For more on the *Adhyātma rāmāyaṇa* see Glasenapp, 'Zwei philosophische Rāmāyaṇas', pp. 73–98.

[83] Whaling, *The Rise*, p. 105.

[84] *The Adhyatma Ramayana*, tr. Rai Bahadur Baij Nath, Delhi: Oriental Reprint, 1979 (1st published 1913), p. III; Glasenapp, 'Zwei philosophische Rāmāyaṇas', pp. 493–4; Bulke, *Rāmkathā*, p. 171; Brockington, *Righteous Rāma*, p. 252, n. 51; Gonda, *Medieval Religious Literature*, p. 274 and Vijayśrī, *Adhyātma rāmāyaṇa*, pp. 27–33.

[85] Depicting Sītā as the personification of the creative power (*prakṛti*) of Rāma the Absolute also seems to suggest Tantric influences. Cf. George A. Grierson, 'On the Adbhuta Ramayana', *Bulletin of the School of Oriental Studies*, vol. 4, no. 1, 1926–8, p. 12.

[86] For more on the structure of the *Rāmcaritmānas* see Chapter Two in this study.

To this day, it is held in high esteem (even if nominally) by devotees, and especially that part known as the *Rāmagītā* (7.5),[87] which is often transmitted and commented on independently and probably may be older than the rest of the work.[88]

The *Adbhuta rāmāyaṇa*[89] is also known as the *Adbhutottarakāṇḍa* and the latter title refers to the traditional assumption that it was written by Vālmīki as the last book, supplementing his poem.[90] It has not exerted such an influence on later authors as the *Adhyātma rāmāyaṇa* most probably because of its definite Shakta orientation but it fascinates with an original treatment of the story, in which Sītā plays an important role. According to a legend, out of a milliard (*śatakoṭi*) verses of the *Rāmāyaṇa* known in the heaven of Brahmā (*brahmaloka*) only twenty-five thousands are known on earth.[91] The *Adbhuta rāmāyaṇa* is said to originate from these 'heavenly' verses and its aim is to praise the greatness of Sītā (*Sītāmāhātmya*; 1.3ff).[92] Vālmīki narrates it at the request of the sage Bharadvāj. It is divided into twenty-seven chapters (*sarga*) of different length and in its longest twenty-fifth chapter Rāma praises Sītā with a thousand names. Sītā is not only his *śakti*, the energy – she is exalted to the position of Devī, the Goddess. It is particularly apparent in the treatment of the events after the victory of Rāma over Rāvaṇa. When the most prominent sages arrive at Ayodhya to celebrate it and start to praise Rāma, Sītā

---

[87] See e.g. a Hindi translation of the *Adhyātma rāmāyaṇa* and its commentary: *Śrīrāmagītā (Adhyātma rāmāyaṇa)*, comment. Svāmī Cinmayānanda, Hindi tr. Rāv Raṇbahādur Siṁh, Kānpur: Sentral Cinmay Miśan Ṭrasṭ, 1994, or a *Rāmgītā* in Hindi based on Tulsīdās's *Rāmcaritmānas: Śrīrāmgītā. Tulsīrāmāyaṇ par ādhārit*, Bambaī: Sentral Cinmay Miśan Ṭrasṭ, 1989.

[88] Gonda, *Medieval Religious Literature*, p. 274 and Whaling, *The Rise*, p. 141.

[89] Its date is difficult to determine. Most commonly, it is claimed to be later than the *Adhyātma rāmāyaṇa*; see e.g. Bulke, *Rāmkathā*, p. 133 and Brockington, *Righteous Rāma*, p. 255.

[90] Grierson, 'On the Adbhuta Ramayana', p. 12 and Brockington, *Righteous Rāma*, p. 255.

[91] Cf. n. 94 further in this Introduction. An echo of this legend can be also found in the *Rāmcaritmānas* 1.33.3–4.

[92] *Adbhuta rāmāyaṇa*, ed. Rām Kumār Rāy, Vārāṇasī: Prācya Prakāśan, 1982, pp. 1–5. Cf. Grierson, 'On the Adbhuta Ramayana', pp. 12–15.

cannot stop herself and bursts out laughing. She reveals to all that the killing of Rāvaṇa is nothing when his one-thousand-headed namesake brother (Sahasramukha-rāvaṇa) is still alive and poses a threat to the gods. Rāma rushes to destroy him but fails and is defeated. Therefore Sītā intervenes. As a terrible Devī in a garland of skulls and bracelets of bones, she defeats Rāvaṇa and his army. After her victory, she prepares a garland of Rāvaṇa's heads but suddenly feels a desire to play with them as with balls. Hordes of dreadful goddesses emanate from her body and join her in this game. Because earth begins to shake and finally falls in due to that awful burden, it is Śiva-Mahādeva who tries to intervene. However, Sītā's might is such that Brahmā has to revive Rāma and seek his help. This is the moment when Rāma praises Sītā with her thousand names and, mollifying her, brings her back to her normal state. This essential part of the *Adbhuta rāmāyaṇa* is much under the influence of Shakta mythology and the *Devī-māhātmya*, as well as folk traditions.[93]

Diverse influences are apparent in the *Ānanda rāmāyaṇa* as well which, like the previously-discussed texts, also claims the authorship of Vālmīki.[94] This work in the form of a dialogue between Śiva and Pārvatī is divided into nine books but only one of them – under a very significant title *Sārakāṇḍa* (*sāra* lit.

---

[93] Cf. Rocher, *The Purāṇas*, p. 195; Brockington, *Righteous Rāma*, pp. 255–6 and Bulke, *Rāmkathā*, pp. 133–4. For more on the Goddess tradition and the *Devīmāhātmya* see Thomas B. Coburn, *Devī Māhātmya: The Crystallization of the Goddess Tradition*, Delhi: Motilal Banarsidass, 1997 (1st published 1984) and idem, 'Consort of None, Śakti of All: The Vision of the Devī-māhātmya', in John Stratton Hawley and Donna Wulff, eds, *The Divine Consort: Rādhā and the Goddesses of India*, Boston: Beacon Press, 1982, p. 153.

[94] The colophons after each of its books (*kāṇḍa*) end with a formula that this is one of a milliard [of versions of] the story of Rāma [created by] Vālmīki; *Ānanda rāmāyaṇa*, ed. and comment. Rāmtej Pāṇḍey and Yugal Kiśor Dvivedī, Kāśī: Paṇḍit Pustakālay, 1958. Its date is uncertain but it was known to Eknāth (1533–99), one of the most important Marathi poets of the Bhakti period, the author of the *Bhāvārtha rāmāyaṇa* in Marathi and Bulke, *Rāmkathā*, p. 134. For more on Eknāth see Shankar Gopal Tulpule, *Classical Marāṭhī Literature: From the Beginning to A.D. 1818*, Wiesbaden: Otto Harrassowitz, 1979, pp. 354–9 and further in this Introduction.

'essence') – narrates the traditional story beginning with Rāma's birth and ending with Rāmarājya. Next, it introduces the story of his life in an original, non-traditional way that is continued through the rest of the books. For example, there is no intrigue of Kaikeyī – Rāma himself informs Sītā that has to go to the forest in order to kill Rāvaṇa and tells her to stay in Ayodhya. However, she asks Rāma to take her to the forest with him, justifying her request with an argument that she has never heard of any *Rāmāyaṇa* in which Rāma would go to the forest without Sītā (1.6.11–12).[95] And of course, Rāma had to keep with tradition! Rāvaṇa knows that Rāma is Viṣṇu and Sītā is his consort – Lakṣmī (Padmā). He captures Sītā in order to die at the hands of Rāma and thus attain heaven (*paramaṃ padam*; 1.11.243–245). In his conflict with Rāma, he is assisted by two twin-like demon friends who seize the sleeping Rāma and Lakṣmaṇa and take them to the underworld from where they are rescued by Hanumān. This motif known from an earlier work, the *Mairāvaṇacarita*,[96] with time gained popularity and in different forms is found in a number of tellings especially from eastern India (Bengal, Assam and Orissa).[97] Its second and third books, *Yātrākāṇḍa* (Journey Book) and *Yāgakāṇḍa* (Sacrifice Book), are very interesting. In the first of them Rāma goes on a pilgrimage all over India and after his return performs the sacrifice of *aśvamedha*.[98] Apart from the fact that this account forms a unique map of the holy places of Hinduism, it appears that one can understand it as a symbolic, triumphant advance of the cult of Rāma in India and its final stabilization on the subcontinent that the *aśvamedha* performed by Rāma seems to indicate. A thorough analysis of this material in

---

[95] Similar words of Sītā can also be found in the *Adhyātma rāmāyaṇa* (2.4.76); cf. Whaling, *The Rise*, p. 121.

[96] Bulke, *Rāmkathā*, pp. 141, 478.

[97] For more on this subject see ibid., pp. 478–81; Saraswathi Venugopal, 'Ramayana Episodes in South Indian Folk Literature', in Singh and Datta, *Rama-katha*, pp. 101–2 and W.L. Smith, *Rāmāyaṇa Traditions in Eastern India: Assam, Bengal, Orissa*, Delhi: Munshiram Manoharlal, 1994 (1st published 1988), pp. 146–53. Also see William L. Smith, 'Mahiravana and the Womb Demon', *Indologica Taurinensia*, vol. 10, 1982, pp. 215–22.

[98] An ancient Vedic horse-sacrifice performed commonly by a king in order to assert his authority over his territory.

this direction could bring promising results, allowing for a more complete understanding of the history of the development of the Rāma cult.

Krishnaite influences, and especially the influence of *Kṛṣṇa-līlā*, or the love exploits of Kṛṣṇa, are also evident in the *Ānanda rāmāyaṇa*.[99] It is said (4.31–50) that women at the sight of Rāma were seized with love and desire. Rāma invariably used to tell them that he would fulfil their wishes in his next incarnation, i.e. when he would be Kṛṣṇa. In such a way his vow of faithfulness to one wife, was to be rewarded in future!

The text of the *Ānanda rāmāyaṇa* also includes the *Rāma-rakṣāstotra*[100] (Hymn to Rāma for [His] Protection), which is a specific encapsulation of Rāma's deeds in the form of his epithets similar to a litany. It functions independently from the *Ānanda rāmāyaṇa*, as a separate text, and has been especially popular in Maharashtra.

Bhuśuṇḍi who, as has been mentioned, appears in the already-discussed *Yogavāsiṣṭha rāmāyaṇa*, also features in the *Bhuśuṇḍi rāmāyaṇa*.[101] The date of this work is uncertain. Commonly it is considered as one of the sources of Tulsīdās (1574);[102] some scholars claim that it was composed in the

---

[99] Mostly in Book 4, i.e. *Vilāsakāṇḍa* (Book of [Sensuous] Pleasure).

[100] For more on this text, its different versions, history and its religious practice see Gudrun Bühnemann, *Budha-Kauśika's Rāmarakṣāstotra: A Contribution to the Study of Sanskrit Devotional Poetry*, Vienna: University of Vienna, 1983. Bühnemann is of the opinion that the *Rāmarakṣāstotra* was incorporated into the *Ānanda rāmāyaṇa*; ibid., p. 25.

[101] Known also as the *Brahma-Bhuśuṇḍa-saṃvāda*, the *Brahma rāmāyaṇa* and the *Ādirāmāyaṇa*. V. Raghavan, 'English Introduction', in *Bhuśuṇḍi rāmāyaṇa. Pūrva khaṇḍa*, ed. Bhagavatīprasād Siṁh, Vārāṇasī: Viśva-vidyālay Prakāśan, 1975, p. 2. The rest of the text was published as: *Bhuśuṇḍi rāmāyaṇa: Dvitīya bhāg (dakṣiṇa khaṇḍa)*, Gorakhpur: Avadh Sāhitya Mandir, no date and *Bhuśuṇḍi rāmāyaṇa. Tṛtīya bhāg (paścima-uttara khaṇḍa)*, Gorakhpur: Avadh Sāhitya Mandir, no date ('Introduction' was written in 1983); all these volumes were edited by Bhagavatīprasād Siṁh.

[102] E.g. Charlotte Vaudeville, *Étude sur les sources et la composition du Rāmāyaṇa de Tulsī-dās*, Paris: Adrien-Maisonneuve, 1955, pp. XX–XXI, 317–19, 323–4.

fourteenth[103] or even in the twelfth century.[104] For years, it was known by its title only and even such experts on the Rāmāyaṇa as George A. Grierson or Charlotte Vaudeville could only presume its existence.[105]

It consists of four parts (*khaṇḍa*): *Pūrva, Dakṣiṇa, Paścima* and *Uttara*. Like the *Ānanda rāmāyaṇa*, it has the strong Krishnaite flavour of the *Bhāgavata purāṇa*, as well as Jayadeva's *Gītāgovinda* and Līlāśuka's *Kṛṣṇakarṇāmṛta*, especially in the presentation of Rāma's childhood and adolescence. Shakta and Tantric influences are also evident,[106] especially in the way of presenting Sītā as Rāma's *śakti* and in her epithets (Sahajā or Sahajānandinī). The abode she dwells in with Rāma is called symptomatically 'Sītā's World' (*Sītāloka*) or 'Sītā's Vaikuṇṭha' (*Sītāvaikuṇṭha*).[107] A special emphasis on the presen-tation of the love sports of Rāma and on esoteric Bhakti is probably the reason why the *Bhuśuṇḍi rāmāyaṇa* was 'really esoteric' and not known to a wider public.

The *Rāmagītā* occurs twice in different contexts and forms in this text[108] but unlike in the *Adhyātma rāmāyaṇa* it is based on Viśiṣṭādvaita (and not on Advaitavedānta), which is crucial for the Bhakti way of perceiving God.[109] Undoubtedly, one can only agree with B.P. Singh, the editor of the *Bhuśuṇḍi rāmāyaṇa* who revealed it to the scholarly world, that it is a text not only important to devotees of Rāma but also a valuable source for the

---

[103] V. Raghavan, 'English Introduction', p. 21; in another of his works Raghavan considers it earlier from the *Adhyātma rāmāyaṇa*: 'The Ramayana in Sanskrit Literature', in V. Raghavan, ed., *The Ramayana Tradition in Asia*, Delhi: Sahitya Akademi, 1980, p. 17. Cf. Brockington, *Righteous Rāma*, p. 257.

[104] Bhagavatīprasād Siṁh/B.P. Singh, 'Prastāvnā', in *Bhuśuṇḍi rāmāyaṇa. Pūrva khaṇḍa*, p. LXI and idem, 'Bhuśuṇḍi Rāmāyaṇa and Its Influence on the Medieval Rāmāyaṇa Literature', in Raghavan, *The Ramayana Tradition*, p. 487.

[105] C. Bulcke, working on his book, already knew about the discovery of its manuscripts but had no chance to examine them himself; Bulke, *Rāmkathā*, p. 138.

[106] Singh, 'Bhuśuṇḍi Rāmāyaṇa', pp. 479–85.

[107] Vaikuṇṭha – the heaven of Viṣṇu.

[108] *Pūrva* 43–59 and *Uttara* 9–25.

[109] See further in this Introduction.

specialists of Ramaite tradition and cults prior to it.[110] Due to its syncretic character the *Bhuśuṇḍi rāmāyaṇa* is a real mine of information on different beliefs and practices.

* * *

The foregoing survey of philosophical and theological Rāmāyaṇas graphically represents the potential lying dormant in the story. The fact that Rāma acts as the Ultimate Being (*nirguṇa Brahman*) who out of the well-being of his worshippers also appears as qualified, personal God (*saguṇa Brahman*) is of much importance from the point of view of later developments. Concurrent with the appearance of these texts was also the rise of the significance of his name. Repeating it with time became an indispensable element of Rāma's worship and at times it can even replace all its other forms. It is feasible that these texts were an important source of the conviction about the identity of the words 'Rāma' and 'God' most explicitly manifested in a different context in the Hindi poetry of Kabīr (*c.*1450–1518).[111]

In some of these Rāmāyaṇas, an important, at times even supreme, role of Sītā is noteworthy. An evidently Shakta influenced concept of Sītā as Mother Goddess that anyway has not gained wider following, although very interesting, is beyond the scope of this study. I would like to pay attention to the Tantra influenced presence of the couple of Sītā-Rāma who reign in heaven and on earth, which is of special importance in Mādhurya Bhakti (lit. 'sweet devotion').[112] It is an essential, new element that, having crossed sectarian boundaries, has become part and parcel of everyday Hindu custom, expressing itself, for example, in the form of a Hindi greeting: *Sītā-Rām/Siyā-Rām* or *Sītā-Rām kī jay* (Hail to Sītā and Rām)

These Rāmāyaṇas, although in the main known for a long time, have not been systematically analysed, especially from the point of view of their mythological and ritual contents. Maybe their late date and syncretism have discouraged scholars

[110] Singh, 'Bhuśuṇḍi Rāmāyaṇa', p. 504.

[111] Kabīr's dates after David N. Lorenzen, *Praises to a Formless God*, New York: State University of New York, 1996, p. 266.

[112] See further in this Introduction.

interested in texts of a more 'established reputation?' It is to be hoped that such a text as, e.g. the *Bhuśuṇḍi rāmāyaṇa* will finally be thoroughly examined and discussed. It is very much desired not only because of its alleged influence on Tulsīdās's *Rām-caritmānas,* the most important devotional text of north India, but also because of its role in the formation and practice of Mādhurya Bhakti that still awaits more investigation.[113]

BUDDHIST AND JAINA TELLINGS

As I have already mentioned, the story of Rāma does not limit itself to Hinduism but is also well-known in Buddhism and Jainism. Although the role of Buddhist and Jaina versions in the formation of the later Rāmāyaṇa is not so evident, nevertheless, one should remember that they both endowed Rāma with a special status, elevating him above the level of a common man. He can be found in Buddhist Jātakas that deal with Buddha's former births. Thus, for example in the *Dasaratha jātaka*[114] he figures as a bodhisattva, i.e. as a Buddhist saint before attaining the supreme state of Buddha. In Jaina Rāmāyaṇas, he is commonly known as Padma[115] who is one of the sixty-three great men (*śalākā puruṣa*).[116] This testifies to the potential of Rāma as

[113] The pioneering work of B. Siṁh is more than fifty-years old now: Bhagavatīprasād Siṁh, *Rāmbhakti mẽ rasik sampradāy,* Avadh Sāhitya Mandir: Balrāmpur, 1957.

[114] For more see Richard Gombrich, 'The Vessantara Jātaka, the Rāmāyaṇa and the Daśaratha Jātaka', *Journal of American Oriental Society,* vol. 105, no. 3, 1985, pp. 427–37 and Frank E. Reynolds, 'Rāmāyaṇa, Rāma Jātaka, and Ramakien: A Comparative Study of Hindu and Buddhist Traditions', in Richman, *Many Rāmāyaṇas,* pp. 50–63. For the English translation of its text see *The Jātaka or Stories of the Buddha Former Births,* ed. E.B. Cowell, Oxford: The Pali Text Society, 1990 (rpt.), vol. 4, pp. 78–82.

[115] It is also an epithet of Viṣṇu. The name Rāma and his other epithets are also used; V.M. Kulkarni, *The Story of Rāma in Jain Literature as Presented by the Śvetāmbara and Digambara Poets in the Prakrit, Sanskrit and Apabhraṁśa Languages,* Ahmedabad: Saraswati Pustak Bhandar, 1990, pp. 75–6.

[116] Kulkarni, 'Jain Rāmāyaṇas and Their Source', in Raghavan, *The Ramayana Tradition,* p. 226.

a paragon of righteousness and a culture figure, recognized by major Indian religious traditions.

The mutual relation between Buddhism and the Rāmāyaṇa tradition, especially where the figure of Rāma is concerned, seems worth considering. Could it not be shaped under the influence of Buddhist teachings? Rāma is a warrior, Kshatriya, but almost in a perfect way controls his emotions, the trait that is so characteristic of Buddhist teachings. Of significance in this context can also be the fact that the *Rāmāyaṇa* in comparison with the *Mahābhārata* is calmer in the emotional sphere – conflicts and violent passions are subdued. The geographical and thus also cultural closeness between the alleged place of origin of the *Rāmāyaṇa*, i.e. north-eastern India, and the bosom of Buddhism could be at work here. Of course, it is very difficult, if possible at all, to ascertain this with such highly transformed material as we have at our disposal. However, it seems highly plausible that the Rāmāyaṇa tradition functioned in the circle of the same ideas from which Buddhism developed.[117]

The earliest Jaina Rāmāyaṇa, i.e. the *Paümacariya*[118] by Vimalasūri in Prakrit (*jaina māhārāṣṭrī*), was followed by a number of other tellings. The most important among them are the *Vāsudevahiṇḍi* in Prakrit by Saṅghadāsa[119] and the *Uttara purāṇa* (AD 897) in Sanskrit by Guṇabhadra.[120] Popular were also: the *Padma purāṇa* (AD 678) by Raviṣeṇa, a rather faithful Sanskrit version of Vimalasūri's *Paümacariya*, the *Paümacariü* (probably mid eighth century) in Apabhransha by Svayambhū, the *Mahāpurāṇa* (AD 965) also in Apabhransha by Puṣpadanta and the

---

[117] Cf. Bulke, *Rāmkathā*, pp. 77–8.

[118] Commonly dated as the late third or early fourth century AD, although the text itself claims its origin in the first century AD; for more on its date see V.M. Kulkarni, 'Introduction', in *Ācārya Vimalasūri's Paumacariyam (with Hindi translation)*, ed. H. Jacobi, 2nd edn, Varanasi: Prakrit Text Society, 1962, pp. 1, 5–6, 8–15 and Kulkarni, *The Story of Rāma*, pp. 51–9; cf. Winternitz, *A History of Indian Literature*, vol. 2, pp. 477–8.

[119] Probably not later than the early seventh century AD; cf. Kulkarni, 'Introduction', p. 1 and Brockington, *Righteous Rāma*, p. 266.

[120] Kulkarni, 'Introduction', pp. 1–2; idem, 'Jain Rāmāyaṇas', pp. 227–9; Kulkarni, *The Story of Rāma*, pp. 12ff.; Bulke, *Rāmkathā*, pp. 58–60, 173–4 and Brockington, *Righteous Rāma*, p. 266.

so-called *Jaina rāmāyaṇa* (around mid twelfth century) in Sanskrit by Hemacandra that is a part of the *Triṣaṣṭiśalākāpuruṣacarita* (Deeds of Sixty-three Great Men).[121] In Jaina Rāmāyaṇas, due to the stress on non-violence (*ahiṃsa*) and high morals of Rāma who cannot commit himself to it, the direct opponent of Rāvaṇa is Lakṣmaṇa (he kills Rāvaṇa!). One of the most interesting of their characteristic features is their critical attitude towards Hindu tellings that are considered to be absurd and deceitful. A strong rational outlook or, rather, rationalizing what was unacceptable to Jainas distinguishes these works. Therefore, when Vimalasūri calls Rāvaṇa Daśamukha ('Ten-faced'), he does so not because Rāvaṇa was Ten-faced or Ten-headed as in Vālmīki but because his (one) face was reflected in nine jewels of a necklace given to him by his mother. Monkeys known from the traditional story are not real monkeys but a kind of supernatural beings (one would like to ask if it is still rationalizing?!), whose totem is a monkey and from this their name originates.[122] This rationalizing attitude is considered to be the proof of the later provenance of the Jaina Rāmāyaṇas, although their authors claim their independence of and seniority to Hindu tellings. However, the fact that they are absent from the Jaina canon seems to corroborate their late origin. Most probably, Jainas took them up later with an intention of popularizing Jaina teachings through this very popular medium.[123]

RĀMĀYAṆAS IN REGIONAL LANGUAGES OF INDIA

The earliest rendering of the Rāmāyaṇa in an Indian language other than Sanskrit or Prakrit is a Tamil poem the *Irāmāvatāram* by Kampaṉ, dated between the ninth and twelfth century[124] and

---

[121] Kulkarni, 'Jain Rāmāyaṇas', p. 227; idem, *The Story of Rāma*, p. 12 and Brockington, *Righteous Rāma*, p. 266, n. 16.

[122] Cf. Kulkarni, 'Introduction', p. 31 and idem, *The Story of Rāma*, pp. 18–19.

[123] Kulkarni, *The Story of Rāma*, pp. 230, 240–1.

[124] See Kamil Veith Zvelebil, *Tamil Literature*, Wiesbaden: Otto Harrassowitz, 1974, pp. 146–7; Ramakrishnan, *The Epic Muse: The Ramayana and the Paradise Lost*, Delhi: People's Publishing House, 1977,

commonly known after its author's name as the *Kamparāmāyaṇam*. Its origin is related to the Bhakti poetry of *āḻvārs* (from around seventh to tenth century AD), i.e. Vishnuite mystic Tamil poets, such as Periyāḻvār, Nammāḻvār, Tirumaṅkaiyāḻvār and Kulacēkarāḻvār.[125] The poetry of *āḻvārs*, lyrical and not narrative in its character, is permeated with fervent devotion, Bhakti, to an incarnate deity and such an attitude also characterizes the *Irāmāvatāram*.[126] Kampaṉ's Rāma is Viṣṇu who descended to the earth and even his opponent, Rāvaṇa, recognizes his real nature.[127] Some interesting changes in the presentation of certain episodes are aimed at showing Rāma in the spirit of Bhakti as the merciful and kind Lord. For example, Lakṣmaṇa mutilates Śūrpaṇakhā not at the behest of Rāma but on his own initiative. It may be added here that he cuts not only her nose and ears but breasts as well.[128] This episode, raising a question of the socially non-acceptable behaviour and of imminent punishment, was enriched by Kampaṉ with local colour. According to Tamil tradition, a woman who is impure loses not only her honour, which is symbolized with cutting of her nose,[129] but also her power that abides in her breasts. In the *Irāmāvatāram*, there is also a mention that during the fourteen years of the exile Lakṣmaṇa

---

pp. 171–5 and David Shulman, 'The Fire and Flood: The Testing of Sītā in Kampaṉ's Irāmāvatāram', in Richman, *Many Rāmāyaṇas*, p. 89.

[125] P.K. Bālasubrahmaṇyam, 'Tamilnāḍu mē rāmsaṁskṛti', in Siṁh, *Śrī Rām viśvakoś*, pp. 534–5 and Zvelebil, *Tamil Literature*, p. 146.

[126] Brockington, *Righteous Rāma*, p. 269.

[127] Zvelebil, *Tamil Literature*, p. 147. For more on the divinity of Rāma in the *Irāmāvatāram* see David Shulman, 'Divine Order and Divine Evil in the Tamil Tale of Rama', *Journal of Asian Studies*, vol. 38, no. 4, 1979, pp. 651–69.

[128] This motif is also known to the *Ānanda rāmāyaṇa*; Bulke, *Rāmkathā*, p. 335.

[129] In many contemporary Indian languages, the concept that the nose is the symbol of one's honour is reflected in rich phraseology. On the one hand, its origin should be traced to traditional Indian law, in which cutting of the nose was a punishment for adultery and losing one's chastity. On the other hand, it results from the conviction that the honour of a family depends on the chastity of its women; cf. Kathleen M. Erndl, 'The Mutilation of Śūrpaṇakhā', in Richman, *Many Rāmāyaṇas*, pp. 81–2.

does not sleep at all, standing guard over Rāma and Sītā's security.[130] The lack of his sleep is known to the *Adhyātma rāmāyaṇa* and the *Adbhuta rāmāyaṇa* and by some authors is enhanced with fasting or, as in Keśavdās's *Rāmcandrikā* in Hindi, with a vow of chastity.[131]

How far from Kampaṉ's Bhakti attitude is an interpretation offered by Ī.Ve. Rāmacāmi Nāyakkar (1879–1973)[132] in his two works *Irāmāyaṇappāttiraṅkaḷ* (Characters of the Rāmāyaṇa; 1930) and *Irāmāyaṇakkuṟippukaḷ* (Notes on the Rāmāyaṇa; 1964).[133] Although they are not literary works, they have to be mentioned in a survey of the Rāmāyaṇa tradition in Tamil because their viewpoint, among other things, discredited the moral character of Rāma and Sītā. It was enthusiastically received by lots of Tamils and till this day has a very wide following among them.[134]

Kampaṉ's *Irāmāvatāram* was also popular in the Kannada-speaking area, likely because of the Jaina character of the earliest Kannada Rāmāyaṇa, i.e. the *Pampa rāmāyaṇa*[135] by Nāgacandra,

---

[130] Brockington, *Righteous Rāma*, p. 272. For the English translation of Kampaṉ's work see *Kamba–Rāmāyaṇa*, tr. Shanti Lal Nagar, Delhi: Parimal Publications, 2008.

[131] See Bulke, *Rāmkathā*, pp. 329–33. However, Bulcke (ibid., p. 329) erroneously suggests that this motif first appears in the *Adhyātma rāmāyaṇa*.

[132] Ī.Ve. Rāmacāmi Nāyakkar/E.V. Ramasami Naicker (Nāyakkar is his caste name that he ceased to use in later times), called also Periyār; he was a founder of a south Indian nationalist party DK (Dravidar Kazhagam/Tirāviṭar Kaḻakam) and one of the most influential leaders of the Dravida movement. Cf. Paula Richman, 'E.V. Ramasami's Reading of the Rāmāyaṇa', in idem, *Many Rāmāyaṇas*, pp. 176, 197. For more see Anita Diehl, *E.V. Ramaswami – Periyar: A Study of the Influence of a Personality in Contemporary South India*, Stockholm–Göteborg–Lund: Esselte Studium, 1977.

[133] The English translation of the first of them was published under a very symptomatic title: *The Ramayana: A True Reading* (1959); Richman, 'E.V. Ramasami's Reading', pp. 180, 199.

[134] For more on this see Zvelebil, *Tamil Literature*, p. 159; Richman, 'E.V. Ramasami's Reading', esp. pp. 175–6, 181–6, 193–4, 198 and Bālasubrahmaṇyam, 'Tamilnāḍu mē rāmsaṁskṛti', p. 539.

[135] Probably composed around the end of the eleventh century; Brockington, *Righteous Rāma*, p. 272.

better known as Abhinava Pampa.[136] A reasonable popularity gained by the *Torave rāmāyaṇa* by Narahari, better known as Kumāra Vālmīki,[137] which was imbued with the spirit of Bhakti. It gave rise to the ample growth of Rāma-related literature in Kannada, however, it is not very interesting from the point of view of the development of the tradition.[138]

In the neighbouring Telugu-speaking area, three Rāmāyaṇas are of major importance: the thirteenth-century *Dvipada rāmāyaṇa*, commonly known as the *Raṅganātha rāmāyaṇa* after the name of its author, the fourteenth-century *Bhāskara rāmāyaṇa* by Hulakki Bhāskara and, apparently, the most popular of Telugu Rāmāyaṇas – the sixteenth century *Molla rāmāyaṇa* by Molla / Mollā, a woman of a low caste of potters.[139]

The beginning of the Rāmāyaṇa tradition in Malayalam, the youngest of the Dravidian languages, marks the beginning of Malayalam literature itself, as the *Rāmacaritam* of the twelfth or thirteenth century is the oldest known work in this language.[140] More or less its contemporary was the *Rāmakathappāṭṭu*[141] and of a somewhat later date (fourteenth or fifteenth century)[142] is the *Kaṇṇaśśa rāmāyaṇam*, permeated with Bhakti, by Rāma Paṇikkar that served as a source of inspiration for Eḻuttaccan̠, the most renowned Bhakti poet of Malayalam literature and the author of the *Attiyātuma rāmāyaṇam*, the best-known Malayalam telling of the Rāmāyaṇa, composed either in the end of the sixteenth or the beginning of the seventeenth century.[143]

---

[136] Ibid., pp. 272–4. Cf. Bulke, *Rāmkathā*, p. 59.

[137] Dated either to the sixteenth or mid seventeenth century; Bulke, *Rāmkathā*, pp. 180–1 and Brockington, *Righteous Rāma*, p. 274. For its English translation see *Torvey Rāmāyaṇa*, tr. Shantilal Nagar, Delhi: B.R. Publishing Corporation, 2004.

[138] Bulke, *Rāmkathā*, pp. 180–1.

[139] Brockington, *Righteous Rāma*, p. 276 and Bulke, *Rāmkathā*, pp. 178–80.

[140] Cf. Bulke, *Rāmkathā*, p. 180; Brockington, *Righteous Rāma*, p. 274 and Taṅkamaṇi Ammā, 'Keral mẽ rāmsaṁskṛti', in Siṁh, *Śrī Rām viśvakoś*, pp. 546–7.

[141] Taṅkamaṇi Ammā, 'Keral mẽ rāmsaṁskṛti', p. 547.

[142] Cf. Brockington, *Righteous Rāma*, p. 276; Bulke *Rāmkathā*, p. 180 and Taṅkamaṇi Ammā, 'Keral mẽ rāmsaṁskṛti', ibid.

[143] Bulke, *Rāmkathā*, p. 180 and Brockington, *Righteous Rāma*, pp. 274–6.

Different tellings of the Rāmāyaṇa of eastern origin are based on the north-eastern recension of Vālmīki's *Rāmāyaṇa*.[144] The oldest of them is the fourteenth-century Assamese version of Mādhava Kandalī, close to Vālmīki but also containing elements popular in Assam.[145] Most probably in the beginning of the sixteenth century,[146] Durgāvara composed his *Gīti rāmāyaṇa* in the form of a collection of songs, based on Mādhava Kandalī's work.[147]

However, the most famous in eastern India is the Bengali *Rāmāyaṇa* by Kṛttivās Ojhā, probably of the late fifteenth century.[148] The immense popularity of this work has made it absorb a lot of material of varied character that is responsible for its different local variants or even traditions.[149] Its text has been constantly reworked and some scholars even say that not much remains of the original.[150] It is worth mentioning here that in Kṛttivās's work, as in other Rāmāyaṇas from eastern India, Shaiva

---

[144] Bulke, *Rāmkathā*, p. 187.

[145] For more see Smith, *Rāmāyaṇa Traditions*, pp. 27–8, 35–6; Brockington, *Righteous Rāma*, pp. 278–9; Bulke, *Rāmkathā*, pp. 187–8; Satyendra Nath Sarma, 'Folk Versions of Rama-katha in Early Assamese', in Singh and Datta, *Rama-katha*, pp. 110–11. For its English translation see *Mādhava Kandalī Rāmāyaṇa*, tr. Shanti Lal Nagar, 2 vols, Delhi: Munshiram Manoharlal, 2000.

[146] Smith, *Rāmāyaṇa Traditions*, p. 28; Prabin Chandra Das, 'Durgavari: An Assamese Version of the Ramayana', in Singh and Datta, *Rama-katha*, p. 141 and Bulke, *Rāmkathā*, p. 188.

[147] For more on the Assamese Rāmkathās see Birendranath Datta, 'Rama-katha in Assam and its Neighbourhood: Popular and Folk Traditions', Singh and Datta, *Rama-katha*, pp. 119–30; Das, 'Durgavari: An Assamese Version of the Ramayana', pp. 137–52; Bhrigu Mohan Goswami, 'The Ramayana-based Ojapalis of Assam', in Singh and Datta, *Rama-katha*, pp. 153–60; Smith, *Rāmāyaṇa Traditions*, pp. 27–30 and Bulke, *Rāmkathā*, pp. 187–9.

[148] Smith, *Rāmāyaṇa Traditions*, p. 30 and Bulke, *Rāmkathā*, p. 189. Dušan Zbavitel expresses the opinion that it was composed in the beginning of the fifteenth century; idem, *Bengali Literature*, Wiesbaden: Otto Harrassowitz, 1976, pp. 135, 141.

[149] Smith, *Rāmāyaṇa Traditions*, pp. 41–2; cf. Zbavitel, *Bengali Literature*, p. 142 and Bulke, *Rāmkathā*, p. 189.

[150] See S. Sen's opinion quoted in Smith, *Rāmāyaṇa Traditions*, p. 30.

and Shakta influences are visible. For example, Rāma's victory over Rāvaṇa is a result of *pūjā*, a sacrifice for Devī, Goddess.[151]

Judging by the number of titles, it seems that the fame of Kṛttivās's telling did not discourage other Bengali authors from composing their own versions. Among them, there was also Candrāvatī, the earliest known Bengali poetess,[152] who probably in the end of the sixteenth[153] or the beginning of the seventeenth[154] century composed her *Rāmāyaṇa* that circulated orally until quite recently.[155] One can also mention the seventeenth-century *Adbhuta rāmāyaṇa* by Nityānanda Ācārya alias Adbhutāćārya (hence the title of the work)[156] and probably a century later[157] the *Viṣṇupurī rāmāyaṇa* by Śaṅkara Kavicandra, while the end of traditional style Bengali poetry on Rāma is said to be marked by the *Śrīrāmarasāyana* (1831?) by Raghunandan Gosvāmī.[158]

Even in a short survey of Bengali works related to the Rāmāyaṇa tradition, one should not omit a modern poem *Meghanādavadha kāvya* (1861) by Madhusūdan Datta (1824–73). Although it does not deal with the entire story but mainly with the motif of the struggle between Rāma and Rāvaṇa's son, it deserves attention because of its originality and the discussion which it provoked; its evaluation is inconclusive till this day.[159] The complex structure of this work evokes in its Indian readers a non-traditional reaction, sympathetic towards Rāvaṇa, Rāma's foe.[160] As Nirad C. Chaudhuri puts it, indicating clearly one of the

---

[151] Smith, *Rāmāyaṇa Traditions*, pp. 127–53. Also see Brockington, *Righteous Rāma*, pp. 276–7 and Bulke, *Rāmkathā*, pp. 191, 588.

[152] Smith, *Rāmāyaṇa Traditions*, p. 31.

[153] Brockington, *Righteous Rāma*, p. 276.

[154] Bulke, *Rāmkathā*, p. 191.

[155] Smith, *Rāmāyaṇa Traditions*, pp. 26, 31, 42.

[156] Ibid., p. 30; Zbavitel, *Bengali Literature*, pp. 142, 145 and Bulke, *Rāmkathā*, p. 192.

[157] Smith, *Rāmāyaṇa Traditions*, p. 31 and Bulke, *Rāmkathā*, p. 192.

[158] Ibid., pp. 32, 93–4, 113 and ibid., p. 193.

[159] For more on its evaluation see Clinton Seely, 'The Raja's New Clothes: Redressing Rāvaṇa in Meghanādavadha Kāvya', in Richman, *Many Rāmāyaṇas*, pp. 149–52.

[160] Ibid., pp. 142–9.

sources of Datta's inspiration:[161] 'When we were thinking of demons and of gods (...), Dutt was thinking of the Trojans and the Achaeans. (...) Ravana's city, which to us was the Citadel of Evil, was to Dutt a second Holy Troy'.[162] And indeed, the poet's approach to Rāma was not traditional, although not unique in the Rāmāyaṇa tradition.[163] It is best expressed in his own words from a letter to his friend: 'People here grumble that the sympathy of the Poet in Meghanad is with the Raksasas. And that is the real truth. I despise Ram and his rabble, but the idea of Ravan elevates and kindles my imagination; he was a grand fellow'.[164] Datta's interpretation of the traditional story may be linked to the situation of India, and especially of Bengal, of the poet's time. Colonialism and the presence of the British resulted in, among other things, the transformation of the traditional value system – 'what was native seemed despicable; what was English, grand and glorious'.[165] Referring to Ashis Nandy, we may say that Datta's poem can be seen as an attempt to redefine 'popular mythology to fit the changing values under colonialism'.[166]

The Oriya language is also no exception as far tellings of the Rāma story are concerned. However, the earliest of them, the work by Siddheśvar Pariḍa (fifteenth century), commonly known as Sāraladās, has not survived.[167] The oldest, extant Rāmāyaṇa in Oriya is the *Jagamohana rāmāyaṇa* by Bāḷarāmdās, probably of the

---

[161] For more on the sources of Datta see Clinton Seely, 'Homeric Similes, Occidental and Oriental: Tasso, Milton, and Bengal's Michael Madhusudan Dutt', *Comparative Literature Studies*, vol. 25, no. 1, 1988, pp. 35–56.

[162] Nirad C. Chaudhuri, *The Autobiography of an Unknown Indian*, 3rd impression, Bombay: Jaico Publishing House, 1969, p. 195.

[163] E.g. in Jaina Rāmāyaṇas. Cf. Ashis Nandy, *The Intimate Enemy: Loss and Recovery of Self Under Colonialism*, Delhi: Oxford University Press, 1993, p. 19.

[164] Quoted after Seely, 'The Raja's New Clothes', p. 137; cf. Zbavitel, *Bengali Literature*, p. 233.

[165] Quoted after Seely, 'The Raja's New Clothes', p. 150.

[166] Nandy, *The Intimate Enemy*, p. 18; cf. Chaudhuri, *The Biography*, p. 195.

[167] Cf. Bulke, *Rāmkathā*, p. 193 and Smith, *Rāmāyaṇa Traditions*, pp. 23, 33.

late fifteenth or early sixteenth century, popularly known as the *Dāṇḍi rāmāyaṇa*.[168]

The *Bhāvārtha rāmāyaṇa* by a Marathi poet Eknāth[169] is the oldest and most respected Rāmāyaṇa in western India. Its narrative is based mostly on Vālmīki as well as on the *Ānanda rāmāyaṇa*, while the *Adhyātma rāmāyaṇa* was the source of the Bhakti stand. Its philosophical and theological orientation is overwhelming.[170] This work is viewed as the sixteenth-century interpretation of the Rāmāyaṇa with the leading theme of Rāmarājya understood as the kingdom of God on earth with Rāma, God-King, the upholder of dharma.[171]

A somewhat later Marathi poet Rāmadāsa (1608–81), an ascetic Rāma devotee,[172] composed two narrative poems based on Book 5 and 6 of the Rāmāyaṇa. The choice of these books is said to originate from the poet's desire to depict this period in Rāma's life, in which gods and people were definitely released from the oppression of Rāvaṇa by analogy with the liberation-to-be of Hindus from the Muslim oppression. The only means to attain this goal was Bhakti, the devotion to God.[173] With time, Rāmadāsa gathered a group of disciples with one female, Veṇābāī alias Veṇusvāmī (1628–1700). She is the author of a touching poem entitled *Sītāsvayaṁvara*, as well as of an incomplete version of the Rāmāyaṇa.[174] Very popular till this day is the *Rāmavijaya* (1703) by Śrīdhara that is under the evident influence of Eknāth.[175] The works of Moropanta (1729–94), considered the last Marāṭhī classical poet, are also interesting. He became famous for, among other things, his *Mantra*[176] *rāmāyaṇa*s. According to tradition, he

---

[168] Smith, *Rāmāyaṇa Traditions*, pp. 23, 25, 32–3; Bulke, *Rāmkathā*, pp. 193–4; and Brockington, *Righteous Rāma*, p. 279.

[169] See n. 94 in this Introduction. It was composed in the latter part of Eknāth's life; left incomplete, probably finished by one of his disciples.

[170] Tulpule, *Classical Marāṭhī Literature*, p. 356.

[171] Ibid. and Brockington, *Righteous Rāma*, pp. 284–5.

[172] Tulpule, *Classical Marāṭhī Literature*, p. 394.

[173] Ibid., pp. 395–6.

[174] Ibid., pp. 400–2, 410; cf. Bulke, *Rāmkathā*, p. 257 and Brockington, *Righteous Rāma*, p. 285.

[175] Tulpule, *Classical Marāṭhī Literature*, pp. 407–8 and Bulke, *Rāmkathā*, p. 204.

[176] *Mantra* 'a sacred formula'.

composed 108 such works, in which a given *mantra* is repeated regularly, e.g. *Śrī Rāma, jaya Rāma, jaya jaya Rāma* (Oh, respected Rāma, glory/victory to Rāma, glory, glory to Rāma!); a certain phonetic rule (also considered to be a *mantra*) can be implemented, e.g. a total evasion of labial consonants (*niroṣthya*).[177] This device was by no means Śrīdhara's invention. It was well known in the tradition of classical Indian poetry, Kāvya, which he was continuing. The main difference between Moropanta and his Sanskrit predecessors was that he offered his mastery of word to his God and not a patron-king.

Although in Gujarat the story of Kṛṣṇa's life was more popular than Rāmkathā, according to C. Bulcke, in the extant data on Gujarati poets active between 1370 and 1852 out of 372 authors fifty of them devoted their works to Rāma.[178] Among them, the most popular till the present day is the *Rāmāyaṇa* (1837)[179] of Girdhara (1783–1852)[180] that obscured at least three earlier tellings. Nevertheless, it is also true that because of the Kṛṣṇa devotion that is prevalent in Gujarat and, related to this, the lack of places important for the cult of Rāma, his devotees felt the need of direct contact with such Ramaite centres as Ayodhya or Chitrakut in the eastern part of north India. And because this area is under the – religious, social as well as literary – influence of the *Rāmcaritmānas,* it is not surprising that Tulsīdās's work gained reasonable popularity in Gujarat. It is not only recited in the original,

---

[177] Tulpule, *Classical Marāṭhī Literature,* pp. 422–4 and Brockington, *Righteous Rāma,* p. 285.

[178] Bulke, *Rāmkathā,* pp. 204–5. Some songs with a Rāma theme are also found in Gujarati folklore; in a collection of *c.* 4000 songs, a little more than 3 per cent are devoted to Rāma, while to Kṛṣṇa 15 per cent; Hasu Yajnik, 'The Oral Tradition of Rāmkathā in Gujarātī Folk Songs', in Alan W. Entwistle et al., eds, *Studies in Early Modern Indo-Aryan Languages, Literature and Culture,* Delhi: Manohar, 1999, p. 411.

[179] Devdatta Joshi, 'Contemporary Rāmāyaṇa Tradition in Gujarat', *Journal of the Oriental Institute* (Baroda), vol. 37, nos 3–4, 1988, p. 245 and Brockington, *The Sanskrit Epics,* p. 503. For its English translation see *Giradhara Rāmāyaṇa,* tr. Shanti Lal Nagar and Tripta Nagar, Delhi: Munshiram Manoharlal, 2003.

[180] Joshi, 'Contemporary Rāmāyaṇa', p. 245.

especially Book 5, and commented on in Gujarati but also translated as a whole or in fragments.[181]

In north India outside the Hindi-speaking area it is Punjab that can claim perhaps the most eminent of the representatives of the Rāmāyaṇa tradition, namely Guru Gobind Siṅgh (1666–1708[182]), the tenth and last personal Guru or spiritual leader of the Sikhs. The major language of his literary expression was Braj (written in the Gur(u)mukhī script), then the most important literary medium in north India, in which he composed his *Rāmāvatār [kathā]* (1698).[183] It is a part of the *Dasam granth*, a collection of Guru Gobind's works that is contained in the *Caubīs avatār* (Twenty-four Avataras).[184]

A number of Rāmāyaṇa manuscripts found in different libraries in Punjab testify to its presence in this part of India as well as a close relationship with Hindi literature. For example, one of the authors[185] enumerates thirty-three works related to the story in Braj with a bigger or lesser admixture of Punjabi. He makes a very important observation, namely that the access to them is relatively limited because those who know the Punjabi language and its Gurmukhī script usually do not know Braj, and vice versa, those knowing Braj mostly do not know the script of Punjabi.[186]

A varied Rāmāyaṇa tradition also developed in Kashmir, the northernmost part of India, although due to different reasons not much has been published of this lore till now. The late eighteenth-

---

[181] Ibid., esp. p. 246.

[182] W.H. McLeod, *Historical Dictionary of Sikhism*, Delhi: Oxford University Press, 2002 (1st published 1995), pp. 86–7. Cf. Sant Sikh Sekhon and Kartar Singh Duggal, *A History of Punjabi Literature*, Delhi: Sahitya Akademi, 1992, p. 57 and R.S. McGregor, *Hindi Literature from Its Beginnings*, Wiesbaden: Otto Harrassowitz, 1984, p. 140.

[183] Baljit Tulsi, 'Rāmāvatār (Rāmāyaṇa) by Guru Gobind Singh', in Raghavan, *The Ramayana Tradition*, p. 518; Vinod Kumār, *Govind Rāmāyaṇ: Guru Govind Siṁh praṇit Rāmāvatār kathā*, Delhi: Sanmārg Prakāśan, 1969, p. 105 and Bulke, *Rāmkathā*, p. 202.

[184] McLeod, *A History*, p. 61.

[185] Manmohan Sahgal, the editor of the eighteenth-century *Rāmcaritra* by Kṛṣṇalāl; see Kṛṣṇalāl, *Rāmcaritra*, ed. Manmohan Sahgal, Delhi: Sanmārg Prakāśan, 1978, pp. 14–15.

[186] Ibid., pp. 5–13.

century[187] *Rāmāyaṇa* of Divākara Prakāśa Bhaṭṭa was most probably preceded by an old oral tradition in Kashmiri. Such a contention seems to be corroborated by the texts of many folk songs and the Kashmiri language itself, which is rich in sayings and idioms referring to the story of Rāma.[188]

* * *

A great diversity that transpires from the material included in the foregoing presentation, by no means pretending to be exhaustive, is a telling exemplification of about twenty-five hundred years of continual wandering and mutual intertwining of the motifs of different origins whose provenance is sometimes impossible to identify unequivocally. The story's unprecedented popularity and exceptional universality is testified to by the large numbers of authors hailing from different parts of India and representing different religious traditions: Hinduism, Buddhism and Jainism (it is worth remembering that it has also found its place in the tribal lore of India). They all tried to elaborate on certain episodes that seemed, for different reasons, especially attractive to them. Many authors, including those belonging to the Hindu tradition, attempted to elucidate these incidents and their circumstances, such as those related to Rāma's exile or the banishment of Sītā, which with time ceased to be comprehensible to their audiences, became unconvincing or appeared to cast a shadow on the impeccable character of Rāma. Apart from the strongest and most conspicuous influence of Vaishnava philosophy and theology, thanks to which Rāma with time was elevated to the status of the Supreme Being, in many Rāmāyaṇas – to a different degree –

---

[187] *The Kāshmīrī Rāmāyaṇa, Comprising the Śrīrāmāvatāracarita & the Lavakuśayuddhacarita of Divākara Prakāśa Bhaṭṭa*, ed. George A. Grierson, Bibliotheca Indica no. 253, Calcutta: Asiatic Society of Bengal, 1930, p. XI; Bulke, *Rāmkathā*, p. 186 and Brockington, *Righteous Rāma*, p. 285. P.N. Pushp maintains that it was composed in 1846; idem, 'Rāmāyaṇa in Kashmiri Literature and Folk-lore', Raghavan, *The Ramayana Tradition*, p. 541. It was published at least six times: thrice in the Arabic script, twice in the Devanāgarī script and once in the Roman script (Grierson's edition); ibid., p. 541. For its English translation see *Rāmāvatāracarita*, tr. Shanti Lal Nagar, Delhi: Munshiram Manoharlal, 2001.

[188] Pushp, 'Rāmāyaṇa in Kashmiri', pp. 534–41.

Shaiva, Shakta or Tantric influences are also apparent and sometimes they determine in a clear-cut manner the ideological strata of a given work.

Of no less importance for the development of the Rāmāyaṇa tradition, especially in more recent pasts, seems the impact on the authors of the arrival and settling in India first of Muslims and then of the British that resulted in a new understanding of and new insights into the story. For example, in the case of Rāmadāsa's Marathi telling the traditional interpretation of the victory of Rāma over Rāvaṇa in terms of the victory of good over evil gained a new element of utmost importance. It was a new interpretation of the borderline between good and evil understood as a boundary between Hindus ('us') fighting on the side of good and destined to win and Muslims ('them') fighting on the side of evil and destined to lose. A similar mechanism operated later in the case of the presence of the British which was evident in Datta's poem. To a considerable degree the penetration of western socio-political thought in India influenced the already-mentioned very interesting trend in the interpretation of the story of Rāma in south India in the last century where the Rāmāyaṇa has become a very convenient tool in the struggle for the Dravidian identity.

A Western reader may feel puzzled that the results of such rich growth with such diverse ideological (religious, philosophical as well as political) contents that at times are contradictory can be contained in one tradition. The simplest and the most appropriate explanation of this seems to suggest that this is the very phenomenon of the Rāmāyaṇa, a mapping of Indian culture on a smaller scale – constantly remodelling itself (or constantly being remodelled) by way of additions to, polemics with and expansion of the already-existing basis, and not abandoning it in order to build on entirely new foundations. What is more, the story of Rāma despite (or maybe: because of?) the differentiation of all its versions invariably seems so attractive and relevant to authors and their audiences that it is told anew generation by generation. As I will try to demonstrate further in this study, although much can change in its form and content, it retains a certain basis on which authors build their retellings. What seems most fascinating in them all from the point of view of the development of the Rāmāyaṇa tradition, besides the extraordinary diversity of their ideological frames, is the unique multidimensionality or even the 'plasticity' of the story which being retold time after time can contain such differing contents and despite this still remains the story of Rāma.

NOTES ON THE CULT OF RĀM (RĀMBHAKTI)

INTRODUCTION

The foregoing sections have primarily been focused on the growth of the literary tradition of the Rāmāyaṇa from the point of view of its main achievements. However, more than once the evolution in the religious strata of the text, manifesting itself in different conceptions of Rāma, has also been referred to. In terms of theology, Rāma first evolved into an avatāra of Viṣṇu, then he was identified with Viṣṇu and finally he transcended Viṣṇu and was elevated to the status of the Supreme Being.[189] In this context, F. Whaling's observation that Vālmīki's Rāma is neither yet worshipped as God nor is yet God in his fullness but rather a symbol of God[190] is of great significance for the understanding of the process of the evolution of the figure of Rāma. At a certain moment, a community of his worshippers also came into existence and the basis of their religious identity was total devotion to Rāma. These changes, connected with the development of different philosophical and theological ideas/ doctrines, exerted an essential influence on the literature composed in new Indo-Aryan languages. The culmination of this process was the development and spontaneous growth of the cult of Rām or Rāmbhakti, especially in the Hindi-speaking area of north India. This development, as pointed out by F. Whaling,[191] can be seen as a specific paradigm of the unfolding of Indian religious tradition characterized by the willingness to accept new elements to the existing basis that promotes the process of transformation. It is not a closed model but a model informed by the openness that has frequently expressed itself in traditional Indian culture.

---

[189] Cf. Whaling, *The Rise*, p. 7.
[190] Ibid., p. 92.
[191] Ibid., p. 5.

The research on the rise and growth of Rāmbhakti, as has been already mentioned, till this day has not been exhaustive which seems surprising if we take into account the significance of this cult especially in the Hindi-speaking area. It seems plausible that the interdisciplinary, multifaceted character of this problem, i.e. the need on the side of a researcher to refer to many disciplines such as philology and textual criticism, archaeology, religious studies, philosophy, history, etc. may have deterred individual scholars from dealing with it. In more recent times, of no less significance may also be a political entanglement of Rām-related issues especially due to the aftermath of the 1992 demolition of Babri Masjid in Ayodhya. The most important studies on the cult of Rām by the already-mentioned Frank Whaling as well as by Hans Bakker are an exception in this regard. Whaling, discussing the rise of the religious significance of Rām, based his analysis exclusively on literary sources, i.e. the three most important Rāmāyaṇas: Vālmīki's *Rāmāyaṇa*, the *Adhyātma rāmāyaṇa* and Tulsīdās's *Rāmcaritmānas*. Bakker in his studies combined the analysis of ritual texts (especially the *Agastyasaṃhitā*) with archaeological findings.[192] What is very commendable about the works of Whaling and Bakker, differing much in their character and thus being complementary to one another, is their authors' attempt to treat the developments in the tradition as an integral process.[193] Undoubtedly, they are basic reading for all those interested in the nature of Rām himself and the rise of Rāmbhakti. To these works, one should also add an already-mentioned study by Bhagavatīprasād Siṁh[194] that deals for the most part with an interesting current of Rāmbhakti, i.e. the esoteric sect of Rasik Sampradāy (for more details see below).

In the discussion devoted to the rise and growth of the cult of Rām, it seems useful to refer to the proposal of Hans Bakker who conveniently divided the history of Rāmbhakti into four

---

[192] Esp. Hans Bakker, *Ayodhyā*, Groningen: Egbert Forsten, 1986; idem, 'The Rise of Ayodhyā as a Place of Pilgrimage', *Indo-Iranian Journal*, vol. 24, 1982, pp. 103–26 and idem, 'Reflections on the Evolution of Rāma Devotion in the Light of Textual and Archaeological Evidence', *Wiener Zeitschrift für die Kunde Südasiens*, vol. 31, 1987, pp. 9–42.

[193] Whaling, *The Rise*, pp. 86–7, 90–1.

[194] Siṁh, *Rāmbhakti*.

periods: 1. the pre-Muslim period; 2. the age of the Delhi Sultanate; 3. the period of the Great Moguls; 4. the eighteenth to twentieth centuries.[195] Thus, the first period embraces the time before the twelfth century when Muslims were already in India but their power was yet to be consolidated. The second period, i.e. the thirteenth to fifteenth centuries, witnessed the consolidation of Muslim power. The third period embraces the sixteenth to eighteenth centuries, i.e. the peak of Muslim power, and it seems that the closing date of the fourth period, characterized with the strengthening of the cult as it is known and practised today, can be conveniently extended till the present day.

As I have tried to show in the foregoing presentation, the Rāmāyaṇa had become very popular long before the process of the formation of its oldest known version, i.e. the *Rāmāyaṇa* of Vālmīki, was closed. The *Rāmopākhyāna,* in which – unlike in other parts (evidently later) of the *Mahābhārata* – Rāma is not conceived as an avatāra, is the earliest exemplification of this.[196] Rāma as an avatāra is dealt with by such earlier Purāṇas as the *Viṣṇu purāṇa,*[197] the *Vayu purāṇa,*[198] the *Matsya purāṇa*[199] and the *Brahmāṇḍa purāṇa.* However, neither these Purāṇas nor Puranic literature as such developed one coherent concept of avatāras – they include various lists of avatāras and differ in their methods

---

[195] Bakker, 'Reflections', p. 9. Cf. Siṁh, *Rāmbhakti*, p. 51. According to Siṁh, however, the development of *Rāmbhakti* can be divided into the following three periods, namely 1. *ālvār yug* from 800 to 1100; 2. *ācārya yug* from 1100 to 1400, and 3. *rāmāvat yug* from 1400 until the present, thus Siṁh's proposal partly overlaps with Bakker's design.

[196] For obvious reasons I refer here neither to Buddhist nor to Jaina sources.

[197] Most probably composed between the fourth and fifth century AD; Rocher, *The Purāṇas*, p. 249 and Bulke, *Rāmkathā*, p. 123.

[198] Dated between the fourth and fifth century AD, most probably later than the *Viṣṇu purāṇa;* Rocher, *The Purāṇas,* p. 245; Brockington, *Righteous Rāma*, p. 234 and Bulke, *Rāmkathā*, p. 123.

[199] Dated between the third and fifth century AD, not later than the sixth century; Rocher, *The Purāṇas,* p. 249. It is considered the earliest Purāṇa that describes Rāma's image. The earliest descriptions of the way Rāma's idols should be made come from the *Viṣṇudharmottara purāṇa* (around fifth century AD) and Varāhamihira's *Bṛhat saṁhitā* (around mid sixth century AD); Bulke, *Rāmkathā*, p. 118 and Siṁh, *Rāmbhakti*, p. 50.

of presentation. In the case of Rāma, it means that they endow him with different degrees of divinity: sometimes he is only a partial avatāra together with his brothers, at other times he is a full avatāra on his own. It is noteworthy that the concept of avatāras, or descents from heaven of a deity (particularly of Viṣṇu), had been preceded with an older idea of God's earthly manifestations, i.e. *prādurbhāva*, which was substituted by the newer concept and term, i.e. avatāra, around the times of Kālidāsa.[200]

Archaeological material related to Rāma is very sparse throughout the first millennium, though later also one cannot consider it profuse.[201] However, although scant, the extant temple relics seem sufficient to deduce a gradual evolution of the figure of Rāma. First, his images accompany Viṣṇu which is the practice originating in the idea of Rāma's being his avatāra. Later the identity between the two of them can be noticed and finally Rāma becomes an independent object of a cult.[202] The existence of a few early sanctuaries devoted to Rāma is documented. H. Bakker suggests that they may have originated from an additional altar (an idol?) in the main Viṣṇu-Nārāyaṇa sanctuary.[203] The best known among them is the Rājīvalocana[204] temple in Rajim (Madhya Pradesh), built in the seventh century and dedicated to Viṣṇu. After renovation, in 1145 AD it was consecrated and

---

[200] For more on the development of the concept of avatāras see Paul Hacker, 'Zur Entwicklung der Avatārlehre', *Wiener Zeitschrift für die Kunde Südasiens*, vol. 4, 1960, pp. 47–70 and Tapeśvar Nāth Prasād, *Madhyakālīn rāmkāvya dhārā par kṛṣṇabhāvnā kā prabhāv*, Vārāṇasī: Caukhambha, 1981, pp. 5–10; cf. Bakker, *Ayodhyā*, pp. 60–3.

[201] I refer here almost exclusively to the representations of Rāma that were related to ritual, i.e. functioned in his cult. Thus, I exclude numerous reliefs and sculptures looking upon Rāma primarily as an epic hero or a king. For more on the latter type of Rāma's images see e.g. John Brockington, 'Visual Epics', in Danuta Stasik and John Brockington, eds, *Indian Epic Traditions – Past and Present* (*Rocznik Orientalistyczny*, vol. 54, no. 1, 2002), pp. 111–31. For illustrations see e.g. P. Banerjee, *Rama in Indian Literature, Art and Thought*, vol. 2, Delhi: Sundeep Prakashan, 1986 and C. Shivaramamurti, *Rāmo Vigrahavān Dharma: Rāma Embodiment of Righteousness*, Delhi: Kanak Publications, 1980.

[202] Bakker, *Ayodhyā*, pp. 64ff.

[203] Ibid., pp. 64–5.

[204] Lit. 'Lotus-eyed', one of the most popular epithets of Rām.

dedicated to Rāma. Very symptomatically, the temple idol embodies Viṣṇu without any attributes characteristic of Rāma. This seems to indicate the tendency in the Ramaite tradition of continuation and modification of previous forms of cult.[205]

BHAKTI

Before dealing with the development of the cult of Rām, i.e. Rāmbhakti, it would be advisable to consider the meaning of the indigenous key-term 'Bhakti'[206] that has already been appearing on the foregoing pages. Basically, it designates the form of devotion dominant in contemporary Hinduism that is, first of all, characterized by a total emotional (less commonly also intellectual) dedication to a chosen deity, conceived as God. A devotee (*bhakta*) while adoring God strives to actively participate in his nature and in return God bestows on his worshipper his grace (*prasāda*), protection and loving affection.

Without going into too many details, it can be said that in the Bhakti type of devotion there are two main ways of perceiving God: firstly, as the unmanifest (*nirguṇa*, i.e. 'without attributes') Ultimate Being and, secondly, as manifest (*saguṇa*, i.e. 'with attributes'), personal God. This differentiation results in the two traditions of Bhakti: *saguṇa*, which is predominant, and *nirguṇa*. In the *saguṇa* Bhakti bhaktas worship basically an anthropomorphic manifestation of God (Viṣṇu, Śiva or Devī, i.e. the Goddess), while in the *nirguṇa* Bhakti bhaktas worship God who has no form but His Name, Word, a guru and *sant*s can act as his partial manifestations.[207] *Saguṇa* Bhakti is essentially rooted in the

---

[205] Bakker, *Ayodhyā*, p. 67.

[206] Bhakti (S. *bhakti*) – the noun from the verbal root *bhaj* ('to partake of; enjoy; feel; serve; honour; love; adore') that means, among other things: '(the being) a part of; belonging; attachment; devotion (to); worship; piety; faith; love'; cf. Monier-Williams, *A Sanskrit-English Dictionary*, p. 743.

[207] In this context, an observation of A.K. Ramanujan concerning the poetry devoted to Śiva is of great significance: 'All devotional poetry plays on the tension between *saguṇa* and *nirguṇa*, the lord as person and the lord as principle. If he were only a person, he would not be divine, and if he were entirely a principle, a godhead, one could not make

mainstream of Hinduism enriched with elements of different local cults. In its commonest form, it is a deintellectualized form of earlier Hinduism dominated by a small, exclusively male Brahmin elite, a result of the opening up of this (orthodox) elite for the rest of Hindu society, i.e. Shudras and women who previously had no ritual rights, and their inclusion in the ritual practice. Thus, it can be seen as an expression of Brahmin ideology addressed to all strata of Hindu (*varṇa*) society. The tradition of *nirguṇa* Bhakti, contesting the authority of the Vedas and Brahmins, is an interesting fusion of different, also unorthodox, Hindu ideas and practices, as well as elements of Islam, especially Sufi mysticism.[208] Its origin is rooted in a strong opposition of the lowest strata of society[209] to the ideology of the mainstream Hinduism dominated by Brahmins. That is why in recent studies the differentiation between these two currents of Bhakti tends to be defined rather in ideological than theological categories which is justified by the contention that different theologies result from different social ideologies and the separate identities of the groups supporting them.[210]

One of the most important new aspects of Bhakti was the substitution of a complicated Vedic sacrifice, made not by a devo-

---

poems about him'. A.K. Ramanujan, 'The Myths of Bhakti: Images of Śiva in Śaiva Poetry', in Vinay Dharwadker, ed., *The Collected Essays of A.K. Ramanujan*, Delhi: Oxford University Press, 2004, p. 295.

[208] The best known, fullest expression of *nirguṇ* type of Bhakti is exemplified by the oeuvre of Kabīr; see e.g. Kabīr, *Bījak*, ed. Śukdev Siṁh, Ilāhābād: Nīlābh Prakāśan, 1972, esp. pp. 84, 91, 113, 138. Cf. Edmour J. Babineau, *Love of God and Social Duty in the Rāmcaritmānas*, Delhi: Motilal Banarsidass, 1979, p. 71. It is noteworthy that for Kabīr the word 'Rāma' (like 'Allah') is a synonym of the word 'God'. Also see Charlotte Vaudeville, *Kabīr*, vol. 1, Oxford: Oxford University Press, 1974, pp. 94ff.

[209] I.e. nominally Hindus (like Shudras) and formally non-Hindus who existed on the fringes of Hindu society and were denied any ritual status.

[210] For more on this subject, see David N. Lorenzen, 'Introduction: The Historical Vicissitudes of Bhakti Religion', in idem, ed., *Bhakti Religion in North India: Community Identity and Political Action*, Albany: State University of New York, 1995, pp. 1–32; also see Prasād, *Madhyakālīn rāmkāvya dhārā*, pp. 123–43.

tee but by a priest, with a sacrifice made directly by a worshipper, i.e. with *pūjā*,[211] in the form of flowers, fruit, incense or just repeating or remembering the Name of God (*jap*, *nām sumiran*). Also of great significance was active participation in the communal religious life, the so-called 'association with the good' (*satsaṅg*), in order to join in religious disputes, the singing of devotional songs and hymns (*bhajan*), listening to public sermons (*pravacan*) and recitations of sacred texts (*pāṭh*), as well as going on pilgrimages (*tīrthyātrā*).[212] As Arthur L. Basham observed[213] Bhakti is neither complicated nor does it involve special expenditure, costly offerings or severe penances – God's grace can be attained without elaborate process expounded in treatises and by religious teachers. God will be satisfied with an offering of a flower or a libation of water given with sincere devotion. In other words, Bhakti can be seen as a specific shortcut to the highest spiritual states that otherwise can be achieved only as a result of arduous exertion and renouncement.[214] Therefore, it took Brahmin orthodoxy some time to acknowledge Bhakti which was considered to be an inferior way to salvation associated with the lower strata of society and as such a primitive type of devotion.

In the development of Bhakti, three main stages can be distinguished. The first of them, which is quite loosely connected with the remaining two, relates to such Upaniṣads as the *Kaṭha upaniṣad* and the *Śvetāśvatara upaniṣad* (probably around the fourth or third century BC) where the nucleus of Bhakti can be sought, while the *Bhagavadgītā* (between the second century BC and second century AD) is an isolated example of the well-formed Bhakti of the intellectual type that suggests a long process in its development. Texts dealing with the theory and practice of Bhakti, such as the *Bhaktisūtra*s (around the tenth century) by Nārada and Śāṇḍilya or the *Bhāgavata purāṇa*, are much later. In the second period, i.e. the period of its proper development, Bhakti emerged as a spontaneous devotional movement in Tamil

[211] For more on *pūjā* see Gudrun Bühnemann, *Pūjā: A Study in Smārta Ritual*, Vienna: University of Vienna, 1988.

[212] Cf. Lorenzen, 'Introduction', p. 24.

[213] A.L. Basham, *The Sacred Cow: The Evolution of Classical Hinduism*, ed. Kenneth G. Zysk, London: Rider, 1990, pp. 91–2.

[214] Ibid.

Nadu, with the greatest intensity between the latter half of the seventh and the ninth century, and then it gradually swept through India. In literature this period is characterized by the use of vernaculars (first in the south and then in north India), serving as a common medium of communication, that with time superseded the prestigious medium of expression, i.e. Sanskrit.[215] The third period can be conveniently dated from around the twelfth century onwards, when Bhakti first reached central and north India. An important role in spreading Bhakti all over India was played by the already-mentioned Rāmānuja who polemicized with the strict monism (*advaitavedanta*) of Śaṅkara (around the second half of the eighth century AD), thus laying the foundations for the doctrine of qualified monism (*viśiṣṭādvaita*[216]). According to Rāmānuja, the Absolute (*Brahman*) is the only reality that manifests itself as personal God, Viṣṇu-Nārāyaṇa, omniscient and infinite in his kindness and grace as well as affection.[217] Rāmānuja, although he did not break ties with the tradition of caste divisions in his philosophy, in actual practice rose above them and provided foundations for the availability of devotion to all groups of Hindu society and also to those from the outside, in which all people were equal before God irrespective of their social status.[218]

Bhakti spread in India both directly through wandering teachers and devotees representing the attitude of Bhakti as well as indirectly through the channels of folk traditions and took roots in north India around the thirteenth century.[219] As has already been mentioned, this was the period marked by a greater and greater presence of Muslims. Their monotheistic and egalitarian religion (relatively simple in its ritual practice), for some people was an attractive alternative to the exclusivist, restrictive and complicated pre-Bhakti Hinduism.

---

[215] Stasik, *Opowieść*, p. 129.

[216] See n. 14 above; cf. e.g. J.L. Brockington, *The Sacred Thread: Hinduism in Its Continuity and Diversity*, Edinburgh: Edinburgh University Press, 1981, pp. 150–6.

[217] Tokarz, *Z filozofii indyjskiej*, p. 50 and Stasik, *Opowieść*, p. 130.

[218] Brockington, *The Sacred Thread*, pp. 154–5; also see Stasik, *Opowieść*, pp. 130–1.

[219] Brockington, *The Sacred Thread*, pp. 168ff.

RĀMBHAKTI IN NORTH INDIA

Although archaeological, epigraphical and other evidence indicates that the adoration of Rāma in his supreme form existed before the twelfth century, Hans Bakker points to the fact that the worship of Rāma in his own right emerged during the twelfth and thirteenth centuries. This means that till then Rāma was regarded just as one of the forms of Viṣṇu, with Viṣṇu as the supreme deity.[220] Bakker explains it vividly: 'The rise of the Rāma cult should be understood as an aspect of the gradual development of Viṣṇuism (...) towards a more personal (humanised) conception of god that had a greater emotional appeal. Figuratively speaking, one may say that it was not a diversion of the stream of devotees from the main sanctum to a subsidiary shrine of Rāma, resulting in a gradual supersedence of the former by the latter, but an evolution within the main sanctum itself whereby Viṣṇu was turned into Rāma'.[221] He also postulates the view that Ramaite form of Vaishnavism should rather be seen not as a divergence from the orthodox Vaishnava tradition but as 'modified continuity' within its fold. Therefore, Bakker proposes defining the cult of Rāma as '(the participation in) a set of Vaiṣṇava doctrines and practices that centres on the worship of a supreme god who is invoked as Rāma and who is incarnate in a (temple) idol which is conceived of as representing him'.[222]

Very significantly, the cult of Rām began to gain prominence during the latest period of independent Hindu rule in north India and despite the great popularity of the Rāmāyaṇa the development of the cult itself was relatively slow until it found favourable circumstances in which to flourish and spread. It was possible thanks to the tide of emotional devotion, known as Bhakti, of a very egalitarian character, especially within the fold of Vaishnavism, which, as has just been mentioned, swept through India and transformed the character of Hinduism.[223]

In the context of the emergence of the cult of Rāma, one should not lose sight of the Ramaite cult texts. The oldest of them

---

[220] Bakker, *Ayodhyā*, pp. 66–7 and idem, 'Reflections', p. 9; cf. Siṁh, *Rāmbhakti*, p. 51.

[221] Bakker, *Ayodhyā*, p. 67.

[222] Ibid.

[223] Ibid., p. 66.

are the *Agastyasaṃhitā* (probably twelfth century[224]), the *Rāma-(pūrva)tāpanīya upaniṣad* (thirteenth to fourteenth century[225]) and the already-mentioned *Rāmarakṣāstotra*. H. Bakker points out that three strands intermingle in these texts: '1. worship (*pūjā*) of Rāma as highest god, 2. veneration of Rāma as exemplifying Hindu kingship (*kṣatra*), and 3. the power assigned to His Name, the ultimate *mantra*, which guarantees success (*siddhi*), be it in spiritual (*brahman*) or political and worldly affairs (*kṣatra / artha*). In other words, the multifarious figure of Rāma serves as a symbol and focus of truth / reality (*satya*) and *dharma*'.[226] These strands, as it will become further apparent in this study, were continued and developed by later vernacular authors such as Tulsīdās. These texts appear to provide convincing evidence of the existence of the Ramaite sects, although some scholars[227] consider the testimony of the *Adhyātma rāmāyaṇa* as more conclusive in this regard, indicating that a community of Rāmbhaktas emerged in north India not later than the fourteenth to fifteenth century.

Although the majority of Rāmbhaktas worship basically the *saguṇ* form of Rām, i.e. his anthropomorphic manifestation, the cult of His Name is also very significant. The most important Ramaite mantra, the Rām(a)mantra (*rāṃ rāmāya namaḥ*),[228] also called Rājamantra, can be considered as at least the harbinger of the worship of Rām's name which became a common practice in north India at the end of the fourteenth century, and in the fifteenth century the word 'Rām(a)' became the most frequently used synonym of the word 'god'. Interestingly, this practice, undoubtedly rooted in Indian tradition ascribing exceptional power to uttered formulas (*mantras*), became common in the time of the most repressive Muslim measures against Hindu temple cult and idolatry.[229] What

---

[224] Ibid., p. 70.

[225] Ibid., p. 122, n. 23.

[226] Bakker, 'Reflections', p. 23.

[227] Whaling, *The Rise*, pp. 105, 112, 170–1 and Babineau, *Love of God*, pp. 77–8.

[228] Siṁh, *Rāmbhakti*, p. 183.

[229] Bakker, *Ayodhyā*, pp. 119–24. Cf. R.S. McGregor, 'The Rama Story and Rama Devotion in North India', in Lallan Prasad Vyas, ed., *Ramayana: Its Universal Appeal and Global Role*, Delhi: Har-Anand Publications, 1992, p. 17 and Babineau, *Love of God*, pp. 55–6.

is more, in north India the Muslim penetration was the longest and the most intense. Therefore, it is plausible to consider it one of the reasons why in the Hindi-speaking area of north India the cult of Rām is the strongest and characterized by a relatively low occurrence of the temple worship of his images as well as a concurrent strong tradition of reciting and reading the story of his life and deeds (most commonly but not exclusively in the form of the *Rāmcaritmānas*), listening to it, contemplating Rām's name and worshipping his lotus feet which are imprinted in the hearts of all bhaktas. It is very important not to lose sight of this, while talking about the cult of Rām. Although he is God of a decidedly phenomenal, anthropomorphic character (*saguṇ*), whose deeds can be enacted, e.g. during famous Rāmlīlā performances,[230] at the same time he is also the Ultimate Being (*Brahman*), i.e. God without qualities (*nirguṇ*), whose possible visualisation is his Name. The most evident and famous literary exposition of such an image of Rām is contained in Tulsīdās's *magnum opus.*

RASIK SAMPRADĀY OR ESOTERIC RĀMBHAKTI

Rāmbhaktas, in their majority, worship Rām as his most devoted servants (*dās*), full of unselfish love for their Lord and ever ready to attend him. This mainstream tradition of Rāmbhakti, propagated in the sixteenth-century *Rāmcaritmānas* of Tulsīdās, is termed *dāsya-bhakti*, lit. 'devotion typical of a servant', i.e. full of humility. However, around the mid sixteenth century, another mode of worship emerged under the influence of Kṛṣṇabhakti,[231] in which the object of worship is the divine couple Sītā-Rām, referred to as the *yugalsarkār* (lit. 'couple-lord, couple-master'), who exercise

---

[230] Rāmlīlās are enacted during the month of Aśvin (September–October). They usually last ten days, although the best-known Rāmlīlā in Rāmnagar lasts the whole month. Rāmlīlās are commonly based on the *Rāmcaritmānas.* For more see Anuradha Kapur, *Actors, Pilgrims, Kings and Gods: The Ramlila at Ramnagar*, Calcutta: Seagull Books, 1990.

[231] Siṁh, *Rāmbhakti*, p. 143 and Peter van der Veer, *Gods on Earth: The Management of Religious Experience and Identity in a North Indian Pilgrimage Centre*, London–Atlantic Highlands, NJ: Athlone Press, 1988, p. 170; cf. Bulke, *Rāmkathā*, p. 200.

their sweet play (*mādhuryalīlā*) in the divine world (*divyalok*) of Sāket, the heavenly Ayodhya. This type of devotion, called *mādhuryabhakti* (sweet, delightful Bhakti) is fundamental in the Ramaite sect known as Rasik Sampradāy,[232] which emerged around the end of the seventeenth century.[233]

The key-term in the understanding of this current of Bhakti, i.e. *rasik*, calls for devoting more attention to it.[234] Its etymology refers to the Sanskrit noun *rasa* which in Indian poetics functions as a designation for an 'aesthetic sentiment' or 'aesthetic taste'. According to the theory of *rasa*, the main human emotions/sentiments (*sthāyī bhāva*) can, in certain circumstances, be transformed into aesthetic emotions/tastes (*rasa*).[235] Most commonly nine *rasa*s, arising from nine *bhāva*s, are distinguished:

1. erotic (*śṛṅgāra*) ← love (*rati*);
2. comic (*hāsya*) ← laughter (*hāsa*);
3. pathetic (*karuṇa*) ← sorrow (*śoka*);
4. furious (*raudra*) ← anger (*krodha*);
5. heroic (*vīra*) ← energy/effort (*utsāha*);
6. terrible (*bhayānaka*) ← fear (*bhaya*);
7. odious (*bībhatsa*) ← disgust (*jugupsā*);
8. marvellous (*adbhuta*) ← astonishment (*vismaya*);
9. quietism (*śānta*) ← tranquillity (*śama*).

Therefore, originally *rasik* means 'the one who is able to savour aesthetic sentiments', i.e. a 'connoisseur'. In the context of

---

[232] For more details see the most comprehensive study on this sect, viz. Siṁh, *Rāmbhakti*; also see Bhuvaneśvarnāth Miśra 'Mādhav', *Rāmbhakti mẽ madhur upāsanā*, Paṭnā: Bihār Rāṣṭrabhāṣā Pariṣad, 1957; Prasād, *Madhyakālīn rāmkāvya dhārā*; Philip Lutgendorf, 'The Secret Life of Rāmcandra of Ayodhya', in Richman, *Many Rāmāyaṇas*, pp. 217–34; Paraśurām Caturvedī, 'Rāmopāsakõ kā "Rasik Sampradāy"', *Hindustānī*, vol. 19, no. 3, 1958, pp. 3–42 and van der Veer, *Gods on Earth*, esp. pp. 159–72.

[233] Siṁh, *Rāmbhakti*, p. 119.

[234] For more see ibid., pp. 141–3.

[235] For more on the theory of *rasa* see Bharatamuni, *The Nāṭyaśāstra (A Treatise on Ancient Indian Dramaturgy and Histrionics)*, ed. Manmohan Ghosh, vol. 1, 3rd edn, Calcutta: Manisha, 1995, esp. pp. 77–116.

Rāmbhakti, however, this term acquired a new meaning. Thus, in the sixteenth century, Bengali Krishnaites cultivating mainly the *puṣṭimārgīy* tradition of Vallabha (1479–1531) and the *gauḍīya* tradition of Caitanya (1486–1533) settled in the region of Braj, the 'birth place' of Kṛṣṇa,[236] from where the teachings of their gurus, especially of Rūpa Gosvāmin and his nephew, Jīva Gosvāmin, quickly spread in north India. Their theology, which proved so attractive, combining religious contents with an explicitly erotic emotional aspect, was based on the theory of *Bhaktirasa* founded on the already-mentioned theory of *rasa* of Sanskrit poetics. The main difference between these two theories is that in the *Bhaktirasa* theory the connoisseur of a literary work was replaced with a devotee and aesthetic pleasure was substituted by the devotional pleasure of savouring Kṛṣṇa's love.[237] According to this theology, appropriated and modified by Rām's devotees,[238] bhakta can assume towards God one of five attitudes full of devotion (*bhāva*). These *bhāva*s, especially thanks to the help of one's guru, can transform into a new quality and make a devotee experience a essence of the real emotional relationship with God – a devotee can thus relish the real 'taste' of a given emotion/sentiment (*rasa*). There are five such attitudes (*bhāva*) and their correlate sentiments (*rasa*):

1. attitude characterized with tranquillity, quietism (*śāntabhāva*), in which Rām is contemplated as God, the Ultimate Being; this attitude leads to experiencing the real nature of quietism (*śāntarasa*);

2. an attitude typical of a servant (*dāsyabhāva*), when a devotee considers God as his master, to whom he serves and feels respect for; this attitude allows a devotee to savour the sentiment of serving (*dāsyarasa*);

---

[236] For more see Prasād, *Madhyakālīn rāmkāvya dhārā*, esp. pp. 209–331; also see Edward C. Dimock, 'Doctrine and Practice Among the Vaiṣṇavas of Bengal', in M. Singer, ed., *Krishna: Myths, Rites and Attitudes*, Chicago: University of Chicago Press, 1968, pp. 48–50 and Bakker, *Ayodhyā*, p. 139.

[237] Dimock, 'Doctrine and Practice', pp. 48–50.

[238] See Siṁh, *Rāmbhakti*, p. 261 and Prasād, *Madhyakālīn rāmkāvya dhārā*, pp. 209–331.

3. an attitude characterized by an affection towards a child (*vātsalyabhāva*), in which a devotee appropriates the role of a parent and thus experiences the taste of an affection for a child (*vātsalyarasa*);

4. an attitude typical of a friend (*sākhyabhāva*), when God is bestowed with a feeling of friendship and a devotee can experience the sentiment of friendship (*sākhyarasa*);

5. an attitude of tender, sweet loving affection, love (*mādhurya-bhāva* or, more commonly, *śṛṅgārabhāva*) as between lovers, which is most valued, allows a devotee to savour the feeling of love (*mādhurya/śṛṅgārarasa*).[239]

Although these five types of relations that arise thanks to the appropriation of a certain attitude by a devotee (with the highest status of the relationship born out of the attitude of love) can be understood as five paths leading to God,[240] actually they are five varieties of the superior relationship that allows one to savour the devotional love, devotional surrender (*Bhaktirasa*).[241]

Summing up, one can say that *rasik* denotes a person who is capable of savouring love for God and love of God. Thus, a Rām Rasik is a devotee who bestows upon Rām his love and savours the reciprocated affection. The community of Rām Rasiks, i.e. Rasik Sampradāy, and their literature are usually referred to in English as 'emotional' or 'erotic'. However, other names of the sect are also current in Hindi, such as Jānakī Sampradāy (Community/Sect of Jānakī [devotees]), Siyā Sampradāy (Community of Siyā)[242] or Rahasya Sampradāy (Secret/Esoteric community).[243] It seems that the last designation, 'esoteric' (*rahasya*), pointing to the exclusive character of their teachings and

---

[239] Siṁh, *Rāmbhakti*, pp. 143–4, 263–5, 282–3; Prasād, *Madhyakālīn rāmkāvya dhārā*, pp. 18–24, 181–98, 391–431; Dimock, 'Doctrine and Practice', pp. 48–50 and idem, *The Place of the Hidden Moon: Erotic Mysticism in the Vaiṣṇava-sahajiya Cult of Bengal*, Chicago: University of Chicago Press, 1966, pp. 22–3.

[240] Siṁh, *Rāmbhakti*, pp. 141–3. Cf. Allan M. Keislar, 'The *Rasik* Concept of Transcendental Sexuality', in Entwistle, *Studies in Early Modern Indo-Aryan Languages*, pp. 179–86.

[241] Cf. Gopināth Kavirāj, 'Bhūmikā', in Siṁh, *Rāmbhakti*, p. II.

[242] The form of Sītā's name in some Hindi dialects, e.g. Avadhi.

[243] Siṁh, *Rāmbhakti*, p. 140.

practices, available only to initiates,[244] is the most appropriate as it very aptly characterizes this current of Rāmbhakti.[245]

Thus, the doctrine and practice of the sect is esoteric, although in principle it is said to belong to the mainstream of Rāmbhakti based on Tulsīdās's *Rāmcaritmānas* and Tulsīdās is much venerated by them.[246] However, the fact that for Rasiks the most important period, practically the only one that really matters, is the time when Rām and Sītā live together in Ayodhya, becomes the cause of their departure from the common, widespread practices and beliefs of other Rāmbhaktas.

According to the doctrine of Rasiks, the abode of Rām can be visualized and perceived on two levels. Firstly, it is the earthly, real (*laukik*) Ayodhya, the physical dimension of which can be experienced empirically (*bhūlok*). Secondly, it is the heavenly, transcendent (*alaukik*) Saket, attainable only by means of esoteric practices (*divyalok*), in which Sītā and Rām perform their divine play (*līlā*). They function as archetypal actors performing their cosmic drama for their audience, i.e. Rasiks, the initiated devotees, who are capable of savouring its *ras*, the essence.[247]

The fundamental feature of this cult, i.e. worshipping the couple jointly and a very strong stress on its propriety (*maryādā*),[248] pose a problem – how can men serve the *yugalsarkār* without robbing Sītā of her dignity? In order to prevent such a situation, a male bhakta has to think of himself as Sītā's female attendant (*sakhī*), practicing thus the *sakhībhāv upāsanā*.[249] According to tradition, this idea turned up when Rām and Sītā returned to Ayodhya, and Hanumān together with Rām's brothers sought Rām's permission to serve not only him but Sītā as well. Thus, they all became first *sakhī*s of Sītā; Hanumān was given the name

---

[244] Ibid., pp. 66, 175.

[245] Cf. ibid. and idem, *Rāmkāvyadhārā: anusandhān evam anucintan*, Ilāhābād: Lokbhāratī Prakāśan, 1976, p. 25.

[246] Siṁh, *Rāmbhakti*, p. 159.

[247] Ibid., pp. 273–8 and Lutgendorf, 'The Secret Life of Rāmcandra', p. 220–1.

[248] For more on this see Siṁh, *Rāmbhakti*, pp. 154–7.

[249] Lit. 'the worship / adoration characterized with the attitude typical of a female friend'; for more on this see Prasād, *Madhyakālīn rāmkāvya dhārā*, pp. 317–31 and Siṁh, *Rāmbhakti*, pp. 157–9, 162–3.

Cāruśīlā, Lakṣmaṇ – Lakṣmaṇā, Bharat – Subhagā and Śatrughna – Hemā. In this context, it is also worth noting that while many of Rām's devotees have names ending in *-dās* (lit. 'servant'), Rasiks traditionally have been given names ending in *-śaraṇ* (lit. 'refuge, shelter'); the endings *-maṇi* and *-sakhā* are also common.[250]

The Rasik type of Bhakti found its expression in ample literature both in Sanskrit and in Hindi.[251] Among the most important works in Sanskrit, e.g. the *Bhuśuṇḍi rāmāyaṇa*, the *Śiva-saṃhitā*, the *Hanumatsaṃhitā*,[252] the *Bṛhatkośalasaṃhitā* and the *Rāmaliṅgāmṛta* of one Advaita[253] can be named. As far as a very interesting and diverse literature in Hindi is considered, the name of Agradās (second half of sixteenth century),[254] also known as Agraalī, the founding father of the sect,[255] Bālkṛṣṇ, better known as Bālalī, or the much later Banādās (1821–92)[256] are merely mentioned here as their works will be discussed in more detail in the later chapters of this work.

Some scholars maintain[257] that had Tulsīdās not created the *Rāmcaritmānas* in the second half of the sixteenth century, Rasik Sampradāy would have gained greater significance much earlier, in Tulsīdās's times. The *Rāmcaritmānas* is thus supposed to have restrained the development of the sect in such a way that its popularity was confined mostly to Ayodhya and to a much lesser extent also to other Ramaite centres (Chitrakut and Janakpur in Mithila). However, it seems that ascribing such a great potential

---

[250] Siṁh, *Rāmbhakti*, pp. 182–3.

[251] Bhagavatīprasād Siṁh maintains that more than two-thirds of the available Ramaite literature has been composed by Rasiks; ibid., p. 67.

[252] It can probably be dated not later than 1658, which is the year of its oldest extant manuscript; ibid., p. 98.

[253] It is differently dated, e.g. *c.*1473 or *c.*1608; see respectively Rāmlakhan Pāṇḍey, *Tulsīdāsottar hindī rāmsāhitya*, Ilāhābād: Vibhā Prakāśan, 2003 (1st published 1972), p. 71 and Siṁh, *Rāmbhakti*, p. 97; cf. Miśra 'Mādhav', *Rāmbhakti mẽ madhur upāsanā*, pp. 107ff. and Prasād, *Madhyakālīn rāmkāvya dhārā*, p. 381.

[254] Siṁh, *Rāmbhakti*, p. 379 and idem, *Rāmkāvyadhārā*, p. 78.

[255] Siṁh, *Rāmbhakti*, pp. V, 88 and Bakker, *Ayodhyā*, p. 139.

[256] Bhagavatīprasād Siṁh, *Mahātmā Banādās: jīvan aur sāhitya*, Vārāṇasī: Viśvavidyālay Prakāśan, 1976, pp. 4, 52.

[257] Prasād, *Madhyakālīn rāmkāvya dhārā*, p. 470 and Pāṇḍey, *Tulsīdāsottar hindī rāmsāhitya*, p. 67.

to this mode of worship is exaggerated. First of all, for obvious reasons, its esoteric character conditions exclusive and not unrestricted participation. There is not much evidence that would testify to the overwhelming popularity of the doctrine of Rasiks either in more distant or more recent pasts. It should not be forgotten that many facets typical of this doctrine are in obvious disagreement with the image of Rām well-known from the Rāmāyaṇa tradition and worshipped by the majority of people in north India. Thus, one should not be surprised to see the genuine astonishment of many Hindus when they hear, apparently for the first time in their lives, of the love exploits of Sītā and Rām in the heavenly Saket.

* * *

The foregoing outline of the development of Rāmbhakti clearly indicates that the most crucial moment in this process was the emergence from among the ranks of the Vaishnava community of a group for which Rām(a) became God. The circumstances under which it happened are not known in detail. However, it took place most probably around the eleventh or twelfth century and from that moment the separate cult as not merely one of the forms of the cult of Viṣṇu can be spoken of. The character of this cult, in which from the very beginning the worship of the name in the form of meditation upon it as well as upon the story were of significant importance, repeating the name and the story, as well as absolute devotion and steadfast service for Lord Rām(a) had been forming much earlier. It is noteworthy that the basic traits of Rāma as God are already present in Vālmīki's *Rāmāyaṇa*; the unfolding tradition appropriated that model, adding new elements and modifying the old ones.

The time in which the cult was getting stronger (between thirteenth and fifteenth century) coincided with the more and more pronounced Muslim presence in north India. In the sixteenth century, it yielded an outstanding text, the *Rāmcaritmānas*, important not only because of its literary values but also because of its religious and socio-cultural message. This quintessence of Rāmbhakti with time has become an object of adoration itself as a specific manifestation of God. That entire period is poorly recorded as far as material objects are concerned. No doubt, it should be partly related to the presence of Muslims and their attitude towards temple cult and idolatry but more important in this context there seems to have been a strong stress laid upon the role of Rām's name. Nevertheless, it is difficult to detach these two elements from each other and assuredly determine which was the cause and which the consequence. There is no denying that many traditions fused into what resulted in Ramaite Bhakti which almost from the beginning had much the same form as is known today with the main difference that until the eighteenth century the temple cult, the cult of Rām's idols and pilgrimages were much less common than today (although one should remember that even today temples solely devoted to Rām are not very common outside the Ramaite cult centres). The steady weakening of the centralized Muslim rule from around the eighteenth century resulted in a transformation in the religious sphere. In the case of Rām, it meant first of all an unprecedented flowering of such pilgrimage centres as Ayodhya, Chitrakut or Janakpur. That blossoming also found its expression in Hindi works devoted to Rām (many of them are related to Rasik Sampradāy), although their numbers do not go hand in hand with their quality and most of them lack the accomplished character of Tulsīdās's poem that till the present day has not been ousted by the oeuvre of the following generations of authors and religious teachers.

PART ONE

THE STORY AND ITS AUTHORS

CHAPTER ONE

Before Tulsīdās: The Beginnings of the Rāmāyaṇa Tradition in Hindi Literature[1]

INTRODUCTION

Some authors[2] assert that the oldest Hindi Rāmkathā is as old as Hindi literature itself and refer to the *Pṛthvīrājrāso*[3] ascribed to one Cand[4] or Cand Bardāī. This story of Rām's deeds forms a part of Chapter 2 (*Samaya Do*) of the poem's largest edition, or the so-called largest recension (*bṛhat rūpāntar*), which was published between 1904 and 1914 by Nāgrī Pracāriṇī Sabhā (NPS),[5] and is included in

---

[1] An earlier version of this chapter was published under the same title in *Rocznik Orientalistyczny*, vol. 55, no. 2, 2003, pp. 87–95.

[2] See e.g. Bhagīrath Miśra's preface to: Loknāth Dvivedī 'Silākārī', ed., *Viṣṇudāskṛt rāmāyaṇkathā*, Ilāhābād: Sāhitya Bhavan, n.d. [1972], p. 33.

[3] *Rāso* (also *rāsau*) – a literary genre of the earliest period of Hindi literature often compared to heroic poems or ballads. *Rāso*s are believed to have been composed between *c.*1000–1400 (or even earlier). R. Śukla named this period in Hindi literature as *vīragāthākāl* after them, i.e. a period of heroic/bardic poetry; Rāmcandra Śukla, *Hindī sāhitya kā itihās*, 13th edn, Kāśī: Nāgrī Pracāriṇī Sabhā, 1961, p. 3. It is possible that *rāso*s are the oldest specimens of Hindi literature, though the language and structure of their present form leave it beyond doubt that they are an outcome of the work of many generations of different authors and scribes. For more on this subject see McGregor, *Hindi Literature from Its Beginnings*, pp. 16–21.

[4] Cand is traditionally believed to be a court bard and a confidant of the prince Pṛthvīrāj Cauhān of Delhi (*c.*1192) but his historical identity has not been unanimously established by scholars. For the meaning and etymology of the word *bardāī* see e.g. *Pṛthvīrāj rāsau*, ed. Mātā Prasād Gupta, Cirgā̃v (Jhā̃sī): Sāhitya-Sādan, 1963, pp. 169–170 and *Saṅkṣipt Pṛthvīrāj rāso*, ed. Hazārīprasād Dvivedī and Nāmvar Siṁh, 8th revd edn, Ilāhābād: Sāhitya Bhavan, 1990, p. 179; cf. McGregor, *Hindi Literature from Its Beginnings*, p. 17.

[5] NPS – a society established in Banaras in 1893 with the aim of propagating the Hindi language and Hindi literature; one of its important tasks, among other things, was the search for manuscripts of old

the description of the ten avatārs of Viṣṇu.[6] Judging from the number of lines devoted to each of the avatārs, it was Kṛṣṇa (656 lines) who was of special interest to the author(s) of this poem. Rām, to whom 148 lines are devoted, comes third after Nṛsiṁha, or Man-Lion, with 155 lines. The main part of the story is devoted to the events related to the war on Lanka, which seems to be influenced by the character of the poem itself.[7] However, in view of many doubts concerning the authenticity of the extant text of *Pṛthvīrājrāso* and the fact that only one, i.e. the largest, of its recensions contains the story of Rām's life, it seems that this version should be treated with extreme caution.

Īśvardās,[8] who is considered to be the author of the earliest extant work written in Avadhi (*Satyavatīkathā*; 1501[9]), wrote also two works – the *Bharat bilāp/vilāp* (Bharat's Lamentation)[10] and the *Aṅgad paij* (Angad's Vow; 1502) concerned with the story of Rām's deeds. These two works were mentioned in the NPS reports on the search for Hindi manuscripts. The first of them is mentioned in the report for the years 1923–25, while the report for the years 1944–46 contains the description of them both along with short

---

works. Mohanlāl Viṣṇulāl Pāṇḍya, Rādhākṛṣṇa Dās and Śyāmsundar Dās were the editors of the first two parts of the NPS edition; later parts were edited by Pāṇḍya and Śyāmsundar Dās with the assistance of Kūvar Kanhaiyā; *Pṛthvīrājrāso*, vol. 1, 2nd new edn, Kāśī: NPS, 1994 (vol. 2 – 1995).

[6] *Pṛthvīrājrāso*, vol. 1, pp. 181–258.

[7] Cf. Dvivedī, *Viṣṇudāskṛt rāmāyaṇkathā*, pp. 33–4.

[8] He is supposed to have been active during the reign of Sultan Sikandar Lodī (1489–1517); Śukla, *Hindī sāhitya kā itihās*, p. 74 and Sītārām, 'Satyavatī kathā', *Hindustānī*, vol. 6, no. 4, Aktūbar 1936, pp. 464–5. Also see *Īśvardāskṛt Aṅgad paij tathā Svargārohiṇī kathā*, ed. Rāmkumārī Miśra, Śivgopāl Miśra, Ilāhābād: Vijñān Pariṣad, 1979, pp. I–II.

[9] For more on its date, see Sītārām, 'Satyavatī kathā'. Also see Īśvardās, *Satyavatī tathā anya kṛtiyā̃*, ed. Śivgopāl Miśra, Gvāliyar: Vidyāmandir Prakāśan, 1958.

[10] Premśaṅkar, *Rāmkāvya aur Tulsī: sāṁskṛtik sandarbh mẽ*, Dillī: Neśanal Pabliśiṅg Hāus, 1977, pp. 21–3. This work is also referred to as *Bharat milāp*; cf. e.g. Dhīrendra Varmā, ed., *Hindī sāhitya*, vol. 2, Prayāg: Bhāratīy Hindī Pariṣad, 1959, p. 305. A work with this title was published in 1902: Īśvarīdās, *Bharat milāp*, Kalkattā: Śrī Nṛtyalāl Sīl, 1309 (1902); quoted after: Pītāmbar Nārāyaṇ, Bhāskaran Nāyar, ed., *Hindī-sāhitya-sāriṇī*, Hośyārpur: Viśveśvarānand Saṁsthan, 1971, p. 8.

extracts.[11] *Bharat bilāp*, whose date is unknown, was edited by Śivgopāl Miśra on the basis of several late manuscripts and published in 1958.[12] Its editor observes that although all these manuscripts display much similarity as far as the text is concerned, nevertheless, at the same time they claim authorship by different poets. For example, the oldest manuscript used by Miśra (dated 1759) names Tulsīdās as the author of the poem, most probably to add prestige to the text.[13] The second text of interest to us, i.e. the *Aṅgad paij*, was published in 1979 in the edition of Rāmkumārī and Śivgopāl Miśra, based on two partly incomplete manuscripts, one of which is dated 1733.[14] Some scholars suggest that both poems in their extant form in fact may be fragments of a longer work devoted to the whole story of Rām's life.[15] Undoubtedly it is an interesting hypothesis but it is also a fact that both texts still wait for a thorough examination and critical edition, as the available published versions can be treated only as provisional.

Yet another Hindi telling of Rāmkathā that forms a part of a larger whole, the beginnings of which may slightly predate Tulsīdās or are contemporary with him, is the famous *Sūrsāgar* of Sūrdās. Taking into consideration its place not only in Hindi literature but also in the religious life of north India, this version calls for our special attention.

RĀM'S STORY IN THE *SŪRSĀGAR*

The *Sūrsāgar* is considered to be not only one of the most important works of the Bhakti period (*bhaktikāl*) but also of Hindi literature in general. It is admired as one of the most splendid achievements of poetry devoted to Kṛṣṇa and although first of all it glorifies his deeds, it also contains a pleasing rendering of the

[11] Cf. Premśaṅkar, *Rāmkāvya aur Tulsī*, p. 21 and Kauśalyā Bhāradvāj, *Hindī rāmkāvya mẽ svabhāvokti (san 1450 se 1650 tak)*, Rohtak: Manthan Pablikeśans, 1982, p. 11; cf. Īśvardās, *Satyavatī*, p. 107.

[12] Īśvardās, *Satyavatī*, pp. 97–102.

[13] Ibid., p. 107.

[14] *Īśvardās kṛt Aṅgad paij*, pp. II–III.

[15] Premśaṅkar, *Rāmkāvya aur Tulsī*, p. 21 and Rāmkumārī Miśra and Śivgopāl Miśra in *Īśvardās kṛt Aṅgad paij*, p. III.

story of Rām. However, while talking about the *Sūrsāgar*, it is important to remember that its history until the present day has provoked a lot of discussion.[16]

The tradition originating from hagiographic sources, notably the *Caurāsī vaiṣṇavan kī vārtā* ascribed to Gokulnāth (1551–1640[17]), maintains that Sūrdās was born in 1478 to a Brahmin family living in Sīhī, a village near Delhi. He is also said to have been blind from birth but thanks to his gift of inner vision he could perceive all forms of the divinity of Kṛṣṇa.[18] In early youth, Sūrdās met Vallabha (1479–1531), the founder of the *puṣṭimārgī* sect, and became his follower. He spent the rest of his life composing and singing songs devoted to Kṛṣṇa. This tradition also maintains that Sūrdās died in 1582.[19]

The enormous popularity of Sūrdās's songs (*pad*)[20] must have influenced the development of his legend, which with time grew and was transformed by oral transmission within and without the Vallabhite sect traditions. Parallel to this development, the number of *pad*s with the name of Sūrdās, i.e. with his poetic signature (*bhaṇitā* or *chāp*), also increased thanks to other poets and compilers 'signing' various songs with his name.[21] Finally, these songs were collected and modelled after the *Bhāgavata purāṇa*. The result of this process can be seen in the current standard *Sūrsāgar* published by the NPS,[22] which contains some 5000 *pad*s (exactly 4,927) out of 125,000 ascribed to Sūrdās by

---

[16] For more on this subject see John Stratton Hawley, 'The Early *Sūrsāgar* and the Growth of the Sur Tradition', in idem, *Three Bhakti Voices: Mirabai, Surdas, and Kabir in Their Time and Ours*, Delhi: Oxford University Press, 2005, pp. 194–207.

[17] Or 1647; Hawley, *Three Bhakti Voices*, p. 95.

[18] See e.g. ibid., pp. 209–10.

[19] See the discussion in Dhīrendra Varmā, ed., *Hīndī sāhitya koś*, vol. 2, Vārāṇasī: Jñān Maṇḍal, 1986, p. 642; cf. McGregor, *Hindi Literature from Its Beginnings*, pp. 76–7.

[20] *Pad* – devotional, metrically simple poetry functioning mostly as songs performed with an instrumental accompaniment during the Vaishnav prayer meetings.

[21] For more on the problem of authorship in Bhakti poetry see Hawley, 'Author and Authority', in idem, *Three Bhakti Voices*, pp. 21–47.

[22] *Sūrsāgar*, ed. Nanddulāre Vājpeyī, vols 1 and 2, 3rd edn, Vārāṇasī: NPS, 1958.

tradition.[23] Contemporary scholars have no doubts that the *Sūrsāgar* should be viewed as a compilation representing 'the Sūrdās tradition' and not as an integral corpus which could be ascribed to a historical figure whose name was Sūrdās.[24] Moreover, the question of 'authenticity' of what is available to us at present is further complicated by the fact that no complete critical edition of the *Sūrsāgar* is as yet available.[25]

The *Sūrsāgar* in the present standard form, i.e. in the NPS edition,[26] consists of twelve books called *skandha*, following the *Bhāgavata purāṇa* model. They differ in length significantly, with the number of *pads* ranging from four in Book 5 up to as many as 4,309 in the longest Book 10. It is worth mentioning here that Books 1–9 and 11–12, with the number of different length *pads* totalling 618, constitute about one sixth of the whole *Sūrsāgar*. The longest *skandha*, which is also the most popular, is devoted to Kṛṣṇa and is commonly known as *Kṛṣṇāyaṇa*.

The fact that Rāmkathā also found its place in the *Sūrsāgar* complies with the tradition originating from the *Bhāgavata purāṇa*, where ten avatārs of Viṣṇu, with Kṛṣṇa as the most prominent among them, are discussed. Thus there can be no doubt that the chosen deity (*iṣṭadev*) of Sūrdās is Kṛṣṇa. He appears here as the Absolute, performing different acts of his divine play or *līlā*. One of the most important elements of this play is acquiring a form and name (*nāmrūp*), meaning here primarily the incarnation of

---

[23] Kenneth E. Bryant, *Poems to the Child-God: Structures and Strategies in the Poetry of Sūrdās*, Berkeley: University of California Press, 1978, p. IX.

[24] Ibid., pp. IX–X. Also see N.M. Sazanova, *'Okean poėzii' Sur Dasa*, Moskva: Izdatel'stvo Moskovskogo Universiteta, 1973, esp. pp. 53–96.

[25] An effort of J.S. Hawley and K.E. Bryant should be noted here: J.S. Hawley and Kenneth E. Bryant, *Sūr's Ocean*, 2 vols, New York: Oxford University Press, forthcoming. Also see Javāharlāl Caturvedī, ed., *Sūrsāgar*, Kalkattā: Śrīnand Mīnānī, 1965; Kenneth E. Bryant, 'Toward a Critical Edition of the Sūrsāgar', in W.M. Callewaert, ed., *Early Hindi Devotional Literature in Current Research*, Leuven: Katholieke Universiteit, 1980, pp. 5–12; idem, 'The Fatehpur Manuscript and the Sūrsāgar Critical Edition Project', in Monika Thiel-Horstmann, ed., *Bhakti in Current Research, 1979–1982*, Berlin: Dietrich Reimer Verlag, 1983, pp. 38–44 and Kenneth E. Bryant, 'The Bottom of the Page: Representing Variation in an Oral Tradition', in Entwistle, *Studies in Early Modern Indo-Aryan Languages, Literature and Culture*, pp. 87–100 and Hawley, 'The Early *Sūrsāgar*'.

[26] *Sūrsāgar*, ed. Nanddulāre Vājpeyī.

Kṛṣṇa, but he is also simultaneously Hari, Viṣṇu, Rām and all that exists – he is the prime cause of creation (e.g. 1.2–4). Thus Rām and Kṛṣṇa are in fact two names of the same Lord and many passages attest to such an attitude.

The *Sūrsāgar*'s Rāmāyaṇa constitutes almost the entire Book 9, comprising 157 *pad*s out of the total of 174 (9.15–172). The basic narrative essentially follows Vālmīki, although an obvious influence of the rich Rāmāyaṇa tradition, mainly that of Purāṇas and Sanskrit retellings, can be also seen. It omits a number of episodes and among them is, e.g. the banishment of Sītā included in the traditional Book 7 because it would not be in agreement with the Bhakti concept of merciful Lord. Therefore, the *Sūrsāgar* ends with the description of Rām's return to Ayodhya and his coronation. Apart from this extensive narrative in Book 9, we can also find other major and minor references to the story, e.g. 1.3, 4, 11, 13, 18, 35, 43, 59, 61, 90, 92, 176 or 7.2. One of the most charming of such passages concerned with Rāmkathā is the episode in which Yaśodā is trying to lull little Kṛṣṇa to sleep and tells him the story of Rām's deeds (10.198–199).[27] When she says that Sītā was captured by Rāvaṇ, baby-Kṛṣṇa awakes and leaps to his feet, crying: 'Bow, [my] bow, Lakṣmaṇ! Give me [my] bow!',[28] which testifies convincingly not only to the identity of Kṛṣṇa's and Rām's deeds but also to the identity of the two of them, which makes his Mother Yaśodā stand in awe of him.[29]

Although Sūr's attitude towards Rām is typical of Bhakti, i.e. it is full of devotion, his Rām – when compared to that of Tulsīdās – is more mundane, more human. Here one is continuously reminded neither of his divinity nor of his valour and chivalrous nature. The poet is more interested in Rām's inner world: in his tender feelings towards his beloved Sītā, his pangs of separation from her or his fears whether he will be able to recover her from Rāvaṇ.[30] A lovely exemplification of this is the lamentation of Rām

---

[27] *Pad* 9.199 repeats the same story in a slightly different, shorter form.

[28] *cāpa-cāpa (...) lachimana dehu* (10.198); *lachimana dhanuś dehu* (10.199).

[29] For an analysis of the whole passage see Bryant, *Poems to the Child-God*, pp. 53–60.

[30] Cf. Varmā, *Hīndī sāhitya koś*, vol. 2, p. 648; Bryant, *Poems to the Child-God*, pp. 69–70 and Yuriy V. Cvetkov, *Surdas i ego poėzija*, Moskva: Nauka, 1979, pp. 84–5.

(*Rāmvilāp*; 9.62–4) after he learns that Sītā has disappeared. He behaves like many other men would do in such a situation – he is so desperate in his search for his beloved, so overwhelmed with love for her that he forgets everything else, even his divine omnipotence (*sūradāsa prabhu priyā-prema-basa, nija mahimā bisari*; 9.63)! It seems that this feature of Sūr's Rāmkathā, its emotional character should be directly connected with the history of his poetry, stemming not from the tradition of epic narration but from the lyrical tradition of devotional songs.[31]

The story of Rām's life in the *Sūrsāgar* is not equal as far as its compositional and stylistic values are concerned, which is not surprising in view of its origin. For example, more than once a presentation of characters and the circumstances in which they act is so brief that it lacks deeper insight. Y. Cvetkov was right, to a large extent, to note that 'Sūrdās simply has no time for a poetical description of events, for creating vivid artistic images; he is in a hurry to reach his heart's most dear aim – the presentation of Kṛṣṇa's life'.[32] It does not mean, however, that in Sūrdās's telling of Rām's life (*Rāmāvatār*) one cannot find passages, which are distinguished for their undeniable artistic values. On the contrary, a number of them are distinguished by dramatic tension that reveals the psychological depth of different characters; many of them are composed in a lively, very imaginative language. Among them we may count, e.g. Rāvaṇ's words addressed to Sītā when he is ready to make her his principal wife, the mistress of 14,000 maid-servants, and share his kingdom with her (*Rāvaṇ-vacan Sītā-prati*; 9.79); the meeting of Hanumān with Sītā (*Hanumān-Sīyā-milan*; 9.83–95); Mandodarī's plea to Rāvaṇ to give Sītā back to Rām (*Rāvaṇ-Mandodarī-saṁvād*; 9.114–19) or the episode before the construction of the causeway in which Rām persuades the ocean to let his army cross over to Lanka (*Rām-sāgar-saṁvād*; 9.121–3).

Taking into consideration the fact that Sūr and his tradition were devoted to Lord Kṛṣṇa, it should not be surprising that relatively little attention is paid to Rām. It seems interesting, however, that Rāmkathā has found its place here and its significance cannot be overshadowed by the fact that most

---

[31] Cf. Premśaṅkar, *Rāmkāvya aur Tulsī*, p. 33.
[32] Cvetkov, *Surdas i ego poėzija*, p. 85.

probably it happened out of the need to comply with the tradition of the *Bhāgavata purāṇa.* As a result we have in our hands a revealing record of a way in which God can be perceived, a way that though it was not the most prevalent among the devotees of Kṛṣṇa[33] has, nevertheless, never been abandoned in later times. The present-day Sūrdās tradition bears witness to this. From the *pads* collected in contemporary editions of the *Sūrsāgar*, sung and recited both during public Vaishnav prayer gatherings and at home, in privacy, emerges an image of a Lord who has many names and one of them is also Rām – the image created by his faithful servant Sūr.

Viṣṇudās and His Rāmāyan: The Poet's Life and Works

The fifteenth-century *Rāmāyankathā*[34] of Viṣṇudās is the oldest extant, independent Rāmkathā in Hindi.

The name of Viṣṇudās first appeared in Western sources on Hindi literature more than one hundred and fifty years ago, as of an author inspired by the *Mahābhārata,* thanks to Garcin de Tassy. In his famous *Chrestomathie hindie et hindouie* (1849), he included an excerpt from Viṣṇudās's text on *kaliyuga,* adapted from the *Mahābhārata* episode of Yudhiṣṭhira's ascent to heaven.[35] The next mentions of Viṣṇudās appear much later in the NPS reports for the years 1906–8, where his name is connected with two titles: *Mahābhāratkathā* and *Svargārohaṇ.*[36] Later reports (1941–3) also

---

[33] Varmā, *Hīndī sāhitya koś*, vol. 2, p. 306 and Premśaṅkar, *Rāmkāvya aur Tulsī*, p. 34.

[34] Such a spelling, i.e. with dental 'n', is used in the text of the first edition of the text; see *Viṣṇudāskṛt rāmāyaṇkathā.*

[35] Garcin de Tassy, *Chrestomathie hindie et hindouie,* Paris: Imprimerie Nationale, 1849, pp. III, 83–90; R.S. McGregor, 'An Early Hindi (Braj-bhāṣā) Version of the Rāma Story: The Rāmāyaṇkathā (A.D. 1442) of Viṣṇudās', in Diana L. Eck and Françoise Mallison, ed., *Devotion Divine: Bhakti Traditions from the Regions of India,* Groningen: Egbert Forsten, Paris: École Française d'Extrême-Orient, 1991, p. 182.

[36] *Khoj,* vol. 3, 1906–8, p. 92. In different reports three titles can be encountered: the *Mahābhāratkathā,* the *Svargārohaṇ* and the *Svargārohaṇ parva;* according to some scholars, they are slightly different versions of the same work entitled by the author the *Svargārohaṇ;* Dvivedī, *Viṣṇudās-kṛt rāmāyaṇkathā,* pp. XLIII–XLIV.

record other manuscripts with *Bhāṣā vālmīki rāmāyaṇ* among them.[37] The reference to Viṣṇudās can also be found in *Miśrabandhu vinod,*[38] the work of the Miśra brothers, which is traditionally considered as the first history of Hindi literature written by Indians.

The works ascribed to Viṣṇudās indicate that he lived in Gopācalgaṛh (contemporary Gwalior) and was a court poet of the king Ḍoṅgarsiṁh of the Tomar dynasty. The years of his life[39] are not explicitly given but his poems are dated – his version of the *Mahābhārata* was composed in 1435 and the *Rāmāyaṇa* in 1442.[40]

Stuart McGregor notes that in the first part of the fifteenth century Gwalior witnessed the birth of narrative poetry on Kṛṣṇa and Rām themes in early Brajbhasha which was used – as inscriptions in Braj testify – at the court of the Tomars for official purposes.[41] Thus, though we can talk of certain Brajbhasha traditions before Viṣṇudās, nevertheless he should be considered as 'a leading inaugurator of the Brajbhāṣā tradition of Hindi'.[42] It is even said that he is the first to use the language, which in the 17th century came to be regarded 'the most accomplished literary language of India'.[43] The fact that exactly at that time, in Gwalior, Viṣṇudās used Braj to narrate the traditional story of Rām is worth noting here. It is probable that the acquisition of Braj as a new means of literary expression was, to a certain extent, a reaction to a new socio-political situation caused by the Muslim expansion. It

---

[37] Ibid., pp. XXXIX–XL, McGregor, 'An Early Hindi (Brajbhāṣā) Version', pp. 181–2 and Premśaṅkar, *Rāmkāvya aur Tulsī*, p. 15.

[38] *Miśrabandhu vinod,* vol. 1, Lakhnaū: Gaṅgā Pustak Mālā, 1972 (1st published 1913), p. 106.

[39] For more on his life see Mohansiṁh Tomar, *Hindī rāmkāvya aur Viṣṇudās kī rāmāyan kathā,* Dillī: Takṣaśilā Prakāśan, 1979, pp. 17–26.

[40] Ibid. and McGregor, 'An Early Hindi (Brajbhāṣā) Version', p. 182. Bhagīrath Miśra supposes his dates to be 1393–1443; cf. 'Introduction' in Dvivedī, *Viṣṇudāskṛt rāmāyaṇkathā*, pp. XXXII, XXXV and Balbhadra Tivārī, *Kavivar Viṣṇudās aur unkī rāmāyan kathā*, Ilāhābād: Sāhitya Bhavan, 1976, pp. 32 and 58.

[41] McGregor, 'An Early Hindi (Brajbhāṣā) Version', p. 183.

[42] Ibid. and McGregor, 'The Progress of Hindi, part 1: The Development of a Transregional Idiom', in Sheldon Pollock, ed., *Literary Cultures in History: Reconstructions from South Asia*, 1st Indian edn, Delhi: Oxford University Press, 2004, p. 914.

[43] Dvivedī, *Viṣṇudāskṛt rāmāyaṇkathā*, p. XLII; cf. McGregor, 'An Early Hindi (Brajbhāṣā) Version', p. 183.

also bears witness to the decline of the hitherto strong tradition of Apabhransha, i.e. a Middle Indo-Aryan language, there and a growing potential of Brajbhasha, i.e. a New Indo-Aryan language.[44] Nevertheless, it should also be noted here that Balbhadra Tivārī considers the language of Viṣṇudās to be Bundeli mixed mainly with Braj but also with a significant number of Sanskrit *tatsamas*, as well as a discernible Perso-Arabic lexicon, which he labels with an anachronic designation of Urdu.[45]

Viṣṇudās's *Rāmāyan* was published in 1972. Its text is based on a manuscript, prepared in 1863, from the collection of the university library in Sagar.[46] This edition has to be dealt with great caution, not only because it is based on one late manuscript but also because its text, the present state of which was undoubtedly influenced by the untimely death of its editor,[47] is full of obscure passages with dotted lines or question marks. They are neither commented on nor explained in any way; an appropriate introduction, stating clearly such points as, e.g. whether the editor left these fragments unfinished for further analysis or they are obscure in the manuscript itself, is also lacking. Moreover, this edition differs significantly from the fragments of the *Bhāṣā vālmīki rāmāyaṇ* included by Hariharnivās Dvivedī in his edition of Viṣṇudās's *Mahābhārat*.[48] For all these reasons it seems right to treat Loknāth Dvivedī's edition as provisional.[49]

The text of this edition is mostly in fifteen-mora *caupahīs*[50] interspersed occasionally with *dohās*[51] and other metres (also some

---

[44] McGregor, 'An Early Hindi (Brajbhāṣā) Version', p. 184; cf. R. Stuart McGregor, 'Viṣṇudās and His Rāmāyan-kathā', in Entwistle, *Studies in Early Modern Indo-Aryan Languages*, p. 239. For an opinion raising doubts 'whether Viṣṇudās should be considered a specifically Brajbhāṣā poet' see Allison Busch, 'Questioning the Tropes about "*Bhakti*" and "*Rīti*" in Hindi Literary Historiography', in Monika Horstman, ed., *Bhakti in Current Research, 2001–2003*, Delhi: Manohar, 2006, p. 43 n. 24.

[45] Tivārī, *Kavivar Viṣṇudās*, pp. 138–48.

[46] Dvivedī, *Viṣṇudāskṛt rāmāyaṇkathā*.

[47] Ibid., p. XXXVI.

[48] McGregor, 'An Early Hindi (Brajbhāṣā) Version', p. 182.

[49] Dvivedī, *Viṣṇudāskṛt rāmāyaṇkathā*, pp. XXXVI, XLVII; McGregor, 'An Early Hindi (Brajbhāṣā) Version', ibid. and McGregor, 'Viṣṇudās and His Rāmāyan-kathā', p. 245.

[50] *Caupahī* or *caupaī* – a quatrain that is a variation of a very popular Hindi moric (*mātrā*) metre known as *caupāī* with a half-line (*pād*) of

Sanskrit *ślokas*). The style of the work indicates that it was meant for oral performance.[52]

The main story seems to be based on Vālmīki but the structure of the work is non-traditional. It is divided into three books whose titles – *Bālkāṇḍ, Sundarakāṇḍ* and *Uttarakāṇḍ* – are, however, borrowed from the seven-book traditional version. The first of them is divided into thirty-one sections (*sarga*)[53] and narrates the events up to Hanumān's departure for Lanka, i.e. the events that are included in Books 1–4 of the traditional version. Almost every *sarga* is a self-contained entity and ends with a formula, usually containing the *sarga*'s title that indicates the main episode, e.g.: 'This is a *sarga* of the "Childhood Book of the Rāmāyaṇa" entitled "Daśaratha's conversation with a minister about the arrival of Śṛṅgī"'[54] or 'This is a *sarga* of the "Childhood Book of the Rāmāyaṇa" entitled "The Lamentation of Tārā"'.[55] Book 2, *Sundarkāṇḍ,* consists of thirteen *sargas*[56] and covers the main story of the traditional Books 5 and 6, starting from Hanumān's mission to Lanka. It is followed by a detailed account of the war (five *sargas*[57]) and the killing of Rāvaṇ up to the description of Rām's return to Ayodhya and his coronation; it ends with Rāmrājya, i.e. Rām's righteous rule. The last book is divided into nine sections that supplement the main story. They deal with, among

sixteen morae. Single lines of a *caupāī,* often functioning as an individual entity, are called *ardhālī.* For more on *caupāī* and *caupaī* in particular and Hindi prosody in general, see Dhīrendra Varmā, ed., *Hindī sāhitya koś,* vol. 1, Vārāṇasī: Jñān Maṇḍal, 1985 (different entries); S.H. Kellogg, *A Grammar of the Hindi Language*, London: Routledge & Kegan Paul, 1965 (1st edn in 1875), pp. 546–84 and R. Snell, *The Hindi Classical Tradition: A Braj Bhāṣā Reader*, London: School of Oriental and African Languages, 1991, pp. 19–28.

[51] *Dohā* – the most common couplet moric metre in Hindi poetry that consists of 24 *mātrās* per line with a caesura after the thirteenth *mātrā.* For more on *dohā,* see Snell, ibid. For more on the *caupāī-dohā* pattern, see below chapter 2.2 'The poem's structure'.

[52] Premśaṅkar, *Rāmkāvya aur Tulsī,* p. 20.

[53] Dvivedī, *Viṣṇudāskṛt rāmāyaṇkathā,* pp. 1–90.

[54] *iti śrī rāmāyane bālakāṇḍai sriṅgī āgamane daśaratha-mantrī-saṁvādo nāma sargaḥ;* orthography as in Dvivedī, *Viṣṇudāskṛt rāmāyaṇkathā,* p. 3.

[55] *iti śrī rāmāyane bālakāṇḍe tārā pralāpo nāma sargaḥ;* ibid., p. 50.

[56] Ibid., pp. 91–204.

[57] Ibid., pp. 147–92.

other things, the origin and doings of *rākṣasas*, the story of Ahalyā, the banishment of the pregnant Sītā and Rām's killing of a Shudra practicing austerities. The work culminates with the depiction of Rām's just rule and then the voice from heaven (*ākāśvāṇī*) tells him that the time to ascend to heaven has come for him. Therefore, Rām hands over the kingdom to his sons, Lav and Kuś, and prepares for his departure.

The length of individual sections of the poem differs and it seems that the more popular a given episode was, the more attention was devoted to it. *Sundarkāṇḍ*, here dealing mostly with the direct conflict between Rām and Rāvaṇ, is the longest book and occupies the most prominent position, constituting more than one third of the whole poem. This may indicate that the conflict between Rām and Rāvaṇ was the most attractive topic for the poet.[58]

As has already been mentioned, the main source of inspiration for Viṣṇudās was the tradition of Vālmīki's *Rāmāyaṇa*. However, Viṣṇudās treated it quite freely and altered it in a significant number of places, especially when the original abounds in long mythological stories that are not directly connected with the main narrative. This feature of reworking the story by omitting or contracting certain episodes and expanding or elaborating on other events is, as the Rāmāyaṇa tradition itself testifies century by century, author by author, one of its most typical features. This is the way, it lives on, endlessly retold and reinterpreted. Viṣṇudās, while retelling the story, was most evidently adopting from the tradition all that which, in his opinion, seemed to be worth attention. However, as Stuart McGregor rightly observes: 'there can be no doubt that Viṣṇudās's intention was to recreate, rather than reinterpret, Vālmīki's *Rāmāyaṇa*'.[59] And Dvivedī's edition reveals Viṣṇudās as a genuine storyteller (*kathāvacak*)[60] who addresses his audience using a language that combines charm with simplicity and through narrating the story of his deeds he praises Rām's name. However, while trying to estimate his place among other Hindi authors, one cannot but repeat after Stuart McGregor that '(t)he importance of

[58] Cf. McGregor, 'Viṣṇudās and His Rāmāyan-kathā', pp. 240–1 and McGregor, 'An Early Hindi (Brajbhāṣā) Version', p. 184.

[59] McGregor, 'Viṣṇudās and His Rāmāyan-kathā', p. 244.

[60] Cf. Premśaṅkar, *Rāmkāvya aur Tulsī*, p. 21.

his demonstration of the capacities of Brajbhasha goes beyond the literary merits of his work'.[61]

For a long time, important sources on the history of Hindi literature almost totally neglected Viṣṇudās's poem.[62] Most probably, this was influenced to a great extent by the title under which the poem was entered in the NPS reports – *Bhāṣā vālmīki rāmāyaṇ*, i.e. 'Vālmīki's Rāmāyaṇ in the [Hindi] Language'. Thus, researchers considered it not an original work but a mere translation, which did not deserve any attention.[63] However, there can be no doubt that this work does deserve the attention of the scholarly world for at least two reasons. Firstly, because it is the earliest extant, so extensive, Rāmkathā in Hindi literature. Secondly, because its author narrated it in such an interesting and pleasing manner that some consider it to be 'the first jewel in the garland of Ramaite poetry' (*Rāmkāvyamālā ... [kī] pahlī maṇi*).[64] In view of all these arguments, there is no doubt that a sound critical edition of Viṣṇudās's text would be very desirable.[65]

* * *

From the foregoing discussion, it should be thus clear that the beginnings of the Rāmāyaṇa tradition in Hindi literature are closely related to Vālmīki whose poem was the main source of inspiration for early Hindi authors interested in Rāmkathā and 'the accepted archetype'[66] for them. This is not surprising in view of the role played by Vālmīki in the whole Rāmāyaṇa tradition. That situation was soon to be changed with the advent of the fervent Rāmbhakti embodied in Tulsīdās's *Rāmcaritmānas*, which – as Philip Lutgendorf very aptly observes – 'has become (...) the archetypal Ramayan text for Hindi speakers'.[67]

---

[61] McGregor, 'The Progress of Hindi', p. 919.

[62] See e.g. Śukla, *Hindī sāhitya kā itihās;* Varmā, *Hīndī sāhitya koś*, vol. 2 and Varmā, *Hindī sāhitya*, vol. 2, p. 305.

[63] Premśaṅkar, *Rāmkāvya aur Tulsī*, pp. 16–17. Cf. Varmā, *Hindī sāhitya*, ibid.

[64] Bhagīrath Miśra in Dvivedī, *Viṣṇudāskṛt rāmāyaṇkathā*, p. XXXVI.

[65] See McGregor, 'Viṣṇudās and His Rāmāyan-kathā', p. 245.

[66] The phrase by Philip Lutgendorf, in idem, *The Life of a Text*, p. 12.

[67] Ibid.

CHAPTER TWO

In the World of Tulsīdās's Rāmkathās[1]

INTRODUCTORY REMARKS ON TULSĪDĀS'S LIFE AND WORKS

The name of Tulsīdās (1532–1623) is famous not only in the Hindi-speaking region but well beyond it thanks to the poet's *magnum opus*, the religious epic *Rāmcaritmānas* (The Mānas [Lake] of Rām's Deeds[2]). This work, considered to be the greatest achievement of Hindi literature, is undoubtedly the quintessence of its own times' spirituality and has exerted an immense influence upon religious life in north India. Nevertheless, many people familiar – in one way or another – with the *Rāmcaritmānas* are not aware of the fact that Tulsīdās retold the story of Rām's deeds also in his other works, which are written not only in Avadhi but in Braj as well. It may seem interesting, sometimes even surprising to literary educated native speakers of Hindi, that apart from singing the glory of Rām, to whom he devoted the majority of his poetry, Tulsīdās also composed works praising other gods – Śiv and his consort Pārvatī, and Kṛṣṇa. However, it is true that these works have not achieved such fame and popularity as the *Rāmcaritmānas*, which has been claimed by Western scholars, aware of its significance, as the Bible of Hindustan.[3]

---

[1] Parts of this chapter were published in an earlier version in 'In the World of Tulsīdās's *rām-kathās*', *Rocznik Orientalistyczny*, vol. 58, no. 2, 2006, pp. 114–31.

[2] On the meaning of the poem's title see Lutgendorf, *The Life of a Text*, pp. 12, 18–22 and further in this chapter.

[3] Though this term is a good example of something that can be termed 'cultural anachronism', it is very convenient and has a long tradition; see e.g. George A. Grierson, *The Modern Vernacular Literature of Hindustan*, Calcutta: Asiatic Society of Bengal, 1889, pp. XX, 42–3. Cf. the opinion of Ralph T.H. Griffith, the translator of Vālmīki's *Rāmāyaṇa* into English (*The Rámáyan of Válmíki*, London: Trübner & Co., Benares: E.J. Lazarus & Co., 1870–4): 'The Rámáyan of Tulsi Dás is more popular and more honoured by the people of the North-Western Provinces than the Bible is by the corresponding classes in England'; quoted after the title page of *The Rámáyana of Tulsi Dás*, tr. F.S. Growse, 6th edn, Allahabad: Ram Narain Lal, 1914.

Our knowledge of Tulsīdās's life is based more on legends than reliable accounts.[4] As a result, it abounds in unusual or miraculous events and 'facts' that cannot be verified. Apart from very few autobiographical mentions in his own works that practically do not tell us much beyond confirming Tulsīdās's existence and his great devotion to Rām, the earliest information about him comes from the famous hagiographical work the *Bhaktamāl* (*c.*1600) by Nābhādās.[5] It forms a six-line stanza (*chappay*), whose opening verse is repeated at the end and says: 'Vālmīki was reborn as Tulsī in order to deliver living creatures from the wicked Kali [age]'.[6] This passage was later elaborated on in Priyādās's *Bhaktirasbodhinī* (1712), a famous commentary on the *Bhaktamāl*. Other yet more uncertain and very dubious hagiographies nevertheless abounding with details, such as: the *Gautamcandrikā* (?1624), the *Mūlgosāĩcarit* (?1630) and the *Tulsīcarit* (?1770), to this day provoke discussion among scholars.[7] Thus, we have not much sound knowledge of Tulsīdās's life; even the most commonly accepted date of his birth, i.e. 1532, is at best the most probable of other propositions.[8] Brief notes in his poems – the *Kavitāvalī* (7.57 and 7.73) and the *Vinaypatrikā* (275.1–3 and 276.1–3) – suggest that in early childhood his parents abandoned him. Suffering loneliness

---

[4] For more on the problems concerned with the biography of Tulsīdās, see Philip Lutgendorf, 'The Quest for the Legendary Tulsīdās', in Winand M. Callewaert and Rupert Snell, *According to Tradition: Hagiographical Writing in India*, Wiesbaden: Otto Harrassowitz, 1994, pp. 65–85.

[5] Ibid., p. 72. On the dates of Nābhādās see e.g. Varmā, *Hindī sāhitya koś*, vol. 2, p. 301 and McGregor, *Hindi Literature from Its Beginnings*, pp. 108–9.

[6] *kali kuṭila jīva nistāra heta bālmīka tulasī bhayau*; 636 (207). Sītārāmśaraṇ Bhagvānprasād Rūpkalā, *Śrībhaktamāl*, 8th edn, Tejkumār Bukḍipo–Navalkiśor Bukḍipo: Lakhnaū, 2005, p. 756; cf. *The Rámáyana of Tulsi Dás*, p. v.

[7] For the most recent discussion of these sources see Lutgendorf, 'The Quest for the Legendary Tulsīdās'.

[8] See e.g. Mātā Prasād Gupta, *Tulsīdās: Ek samālocnātmak adhyayan*, 5th edn, Prayāg: Hindi Pariṣad Prakāśan, 1972, esp. pp. 141–3; McGregor, *Hindi Literature from Its Beginnings*, p. 109; F.R. Allchin's 'Introduction', in Tulsī Dās, *Kavitāvalī*, tr. F.R. Allchin, London: George Allen & Unwin, 1964, p. 33 and Lutgendorf, 'The Quest for the Legendary Tulsīdās', p. 69.

and hunger, most probably he was saved by Vaishnav sadhus who introduced him to the devotion of Rām. From the *Rāmcaritmānas* we know that Tulsīdās's life led him to Ayodhya, the supposed birthplace of his favoured deity Rām, and later to Banaras, where he died in 1623.[9] Luckily, however, we have much more certainty about his oeuvre.

Commonly, it is presumed that apart from the *Rāmcaritmānas* Tulsīdās is the author of at least eleven other works.[10] The most probable chronology of the works whose authorship is unanimously acknowledged is as follows: the *Rāmlalānahachū* (undated; Avadhi[11]); the *Rāmājñāpraśna* (1564; Avadhi); the *Jānakīmaṅgal* (undated; Avadhi); the *Rāmcaritmānas* (1574; Avadhi); the *Pārvatīmaṅgal* (1586; Avadhi); the *Gītāvalī*, the *Kṛṣṇagītāvalī* and the *Vinaypatrikā* (these three works in Braj are undated but they may have been composed sometime during the last decade of the sixteenth and the first years of the seventeenth century); the *Barvai rāmāyaṇ* (undated; Avadhi); the *Kavitāvalī* (undated; Braj). Many scholars traditionally ascribe to Tulsīdās the *Dohāvalī* (undated), comprising over 500 verses, and *Satsaī*, comprising some 700 verses. They both share *c.*130 verses and are commonly referred to

---

[9] For more details on Tulsīdās's life see e.g. Gupta, *Tulsīdās*, pp. 141–206; Śivnandan Sahāy, *Gosvāmī Tulsīdās*, 2nd edn (1st published in 1916), Paṭnā: Bihār Rāṣṭrabhāṣā Pariṣad, 2000, pp. 2–118; Rāmkumār Varmā, *Hindī sāhitya kā ālocnātmak itihās (saṁvat 750–1750)*, 5th edn, Ilāhābād: Rāmnārāyaṇ Lāl Benī Mādhav, 1964, pp. 337–48 and Vedvrat Śāstrī, 'Tulsī kā jīvanvṛtt', in Rāmsvarūp Ārya and Girirājśāraṇ Agravāl, *Tulsī mānas sandarbh*, Sambhal: Mānas Catuśśatī Ayojan Samiti, 1974, pp. 1–11; Rāmdatt Bhāradvaj, 'Tulsī kā janma sthān aur sorõ sāmagrī', in Ārya and Agravāl, *Tulsī mānas sandarbh*, pp. 12–39. Also see Varmā, *Hindī sāhityā koś*, vol. 2, pp. 233–5 and W. Douglas Hill, *The Holy Lake of the Acts of Rama: A Translation of Tulasī Dās's Rāmcaritmānas*, Calcutta: Oxford University Press, 1952, pp. IX–XII.

[10] Different sources ascribe to him many different works. For the discussion of almost 40 such works see Gupta, *Tulsīdās*, pp. 132–6; cf. Sahāy, *Gosvāmī Tulsīdās*, pp. 130–1.

[11] As in many cases in the language of Tulsīdās different forms are used it is difficult to make a clear-cut distinction between Avadhi and Braj. Therefore, the names given above in brackets rather indicate the prevailing linguistic character of a particular work than refer to the pure form of Avadhi or Braj.

together (*Satsaī-Dohāvalī*). Apart from that, some scholars also mention two other works: the *Vairāgyasandīpinī* (Braj) and the *Jñāndīpikā* (1565; Avadhi), which – if written by Tulsīdās – may predate the *Rāmcaritmānas*.[12] Thus, just a mere enumeration of his works makes it clear that their overwhelming majority were in one way or the other devoted to his chosen God – Rām.

THE *RĀMCARITMĀNAS*

INTRODUCTORY REMARKS

According to the poet's own testimony, he began the *Rāmcaritmānas* in 1574 in Ayodhya.

> *Now respectfully bowing my head to Shiv,*
> *I recount the pure story of Ram's qualities.*
> *In the year 1631 [of the Vikram era],*[13]
> *I narrate it with my head at Hari's feet.*
> *On Tuesday, the ninth day of the month of Chait,*[14]
> *In Ayodhya city, these deeds have been brought to light.*[15]

From the fact that Book 4 of the poem (*Kiṣkindhākāṇḍ*) begins with an invocation in praise of Banaras (Kāśī),[16] it is commonly

---

[12] G.A. Grierson, 'Notes on Tul'sī Dās', *Indian Antiquary*, vol. 22, 1893, pp. 89–98, 122–9, 197–206, 225–36, 253–74; Gupta, *Tulsīdās*, pp. 132–6, 234–82; Sahāy, *Gosvāmī Tulsīdās*, pp. 130–309; Varmā, *Hindī sāhitya kā ālocnātmak itihās*, pp. 361–71; McGregor, *Hindi Literature from Its Beginnings*, pp. 109–17; Vedprakāś Garg, 'Tulsī kī kṛtiyā̃', in Ārya and Agravāl, *Tulsī mānas sandarbh*, pp. 40–57 and Devakīnandan Śrīvāstav, *Tulsīdās kī bhāṣā*, Lakhnaū: Lakhnaū Viśvavidyālay, 1957, pp. 347–68.

[13] That is AD 1574.

[14] *Madhu māsā* – the month of Cait (March–April). This day, i.e. the ninth day of the light half of Cait, is known as Rāmnavamī and celebrated as Rām's birthday.

[15] *sādara sivahi nāi aba māthā; baranaū bisada rāma guna gāthā./ sambata soraha sai ekatīsā; karaū kathā hari pada dhari sīsā./ naumī bhauma bāra madhu māsā; avadhapurī̃ yaha carita prakāsā;* 1.34.2–3. All quotations from the text of the *Rāmcaritmānas* (henceforth abbreviated in references as RCM) after Tulsīdās, *Śrīrāmcaritmānas*, ed. and comment. Hanumānprasād Poddār, 19th edn, Gorakhpur: Gītā Pres, 1972.

accepted that the poet moved to that city while still working on his poem and finished it there a few years later.

Considering the main line of the story included in the poem, one can say that in general it agrees with the traditional story as told by Vālmīki. However, it should be stressed that in no way is it a translation of the Sanskrit epic, nor its direct successor – Tulsīdās benefited from the rich Rāmāyaṇa tradition to which he points in the one of the opening Sanskrit *śloka*s.[17] He mentions in it different Puranas, *nigama*s and *āgama*s, i.e. the Vedas and *śāstra*s, as well as the *Rāmāyaṇa* itself and other (traditionally transmitted) texts.[18] Charlotte Vaudeville, in her work on the sources of the *Rāmcaritmānas*, considers that apart from the *Rāmāyaṇa* of Vālmīki, the major sources of Tulsīdās were the dramas: the *Hanuman-nāṭaka* and the *Prasannarāghava*, the already-discussed philosophical Rāmāyaṇas such as the *Adhyātma rāmāyaṇa*, the *Yogavāsiṣṭha rāmāyaṇa* and the *Bhuśuṇḍi rāmāyaṇa*,[19] as well as the *Śiva purāṇa* and the *Bhāgavata purāṇa*.[20] As a result, a number of episodes known from Vālmīki's version were omitted by Tulsīdās or changed and still others added. There can be no doubt that Tulsī interpreted the story of Rām's deeds in accordance with the spirit of his own times. Therefore, the poem is expressive not only of its author's ideas but is also one of the best testimonies of those times. We also know that such a practice, i.e. re-telling and re-interpreting a well-known story, is not an exception in the Rāmāyaṇa tradition but typical of it, its essence and life force.

---

[16] RCM 4.0.

[17] Sanskrit *śloka*s open all the books and also close the last one. They can be understood as a kind of tribute paid to traditional Brahmin circles; most probably, the use of Sanskrit was also meant to increase the religious status of the poem.

[18] *nānāpurāṇanigamāgamasammataṃ yad, rāmāyaṇe nigaditaṃ kvacid-anyato'pi* (1 *śloka* 7).

[19] For more on the validity of the contention that the *Bhuśuṇḍi rāmāyaṇa* is one of the sources of the *Rāmcaritmānas,* see my 'Crow Bhuśuṇḍi and His Story of the Deeds of Rām', in Danuta Stasik and Anna Trynkowska, eds., *India in Warsaw: A Volume to Commemorate the 50th Anniversary of the Post-War History of Indological Studies at Warsaw University (2003/2004)*, Warszawa: Dom Wydawniczy Elipsa, 2006, pp. 293–9, esp. pp. 297–8.

[20] Vaudeville, *Étude*, esp. pp. XV–XXIII, 307–24.

As far as the *Rāmcaritmānas* manuscript tradition is concerned, the oldest seventeenth-century manuscripts are very few; more common are the eighteenth-century manuscripts.[21] In this context an interesting feature of this tradition, to which George A. Grierson paid attention[22] as early as the end of the nineteenth century and which Philip Lutgendorf corroborated in his excellent work on the poem's performing traditions,[23] is worth mentioning here. Thus, some 10 percent of manuscripts are written in *kaithī*, the script used by mercantile and scribal castes, and a smaller, but still significant number, in Perso-Arabic script. This seems to suggest the poem's early popularity with the landed aristocracy and mercantile classes, while it had to wait much longer for the full acceptance of Brahmins. Lutgendorf refers[24] to the words of F.S. Growse who in his translation of the *Rāmcaritmānas* published almost 300 years after the poem's creation wrote that 'the professional Sanskrit pandits (...) still affect to despise [Tulsī's] work as an unworthy concession to the illiterate masses'. It is worth adding here that Growse further continues: 'With this small and solitary exception the book is in every one's hands, from the court to the cottage, and is read, or heard, and appreciated alike by every class of the Hindú community, whether high or low, rich or poor, young or old'.[25] Interestingly, it is still true even today.

THE POEM'S STRUCTURE

The *Rāmcaritmānas* is an extensive poem, consisting of seven traditionally named books (the exception is Book 6 entitled *Laṅkākāṇḍ*, the Lanka Book, unlike Vālmīki's *Yuddhakāṇḍa*, the War Book, but following the *Adhyātma rāmāyaṇa*). The longest are

[21] Cf. Gupta, *Tulsīdās*, pp. 216–20.

[22] Grierson discussing the date of the poem referred to the opinion expressed by Paṇḍit Sudhākara Dvivedī that the *Rāmcaritmānas* 'first became popular amongst *Baniyās* and *Kāyasthas*, who began to write the poem in their own alphabet, the *Kaithī*'. Grierson, 'Notes', pp. 93–4.

[23] Lutgendorf, *The Life of a Text*, p. 9; also see Lutgendorf, 'The Quest for the Legendary Tulsīdās', p. 75.

[24] Lutgendorf, *The Life of a Text*, p. 9.

[25] *The Rámáyana*, pp. XVII–XVIII.

the two first books, the Childhood Book and the Ayodhya Book, which together constitute more than a half of the epic.

The entire poem consists roughly of 12,800 lines divided into 1073 units,[26] usually termed by Western scholars as stanza, or strophe.[27] It is a sequence of, most commonly, four *caupāī* couplets followed by a *dohā*. In Indian sources, the whole unit is usually called after the name of the metre that closes it, i.e. *dohā*.[28] The most popular modern editions, e.g. the Gita Press edition, are arranged in such a way that *caupāī*s are numbered within an individual stanza and *dohā*s throughout each book.[29] Even though it facilitates the use of the text, as well as its comprehension (as the testimony of Añjanīnandan Śaraṇ proves),[30] it was not applied in modern printed editions of the poem from the very beginning. For example, in the edition of 1810 no numbers are used at all; in the edition of 1839 both *caupāī*s and *dohā*s are numbered separately throughout each book. A similar method was implemented in one of the two editions of 1869 with a slight difference that each single line of a *caupāī*, and not the entire *caupāī*, is numbered; in the other, *dohā*s and other metres (*chand*s) are numbered but not *caupāī*s.[31] Such variations in the method of editing the *Rāmcaritmānas* seem to suggest that not all editors of the poem were fully aware of the fact that a *dohā* as the closing element of the *caupāī*–*dohā* sequence forms an important feature of the poem's

---

[26] These numbers are quoted after Lutgendorf, *The Life of a Text*, p. 13.

[27] The term stanza is used, e.g. by Lutgendorf in his *The Life of a Text*; Charlotte Vaudeville uses the term strophe in her study *Étude*, pp. xIff. Also see Whaling, *The Rise*.

[28] See e.g. an authoritative RCM commentary: Añjanīnandan Śaraṇ, *Mānaspīyūṣ*, 11th edn, Gorakhpur: Gītā Pres, 1998, vol. 1, pp. IXff.

[29] But see e.g. an important Kāśirāj edition in which each single line of a *caupāī*, i.e. each *ardhālī*, is numbered and the number is given after every four verses; Tulsīdās, *Rāmcaritmānas*, ed. Viśvanāthprasād Miśra, Vārāṇasī: Kāśirāj Nyās, n.d. (1962).

[30] See Śaraṇ, *Mānaspīyūṣ*, vol. 1, pp. IXff.

[31] *Tulsīkṛt rāmāyaṇ*, ed. Sadal Miśra, Calcutta, 1810; *Tulsīdāsgosvāmīkṛt saptakāṇḍa rāmāyaṇagranthaḥ*, ed. (?) Tilakrām Nāthrām, Kalikattā, 1839; *Tulsīkṛt rāmāyaṇ*, ed. Sadāsukh Lāl, Ilāhābād: Nūrula Absār Pres, 1869 and *Tulsīkṛt rāmāyaṇ*, ed. Rāmjasan, Benares: E. Lazarus & Co., 1869 (all from the collection of Cambridge University Library).

structure.[32] Whatever the reason for this, it may also testify to their ignorance of old manuscripts in which the organizing role of the final *dohā* is evident.[33] (As noted above, it was also a problem of A. Śaraṇ, at an earlier stage of his commentarial career. What is more, as noted by Philip Lutgendorf,[34] it also disagrees with the *Rāmcaritmānas* oral performing tradition.) Scholars point to the fact that Tulsīdās was not the first to implement the sequence of *caupāī*s and *dohā*s in his work. The earliest examples of such an arrangement can be found in Apabhransha works of the famous siddha Sarahapā(da) (around the eighth century AD).[35] By the time of Tulsī, it had become quite a well-established literary tradition in Avadhi with such predecessors of Tulsīdās as Maulānā Dāūd and his *Candāyan* (1379)[36] or Malik Muhammad Jāyasī and his *Padmāvat* (1540/1).[37]

Philip Lutgendorf, noting that apart from the more obvious division of the poem into books and stanzas the *Rāmcaritmānas* also has a further implicit division into individual episodes (*prasaṅg*) and dialogues (*saṁvād*), very rightly comments that this feature appears 'to reflect the conventions and constraints of oral story telling and sequential recitation'.[38] In other words, although Tulsīdās did write his poem, it was written not so much to be read in solitude as rather to be heard recited, sung or read, especially by others.[39] One is reminded of this, e.g. in many *phalaśruti*s (lit. 'fruit-hearing'), which designate instructions on gains or

---

[32] Cf. Lutgendorf, *The Life of a Text*, p. 15, n. 39 and Divyānand Sarasvatī, *Mānasvarṇānukramaṇikā*, Ṛṣikeś: Svāmī Divyānand Sarasvatī, 1993, where *dohā* opens the sequence of *caupāī*s.

[33] See Śaraṇ, *Mānaspīyūṣ*, vol. 1, p. IX and facsimiles of two old manuscripts (with the so-called Rājāpur manuscript believed to be handwritten by Tulsīdās) in Grierson, *The Modern Vernacular Literature*, pp. 46–7, 50–1.

[34] Lutgendorf, *The Life of a Text*, p. 15, n. 39.

[35] Hazārīprasād Dvivedī, *Hindī sāhitya kī bhūmikā*, 2nd edn, Dillī: Rājkamal Prakāśan, 1969, pp. 49–50 and John Millis, 'Mallik Muhammad Jāyasī: Allegory and Religious Symbolism in His *Padmāvat*', Ph.D. dissertation, Chicago: University of Chicago, 1984, pp. 60–1.

[36] McGregor, *Hindi Literature from Its Beginnings*, p. 26.

[37] Ibid., p. 67.

[38] Lutgendorf, *The Life of a Text*, p. 17.

[39] Ibid., pp. 35–41.

rewards resulting from communing with the text of the poem and they are scattered throughout it.[40]

Discussing the first of the two explicit interpretive frames built into the structure of the *Rāmcaritmānas*, i.e. the poem's title, Philip Lutgendorf refers to the Hindi tradition that shortens it to its final element, making it simply *Mānas*.[41] In this context, his explanation of his decision is most revealing. He very rightly observes that it 'is not a mere truncation of the title, but a significant condensation that focuses on the central metaphor of the poem'.[42] Trying to avoid the ample repetition of Ph. Lutgendorf's argument based on the *Rāmcaritmānas* commentarial tradition,[43] which he has very competently presented to the English-speaking audiences, let me note that this is the metaphor of the text conceived in Śiv's mind/heart and belonging to it (S. > H. *mānas* < S. *manas* 'mind; heart'[44]). Tulsīdās thus expounds on the origin of the poem.

> *The 'Ramcharitmanas', pleasing sages,*
> *Beautiful and holy, was created by Shiv.* (...)
> *Upon its creation, Shiv put it into his heart,*
> *And when the right time came, he told it Parvati.*
> *Therefore, he had lost himself in contemplation, and then,*
> *Delighted, gave it an excellent title – 'Ramcharitmanas'* (1.35.5–6).[45]

The poem is also equated with Māna(s)sarovar, the Himalayan Manas Lake (1.36.1–5), which is used as a metaphor itself for the mind in its sublime, refined state.[46] This lake of a text – the *Mānas* – is an endless source of the story of Rām's deeds (*Rāmcarit*). The story is one but in Tulsīdās's design there are four storytellers and

---

[40] Cf. ibid., pp. 2, 11.

[41] Ibid., pp. 12, 18–22.

[42] Ibid., p. 12.

[43] See e.g. Śaraṇ, *Mānaspīyūṣ*, vol. 1, esp. pp. 507–606.

[44] For more meanings of this word, see Monier-Williams, *A Sanskrit-English Dictionary*, p. 783.

[45] *rāmacaritamānasa muni bhāvana; biraceu sambhu suhāvana pāvana.*/ (...) *raci mahesa nija mānasa rākhā; pāi susamau sivā sana bhāṣā.*/ *tātẽ rāmacaritamānasa bara; dhareu nāma hiyā̃ heri haraṣi hara.*

[46] Lutgendorf, *The Life of a Text*, p. 20.

their four audiences. At this point one encounters the second explicit interpretive frame in the structure of the *Rāmcaritmānas*.

The poem's narrative is realized through a series of four dialogues[47] (also forming the four narrative frames of the poem), i.e. the dialogues between Śiv and Pārvatī, Bhuśuṇḍi and Garuḍ, Yājñavalkya and Bharadvāj, Tulsīdās and his audience (*sants*).[48] According to Philip Lutgendorf, such a presentation of the narrative 'exemplifies a traditional pattern in Indian literature: the presentation of a text as an oral narration by a particular teller to a particular listener, within a carefully delineated context' and also 'suggests an intimate and unbroken connection between oral and written literature, and a continuing awareness of the former as a source and model for the latter'.[49] However, it should be stressed that they are only seemingly dialogues. In fact, there are, as I have already mentioned, four narrators who, for the most part, use the form of monologue. They are very aware of their audience all the time although usually it is active only during the opening and closing parts of their lines. Put simply, one can say that given threads of the story are evoked by questions of Pārvatī, Garuḍ or Bharadvāj and are followed by answers by Śiv, Bhuśuṇḍi or Yājñavalkya, respectively. One should remember that Tulsīdās's audience, though very much present in the poem's structure, is not active because in fact it cannot be active and voice its doubts or comments in the text itself. The potential of this audience, however, is fully realized in the performing traditions of

---

[47] On an attempt at explaining this as a result of different stages in the composition of RCM see Rāmnareś Trīpāṭhī, *Tulsī aur unkā kāvya*, Dillī: Rājpāl eṇḍ Sanz, 1953, pp. 220ff; Gupta, *Tulsīdās*, pp. 268–81; Vaudeville, *Étude*, pp. 319–24; Whaling, *The Rise*, pp. 229–31 and C. Bulcke, '*Rāmacaritmānasa* and Its Relevance to Modern Age', in Raghavan, *The Ramayana Tradition*, pp. 65–7.

[48] The chronology of the transmission of the story is not clear; see the *Rāmcaritmānas* itself 1.30.1–31.1, as well as Lutgendorf, *The Life of a Text*, p. 24, n. 56 and Linda, Hess, 'Staring at Frames Till They Turn into Loops: An Excursion through Some Worlds of Tulsidas', in Bradley R. Hertel and Cynthia Ann Humes, ed., *Living Banaras: Hindu Religion in Cultural Context*, 1st Indian edn, Delhi: Manohar, 1998, pp. 75ff.

[49] Lutgendorf, *The Life of a Text*, pp. 22–3; cf. also idem, 'The View from the Ghats: Traditional Exegesis of a Hindu Epic', *Journal of Asian Studies*, vol. 48, no. 2, 1989, pp. 272–88.

the *Rāmcaritmānas*, which have been extensively explored by Philip Lutgendorf in his, oft-quoted here, book *The Life of a Text*.

Tulsīdās extends the metaphor of the lake-like text into a comprehensive allegory in which these four dialogues are conceived as four embankments (*ghāṭ*s) of the lake. Significantly, the commentarial tradition considers them to be different methods of 'approaching' the text, viz., its different interpretations. The seven books of the poem are the seven stairs (*sopān*) of a *ghāṭ*. Tulsīdās formulated it in the following way:

> *Exceptionally beautiful, excellent dialogues, created after deep contemplation,*
> *Are the four charming embankments of this holy, delightful lake.*
> *Seven books are beautiful stairs;*
> *Seeing them with the eyes of wisdom, the heart rejoices* (1.36–7.1).[50]

These stairs lead to the deep waters of the lake of Rām's unqualified, constant magnificence (*raghupati mahimā aguna abādhā*; 1.37.1) and of Rām and Sītā's glory (*rāma sīya jasa*; 1.37.2). Thus it becomes clear that reading, reciting, singing the poem or listening to it is an idiosyncratic initiation, the way to reach the core of the mystery of the Rāmkathā. The further the story goes, the closer one is to fathom out this mystery.[51]

In this context, it is worth considering why the number of stairs descending to the lake is seven. The most natural answer to such a question would be that it is due to Vālmīki and the Rāmāyaṇa tradition begun by him, i.e. the tradition of dividing the story of Rām's deeds into seven books, or parts. However, it is well known from this tradition itself that many tellings do not necessarily repeat the division implemented in the *Rāmāyaṇa* of Vālmīki. It seems more than probable that Tulsīdās, creating his poem, which was meant to reward with a release from the bonds of existence, was also referring to Yoga and its practice. The fact

---

[50] *suṭhi sundara sambāda bara birace buddhi bicāri; / tei ehi pāvana subhaga sara ghāṭa manohara cāri. / sapta prabandha subhaga sopānā; jñāna nayana nirakhata mana mānā*. See Śaraṇ, *Mānaspīyūṣ*, vol. 1, pp. 535–47; Lutgendorf, 'The View from the Ghats', pp. 272–9; idem, *The Life of a Text*, pp. 26–7 and Hess, 'Staring at Frames', pp. 73–101.

[51] Stasik, *Opowieść*, pp. 173–5.

that Yoga is mentioned by the poet as one of the inhabitants of the lake (1.37.5), as well as the undeniable structural resemblance between Yogic practices and Tulsīdās's allegory lend credence to such a contention. Without going into too many details, let me observe that in Yoga the ultimate end can be achieved only through following the path of eight stages, lit. 'eight members/ limbs' (*aṣṭāṅga*). They are: moral restraints such as non-violence, truth, chastity and abstention from attachment to possessions (*yama*); physical and ascetic observances (*niyama*); bodily postures thanks to which independence from the stimuli of the exterior world is achieved (*āsana*); the process of respiration that enables one to take control over the vital breath (*prāṇa*) and physiological processes (*prāṇāyāma*); emancipation of sensory activity from the domination of external objects – this is the last stage of psycho-physiological asceticism (*pratyāhāra*); concentration, i.e. fixing the attention on one object (*dhāraṇā*); contemplation of the nature of this object, Yogic meditation (*dhyāna*) and, finally, the highest concentration, merging consciousness with the object of meditation recognized as 'release/liberation', understanding of the ultimate being (*samādhi*).[52] It is also very important to note here that after the realization of the seventh stage supernatural powers (*siddhi*), meaning the ability of going beyond every-day limitations, appear.

Going back to the *Rāmcaritmānas*, it should be noted that the image of the Manas Lake with four *ghāṭs* around it is not restricted to the opening fragments of the poem. As I have already mentioned, each of the seven books following one after another is a consecutive stair (*sopān*) leading to the waters of the lake. Therefore, such activity as the poem's recitation or listening to it can be seen as a stairway to initiation, getting to the bottom of the lake and thus to the secret of the deeds of Rām. In Book 7, the image of the lake is evoked in the dialogue between Bhuśuṇḍi and Garuḍ. Here it forms the epilogue of the narrative and at the same time bridges it into a harmonious whole,[53] so that journey through the seven books-stairs does not end with a step into the void. The next – eighth – step leads one into the waters of the lake, allowing

[52] For more on this subject see Mircea Eliade, *Yoga: Immortality and Freedom*, London: Routledge and Kegan Paul, 1969, esp. pp. 47–104.

[53] Stasik, *Opowieść*, pp. 173–5; cf. Lutgendorf, *The Life of a Text*, p. 22.

immersion in them and going beyond every-day limitations. If one considers that the books of the poem form such a perspective, one can notice a new unusual quality in the form of the whole poem itself!

Thus the wandering, both literary through the successive books of the poem and allegorical through the stairs of *ghāṭ*s, can be understood as a special activity, passing through successive stages and contemplating contents encountered on the way. It also means a gradual exploration of oneself and an attempt at getting to the core of reality – the essence of which is Bhakti, the devotion to Rām – with the help of the poem's text. Summing up these notes on the prologue to the *Rāmcaritmānas* (1.1–43), one point has to be stressed: Tulsīdās was very careful to introduce his audiences to the essential features of his poem's structure from the very beginning, making them acquainted with what he considered important in the process of its interpretation.

The narration of Rām's story proper begins only in stanza 176 with the birth of his adversary, Rāvaṇ, and then in stanza 191 Rām's birth follows. This narration is continued through the rest of the poem and ends with the triumphant return of Rām to Ayodhya after his victory over Rāvaṇ, his enthronement and the depiction of his ideal, just rule, i.e. Rāmrājya. It is worth noting here that Tulsīdās ends his story differently from Vālmīki. There is no banishment of the pregnant Sītā in the *Rāmcaritmānas* and their sons – Lav and Kuś – are born not in Vālmīki's hermitage but in Ayodhya. Rām does not ascend to heaven, ending his earthly existence by drowning himself in the waters of the river Sarayu. In the *Rāmcaritmānas,* having distributed his wealth among his people, Rām leaves Ayodhya together with his brothers and Hanumān. When he grows weary, he retires to a cool mango grove and attended by all his brothers sits on a robe spread for him by Bharat.[54] The commentarial tradition explains this as Rām's departure to Vaikuṇṭha, his heavenly abode.[55] Yet, analysing this passage, one has an irresistible impression that Rāmrājya has not ended, that Rām's just and happy rule still

[54] (...) *gae jahā̃ sītala avārāī. bharata dīnha nija basana ḍasāī; baithe prabhu sevahī saba bhāī.* 7.50.3.

[55] Śaraṇ, *Mānaspīyūṣ,* vol. 7, pp. 310–11.

lasts,[56] that Rām himself is always nearby and could come when any such need arises.

After the main narrative, which concludes in stanza 51 of Book 7, the so-called 'Bhuśuṇḍi Rāmāyaṇa' (7.53.1–125) follows; its basis is the dialogue between Bhuśuṇḍi and Garuḍ. A prelude to it fashions Garuḍ's doubt revealed to Śiv – he is sceptical about the real power of Rām whom, after all, he had to help free himself from the tangle of snakes set on him by Meghnād, the son of Rāvaṇ, during the battle. In order to dispel his doubts, Śiv sends Garuḍ to Crow Bhuśuṇḍi, an immortal creature in the form of an impure bird, literally 'a chandal[57] among birds' (*pacchī caṇḍālā*; 7.112.8), who incessantly narrates the story of Rām's deeds to the birds gathering at the top of Blue Mountain (*nīl parvat/sail*). The crow instructs them about the nature of Rām himself and his worship. It is worth noticing here that Bhuśuṇḍi is shown as a bhakta to whose heart the period of Rām's childhood is especially pleasing. (7.75.1–77 and 114.6–7). He does not regret his present incarnation and his crow body is dear to him, because it is this very form in which a true Rāmbhakti arose in his heart, in this very form he received the blessing of seeing his Lord and was relieved of all doubts (7.114.ka). Thus from Bhuśuṇḍi Garuḍ as well as all those who are interested in hearing his message learn about the extraordinary power of Bhakti and the saving power of Rām's name leading to liberation in the Dark Age of Kaliyug.[58]

Finally, Śiv takes up the narrative and, teaching about the extraordinary qualities of the story of Rām's deeds, he utters the following, very meaningful words:

> *Blessed is the land in which the Ganges*[59] *flows!*
> *Blessed is the wife faithful to her husband!*
> *Blessed is the king who governs rightly!*
> *Blessed is the twice born who does not give up his dharma!*
> *Blessed is the wealth given to others!*[60]

---

[56] Cf. Whaling, *The Rise*, pp. 250–1.

[57] Chandal (*cāṇḍāl*) – 'the lowest of the low in the hierarchy'.

[58] For more on Bhuśuṇḍi's life and his precepts, see Stasik, 'Crow Bhuśuṇḍi'.

[59] In the original 'the river of Gods' (*surasarī*).

Blessed is the mature mind engrossed in virtue!
Blessed are the moments spent in the company of the saints!
Blessed is the life of continuous devotion to Brahmins!

Listen, O Uma! Blessed is the family, holy and venerated by the world,
In which a humble man, devoted to Shriraghubir was born (7.127.3–4, 127).[61]

The poem concludes with the words of Tulsīdās who, in a typical *phalaśruti*, for the last time enumerates the advantages of listening, reading and transmitting the story, followed with two Sanskrit *śloka*s. In the first of them, the author explains that he only verbalized in a vernacular (*bhāṣābaddh*) the *Rāmāyaṇa* composed by Śiv, giving to it the form of *Mānas*.[62] He did it in order to disperse the darkness of his own mind (*svāntastamaḥśāntaye*). The second *śloka* is another *phalaśruti*, this time in Sanskrit.

However, in the case of some editions of the *Rāmcaritmānas* it is not the real end, as they also include an interpolated Book 8, the Lav and Kush Book (*Lavkuśkāṇḍ*). This book makes up for the final episodes that the *Rāmcaritmānas* lacks in comparison with Vālmīki's *Rāmāyaṇa* and many other tellings. It deals with the banishment of Sītā, the birth of Lav and Kuś in Vālmīki's aśram and their later fight with the army under Bharat's and then Rām's command. In the finale, Sītā seated by the Earth upon a bejewelled throne vanishes in the netherworld and Rām departs for his abode, disappearing in the waters of Sarayu. Although this book is an evident interpolation (the question of its authorship and its

---

[60] *Prathama gati* – lit. 'the first method'. This concept is based on a conviction that wealth can be used in three ways. First, it can be given away to others (*dān*) and this method is considered to be the best one. Second, it can be used for any kind of enjoyment (*bhog*); this method is not as good as the first one but much better than the last one, when wealth is neither given away to others nor used by its owner himself, which means it is spoiled (*nāś*). See Śaraṇ, *Mānaspīyūṣ*, vol. 7, p. 784.

[61] *dhanya desa so jahā̃ surasarī; dhanya nāri patibrata anusarī./ dhanya so bhūpa nīti jo karaī; dhanya so dvija nija dharma na ṭaraī./ so dhana dhanya prathama gati jākī; dhanya punya rata mati soi pākī./ dhanya gharī soi jaba satasaṅgā; dhanya janma dvija bhagati abhaṅgā./ so kula dhanya umā sunu jagata pūjya supunīta;/ śrīraghubīra parāyana jehī̃ nara upaja binīta.*

[62] A pun on the name of the poem and the lake.

date is still open), the fact that many Hindus are convinced that Tulsīdās's Rām banished Sītā[63] testifies to its popularity very vividly.

POPULARITY OF THE *RĀMCARITMĀNAS*

Considering the causes of extraordinary popularity that the *Rāmcaritmānas* gained soon after its creation, one's attention, first of all, should be paid to the times in which Tulsīdās created his poem. In the late sixteenth century, India was under Muslim rule, the rule of Akbar, the Great Mogul (1556–1605). As observed by Stuart McGregor, in north India it was 'an age in which confident reassertion of Indian and Hindu values was an important factor' as opposed to the earlier 'period of cultural disorganisation, adjustment and assimilation'.[64] Thus it seems very natural that, on the one hand, those times resulted in a further synthesis of Hindu and Islamic cultures but, on the other hand, and in this context it seems even more important, it also consolidated Hindus' feelings about the greatness of their own tradition and urged them to voice their own cultural values.[65] Therefore, the *Rāmcaritmānas* can be seen as a work that, following important traditions of Hindu India, has become an epitome of the ideal (Hindu) society, state and its ruler – a counter-proposal for the reality in which Tulsīdās and his contemporaries lived.

In north India, the sixteenth century was also the peak of the Bhakti movement that in Vaishnav circles meant first and foremost the opening of Brahmin orthodoxy to other groups of Hindu society and offering them the possibility of attaining salvation.[66] In his poem Tulsīdās employed this idea of Bhakti fully: his work was meant for all Hindus, and the use of Avadhi, the language

---

[63] During my several stays in India between 1993 and 2007, my interlocutors of different social and educational background, living in different parts of the Hindi-speaking area, expressed such a conviction.

[64] McGregor, 'The Rama Story and Rama Devotion in North India', in Vyas, *Ramayana. Its Universal Appeal and Global Role*, p. 19.

[65] Cf. ibid.

[66] For more see Lorenzen, 'Introduction: The Historical Vicissitudes of Bhakti Religion'.

of those not conversant with Sanskrit, called by the poet simply as the 'language' (*bhākhā*), is the most telling evidence of it. Of course, it should be stressed that such an attitude by no means meant a social revolution, an attack on the traditional Hindu hierarchy with Brahmins at the top and Shudras at the bottom, in which clearly defined duties were assigned to each group and anybody not fulfilling his tasks was liable to punishment. Tulsīdās expressed it very definitely in a number of passages and the most telling of them are the words of Vasiṣṭha, serving as a meaningful counterpoint to the 'Blessed' (*dhanya*) passage quoted earlier.

Lament the Brahmin, who is deprived of the Veda,
Who discarded his own dharma and is engrossed in sensual enjoyment!
Lament the king, who does not know what political wisdom is,
And his people are not as dear to him as his own life!

Lament the Vaishya, who – although rich – is miserly,
Who neither knows hospitality, nor is devoted to Shiv![67]
Lament the Shudra, who is talkative, thirsting for recognition,
Proud of his knowledge and disregards Brahmins!

Lament, then, a wicked, quarrelsome and
Wilful wife, deceiving her husband! (2.172.2–4)[68]

Later in this passage, Tulsīdās also mentions those who break their vows (*bratu/vrata*), who do not obey their own parents, guru and other elders, and who hurt other people (2.172.4–173.2). Both here and in the *dhanya* passage, as well as in a number of other fragments of the *Rāmcaritmānas*, the poem – just like the Rāmāyaṇa tradition from which it grew – appears to be a source of ethical

---

[67] According to commentaries the devotion to Śiv promotes growth of wealth; a rich man should entertain guests and serve them properly (*atithisevā*), otherwise wealth can get wasted, be consumed by fire, stolen by a thief or taken over by the king (!); Śaraṇ, *Mānaspīyūṣ*, vol. 4, p. 668.

[68] *socia bipra jo beda bihīnā; taji nija dharamu viṣaya layalīnā. / socia nṛpati jo nīti na jānā; jehi na prajā priya prāna samānā. / socia bayasu kṛpana dhanavānū; jo na atithi siva bhagati sujānū. / socia sūdra bipra avamānī; mukharu mānapriya gyāna gumānī. / socia puni pati bañcaka nārī; kuṭila kalaha priya icchācārī.*

values enriched with other precepts. Tulsīdās throughout his work leaves no doubt that in the sphere of social conduct the most important authority for him is the Veda, but – very symptomatically – together with 'the ways of the world' (*loka/lokahū*[69] *beda*).[70] Thus, describing the story of Rām's life, Tulsīdās has shown what the ideal life of a Hindu should look like. Taking into consideration the fact that the *Rāmcaritmānas* has become one of the greatest authorities, one can but agree that the poet's vision has ideally met the needs of Hindu society.

The presence of Śiv is also very significant. He not only created the story and is one of its four narrators but is also dear to Rām as no one else' (*siva samāna priya mohi na dūjā*; 6.2.3) as well as his most prominent devotee. Therefore, Tulsīdās's poem, being the genuine expression of Rāmbhakti, is also an attempt to reach for an audience from among Shivaites, an attempt at the reconciliation of Rām and Śiv devotees.[71]

Mentioning earlier in this study the four dialogues that form the structural frames of the *Rāmcaritmānas*, I have noted that they, likened to the *ghāṭ*s leading to the Manas Lake, are understood as different ways of 'approaching' the text. One can add here that thanks to these conceptual flights of steps, the text of the epic becomes as accessible as the water of the lake. Very importantly – they are suited to people's different needs and abilities. Thus in the commentarial tradition,[72] the dialogue between Tulsīdās and his audience is likened to a flat, smooth landing, serving as a watering place for cattle (*gaūghāṭ*), as well as an approach for the crippled. It can be accessed without any effort; only the mood of humility (*dainya*) is needed. The dialogue between the sages Yājñavalkya and Bharadvāj is likened to a landing meant for the use of all members of society (*pañcāyatīghāṭ*). This is the path for

[69] *lokahū* – *loka* + emphatic particle -*hū*.

[70] E.g. 1.3.3a, 1.7.4, 1.28.3, 1.324.7, 1.352.1, 2.194.2, 2.196.1, 2.207.2, 2.218.4 or 2.252.4. Cf. Avadhesh Kumar Singh, 'Rāma, His Carita, Mānasa and Kathā', in idem, ed., *Rāmāyaṇa Through the Ages – Rāma-Gathā in Different Versions*, Delhi: D.K. Printworld, 2007, pp. 17–18.

[71] RCM 6.2.4, 6.7.45, 6.97. Cf. Whaling, *The Rise*, pp. 233, 307.

[72] Śaraṇ, *Mānaspīyūṣ*, vol. 1, pp. 541–7. Also see Lutgendorf, 'The View from the Ghats', pp. 277–9 and Rām Kiṅkar, *Mānas ke cār ghāṭ*, Ayodhyā: Rāmāyaṇ Ṭrasṭ, 1997.

those who follow customary observances (*karmakāṇḍ*). The dialogue between Śiv and Pārvatī is likened to a landing used by the nobility (*rājghāṭ*); it is a difficult path of gnosis (*jñān*), available only to those who possess appropriate knowledge. Last but not least, the dialogue between Bhuśuṇḍi and Garuḍ is likened to a secluded landing (*panghaṭ*) where women can bathe and draw water far away from men's gazes; this is a path of esoteric practices, epitomising the devotional worship of the Lord (*bhakti upāsanā*). Such a variety of different approaches to the text once again indicates very clearly that the *Rāmcaritmānas* was meant to suit the different needs of its audiences. The past and present popularity of the poem testifies to the fact that the masses of north Indian Hindus use it in the way which suits best their needs and abilities.

Undoubtedly, one of the most important factors influencing the popularity of the *Rāmcaritmānas*'s is also the way in which Rām is depicted. He is the Supreme Being, Merciful Lord, the best of men and the best of rulers who knows how to protect his people. However, I will leave this subject for the time being, as it will be dealt with in more detail in Part Two of this study.

Summing up the foregoing discussion, one should observe that many authors preceding Tulsīdās and many of those who lived after him, while telling the story of Rām's life, were changing it by adding, extending or removing certain episodes. They tried to make their tellings captivating, quite often they included different moral, philosophical or theological precepts in them, and Tulsīdās is no exception in this regard. The genius of Tulsīdās, however, reveals itself in the fact that in the *Rāmcaritmānas* he offered the vision of cosmos, the harmonious, ordered entity watched over by Rām who decidedly eliminates any signs of chaos if they happen to appear anywhere. Tulsīdās's poem can thus be seen as a clear exposition of the rules that govern the sphere of ritual, religious, social or – just in general – human life. Their transparency and steadfastness to this day are exemplary for many people (not all of them are necessarily Hindi speakers) and are a positive challenge to implement them in their own lives.

Of course, this does not mean that Tulsīdās's work cannot be criticized and as such has not been criticized, it has. As rightly observed by Philip Lutgendorf 'The Ramayana tradition has always had "problems"',[73] and the *Rāmcaritmānas* is no exception in this respect, although open, harsh criticism is a relatively modern phenomenon. The poem and its author have been attacked and criticized for, among other things, propagating the domination of Brahmins, promoting exploitation and unfair treatment of Shudras, low-castes and women, sanctioning reactionary attitudes and the backwardness of Hindu society. Even if there have not been many 'who have straightforwardly attacked the *Mānas*; to do so would be like attacking motherhood or the cow',[74] nevertheless such allegations made in the past[75] and today[76] are an undeniable fact. However, quite paradoxically, this testifies to the important role played by Tulsīdās and his work in shaping the countenance of north Indian society – no one attacks works that are meaningless. Thus, to use Romila Thapar's words: 'Questioning the Ramayana is therefore questioning that which is seen as the norm'.[77]

BEYOND THE *RĀMCARITMĀNAS*

In the introductory part of this chapter, I mentioned that Tulsīdās is traditionally considered to be the author of twelve works. The majority of them, i.e. the *Rāmlalānahachū*, the *Rāmājñāpraśna*, the *Jānakīmaṅgal*, the *Gītāvalī*, the *Vinaypatrikā*, the *Barvai rāmāyaṇ*, the *Kavitāvalī* and of course the *Rāmcaritmānas*, in a more or less explicit way pertain to the story of Rām's deeds. Some of them

---

[73] Lutgendorf, *The Life of a Text*, p. 392.

[74] Ibid., p. 395.

[75] See e.g. Rajnīkānt Śāstrī, *Mānas mīmāṁsā*, Ilāhābād: Kitāb Mahal, 1949 and the discussion of this work in Lutgendorf, *The Life of a Text*, pp. 401–3.

[76] See e.g. Viśvanāth, ed., *Hindu samāj ke pathbhraṣṭak Tulsīdās*, Dillī: Viśvavijay Prakāśan, n.d. This collection of essays, whose very provocative title means 'Tulsīdās: the Misleader of Hindu Society', is one of the best examples of this kind of criticism. For an interesting discussion of more of RCM's critics see Lutgendorf, *The Life of a Text*, pp. 392–409 and for more on 'problems' with the Rāmāyaṇa, see Richman, *Questioning Ramayanas*.

[77] Romila Thapar, 'Foreword', in Richman, *Questioning Ramayanas*, p. VII.

refer to the entire story, e.g. the *Rāmājñāpraśna* or the *Kavitāvalī*, others are devoted to single episodes, viz. the *Rāmlalānahachū* and the *Jānakīmaṅgal* and yet others, i.e. the *Gītāvalī* and the *Vinaypatrikā* relate to the story only loosely. Discussing these works, first I would like to concentrate on two minor works of Tulsīdās, i.e. the *Rāmlalānahachū* devoted to a preliminary marriage ceremony of paring Rām's nails (this rite is not dealt with in the *Rāmcaritmānas*) and the *Jānakīmaṅgal* depicting the marriage ceremony of Sītā and Rām.[78] Though neither of them deals with the entire story, their comparison with relevant passages of the *Rāmcaritmānas* proves to be an interesting exercise that betrays a very significant feature of Tulsīdās's epic.

THE *RĀMLALĀNAHACHŪ* AND THE *JĀNAKĪMAṄGAL*

The *Rāmlalānahachū* consists of 20 *sohar*[79] stanzas (40 couplets).[80] It depicts the rite of *nahachū* as well as *māyan* that precedes it and is dedicated to ancestors who are invoked and invited to the wedding. These ceremonies are performed in the house of King Daśarath in Ayodhya. First, a wedding canopy is erected and Rām is washed in Ganges water. Then the ceremonial square (*cauk*) is prepared and Rām is seated on the throne (1–4). Beautifully dressed women of different menial castes come for the *māyan* rite and bring with them different requisites. Among them is a black-

---

[78] For a more detailed analysis of these texts see Danuta Stasik, 'The Divine Marriage: the Nuptials of Rām and Sītā as Seen by Tulsī', *Cracow Indological Studies*, vol. 1, 1994, pp. 245–51; idem, 'Text and Context: Two Versions of *Rāmlalānahachū*', in Entwistle, *Studies in Early Modern Indo-Aryan Languages*, pp. 379–92 and idem, 'Tulsidas' Vision of the Nuptials of Ram and Sita', *Hindi: Language, Discourse, Writing*, vol. 1, nos. 3–4, October 2000 – March 2001, pp. 295–306.

[79] *Sohar* – a kind of an auspicious song sung by women on occasions that are considered joyful such as, e.g. the birth of a son or a marriage.

[80] All quotations from the *Rāmlalānahachū* (henceforth abbreviated in references as RN), if not otherwise stated, are after the text published in *Tulsī granthāvalī*, ed. Rāmcandra Śukla et al., vol. 2, Kāśī: NPS, 1974, pp. 3–5. For a more detailed analysis of RN's two versions see Stasik, 'Text and Context'.

smith's wife (*loharini*[81]) with an iron ring (*barāyan*), a woman belonging to the caste of *ahīr*, i.e. herdsmen, (*ahirini*) with an auspicious pot of curds (*dahẽṛi*), a betel-seller's wife (*tãbolini*) with *pān*, or betel, in her hand, a tailor's wife (*darajini*) with a suit of clothes, a cobbler's wife (*mocini*) with a pair of shoes, a gardener's wife (*maliniyā*) with a marriage crown (*maur*) and a woman of the *bārī* caste, members of which produce leaf-cups and leaf-plates and who also act as attendants (*bariniyā*), with a parasol (*chātā*) in her hand (5–8). Finally, a barber's wife (*nauniyā*) appears and sings joyously a *gāri/gālī*[82] in the women's apartments (*ranivās*). Kauśalyā, instructed by her *jeṭhi*[83] to start performing the *nahachū* rite, sits with Rām in her lap and covers his head with the end of her sari. Then the barber's wife is called again and she approaches Rām with a nail-parer (*naharnī*) in her hand (9–10). *Nauniyā* sings a *gālī* in which she teases Daśarath's family.

> *Why is Ramji dark and Lakshman fair?*
> *There must have been some deceit by Kaushalya.*
> *Ram is Dasharath's, Lakshman someone else's,*
> *Still Bharat and Shatrughna are Shriraghunath's brothers!* (12)[84]

The barber's wife, very proud of her role, touches Rām's nails with her hand, washes his feet and, having cut the nails, applies red colour (*jāvak*) to them (13–15). Gifts (*nichāvar*) follow the rite; the barber loads them on the cart and takes them home, where his family rejoice over the gifts and sleep undisturbed by troubles

---

[81] Note: Orthography as in the original text!

[82] Playfully impudent or humorously indecent and mockingly insulting songs sung by women during weddings. As William G. Archer observes: 'In these sexual jokes is a release of repressed energy which when applied to the marriage must necessarily make it fertile'; William G. Archer and Barbara Stoler Miller, eds., *Songs for the Bride: Wedding Rites of Rural India*, New York: Columbia University Press, 1985, p. 7.

[83] Here synonymous with *jyeṣṭhā*, 'a senior female [relative]'. Cf. *Jānakīmaṅgal* (henceforth abbreviated in references as JM), in *Tulsī granthāvalī*, stanza 172, p. 51 and Baccūlāl Avasthī, *Tulsī śabdakoś*, vol. 1, Dillī: Buks en' Buks, 1991, p. 363.

[84] *kāhe rāmajiva sā̃vara lachimana gora ho;/ kīdahũ rāni kausilahi parigā bhor ho./ rāma ahahī dasaratha kai lachimana āna ka ho;/ bharata satruhana bhāi tau śrīraghunātha ka ho.*

(16–17). In the meantime, all gathered in the women's quarters sing a *gālī* addressing Rām, play together mimicking one another and the hearts of all are filled with joy. At this sight, the queen feels happy and gives presents in abundance (18–19).

Mātāprasād Gupta, discussing the *Rāmlalānahachū* in his work on Tulsīdās, disclosed that he was in possession of its oldest-known manuscript consisting of 26 couplets, which differed from the widely known published version that I have just introduced. In his analysis of these two versions, M. Gupta showed a very strong bias towards the text of the manuscript in his possession and finally considered it to be authentic, thus denying authenticity to the published version.[85] A comparison of these two versions made by me elsewhere[86] revealed very interesting facts. Gupta doubted the authenticity of the printed version especially on account of an 'unseemly' reaction of King Daśarath at the sight of a young *ahirini*.[87] It is also clear that discussing the above-quoted couplets starting with a question of the barber's wife why Rāmjī is fair and Lakṣmaṇ dark, he overlooks (or wants to overlook?) the fact that the barber's wife in her *gālī* teases the whole family of Rām – four brothers, the queens and Daśarath, and having understood this stanza differently he comes to the conclusion that these lines are faulty.[88] I have paid special attention to these supposed faults, because one often gets the

---

[85] Gupta, *Tulsīdās*, pp. 208–11, 234–40. Cf. also Gupta's article in Varmā, *Hindī sāhitya koś*, vol. 2, pp. 520–1.

[86] Stasik, 'Text and Context'.

[87] *ahirini hātha dahẽṛi saguna lei āvai ho;/ unarata jobanu dekhi nṛpati mana bhāvai ho* (5). Cf., e.g. Miśrabandhu, *Hindī navaratna*, pp. 82, 99, quoted in Gupta, *Tulsīdās*, p. 133, as well as Gupta's own opinion in Gupta, *Tulsīdās*, p. 320.

[88] He wonders: 'When once it is said that Kauśalyā was misled, then how can it be said later that Rām is Daśarath's [son] and Lakṣmaṇ someone else's? Then, how could Bharat and Śatrughna both be called Rām's brothers? Bharat and Rām resembled each other but Śatrughna resembled Lakṣmaṇ (...)' and he quotes the appropriate lines from RCM to corroborate his point (1.311.3B–4A). Gupta, *Tulsīdās*, p. 236. Cf. Bhagavatī Prasād Siṁh, 'Rāmlalā nahachū: punarvicār', in Tribhuvan Siṁh, ed., *Tulsī: sandarbh aur samīkṣā*, Vārāṇasī: Tulsī Śodh Saṁsthān, 1976, pp. 139–40.

impression that the real reason for Gupta's opinion was, in his own words, their 'unconventional/immodest erotic sentiment' (*amaryādit śṛṅgāriktā*). Whether it should be called *amaryādit*, indecent, or not, it should be justly weighed against the relevant evidence and in no case should its role be exaggerated.[89]

The text of the *Jānakīmaṅgal* deals with the nuptial rites of Rām and Sītā. Although this ceremony is dealt with in great detail in the *Rāmcaritmānas*, yet on a number of occasions from the *Jānakīmaṅgal* one can learn such particulars, which are not included in the epic.[90] For example in the *Rāmcaritmānas* (1.287.1, 1.290.1–3) it is said that Janak sends messengers to Ayodhya with a letter inviting the king Daśarath to Janakpur, while from the *Jānakīmaṅgal* (126, 130–1) one learns that Janak sends to Ayodhya his family guru Śatanand with *lagan* [*patrikā*][91] and *tilak* [presents].[92] Then, when time for the post-wedding ceremonies comes, women take the bride and the groom to the nuptial chamber (*kohbar*) (RCM 1.326.8; JM 164). Rām and Sītā offer each other with their own hands some food during the rite called *lahkauri* (RCM 1.327.7–8; JM 167). In this context, the *Rāmcaritmānas* mentions only the atmosphere of merry-making, while the *Jānakīmaṅgal* adds to it the tune of a *gālī* sung by the women of the bride's side. The *Jānakīmaṅgal* (168) also mentions gambling rites (*juvā*), during which *gālī*s addressing both queens are sung.[93]

---

[89] Cf. Bhagīrath Miśra, 'Aiśvaryarūpopāsak maryāda Rāmbhakta kavi', in Devendra Śarmā and Vijayendra Snātak, ed., *Hindī sāhitya kā bṛhat itihās*, vol. 5, Vārāṇasī: NPS, 1974, p. 290.

[90] For a more detailed comparison of JM and RCM see Stasik, 'The Divine Marriage'.

[91] *Lagan-patrikā* – a kind of a letter sent to the groom's side by the bride's side (customarily by the bride's father to the groom's father) that informs about the date of the wedding calculated by astrologers of the bride's side.

[92] *Tilak* – the ceremony during which the vermilion mark is made on the forehead of a groom (most commonly by the bride's father or brother) and different gifts presented to him; it is also synonymous with the *sagāī*, i.e. the betrothal ceremony. See Atul Kumar Agarwala, 'Marriage Songs in Harauti', Ph.D. dissertation, Kiel: Christian-Albrechts-Universität, 1982, pp. 32–7.

[93] Stasik, 'Tulsidas' Vision', pp. 300–1.

Summing up the foregoing discussion, it has to be noted that an analysis of the contents of the *Rāmcaritmānas*, the *Jānakīmaṅgal* and the *Rāmlalānahachū* more than once indicates that the longest of them, i.e. the *Rāmcaritmānas* portion of the Childhood Book, lacks the details present in the two other texts. As I have argued in this chapter and elsewhere,[94] it seems that this interesting difference can essentially be explained by the nature of the *Rāmcaritmānas* itself. First, it is firmly rooted in the Rāmāyaṇa tradition that has to be understood as a repository of moral values, which with the passage of time has been enriched with different precepts and teachings. Second, and this point is closely connected with the first one, it is an epic and as such does not depict actual events but standardized behaviour.[95] Thanks to this, the *Rāmcaritmānas* has become one of the sources of unquestionable moral acceptability, the model of behaviour, setting the pattern to be followed by respectable men, the epitome of the ideal of Hindu life, which has managed to gain a large following among Hindus.[96]

Exploring the text of the *Rāmcaritmānas* as the cultural idiom[97] and comparing it with other works by Tulsīdās, one observes in the *Rāmcaritmānas* an evident tendency towards standardization. Tulsī appears here to be much more careful and sometimes less generous to his audience than may have been expected. On the other hand, the texts of the *Jānakīmaṅgal* and the *Rāmlalānahachū* seem to be relieved, at least to a certain degree, from the burden of standardization (understood as compliance with orthodoxy). At the same time, the much freer atmosphere prevalent in them testifies to their closer ties with folk tradition. Of course, this does not mean that the *Rāmcaritmānas* has no ties with it. Its multiple elements are present in the text of the *Rāmcaritmānas* but they are filtered very carefully. This becomes obvious when one compares Tulsīdās's epic with his other works, as well as with a number of

[94] Idem, 'The Divine Marriage' and idem, 'Tulsidas' Vision'.

[95] Agarwala, 'Marriage Songs', p. 8.

[96] Cf. ibid.

[97] Cf. Romila Thapar, 'A Historical Perspective on the Story of Rama', in Sarvepalli Gopal, ed., *Anatomy of Confrontation: The Babri Masjid–Ram Janmabhumi Issue*, 2nd edn, Delhi: Penguin Books, 1993, esp. pp. 141–2, 151ff.

folk songs (especially marriage songs), which evidently betray some common links with the *Rāmcaritmānas*.

And Tulsīdās untiringly encourages his audience, saying:

> *The everlasting joy to those*
> *who with love sing and listen about Sita and Ram's wedding,*
> *[as] the glory of Ram is the abode of auspiciousness* (RCM 1.361).[98]

ASK RĀM FOR ASSISTANCE – RĀMKATHĀ AS A METHOD OF DIVINATION

The *Rāmājñāpraśna* (Questions [to] Rām [about His] Precepts), also known as the *Dohāvalī rāmāyaṇ*, is a very interesting short work, in which Rāmkathā serves as a method of divination, thus ensuring devotees that they are protected in every possible way. It belongs to the group of Tulsīdās's works whose authorship is not doubted. The date of its composition is included in one of the couplets at the end of the poem;[99] the numerical value of the words used in this chronogram is an equivalent of the year 1621 of the Vikram era, i.e. AD 1564.[100]

Its origin is traditionally connected with one Gaṅgārām, an astrologer and a friend of Tulsīdās.[101] The two of them performed together the customary *sandhyā* prayers in the evenings on the banks of the Ganges in Banaras. One day, much-concerned, Gaṅgārām

---

[98] *siya raghubīra bibāhu je saprema gāvahī sunahī;/ tinha kahū sadā uchāhu maṅglāyatana rāma jasu.*

[99] 7.7.3; all quotations from the *Rāmājñāpraśna* (henceforth abbreviated as RP) are, if not otherwise stated, after the text published in *Tulsī granthāvalī*, pp. 55–84.

[100] This couplet is as follows: *saguna satya sasi nayana guna, avadhi adhika nayavāna;/ hoi suphala subha jāsu jasu, prīti pratīti pramāna* (p. 82). The words: *sasi* ('moon'), *nayana* ('eye'), *guna* ('quality'), *nayavāna* (in other editions figuring as *naya bāna*: 'right or moral conduct, morality'; 'arrow') are equal to 1, 2, 6, 1, which, when read backwards, give the year of the poem's composition. See Gupta, *Tulsīdās*, p. 240; cf. Varmā, *Hindī sāhitya koś*, vol. 2, p. 525 and Varmā, *Hindī sāhitya*, vol. 2, pp. 307–8, 314. For a different opinion on the date of the *Rāmājñāpraśna* see Varmā, *Hindī sāhitya kā ālocnātmak itihās*, p. 380.

[101] G.A. Grierson also refers to an opinion, popular in his times, that the poem was written at the request of Todar Mal, the famous minister of Akbar; however, he simultaneously doubts it. Grierson, 'Notes', p. 96.

told Tulsīdās that he would not be able to go with him to the riverside. When asked by his friend about the reason, he explained that a raja's son had gone hunting and after some time the court was informed that a tiger had killed one of the hunters. However, the identity of the victim was not known. The raja summoned Gaṅgārām to learn from him about the fate of his son. The raja assured the astrologer that he would reward him amply if he received the right answer; otherwise, he would put him to death. Gaṅgārām asked the raja for one-day's delay to consult the stars to the best of his abilities, although he was aware that his astrological knowledge was not sufficient to give a definite answer. Therefore, he was worried about his life. Tulsīdās consoled his friend telling him that Rām would show his kindness to him and everything would end well. After such comforting words, they both went to the bank of the Ganges to perform the usual *sandhyā*. Later Tulsīdās sat down to work and after six hours he gave the results to his friend. Next day Gaṅgārām went to the raja and, having referred to the *Rāmājñāpraśna*, he told him that his son was safe and sound. The raja with his court waited for his son's return but in the meanwhile Gaṅgārām was held captive. The raja set Gaṅgārām free only after the return of his son, when he became convinced about the correctness of the astrologer's words; he also remunerated him amply. Gaṅgārām put all that wealth at Tulsīdās's feet. The poet, after much persuasion, took ten thousands rupees from it and assigned them for the purpose of building ten temples devoted to Hanumān.[102]

This is how the story of Rām's deeds is believed to have taken the form of a work used in divination and has become a kind of oracle. When its chosen lines are properly interpreted – essential instructions are included in the text itself (7.7) and can also be found in popular editions of this work[103] – they can help to make the right decision.

The *Rāmājñāpraśna* from the point of view of its composition should rather be viewed as a collection of loosely connected couplets, which basically are arranged in accordance with the

[102] *Rāmājñāpraśna*, comment. Sudarśan Siṁh, Gorakhpur: Gītā Pres, 1983, pp. III–IV. Also see Varmā, *Hindī sāhitya kā ālocnātmak itihās* and Śukla, *Hindī sāhitya kā itihās*, p. 141.

[103] See e.g. *Rāmājñāpraśna*, pp. V–VIII.

chronology of the story of Rām's deeds. However, due to the size of the work the story is very much condensed, which results in the omission of certain episodes. However, and it seems even more interesting, Tulsīdās included in it some episodes that are absent from his *magnum opus*. Among them is the banishment of Sītā (6.6.4–5), during which she gives birth to her two sons, Lav and Kuś, (6.7.4–5), and at the end she disappears being received by the Earth (6.7.6). These differences between the *Rāmcaritmānas* and the *Rāmājñāpraśna* are supposed to result from different sources that inspired Tulsīdās at the beginning of his career and in later times. At an earlier stage he is said to have been more under the influence of the tradition connected with the story as told by Vālmīki and in earlier Sanskrit literature; at a later stage he is said to have been more under the influence of the *Adhyātma rāmāyaṇa*, the *Hanumannāṭaka* and the *Prasannarāghava*.[104]

The septenary structure of the *Rāmājñāpraśna* seems worth mentioning here. The work consists of seven chapters (*sarga*), which are divided into seven parts, lit. 'heptad' (*saptak*), containing seven couplets in a *dohā* metre. It means that the work consists of 343 *dohās*. This septenary structure can undoubtedly be related to the Rāmāyaṇa tradition, in which, from the times of Vālmīki, a division into seven books (*kāṇḍa*), or more generally – seven parts (depending on the type of work), was very common. Of no less importance is the symbolic meaning of the number 7, which is often used in Indian tradition as, among other things, a symbol of plenitude, completeness, and is considered to be auspicious.[105] Due to the septenary structure of the work, the methods of finding an omen are also related to this number in a natural way.

As I have already mentioned, general instructions on how to use the text of the *Rāmājñāpraśna* are given in the text itself (7.7) and usually additional guidance can also be found in popular editions of the *Rāmājñāpraśna*.[106]

---

[104] Gupta, *Tulsīdās*, pp. 241–2 and Varmā, *Hindī sāhitya koś*, vol. 2, p. 525. Cf. Vaudeville, *Étude*, pp. 307–24 and McGregor, *Hindi Literature from Its Beginnings*, p. 113.

[105] Hardev Bāhrī, *Prācīn bhāratīy saṁskṛti koś*, Dillī: Vidya Prakāśan Mandir, 1988, pp. 409–10.

[106] In the following analysis, apart from the information included in the text of RP, I also refer to different commentaries, including trans-

Thus on the eve of a chosen day, a bhakta should put the text in an appropriate place and pay hom-age to it, announcing to Rām that on the following day he will address him with a question and expects his kindness. It may be added here that Monday, Wednesday, Thursday and Friday are considered auspicious for this purpose, and the most auspicious is Thursday, whose patron is Jupiter, associated with a guru; very important also is the fact that Thursday is both preceded and followed by the days considered to be auspicious.[107]

The following morning, after the usual rituals purifying the body and mind, the text is once again put in the appropriate place and offered flowers, sandal paste, incense and a lamp is lit. The guru, Gaṇeś, Śiv and Gaurī, Sītā and Rām, Lakṣmaṇ and Hanumān are remembered,[108] and only then can the question be asked, preferably aloud.[109] A devotee should take in his hand 108 – preferably lotus – seeds, put them close to the text and divide them into three parts. The seeds in each part should be carefully counted and the resulting number divided by 7 in each case. The remaining seeds in the first of them indicate the number of a *sarga*, in the second one – the number of a *saptak*, and in the third one – the number of a *dohā*.

Three specially designed diagrams, instead of seeds, are often used. They can be either circular (see below Fig. 1[110]) with the circle divided into seven parts – one circle in the middle and six equal segments on its edge and numbered from 1 to 7 – or made of seven equal squares / rectangles (see below Fig. 2[111]) arranged in such a manner that three of them are in the middle row and the

---

lations, and to explanations given to me in February 1999 by Vinubhāī, a Rāmbhakta from Baroda. Because most of the information thus acquired is similar, I use reference notes only in the case when a given method or its detail differ from the rest.

[107] David Frawley, comment., *The Oracle of Rama: An Adaptation of Rama Ajna Praśna of Goswami Tulsidas*, 2nd edn, Delhi: Motilal Banarsidass, 1999, p. 21.

[108] *guru ganesa hara gauri siya, rāma, lakhana, hanumāna;/ (...) sādara sumira saba*; 7.7.4.

[109] Frawley, *The Oracle*, p. 22.

[110] Adapted from *Tulsī granthāvalī*, p. 57; cf. *Rāmājñāpraśna*, p. III.

[111] Adapted from S.P. Bahadur, tr., *Complete Works of Goswami Tulsidas: Minor Works*, vol. 6, Delhi: Munshiram Manoharlal, 1998, p. 39.

remaining four in the upper and lower rows with two in each of them and all are numbered from 1 to 7. A devotee should aim his right ring finger at each of the diagrams and the numbers thus indicated refer to a *sarga*, a *saptak* and a *dohā*.

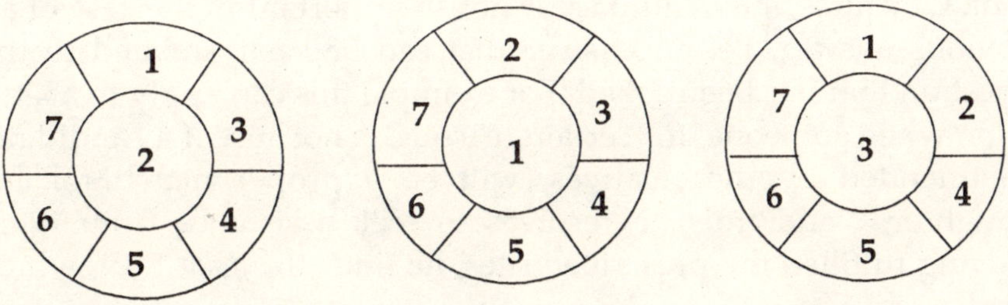

Fig. 1

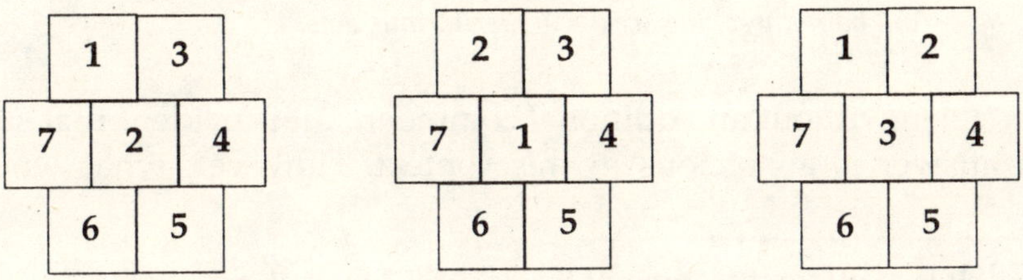

Fig. 2

Coins, or pebbles, numbered from 1 to 7 can be also used. They are shaken in folded hands and thrown, and then three coins should be picked up (one coin at a time) with the thumb and the ring finger of the right hand. The numbers of the coins indicate a *sarga*, a *saptak* and a *dohā*.

When in either of these manners a *dohā* has been chosen, it should be read, as it is an answer to the question asked earlier. The relationship between the contents of the *dohā* and the question is important in this context. If they have nothing in common, it is believed that a devotee did not manage to concentrate adequately in order to create a spiritual atmosphere suitable for acquiring Rām's advice. It can also mean that the question was not important enough to deserve his answer. Although it is postulated that not too many questions should be asked in one day – preferably only one question – the text itself[112] makes it possible to ask three questions a day. The right attitude and good intentions, as well as – what seems to be even more important – a special, intimate association with the text of the *Rāmājñāpraśna*[113] that enables one to interpret the actual meaning of the received answer, are significant. Of course, such intimacy is not so important in the case of an obvious answer, i.e. an answer that can be easily related to the question that has been asked. For example this can apply to a situation when someone, for certain reasons, is not sure if a candidate, commended by the relatives, will be a proper match for his daughter,[114] and thus he resolves to seek assistance from Rām. Having fulfilled the prescribed rites, he finds the *dohā* 1.5.7, which reads:

> *[After] all the sons, the epitomes of auspiciousness,*
> *Were married in a wedding canopy,*
> *Together with Tulsi rejoice people*
> *And both kings, the oceans of meritorious acts.*[115]

Even without an additional comment,[116] it is evident that such an answer is auspicious in this context. However, what would

---

[112] It is a different reading of the *dohā* 7.7.3 quoted in n. 100.

[113] Cf. Bahadur, *Complete Works*, p. 39.

[114] One should remember that in India till today most marriages are arranged either in a traditional way with the help of family members and/or customary matchmakers such as members of the *nāī* caste, i.e. barbers, or in a more modern fashion through matrimonial ads placed in the press.

[115] *eka bitāna bibāhi saba, suvana sumaṅgala rūpa;/ tulasī sahita samāja sukha, sukṛta sindhu dou bhūpa.*

[116] Such comments can be found after a translation of a *dohā* into modern Hindi (see e.g. *Rāmājñāpraśna*, p. 19). However, many such translations (and this applies not only to the text of RP) not entirely – euphemistically speaking – agree with original passages; therefore using them one has to be very cautious. Apart from this, one should remember that especially in the case of the most popular editions – such as these of Gita Press which to a great extent influence a reception of a given text – such 'translations' are not created out of nothing and usually have closer or more distant links with rich commentarial traditions (this holds especially true in the case of RCM).

happen, if this very *dohā*, 1.5.7, served as an answer to a question related to some other vital situation, for example related to a court case? Unfortunately, although this *dohā*'s general meaning is auspicious, in such a situation there is an evident lack of relation between the question and the answer, a discrepancy between two contexts, so the result should, at best, be considered as uncertain.[117]

Apart from this, other examples of omens can be given. It is considered that *dohā*s referring to the wanderings of Rām and Lakṣmaṇ in search of Sītā augur badly for great sorrow and misfortune, while verses referring to the heroic death of Jaṭāyu promise one's salvation after death.[118]

Considering both the form and function of this atypical Rāmkathā, it should be stressed that in his work Tulsīdās once again testified to the extraordinary kindness of Rām – three quarters of the 343 couplets have an auspicious meaning and less than one quarter a decidedly inauspicious meaning (15 *dohā*s have a double meaning). One can risk a conclusion that Tulsīdās also proved to be a skilful psychologist who had taken into consideration the fact that too great a probability of getting a bad omen could deter people from consulting the *Rāmājñāpraśna*. However, in no case did Tulsīdās intend to satisfy people's sheer curiosity; he wanted to come to the assistance of Rām's devotees in difficult moments of their lives, meaning to help those who lived humble lives and at times were not sure of tomorrow. This work proved to suit people who, like Rāmcandra Śukla, see in Rāmkathā 'a sum of all situations in life'.[119]

---

[117] Cf. *Rāmājñāpraśna*, p. VIII.

[118] Hill, *The Holy Lake*, p. XIV.

[119] *Rāmcarit jīvan kī sab daśā kī samaṣṭi hai, iskā pramāṇ 'Rāmājñāpraśna' hai jisse log har ek prakār kī ānevālī daśā ke sambandh mẽ praśn karte aur uttar nikālte haĩ* ('the deeds of Rām are a sum of all situations in life and its proof is the *Rāmājñāpraśna*; people ask it questions and find in it answers to them, concerning all kinds of forthcoming situations'); Rāmcandra Śukla, *Gosvāmī Tulsīdās*, 2nd edn, Vārāṇasī: NPS, 1983, p. 141.

'GLORY-SONGS OF RĀGHUNĀTH':[120] THE *GĪTĀVALĪ*, THE *VINAYPATRIKĀ*, THE *KAVITĀVALĪ* AND THE *BARVAI RĀMĀYAṆ*

This section concentrates on four of Tulsīdās's works that belong to the later period of the poet's life or at least they received their present shape at that time. Although differing a great deal in their treatment of Rāmkathā, they all share the common feature of being of a non-narrative character – they are in fact lyric anthologies revolving around Rāmkathā and Rām-related themes. Two of them, i.e. the *Gītāvalī* and the *Vinaypatrikā*, are song verses (*pads*) with which particular musical *rāgas* are associated.[121] Thus especially these two works, but not only them, can be seen as real 'glory-songs of Rām'.

The *Gītāvalī* (Collection of Songs) is an anthology of 328 *pads*,[122] each conceived as an independent entity, of different length that – as has just been noted – by their nature are meant to be sung. The *Gītāvalī* provides a very fine, lyric presentation of the events known from the tradition but the whole work, because of its form, lacks proper narrative. Thus, a particular *pad* or a group of *pads* concern a given episode and they are all structured according to the chronology of the events in Rām's life and divided into the customary seven books of different length. For example the Kishkindha Book is very short (two *pads*) as is also the Lanka Book (twenty-three *pads*), while the Beautiful Book, which is praised for its poetical values,[123] usually short in other tellings, comprises fifty-one *pads*.[124]

The author's approach to Rāmkathā in this is much influenced by Krishnaite tradition. It is particularly evident in the passages that deal with Rām's childhood (1.7–44), in descriptions

---

[120] The phrase 'glory-songs of Raghunāth' (*raghunātha gunagātha*) is taken from the *Kavitāvalī* (7.29) and given in Raymond Allchin's translation as published in Tulsī Dās, *Kavitāvalī*, p. 143.

[121] For more on this subject, see Tulsī Dās, *Kavitāvalī*, pp. 38–9.

[122] Scholars also refer to a manuscript of this work that contains a shorter, probably earlier, version of the text referred to as the *Padāvalī rāmāyaṇ* (Song-Verse Rāmāyaṇ); Gupta, *Tulsīdās*, pp. 222ff and Varmā, *Hindī sāhitya koś*, vol. 2, pp. 132–3.

[123] Varmā, *Hindī sāhitya kā ālocnātmak itihās*, pp. 399–400.

[124] All references are to the text as published in *Tulsī granthāvalī*, pp. 221–357.

of Rām's beauty enchanting all people including young females (7.2–16) or the atmosphere of merrymaking when Rām and Sītā with their friends and attendants play on a see-saw (7.18). Rām in the *Gītāvalī*, although divine, at the same time is also very human and one can say that he is shown living the life of a prince of Tulsīdās's times, delighting himself in the pleasures and pastimes of life (1.43–4, 7.20–2). This feature of the *Gītāvalī* – its *mādhurya* disposition – also seems to bring it close to the literature typical of the already-discussed Rāmrasik Sampradāy.[125]

The decidedly dominating lyrical mood of the *Gītāvalī* made it difficult for the poet to deal with the war on Lanka and only two short passages are devoted to it. The first of them – that is also longer – concerns the wounding of Lakṣmaṇ by Meghnād and the rescue mission undertaken by Hanumān (6.5–15). The second passage, consisting of only one *pad* (6.16), deals with Rām's victory, or rather the splendour of the victorious Rām (with his brother Lakṣmaṇ at his side) who is in control of everything. The emotionality of Rāmbhakti, however, was not a sufficient reason to spare Sītā banishment in the *Gītāvalī*. Nevertheless, one has to admit that its treatment is not absolutely traditional – Sītā, anticipating Rām's decision, expresses her will to live in the forest in order to serve ascetics and pay homage to them. Therefore, Lakṣmaṇ takes her to Vālmīki's ashram where Lav and Kuś are born (7.25–36).

Essentially, the *Gītāvalī* is an appealing work whose lyricism, emotionality, an individual approach to Rām and contemplation of his more human nature make it an interesting complement to the *Rāmcaritmānas*[126] that, first of all, attempts to expound and spread the essence of Bhakti. However, the *mādhurya* shade of the devotion to Rām, the Supreme Being, in the *Gītāvalī*, as opposed to the *dāsya* orientation of Tulsī's epic, as well as the lack of teachings contained in the *Rāmcaritmānas* have also been criticized.[127]

The *Vinaypatrikā* (Entreaty), another collection of *pads*, is of a very different character from the *Gītāvalī*. In 279 verses,[128] appar-

[125] Cf. Varmā, *Hindī sāhitya kā ālocnātmak itihās*, pp. 403–4 and Varmā, *Hindī sāhitya koś*, vol. 2, p. 133.

[126] Cf. Varmā, *Hindī sāhitya koś*, vol. 2, p. 133.

[127] Varmā, *Hindī sāhitya kā ālocnātmak itihās*, p. 402.

[128] All references, if not otherwise stated, are to the text as published in *Tulsī granthāvalī*, pp. 379–496. An old manuscript entitled the *Rām-*

ently composed over a long period of time, Tulsīdās does not concentrate on the story but primarily strives to demonstrate his absolute devotion to Rām.

In popular printed editions, the contents of the *Vinaypatrikā* is divided into two major sections,[129] although one should rather see it in three parts.[130] The first of them, *pads* 1–64, forms an introductory part consisting of hymns of praise to different gods; among them are Gaṇeś, Sūrya, Śiv, Pārvatī as the Goddess (1–16), to the sacred rivers – Gaṅgā and Yamunā (17–21), to the main characters of Rāmkathā: Hanumān (25–36), Lakṣmaṇ (37–38), Bharat (39), Śatrughna (40), Sītā (41–2), and last but not least to Rām (64). In this section, named aptly by Raymond Allchin 'The Prologue',[131] Tulsīdās tries to win favour with all of them and to prepare the ground for his entreaty. As Viyogī Hari explains it in his 'Remarks' (*vaktavya*) on the composition of the *Vinaypatrikā*,[132] Tulsīdās tormented by the Kali age formulates his plea addressed to Rām. The poet is not in a position to put it forward personally before his Lord; therefore, he needs the help of others. Tulsīdās puts himself here in the position of a servant who tries to approach his master and seeks first to win the favours of his courtiers and favourites in order to secure the success of his cause. This image of Rām's court (*Rāmdarbār*) with gods, his own brothers and companions as his courtiers (*darbārīs*) and favourites (*musāhabs*), and the poet as

---

gītāvalī containing a shorter, probably earlier, version of the *Vinaypatrikā*, is also known; Gupta, *Tulsīdās*, p. 222, Varmā, *Hindī sāhitya kā ālocnātmak itihās*, p. 417 and Varmā, *Hindī sāhitya koś*, vol. 2, p. 567. For the relationship between the *Rāmgītāvalī* and the *Padāvalī rāmāyaṇ* see Gupta, *Tulsīdās*, pp. 222–8 and Varmā, *Hindī sāhitya koś*, vol. 2, p. 567.

[129] See e.g. 'Tables of Contents' in Tulsīdās, *Vinaypatrikā (haritoṣiṇī ṭīkā sahit)*, ed. and comment. Viyogī Hari, Dillī: Sastā Sāhitya Maṇḍal Prakāśan, 1981, p. 34 and Tulsīdās, *Vinaypatrikā (saral bhāvārth sahit)*, 30th edn, Gorakhpur: Gītā Pres, 1983, p. IV.

[130] Tulsīdās, *Vinaypatrikā (haritoṣiṇī ṭīkā sahit)*, pp. 8–10; Varmā, *Hindī sāhitya koś*, vol. 2, p. 567 and R. Allchin's 'Introduction' in Tulsī Dās, *The Petition to Rām: Hindi Devotional Hymns of the Seventeenth Century*, tr. F.R. Allchin, London: George Allen & Unwin, 1966, pp. 48–52.

[131] Tulsī Dās, *The Petition to Rām*, p. 48.

[132] Tulsīdās, *Vinaypatrikā (haritoṣiṇī ṭīkā sahit)*, pp. 8–10.

a humble supplicant seeking a chance to have audience with them is unparalleled in Hindi literature.[133]

The main body of Tulsīdās's entreaty that follows 'The Prologue' is contained in *pads* 65–276, which are traditionally called *vinayāvalī*, i.e. 'a collection of humble requests/entreaties', or *vinaykhaṇḍ*, i.e. 'a section of humble requests'. On the one hand, it is full of the humility of Tulsīdās concerned with his own lot and the fate of all living creatures distressed by the outrages of the Kali age; on the other hand, the greatness and the saving powers of Lord Rām and his name are exalted.

The three-*pad* finale of the *Vinaypatrikā*, 'The Epilogue' in R. Allchin's words, begins in *pad* 277 in which Tulsīdās directly addresses Rām:

> *Father! Read this wretched man's 'Entreaty',*
> *Which Tulsi has written, having looked deep into his heart* (...) (277).[134]

Seeking to receive protection from Rām, the poet asks him for his approval of his *Vinaypatrikā*. Then Tulsī addresses Hanumān, Śatrughna, Bharat and Lakṣmaṇ to intercede for him with Rām and thus help him to find protection under his Lord. In the last *pad* (279), Rām is shown in his court with his brothers and the royal council. Lakṣmaṇ informs Rām about Tulsīdās's petition and recommends it to him. It is fully approved by Rām and thus Tulsī finds himself under his protection.

The *Vinaypatrikā* is considered to form the fullest expression of devotion typical of a servant (*dāsyabhakti*), which essentially means that a devotee surrenders himself or herself to his or her Lord and eagerly awaits winning the Lord's approval. The fact that Rām is the Ocean of Mercy (*kṛpā sindhu*[135]) seems to signify that the expectations of his devotees, *Rām ko gulām* (servant(s) of Rām), will be fulfilled in every respect.

---

[133] Cf. Sahāy, *Gosvāmī Tulsīdās*, p. 275 and Śiv Avatār Rastogī, 'Tulsī aur *Vinaypatrikā*', in Ārya and Agravāl, *Tulsī mānas sandarbh*, pp. 405–6.

[134] *binaya-patrikā dīna kī bāpu! āp hī bā̃co;/ hiye heri tulasī likhi* (...).

[135] One of the most common epithets of Tulsīdās's Rām; cf. e.g. *pads* 71, 145, 147, 153 or 181.

The *Kavitāvalī* (Collection of *Kavit(t)*s[136]) – also known as the *Kavitt rāmāyaṇ*[137] – consists of verses mostly in *kavitt* metre (335 verses in total[138]). It is considered to be the most important work of Tulsīdās apart from the *Rāmcaritmānas*, from which it differs, like the *Gītāvalī* and the *Vinaypatrikā*, in its non-narrative character. The present form of the *Kavitāvalī* is the result of a later editorial process, most probably accomplished in the last phase of Tulsīdās's life, although this work contains verses composed in different periods of his life.[139]

The *Kavitāvalī* is divided into the customary seven books, which are of very unequal length. For example, two books – the Forest Book and the Kishkindha Book – consist of one verse. (In fact, the *Kavitāvalī* stanza of the latter book, deals with the episode of Hanumān's leap across the ocean to Lanka that in major tellings, including the *Rāmcaritmānas*, belongs to the Beautiful Book.) The third shortest book is the Childhood Book (twenty-two verses), which in the *Rāmcaritmānas* is the longest, and the second longest book is the Lanka Book (fifty-eight verses) that is praised for its aesthetic values, in particular the treatment of sentiments (*rasa*), especially of the terrible (*bhayānaka*), heroic (*vīra*) and furious (*raudra*) sentiments. The first six books that form less than a half of the entire work provide some glimpses into the story of

[136] For more on the *kavitt* quatrains and other metres in the *Kavitāvalī*, see Imre Bangha, 'Dynamics of Textual Transmission in Premodern India: The *Kavitavali* of Tulsidas', *Comparative Studies of South Asia, Africa, and the Middle East*, vol. 24, no. 2, 2004, pp. 33–4 and Tulsī Dās, *Kavitāvalī*, pp. 63–4.

[137] Throughout the nineteenth century, most printed editions of this very popular work were published under this very title. For a bibliography of printed editions of the *Kavitāvalī* and other details pertaining to its text see the website of an international research project – the Critical Edition of Tulsīdās *Kavitāvalī* – undertaken by scholars and students from Hungary, Romania and Great Britain: http://tulsi.freeweb.hu. Also see Bangha, 'Dynamics', pp. 33–44.

[138] All references are to the text as published in *Tulsī granthāvalī*, pp. 129–218.

[139] Gupta, *Tulsīdās*, pp. 265–8, Varmā, *Hindī sāhitya kā ālocnātmak itihās*, p. 408, Varmā, *Hindī sāhitya koś*, vol. 2, p. 73 and McGregor, *Hindi Literature from Its Beginnings*, p. 116.

Rām's deeds, most probably those that for certain reasons seemed most attractive to Tulsīdās.[140]

Book 7, the Later, is the longest (183 verses) of the *Kavitāvalī* books. Its subject matter differs from the rest of the work and includes mostly personal material (unusual in the author's earlier works) in the form of autobiographical references, Tulsī's reflections on life and his times (e.g. 7.83–88, 7.96–103), as well as of references to historical, or historically verifiable, events such as the pestilence in Banaras (7.169–177), the cycle of *rudrabīsī* ('the twenty years of Rudra' referring either to 1566–85 or to 1566–1618;[141] 7.170) and the conjunction *mīn kī sanīcarī* (Saturn in Pisces in 1583–5 and/or 1612–4;[142] 7.177). The poet continually evokes the name of Rām, attempting to plumb the depths of the essence of his greatness, its meaning and influence on his own life (e.g. 7.65–82). The beauty and extraordinary emotional charge of the *Kavitāvalī* verses, expressive of Tulsīdās's personality, make it an important work for understanding the author's oeuvre.

It should be noted here that the *Kavitāvalī* in the NPS edition of Tulsīdās's collected works[143] is published with the text of the *Hanumānbāhuk*.[144] Surprising, as it may seem, in the *Hanumānbāhuk* Tulsīdās, suffering from severe pain in his arm spreading all over his body and accompanied by painful boils, 'turned – as Philip Lutgendorf observes – not to the "purifier of the fallen" (*patita-pāvana*), Rama, but to the "liberator from distress" (*saṅkaṭa mocana*), Hanuman, a deity who was invoked by suffering people seeking help in mundane contexts'.[145] This means that the poet turned not

[140] Tulsī Dās, *Kavitāvalī*, p. 65 and Bangha, 'Dynamics', pp. 34–5.

[141] Quoted after Bangha, 'Dynamics', p. 43, n. 24.

[142] Ibid.

[143] *Tulsī granthāvalī* to which I refer here.

[144] Philip Lutgendorf observes that 'The meaning of the title is not readily apparent. Sanskrit *bāhuka* is an adjective meaning "servile", "dependent" (...). In this sense the title may be read as "Hanuman's Dependent". But *bāhuka* can also mean "arm", "strength", and "monkey", and thus punningly allude both to the poet's physical affliction and to Hanuman's desired assistance. I tentatively translate it (sacrificing some of the allusions) as "the arms of Hanuman"'. Philip Lutgendorf, *Hanuman's Tale: The Message of a Divine Monkey*, New York: Oxford University Press, 2007, p. 97, n. 9.

[145] Ibid., p. 99.

to his Lord but his exemplary servant! The text of the *Hanumānbāhuk*, which with time has become very popular and today is commonly published as a separate work (devotees regard it as 'especially good for curing physical ailments'[146]), can be found in a number of pre-nineteenth century manuscripts of the *Kavitāvalī*, where it follows the Later Book of the *Kavitāvalī*. It seems to indicate that it was originally part of the *Kavitavali*.[147] At the same time, a significant number of the *Hanumānbāhuk* manuscripts (both earlier and later) that were found as separate texts may suggests that they might have been two independent works. However, the resemblance between the *Hanumānbāhuk* and, especially, the *Kavitāvalī*'s *Uttarkāṇḍ* in their metrical pattern and a form of prayer cannot be denied.[148] This is yet one more example of Tulsīdās's work(s) that calls for a closer textual study.[149]

The *Barvai rāmāyaṇ* (Rāmāyaṇ in *Barvai*[150]) is one of Tulsīdās's less-studied minor works. Rupert Snell in his excellent study of *barvai* metre notes that 'Indian literature abounds with couplet metres well suited to concise gnomic expression and punchy aphorisms, and in the Hindi part of this realm it is the well-known *dohā* that wears the crown: but compared with the lesser-known *barvai* couplet, the *dohā* seems longwinded and diffuse'.[151] The opinion of Snell, undoubtedly, lets one better understand the reputation of the *Barvai rāmāyaṇ* that because of both its size (sixty-nine couplets[152]) and the metre employed in it is very condensed and regarded as being difficult to understand,

---

[146] Ibid., p. 89.

[147] Bangha, 'Dynamics', p. 42, n. 1; cf. Gupta, *Tulsīdās*, pp. 232–3.

[148] Cf. Varmā, *Hindī sāhitya kā ālocnātmāk itihās*, p. 386.

[149] The results of the above-mentioned project on the Critical Edition of Tulsīdās *Kavitāvalī* seem very promising in this regard.

[150] For more on the *barvai* couplet in general, see Varmā, *Hindī sāhitya koś*, vol. 1, p. 427 and Snell, *The Hindi Classical Tradition*, p. 21; for more on *barvai* in the *Barvai rāmāyaṇ* in particular, see Rupert Snell, '"*Barvai*" Metre in Tulsīdās and Rahīm', in Alan W. Entwistle and Françoise Mallison, ed., *Studies in South Asian Devotional Literature*, Delhi: Manohar – Paris: École Française d'Extrême-Orient, 1994, pp. 373–405.

[151] Snell, '"*Barvai*" Metre', p. 373.

[152] All references are to the original text as it is published in *Tulsī granthāvalī*, pp. 15–22.

especially without good knowledge of Rāmkathā and the intricacies of Indian / Hindi poetics.[153]

All the couplets are arranged in seven books of uneven length. The first thirteen couplets of the Childhood Book, which consist of nineteen *barvai*s altogether, praise Sītā and Rām, describing their exceptional beauty. Only six couplets relate to the story, i.e. to the episode of the bow contest and merrymaking after the wedding of Rām and Sītā. The last couplet, out of sequence, describes a child-Rām with his toy bow who then tries his hand with a real bow. The next five books (the Ayodhya Book – eight couplets, the Forest Book – six couplets, the Kishkindha Book – two couplets, the Beautiful Book – six couplets and the Lanka Book – one couplet) deal only very selectively with some episodes known from the tradition, ending with the only *barvai* of the Lanka Book that praises Rām's army and its unequalled force. The twenty-seven *barvai*s of the Later Book concentrate on praising the greatness of Rām and his name, resembling in this the three works discussed above – the *Gītāvalī*, the *Vinaypatrikā* and the *Kavitāvalī*.

Despite the condensation of the *Barvai rāmāyaṇ* – Rupert Snell, referring to the 'episodes' of this work, even says that they 'are nothing more than the briefest of allusive sketches'[154] – its verse delights with a light though at the same time refined style which conveys a maximum of meaning with a minimum of words.

As far as the use of *barvai* by Tulsīdās is concerned, tradition maintains that he imitated Rahīm (Abdurrahīm Xānxānā; 1556–1627[155]), considered to be a master of this metre. It is said that Rahīm sent several of his *barvai*s to Tulsīdās who, after reading them, felt a desire to write such delighting verses himself.[156] Rupert Snell in his comparative study of these two poets' *barvai*s, however, questions the credibility of such an assertion. He says: 'In terms of the formal construction of metre and (if a more subjective assessment is allowed) of poetic quality, Tulsī's verses

---

153 Cf. Vijaynārāyaṇ Siṁh, *Tulsī ke rāmkathā kāvya*, Dillī: Granthalok, 2007, pp. 160–1.

154 Snell, '"*Barvai*" Metre', p. 377.

155 Cf. McGregor, *Hindi Literature from Its Beginnings*, p. 121.

156 *kavi rahīma baravai racaĩ paṭhae munivara pāsa;/ lakhi tehi sundara chanda maĩ racanā kiyo prakāsa*; Benīmādhavdās, *Mūl gosāĩ carit* (93); quoted after Gupta, *Tulsīdās*, p. 53, also see p. 261.

stand apart from Rahīm's, raising doubts about the authenticity of the allegation that Tulsī was imitating Rahīm in his use of the *barvai*. As elsewhere in his poetry, Tulsī shows himself to be the master and not the slave of his adopted conventions'.[157]

The extant text of the *Barvai rāmāyaṇ* is yet another example among Tulsīdās's works that poses a problem – there are significant differences between its different manuscripts, which suggest that it may have been composed after the author's death on the basis of a core of *barvai*s composed by him.[158] In this context, a very important question posed by R. Snell is worth remembering. Paying attention to the different character of the *Barvai rāmāyaṇ*'s *Uttarkāṇḍ* from the rest of the work, he wonders whether it is 'distinct from the earlier part in origin or period, or are its (rather dimly perceived) differences of style simply a function of its thematic distinctiveness from the narrative part of the text?'[159] Comparing the *Barvai rāmāyaṇ* with other works of Tulsīdās, especially the works discussed in this section, I incline to accept the second supposition. However, the doubts concerning the history of the composition and transmission of the *Barvai rāmāyaṇ*, the fact that its text is the least determined of Tulsīdās's works[160] as well as the problem of its internal differences undoubtedly call for a careful critical and editorial approach to it.

CONCLUSIONS

It is not uncommon that authors dealing with Hindi literature, even those who specialize in Hindi Rāmkathās, claim that Tulsīdās's *Rāmcaritmānas* for long satiated the demand for new tellings on the Hindi literary scene and discouraged potential poets aspiring to compose their own Rāmāyaṇas in Hindi.[161] As I will try to demonstrate in the following chapters, such a contention is

[157] Snell, '"*Barvai*" Metre', p. 397.

[158] Gupta, *Tulsīdās*, pp. 259–62 and Varmā, *Hindī sāhitya kā ālocnātmāk itihās*, pp. 375–6.

[159] Snell, '"*Barvai*" Metre', pp. 397–8.

[160] Gupta, *Tulsīdās*, pp. 230, 259–62.

[161] See e.g. Varmā, *Hindī sāhitya kā ālocnātmak itihās*, pp. 335–6; Bulke, *Rāmkathā*, p. 199 and Pāṇḍey, *Tulsīdāsottar hindī rāmsāhitya*, p. 26.

not completely valid, though at the same time there is no denying that there is a grain of truth in it. The best evidence of this seems Tulsīdās's oeuvre itself. The *Rāmcaritmānas* has become a household name in north India and beyond it. However, anyone working on Tulsīdās should ask a vital question: how many people, meaning first of all the 'lay' Hindi-speaking public, know (well) Tulsī's other works? Undoubtedly, those who have some education in the field of Hindi literature recognize several titles of his works but apart from this do not know much, if anything, more. Is it not symptomatic? Does it not show that the *Rāmcaritmānas* has overshadowed Tulsīdās's other works? To a great extent, the answer is positive, especially if one takes into consideration a common 'layman'. For a bhakta the *Rāmcaritmānas* always remains the revered scripture though he frequently also derives delight by communing with Rām from Tulsīdās's other works, most commonly from the *Kavitāvalī*, as well as from the *Vinay-patrikā* or the *Gītāvalī*, depending on his mood, his situation or the attitude appropriated by the devotee towards Rām (*upāsanā bhāv*).

The analysis carried out in this chapter makes apparent, first of all, the difference between the story-oriented epic *Rāmcaritmānas* and, on the one hand, one-episode centred works of the earlier period of Tulsīdās's life (the *Rāmlalānahachū* and the *Jānakīmaṅgal*), as well as, on the other hand, the meditative, lyric collections attributed to the later period of his life. All these works complement one another in different ways but they are also the meaningful evidence of versatile creative abilities of the poet and – what seems more important in the context of the discussion of different Rāmāyaṇa tellings and their authors – of the extent of his understanding of Rāmkathā and Rāmbhakti. There is no doubt that his *Rāmcaritmānas* and, to a lesser extent, his other works too have shaped the character of north Indian Rāmbhakti and of Hindi Rāmkathās. Many later authors addressed Tulsīdās in the same way as earlier Vālmīki had been addressed. Nevertheless, despite all the work that has been done on Tulsī's oeuvre to this day both inside and outside India, this analysis has more than once proved that there is still a great deal to be done, particularly in the field of critical work on the extant manuscripts of Tulsīdās's texts, on their transmission and reception. Such work is especially desired in view of the rapid changes that have taken place in India in recent years, among other things also in the socio-cultural sphere, where modern life styles are drawing out traditional entertainments and pastimes from the scene. No need to mention here the decaying and disappearing, for different reasons, of old manuscripts and early printed material and the passing away of another generation of people familiar with traditional literary culture. Such work is also needed, since even now one cannot be sure to what extent one is evaluating the authentic work of Tulsī and to what extent a received text. It may also add, apart from many other results, to our present knowledge of the language of Tulsīdās and, among other things, may help us to learn more about the reasons for his use of both Avadhi and Braj. The use of the first of them seems quite natural in view of Tulsīdās's origin from the eastern parts of the Hindi-speaking area, as well as of his primal interest in Rām themes. However, is it all we can say in this regard? The use of Braj is not so obvious. Was it just a result of its status as the main literary vehicle in those times or of the process of Krishnaization of Tulsīdās's Bhakti, Rāmbhakti in general, the development of Rāmrasik Sampradāy or something else?[162] Without further research, which goes far beyond the scope of this study, these and other related questions cannot be fully answered. Nevertheless, is not such a study our obligation to Tulsīdās whom we know from his works – the well- and the lesser-researched ones – as a consummate artist; the works of whom are all very important for our understanding of later developments in Rāmbhakti and Rām literature in Hindi?

---

[162] McGregor, 'The Progress of Hindi', pp. 936–9.

CHAPTER THREE

Rāmkathā in the Seventeenth and Eighteenth Centuries: In the Shadow of Tulsīdās?

INTRODUCTORY REMARKS

While the *Rāmcaritmānas* and the *Sūrsāgar* are the works that belong to the period traditionally referred to in Hindi literature as Bhakti, with Keśavdās (?1555–1617[1]), in fact a contemporary of Tulsīdās and a near contemporary of Sūrdās, one enters another period of Hindi literature. In other words, Keśavdās's works herald the advent of the Rīti[2] period, in which elaborate poetry modelled after the rules of Sanskrit poetics and composed under court patronage dominates. Rīti authors, first of all, were oriented to demonstrating their knowledge of poetics in both theory and practice. This period produced a number of works in one way or another related to Rāmrasik Sampradāy and under its influence. Most of them did not win much renown which can partly be seen as a result of the esoteric character of the sect and partly, which seems even more important, as a result of their meagre poetic value. However, an objective evaluation of this literature is still pending, because many texts are known only by their titles and their manuscripts are inaccessible or irrecoverable.[3]

ARTISTRY OF KEŚAVDĀS

THE POET AND HIS WORKS

Keśavdās was a court poet of Indrajīt Siṁh, a brother of the ruler of Orchha. His place in Hindi literature seems to be sanctioned in a popular saying: 'Sūr is the Sun, Tulsī – the Moon, Keśavdās –

---

[1] Cf. Śukla, *Hindī sāhitya kā itihās,* p. 199; Varmā, *Hindī sāhitya koś,* vol. 2, p. 107 and Ānandnārāyaṇ Śarmā, 'Kavi Keśavdās', in Vijaypāl Siṁh, ed., *Keśavdās,* Dillī: Rādhākṛṣṇa Prakāśan, 1970, p. 41.

[2] Rīti – lit. 'manner, method; style', therefore as the name of a period in Hindi literature it is often translated as 'mannerism'. For the discussion of the correctness of the usage of this term see Busch, 'Questioning the Tropes'.

[3] See e.g. Varmā, *Hindī sāhitya,* vol. 2, pp. 329–30.

the multitude of stars'.[4] He won wide recognition and fame for, among other things, his very refined language, albeit often difficult to grasp.[5] Therefore, Keśavdās is commonly referred to as 'a demon of difficult poetry (*kaṭhin kāvya ke pret*). An anecdote says that if a ruler wanted to get rid of a poet without paying him, he used to ask him the meaning of a verse by Keśavdās.[6] Thus, one can assume that this method was effective enough to go down in the history of Hindi literature.

The exact number of Keśavdās's works has not been unanimously determined. The most authoritative three-volume collected works of Keśavdās include nine works. They are the three best-known poems, i.e. the *Rasikpriyā* (The Connoisseur's Love; 1591), the *Kavipriyā* (The Poet's Love; 1601) and the *Rāmcandracandrikā*[7] (The Moonlight of Rām the Moon; 1601[8]), as well as the *Chandmālā* (A Garland of Metres), the *Śikhnakh* (From Top-knot to Toe-nail), the *Ratanbāvanī* (Fifty-two [Verses] on Ratan; c.1601–7), the *Vīrsiṁhdevcarit* (The Deeds of Virsinhdev; c.1607), the *Jahā̃gīrjascandrikā* (The Moonlight of Jahangir's Fame; 1612) and the *Vijñāngītā* (A Song of Knowledge; 1610).[9]

Keśavdās's telling of the Rāmkathā, the *Rāmcandracandrikā*, commonly known as the *Rāmcandrikā* (The Moonlight of Rām),

---

[4] *sūra sūra tulasī sasī uḍugana kesavadāsa*; Rūpnārāyaṇ Pāṇḍey, 'Bhūmikā', in Keśavdās, *Rāmcandrikā saṭīk*, comment. Jānakīprasād, Lakhnaū: Navalkiśor Pres, 1923, p. I.

[5] Ibid., pp. VI–VII.

[6] *dībo na cāhai bidāī naresa to pūachaṭa kesava kī kabitāī*; ibid., p. I or *kavi ko daina na cahai bidāī, pūchāī kesava kī kabitāī*; Śarmā, 'Kavi Keśavdās', p. 41; cf. Varmā, *Hindī sāhitya koś*, vol. 2, p. 109.

[7] This title appears in the text of the poem itself (e.g. 1.5, 1.6, 1.21), as well as in Sanskrit colophons that come at the end of each chapter; also see *Keśav granthāvalī*, ed. Viśvanāthprasād Miśra, vol. 3, Ilāhābād: Hindustānī Ekeḍemī, 1959, p. XXVI.

[8] Varmā, *Hindī sāhitya koś*, vol. 2, p. 505; Nagendra, ed., *Hindī sāhitya kā itihās*, Dillī: Neśanal Pabliśing Hāus, 1986, p. 266 and Varmā, *Hindī sāhitya*, vol. 2, p. 327; cf. McGregor, *Hindi Literature from Its Beginnings*, p. 127.

[9] The order of works follows *Keśav granthāvalī*, ed. Viśvanāthprasād Miśra, 3 vols., Ilāhābād: Hindustānī Ekeḍemī, 1954–9. Cf. Śukla, *Hindī sāhitya kā itihās*, p. 201 and Deśrājsiṁh Bhāṭī, *Keśavkāvyasudhā (keśav-sāhitya kā ālocnātmak tathā vyākhyātmak adhyayan)*, Dillī: Kalā Mandir, 1974, pp. 5–10.

is the most famous and discussed of his works.[10] This poem, apparently influenced by the socio-political and religious (e.g. Rasik Sampradāy) atmosphere of its times and of the milieu of Keśavdās himself, was very popular not only with literary experts. It is corroborated by a significant number of manuscripts[11] and commentaries, such as for example the commentary of Jānakīprasād written in 1815[12] and the commentary of Lālā Bhagvāndīn published for the first time in 1923 and reprinted till today.[13]

'MOONLIT' RĀMKATHĀ OF THE *RĀMCANDRIKĀ*

The poem consists of thirty-nine chapters, called *prakāś*,[14] of different length, in which a range of many different metres is used.[15] It opens with verses praising Gaṇeś, Sarasvatī and Rām (1.1–3). Keśavdās presents Rām both as the non-manifested Supreme Being and the manifested, personal God, the worshipping and repeating of whose name bring salvation; thus, the spirit of Bhakti is evident here. After a short genealogy of his own lineage and the date of his work, the author gives the reasons for composing the poem: Vālmīki appeared in his dream (1.7) and made him write it. He convinced Keśavdās that thanks to praising Rām's name, the cause of all happiness and fulfilment (1.8–9), the abode of truth (*rām nām. satya dhām*; 1.10), he would attain Rām's heavenly abode and be relieved of sins. Keśav, thus instructed, chooses Rām as his favoured God (*'kesavadāsa' tahĩ karyo rāmcandrajū iṣṭa;*[16] 1.18) and sets to work to compose the poem.

---

[10] Cf. Rameścandra Miśra, 'Keśav kā vyaktitva aur racnā', in Siṁh, *Keśavdās*, p. 29.

[11] Varmā, *Hindī sāhitya koś*, vol. 2, p. 505.

[12] See Keśavdās, *Rāmcandrikā saṭīk*; the year quoted after Śukla, *Hindī sāhitya kā itihās*, p. 387.

[13] Lālā Bhagvāndīn, *Keśavkaumudī arthāt rāmcandrikā saṭīk*, 9th edn, Ilāhābād: Rāmnārāyaṇ Lāl Benī Mādhav, 1961, 2 vols.

[14] *Prakāś* – lit. 'light'; cf. the poem's title. All references are to the text as published in *Keśav granthāvalī*, vol. 2.

[15] Ā. Śarmā states that Keśavdās employed eighty-two metres in the *Rāmcandrikā*; Śarmā, 'Kavi Keśavdās', p. 47.

[16] Orthography as in *Keśav granthāvalī*.

The author begins the story from verse 21, introducing Daśarath and his four sons, and then Ayodhya, the city of gods (*devapurī*), at which the sage Viśvāmitra arrives (1.51). The sage, as in the traditional narrative, takes with him Rām and Lakṣmaṇ to crush demons disturbing his sacrifice (chapters 2 and 3). When Viśvāmitra with the two brothers comes to the capital of Janak, Keśavdās proves himself to be a real court poet – he devotes more than two chapters (3.11–5) to a very lively presentation of different daring contestants (among them Rāvaṇ) boasting about their might before they try to break Śiv's bow in order to win Sītā's hand. As is known from tradition, this remarkable feat was accomplished by Rām. Interestingly, Keśavdās devotes relatively little space to the ensuing nuptial rites of Sītā and Rām (6.6–9) that are of much interest to other authors. For example, Vālmīki devotes to this episode a substantial fragment (1.67–73.7) and Tulsīdās dedicates to it as much as about one-quarter of the Childhood Book (1.283–361). Much more attention than to the ceremony itself Keśavdās devotes to an exchange of politenesses before the wedding feast (6.11–28) and to the feast, accompanied by an interesting *gālī* sung during it (6.29–36). When Rām and Sītā retire for rest, for the author it is an occasion to present Rām at his best, i.e. depicting him from head to toe (6.43–58) and then he devotes only one verse to Sītā (6.59). Devoting so much attention almost exclusively to Rām has to be seen as compliance with modesty (*maryādā*[17]) that does not allow the poet to go on at length about Sītā's physical beauty.[18]

Among the following events connected with the exile, one's attention is drawn by a passage after Kausalyā expresses her willingness to accompany her son (9.10). Rām, motivated by filial duty, teaches her about the responsibilities of a woman and of a widow in particular – as if anticipating the course of events – which may seem conduct unbecoming to a son (9.11–21).[19] On their way to exile, one can witness a tender loving scene, in which Rām, having found an appropriate place, makes it comfortable for Sītā lining it with grass and fans her in order to drive away her tiredness (9.44). Also interesting is the behaviour of Bharat in

---

[17] Lit. 'limit, boundary'.

[18] For more on this see further in this chapter.

[19] Cf. Śukla, *Hindī sāhitya kā itihās*, p. 207 and Gargī Gupta, *Rāmcandrikā kā viśiṣṭ adhyayan*, Dillī: Bhāratī Sāhitya Mandir, 1964, p. 321.

Chitrakut. When Rām dismisses his request to come back to Ayodhya, Bharat says:

It is not a sin not to fulfil an order of the one
Who delights in alcohol and gives in to a woman,
Who during a course of events babbles
And whose [sinful nature] makes others run away.[20]

Thus preached Shiv, Vishnu and Brahma,[21]
And I have understood it thanks to the power of the Veda.
If you dismiss it, sticking to your decision,[22]
I will abandon my body at the bank of the Ganga[23] (10.36–37).[24]

Then, ready to fulfil his threat, he goes to the bank of the river, which takes on the form of a beautiful woman and makes him realize that his brother is in fact the Supreme Being who has become incarnated in order to destroy unrighteousness (*adharma*) in this world. Bharat, convinced by her words, asks Rām to give him his sandals and retires to Nandigram near Ayodhya, where he and Śatrughna will devote all their thoughts to their brother (10.38–44).

In Keśavdās's presentation of this episode, Bharat's reasoning aimed at making Rām return to Ayodhya is very striking. How ever one would wish to interpret his words, they will always mean that one should not bother with orders of an unworthy, vile person. Even though Bharat, according to his own words, only refers to the revealed truths that he has understood thanks to the Veda and does not name anyone explicitly, nevertheless, there can be no doubt that he means Daśarath. How far from tradition he is in his judging and criticizing his own father![25]

---

[20] Cf. Bhagvāndīn, *Keśavkaumudī*, vol. 1, p. 165.

[21] Ibid.

[22] Ibid.

[23] The river Mandakini flowing near Chitrakut is meant here. In Hindu mythology, Mandakini (Mandākinī) is the name of the celestial Ganges (Gaṅgā) and of the Milky Way as well.

[24] *madyapāna rata strījita hoī, sannipātajuta bātula joī;/ dekhi dekhi tinakõ saba bhāgai, tāsu baina hani pāpa na lāgai./ īsa īsa jagadīsa bakhānyo, bedavākyabala tẽ pahicānyo;/ tāhi meṭi haṭikai rahihaũ jau, gaṅgātīra tana kõ tajihaũ tau.*

[25] Cf. Nizām Uddīn, 'Tulsī aur Keśav', in Ārya and Agravāl, *Tulsī mānas sandarbh*, p. 388.

The course of later events, i.e. the stay in Chitrakut and Dandaka and the episode of the mutilation of Śūrpanakhā, is treated in a more traditional way with the difference that on many occasions it has a distinct Bhakti flavour. For example, Mārīc, for whom Rām is an all-pervading being, wants to die at his hands (12.9–11). The kidnapping of Sītā also has an obvious characteristic of the divine play, *līlā*. Rām not only orders her to enter fire, which is supposed to protect the real Sītā against her kidnap by Rāvaṇ, but also tells her that when she has already taken on her shade-shadow form (*chāya-sarīra*), she should ask him to kill a deer, i.e. Mārīc (12.12).

Although in the poem there is no scarcity of very dynamic descriptions of fights during the war on Lanka, Keśavdās is very interested not only in what is happening on the battlefield but also outside it. This portion of the *Rāmcandrikā* includes precepts given by different persons as well. Although they are all related to the war that is taking place there, it is clear that they are of a universal, didactic character. For example, one of Rāvaṇ's ministers instructs him that there are four kinds of kings (17.20–3), four kinds of ministers (17.24–5) and four kinds of advice given by them (17.26–7); Kumbhakarṇa, Rāvaṇ's brother, referring to the four goals of life of a Hindu (*puruṣārtha*), i.e. *dharma, artha, kāma* and *mokṣa*, explains the sense of a king's life (18.7–11).

In the description of the war itself, Keśavdās, utilizing an episode from the *Adhyātma rāmāyaṇa*,[26] tells how Rāvaṇ, after many defeats and the death of his beloved son, Meghnād, sets out to perform a sacrifice for victory. Rām, having learnt about it, orders monkeys to disturb the sacrifice. Monkeys get inside Rāvaṇ's palace and behave bolder and bolder there. At one moment, Aṅgad manages to capture Rāvaṇ's wife, Mandodarī, and pulling her by her hair, drags her out of a picture gallery, in which she had hidden with other women. Her ornaments spill, her bodice gets ripped and discloses her attractive, round breasts. The poet does not spare his effort in describing them (19.29–33), making an original comparison between them and polo balls (*caugān ke ... hālagolā*; 19.32) – just like polo players follow balls during a play, in the same way men's eyes follow the voluptuous breasts of a beautiful woman. At last, Rāvaṇ, alarmed by the cries

[26] This episode originates from the north-western recension of Vālmīki's *Rāmāyaṇa*; Bulke, *Rāmkathā*, p. 464.

of Mandodarī and other women, gets them out of trouble, thus disrupting his sacrifice. In such a way, the goal of the action undertaken by Rām has been achieved and that is why Rāvaṇ drops dead on the battlefield soon after.

After Rām's return to Ayodhya (22), it appears that he does not want to ascend the throne. He is not interested in ruling as he considers it to be the reason for all suffering and in accordance with sin (*rāja hai dukhamūla, saba pāpa ko anukūla*; 23.13). Thus, the poet finds an excuse, which is Rām's will to get released from this world, to demonstrate – by way of Vasiṣṭha's words – the true nature of the incarnate Absolute. When all become familiar with this truth, Rām declares that, though he does not want it, out of consideration for people he is ready to take the burden of rule on himself (24–5). All gathered praise him and the greatness of his name, and the ceremony of coronation takes place (26). Almost the whole of chapter 27 is devoted to praising Rām and his divine nature by the representatives of the fourteen worlds (*caturdaśa-bhuvana*), i.e. of all cosmological regions. The best testimony of Rām's qualities as a king is chapter 28, describing the great prosperity in his state, with all its citizens young, healthy, beautiful, extremely well off and, like their ruler, having only one wife (!).

The next four chapters (29, 30, 31 and 32) are an almost unbroken show of Keśavdās's poetic skills and, at the same time, his most original contribution to Rāmkathā. They are dominated by very evocative, fine descriptions of court life. The author draws in them a picture of splendid palace chambers in which continuous plays and games take place and which are filled with music and enlivened with dances (30.2–4), as well as Rām's extraordinary bedchamber (30.20–5). He depicts grand meals with a variety of fifty-six different dishes (30.28–31), polo matches, Sītā strolling with her companions (*sakhī*) and their games in a pond (32.37–8). There is also an interesting passage, in which Śuk, Rām's companion, describing the beauty of one of Sītā's attendants, which in fact describes Sītā's beauty (31.4–41). Such a device is based on the assumption that if an attendant is so beautiful, how beautiful must be the mistress herself! Here the principle of modesty is once more apparent, proving distinctly that direct descriptions of Sītā's beauty are unbecoming. Thus, here the author uses the same device as in chapter 6, where he described only Rām, hardly hinting at Sītā's beauty.

An original motif appears in the opening fragment of chapter 33 (33.4–7), in which Brahmā addresses Rām, expressing his worries. He is afraid because Rām, who created all the worlds, in fact has become a threat to them. This is so because, giving a chance of attaining salvation to all people disregarding their deeds, there is no difference between a sin and a meritorious act any longer (*miṭi ge saba pāpana punyana ke naga*; 33.5). Rām laughs at these words, understanding that they are hinting at the fact that the time of his mundane existence is coming to the end, and assures Brahmā that he will finish his mission soon.

Keśavdās includes in his poem episodes absent from the *Rāmcaritmānas*: the killing of Śambūk (33.12–19), the banishment of Sītā and the birth of Kuś and Lav in Vālmīki's ashram (33.25–56). The banishment of Sītā is preceded by the interesting reaction of Bharat, who simply laments his fate of having such a mother as Kaikeyī, such a father as Daśarath and a brother who is going to banish his wife without any reason! He even says that if Rām does so, he will depart from this world (33.30–5). Lakṣmaṇ and Śatrughna also try to dissuade Rām from his intention but all to no avail – Rām orders Lakṣmaṇ to take Sītā to the forest.

Keśavdās also devotes much attention to the *aśvamedha* performed by Rām and to the conflict with his sons that ensues as its result (35–9). Rām decides to perform the sacrifice. However, he is afraid that the sin of abandoning Sītā who is thus not present at his side does not make the sacrifice invalid. Therefore, he turns for advice to Vasiṣtha and Viśvāmitra and other sages. This problem is solved by the sage Kaśyap who declares that the sacrifice will be useless (*niṣphal*; lit. 'fruitless') unless Rām has a beautiful idol of Sītā made of gold; with such a golden Sītā he can perform the rite (35.1–6). Thus, the sacrifice begins and an exceptional horse is allowed to roam free, assisted by Rām's army under command of Śatrughna. Finally, it arrives at Vālmīki's ashram where Lav catches the horse (35.11–12). In the ensuing fight, Lav struggles with his uncle, not aware who he is. After a mighty blow by Śatrughna, Lav loses consciousness but Śatrughna is eventually defeated by Kuś. Then both boys one by one fight with Lakṣmaṇ, Bharat and, finally, Rām himself, leaving them all – with their brave soldiers – dead in the field. Sītā is horrified when she learns what has happened. She laments that her sons have become the perpetrators of the death of their father and uncles. Vālmīki tries to quieten her and tells her that with the power of her chastity, she can restore them all to life. In the battlefield, she animates the lives of all the fallen soldiers (39.10). Rām and Sītā meet and together return to Ayodhya. In the closing passage of the *Rāmcandrikā*, Rām, having distributed his kingdom among his sons, nephews and grandsons, instructs them how a good king should govern his kingdom and people. For example, he should not tell lies, befriend fools, take back anything once given to someone, inflict sufferings on his minister and friend (!) or trust an enemy; he should be constant in his feelings, treat his subjects as his own sons, etc. (39.29–34). Rām also teaches them how the security of a state should be maintained and it is a really Machiavellian lesson. According to it, adjacent kingdoms should be treated as foes, thus a wise king should be at war with them. The kingdoms that are the neighbours of neighbours should be treated as friends, peacefully; those that lie the furthest should be treated neutrally and some kind of exchange should be maintained with them (39.35–6).

The poem ends with a *phalaśruti* (39.38–9) specifying the benefits awaiting those who listen to, read or sing about Rām's life depicted in the *Rāmcandrikā*. The reward, irrespective of sex and social status (*nāri kā nara bipra kṣatriya baisya sūdra jū koi*), is a son, a [good] wife and wealth (*putra kalatra sampati*), well-being in this life and salvation after it (*subhukti loka loka anta mukti*). Contact with the story brings the same results as sacrificial gifts or bathing in many sacred places (*jajña dāna aneka tīratha nhāna ko phala hoi*).

CHARACTERISTIC FEATURES OF THE *RĀMCANDRIKĀ*

The beginning of the poem – the appearance of Vālmīki in the poet's dream – indicates that Vālmīki and his *Rāmāyaṇa* were Keśavdās's inspiration. And indeed the story line, as in many other tellings, for the most part follows Vālmīki's *Rāmāyaṇa*. However, taking into consideration that Keśavdās also looked for inspiration to other Sanskrit works, among which Bhavabhūti's *Uttararāmacarita*, Jayadeva's *Prasannarāghava* and the *Hanumannāṭaka* are mentioned,[27] and gives voice to his own imagination, as

[27] Śukla, *Hindī sāhitya kā itihās*, p. 204; Miśra, 'Keśav kā vyaktitva', p. 29 and Gupta, *Rāmcandrikā kā viśiṣṭ adhyayan*, pp. 244–67. For more on

well as shows his noteworthy poetic artistry, one should rather say that the reference to Vālmīki is a symbolic testimony of his place in the Rāmāyaṇa tradition and a well-deserved homage paid to him. In this context, it is worth mentioning here that while Keśavdās is said not to be a master of narrative (a question to which I will come later in this chapter), an outstanding lightness and skilful bringing out of the psychological depth of characters distinguish the dialogues created by him. They have prominent dramatic value, which is also corroborated by the fact of their use in Rāmlīlā performances.[28]

The episode in which Rām orders Sītā to enter fire and ask him to kill a deer when she is already in her shadow form (12.12), on the one hand, is a vivid illustration that in the *Rāmcandrikā* nothing happens by accident and all proceeds in accordance with a given plan, defined rules and roles, i.e. according to *līlā*, the divine play of Rām. On the other hand, the very laconic introduction of this and many other episodes does not seem to justify R. Śukla's opinion about the lack of narrative skills in Keśavdās[29] but, quite the opposite, presents him as an author conscious of the fact that the story he is dealing with is firmly set in a context well-known to his audience. He does not have to narrate the story in its every detail because everyone knows what it is about.[30]

---

the probable sources of Keśavdās see Gupta, *Rāmcandrikā kā viśiṣṭ adhyayan*, pp. 234–75; Vijaypāl Siṁh, *Keśav aur unkā sāhitya*, Dillī: Rājpāl eṇḍ Sanz, 1961, pp. 338–49; Bhāṭī, *Keśavkāvyasudhā*, pp. 5–10 and Hīrālāl Dīkṣit, *Ācārya Keśavdās*, Lakhnaū: Lakhnaū Viśvavidyālay, 1954, pp. 16–17.

[28] Varmā, *Hindī sāhitya koś*, vol. 2, p. 505 and Nizām Uddīn, 'Tulsī aur Keśav', pp. 390–1. For more on dramatic features in the *Rāmcandrikā* see Rāmdīn Miśra, '"Rāmcandrikā" prabandhakāvya nahī̃ apitu ek nāṭya-prabandha', *Hindustānī*, vol. 26, nos 1–2, 1965, pp. 30–9 and Vyāsmaṇi Tripāṭhī, *Rāmcandrikā mẽ nāṭya tatva*, Dillī: Sākṣī Prakāśan, 2003.

[29] Śukla, *Hindī sāhitya kā itihās*, pp. 202–3. While reading Śukla's opinion about Keśavdās (ibid., pp. 199–205), one is under the impression that Śukla, denying Keśav originality as well as poetic sensibility and criticizing him for his seeming predilection for bizarre plays on words and effects, as well as the inability to recognize the vital points in the story, was not objective in his appraisal of the poet; see ibid., esp. pp. 201–4.

[30] Cf. Siṁh, *Keśav aur unkā sāhitya*, pp. 295–6 and Gupta, *Rāmcandrikā kā viśiṣṭ adhyayan*, p. 233.

Undoubtedly, this feature of the Rāmāyaṇa tradition made Keśavdās's concentration on his poetic skills, showing off his erudition as well as mastery of words much easier. The most telling examples of this are those fragments of the poem in which Keśavdās, constructing acutely succinct, elliptic lines and, at the same time, making use of polisemy that is so characteristic of the Hindi language, was so skilled in selecting words that as a result he produced verses having a double or even triple – not infrequently opposite – meaning. For example, when Rāvaṇ addresses Sītā in Lanka trying to win her over and to make her forget about Rām (13.57–69), Keśavdās describes the demon in such a way that his words take on a double meaning. Firstly, Rām is shown as Rāvaṇ's mundane, human enemy; secondly, he is shown as God seen through a bhakta's eyes with Sītā viewed as Rām's (partial) earthly manifestation.[31] A proper understanding of such verses without a commentary, and often also with it, is very difficult. Perfect language competence is not enough here; in order to understand such poetry one has to be a true connoisseur whom Keśavdās addressed while creating his work.[32]

As I have already mentioned, an undeniable Bhakti flavour is present in the *Rāmcandrikā*. Although Keśavdās is said to be a Vaishnav belonging to the tradition of Nimbārka (*c.*1162[33]), and as such a worshipper of Rādhā and Kṛṣṇa and not of Rām,[34] one has to admit that the general tone of the poem stands in agreement with the attitude of a Rām devotee.[35] However, there is no doubt that Keśavdās's intention was not so much to sing the

[31] Bhagvāndīn, *Keśavkaumudī*, vol. 1, pp. 230–2.

[32] A translation of such verses into other languages without losing either of the meanings is very difficult, if possible at all. See e.g. 13.59 with a fragment of the above-mentioned double-meaning description of Rām (*mahā nirgunī nāma tāko na lījai, sadā dāsa mopai kṛpā kyõ na kījai*) or 15.39 with the triple-meaning lines describing Rām's army that can also be understood as a presentation of the majesty of Vibhīṣaṇ as the king and as the approaching of Rāvaṇ's death (*rāmacandrajū kī camū, rājśrī vibhīṣana kī, rāvana kī mīcu darakūca cali āī hai*).

[33] R.G. Bhandarkar, *Vaiṣṇavism, Śaivism and Minor Religious Systems*, Strassburg: Karl J. Trübner, 1913, p. 63; cf. J.N. Farquhar, *An Outline of the Religious Literature of India*, Delhi: Motilal Banarsidass, 1984 (1st published 1920), pp. 239, 376.

[34] *Keśav granthāvalī*, vol. 3, p. XXVII.

[35] Dīkṣit, *Ācārya Keśavdās*, pp. 16–17.

glory of God Rām as to present him as a king, a full-blooded man who knows how to delight in the pleasures of life and how to overcome any hardships. Such a portrayal was certainly influenced by the fact that the *Rāmcandrikā* came into being under court patronage. In this context, the above-mentioned precepts and teachings given on different occasions also come to mind. Their presence can be explained at least in two ways. Firstly, the *Rāmcandrikā* may have been designed as a kind of manual for rulers; secondly, and this relates to the first point, the poem can be seen as an occasion for the poet to take up a role of an erudite mentor. It is not clear, nevertheless, what motivation stood behind Keśavdās's choice of the Rāmkathā as material for his work[36] but it may be presumed that his choosing a well-known story was a real challenge for a poet aspiring to mastery or wanting to authenticate it. Creating a work bewildering with its novelty was enough to achieve this goal! It seems that despite all the criticism (well-deserved and not),[37] the author of the *Rāmcandrikā* managed to produce an accomplished work. In Stuart McGregor's words, it 'conveys (...) an impression of cultural and artistic comprehensiveness: a retelling of a legend now sanctified, and at the same time a showpiece of poetic art'.[38] Unlike in the case of Keśav's other works, even its difficult style and language, i.e. sanskritized Braj with Bundelī elements, did not prevent non-specialists from reading it and from it becoming known outside the specialist circles.[39]

* * *

Discussing the contribution of Keśavdās – a precursor of Rīti literature – to the development of Rāmkathā in Hindi, two other major court poets, i.e. Senāpati (*fl.* the first half of the seventeenth century) and Padmākar Bhaṭṭ (?1753–1833[40]), also deserve a brief mention here.

[36] According to R. Śukla: 'He felt a desire to write a narrative poem as well and for this [purpose] he took Rām's story'; Śukla, *Hindī sāhitya kā itihās*, p. 202.

[37] E.g. ibid., pp. 200–4.

[38] McGregor, *Hindi Literature from Its Beginnings*, p. 127.

[39] Cf. ibid.

[40] Śukla, *Hindī sāhitya kā itihās*, p. 293 and Varmā, *Hindī sāhitya koś*, vol. 2, p. 321; cf. McGregor, *Hindi Literature from Its Beginnings*, p. 183.

Not much is known about Senāpati's life but in his highly valued work *Kavittratnākar* (The Sea of Kavitts; 1649)[41] he proves to be an accomplished poet and true Rāmbhakta. *Kavittratnākar* is a collection of loosely knit verses in *kavitt* metre arranged in five chapters (*taraṅg;* lit. 'wave'), dealing with a specific theme. Two chapters of this work, i.e. chapters 4 and 5, draw inspiration from the Rāmāyaṇa tradition. Thus, chapter 4 the *Rāmāyaṇvarṇan* (Account of Ram's Life) – in seventy-six verses[42] – focuses, according to Senāpati's own words, on some episodes of the story of Rām's deeds.[43] Chapter 5, *Rāmrasāyanvarṇan* (Account of Ram's Elixir), in eighty-six verses,[44] offers an interesting exposition of Senāpati's understanding of Rāmbhakti.

Padmākar, one of the last eminent Rīti authors and a versatile court poet, at the end of his life created the *Rāmrasāyan* (Rām's Elixir'), a sizable work in Braj that is said to be a translation of the *Rāmāyaṇa* of Vālmīki (*padmākar kavikṛt bālmīkirāmāyaṇ kā chandobaddh bhāṣānuvād*).[45] Despite the fact that it has not won much popularity, it seems of interest here, because it draws on the tradition of *caupāī–dohā* metres, so characteristic of the *Rāmcaritmānas*. However, from the point of view of its composition and narrative it follows Vālmīki's *Rāmāyaṇa* and other Sanskrit tellings. Thus, its metrical structure may testify, although not necessarily, to the role of Tulsīdās's poem but its narrative rather points to the fact that the success of the *Rāmcaritmānas* did not mean that previous tellings had sunk into oblivion. Some critics say that the *Rāmrasāyan* is not as accomplished as other works by

---

[41] Senāpati, *Kavittratnākar (bhūmikā, pāṭhāntar tathā ṭippaṇī sahit)*, ed. Umāśaṅkar Śukla, Ilāhābād: Hindī Pariṣad–Prayāg Viśvavidyālay, 1936. For more on Senāpati and his work see e.g. Śukla, *Hindī sāhitya kā itihās*, pp. 214–18; Varmā, *Hindī sāhitya koś*, vol. 2, pp. 76–7, 353–4 and McGregor, *Hindi Literature from Its Beginnings*, pp. 174–5.

[42] Senāpati, *Kavittratnākar*, pp. 72–94.

[43] *senāpati yātaĩ kathā-krama kaũ pranāma kari; kāhū kāhū ṭhaura ke kabitta kachū kīne haĩ*; 4.6, ibid., p. 73.

[44] Ibid., pp. 95–118.

[45] See the title page of its incomplete (only the first three books were published) edition: Padmākar, *Rāmrasāyan*, Kāśī: Bhāratjīvan Pres, 1895. Also see the search reports of NPS for the period between 1901–5; *Padmākar granthāvalī*, ed. Viśvanāthprasād Miśra, Vārāṇasī: NPS, 1956, p. 33.

Padmākar and even doubt his authorship of it,[46] while others, e.g. the editor of Padmākar's collected works, do not agree with such an opinion.[47]

Esoteric Rāmkathas

As I have already mentioned, the beginnings of Hindi Rasik literature go back to Agradās,[48] a pupil of Kṛṣṇadās Payahārī[49] who was one of the spiritual leaders of the Rāmānandī sect. Not much is known about Agradās's life. However, the extant evidence reveals that he was active in the second half of the sixteenth century and the first part of the seventeenth century in Rajasthan, where later in his life he founded a monastery, Raivāsā Gaddī, in Galta near contemporary Jaypur.[50] He composed works overflowing with devotion for Rām under his Rasik name Agraalī, considering himself in them one of Sītā's female friends or attendants.[51] Some sixteen works are ascribed to him,[52] including an important work in Sanskrit the *Aṣṭayāma*,[53] but his best-known poem in Hindi is the *Dhyānmañjarī* (Handmaiden of

---

[46] Śukla, *Hindī sāhitya kā itihās*, p. 295; Pāṇḍey, *Tulsīdāsottar hindī rām-sāhitya*, p. 40 and Varmā, *Hindī sāhitya koś*, vol. 2, p. 321.

[47] *Padmākar granthāvalī*, p. 33. However, it is not included in it on the grounds that it was a translation and not Padmākar's original work; see ibid., p. 39.

[48] Introduction, p. 52. For Rāmcandra Śukla's mistaken ideas on Rasik Sampradāy see Śukla, *Hindī sahitya kā itihās*, pp. 148–50.

[49] His name is differently spelt: Payahārī (e.g. Śukla, *Hindī sāhitya kā itihās*, pp. 118–19; Siṁh, *Rāmbhakti*, p. 379; Prasād, *Madhyakālīn rāmkavya dhārā*, p. 381 and Lorenzen, *Praises to a Formless God*, p. 263); Payāhārī (McGregor, *Hindi Literature from Its Beginnings*, p. 107) and Payohārī (Varmā, *Hindī sāhitya koś*, vol. 2, p. 8).

[50] Siṁh, *Rāmbhakti*, p. 379 and idem, *Rāmkāvyadhārā*, p. 78.

[51] *Alī* – lit. 'a female friend of a woman'; cf. Siṁh, *Rāmbhakti*, p. 8; Balbhadra Tivārī, 'Bhūmikā', in *Agradās granthāvalī (Kuṇḍaliyā̃, Dhyan mañjarī, Sādhan gītāvalī)*, ed. Balbhadra Tivārī, Ilāhābād: Satyendra Prakāśan, 1985, p. VI and Prasād, *Madhyakālīn rāmkāvya dhārā*, p. 381. Varmā, *Hindī sāhitya*, vol. 2, p. 306.

[52] Cf. Siṁh, *Rāmbhakti*, pp. 380–1; Siṁh, *Rāmkāvyadhārā*, p. 82; Śukla, *Hindī sāhitya kā itihās*, p. 142; Varmā, *Hindī sāhitya koś*, vol. 2, p. 8 and McGregor, *Hindi Literature from Its Beginnings*, p. 108.

[53] For more details about this type of work in Hindi see below.

Meditation[54]) also called *Rāmdhyānmañjarī* (Handmaiden of Meditation on Rām).[55] It is a basic text of Rasiks, considered so important that it is even called the 'Gītā of Rasiks'.[56] This work, as its title suggests, is conceived as aid in the contemplation of the real nature of the divine couple Sītā-Rām. Although it does not deal with the entire story of Rām's deeds, it is noteworthy and deserves more attention, as it is the earliest known work associated with Rasik Sampradāy that was composed in a new Indo-Aryan language and not in Sanskrit. It also encouraged later authors to undertake the theme of the love sports of Rām, Sītā's master.

Agradās's *Dhyānmañjarī* is composed in Braj, in eighty couplets in *rolā* metre.[57] After the invocation to Rām (1–2), the author admires the splendour of Ayodhya, its buildings and palaces, market places and streets set with precious stones, which disperse darkness (3–7). In the shade of trees, there are wells, also set with gems, with crystal-clear water (14–15). Nearby flows the Sarayu river that leads to the Vaikuṇṭha mountain, the heavenly abode of Rām and all those who deserve it (18–24). Next, Agradās concentrates on the description of a bejewelled pavilion in which a throne studded with precious stones with a fragrant lotus flower put atop of it is installed. The throne is placed on a golden platform near *kalpa vṛkṣa,* a tree granting all desires (28ff.) and the sixteen-year-old beautiful Rām is seated on it (*ṣoḍaśa varṣa kiśora rāma nita sundara rājaī*; 47). It is considered that the motif of Rām's throne is most probably of Shakta origin, which seems to be

---

[54] The translation proposed by Philip Lutgendorf; idem, 'The Secret Life of Rāmcandra', p. 222. *Mañjarī* – most commonly 'blossom; bunch of flowers'; however, in the context of Rasik Sampradāy it is a designation for one of the classes of female attendants of Sītā. Cf. Siṁh, *Rāmbhakti,* p. 380.

[55] All references are to the text as published in Agradās, *Dhyān mañjarī,* comment. Rāmvallabhāśaraṇ, Ayodhyā: Śrī Rāmkṛṣṇadās Utsavī, 1940; cf. the text published in *Agradās granthāvalī,* pp. 49–57.

[56] *Dhyān-mañjarī (...) rasiksādhakõ kī Gītā mānī jātī hai*; quoted in Siṁh, *Rāmkāvyadhārā,* p. 81.

[57] Cf. Tivārī, 'Bhūmikā', p. VIII and R.S. McGregor, 'The *Dhyān-mañjarī* of Agradās', in Monika Thiel-Horstmann, ed., *Bhakti in Current Research, 1979–1982,* Berlin: Dietrich Reimer Verlag, 1983, p. 238. For more on *rolā* metre see Varmā, *Hindī sāhitya koś,* vol. 1, p. 737; cf. Snell, *The Hindi Classical Tradition,* p. 23 and Kellogg, *A Grammar,* p. 579.

corroborated by a very similar description in the *Sadāśivasaṁhitā* and is also known to the *Bhuśuṇḍi rāmāyaṇa*.[58] It may be mentioned here that this is one of the most common motifs among popular images of Rām (especially on chromolithographic images so popular in India till this day), although there are some common differences in details, e.g. the element of the wish-fulfilling tree is usually absent. Next, the poet gives a detailed description of Rām, from head to toe, and likens this extremely beautiful youth to a blue lotus (*nīla indīvara*; 31). His head is adorned with a crown giving off the intense glare of a multitude of suns (*nikara dinakarakī jyotī*; 32) and the earrings in his ears eclipse the brightness of the moon and the sun (33). At his left sits Sītā clad lavishly (48–65). Rām's brothers and Hanumān assist them. Lakṣmaṇ is holding a parasol above their heads and Bharat has in his hand a flywhisk (*cāvar*) – these two objects being the attributes of royal power – while Śatrughna and Hanumān wait for Rām's orders, singing his praises (67–9). Sītā's female attendants are also present, as well as Śiv, Brahmā and the goddesses.[59] The final couplets (71ff.) are concerned with the importance of the image structured in the *Dhyānmañjarī* that is supposed to help Rasiks to meditate on Sītā and Rām.

The language of the poem, which is little embellished with poetic ornaments, is considered pleasing in its naturalness. It highlights the significance of the contemplation of the divine couple, excelling knowledge (*jñān*), Yoga and ascetic practices.[60]

Agradās, as has been mentioned, is the author of another important text of the sect – the *Aṣṭayāma* (The Eight Yamas of a Day[61]) in Sanskrit, while his pupil, the already-mentioned Vaishnav hagiographer, Nābhādās, is the author of the *Aṣṭayām* written in Braj.[62] Because of the role that the works of this type[63]

---

[58] Siṁh, *Rāmbhakti*, p. 94; McGregor, 'The *Dhyān-mañjarī*', pp. 240–1 and idem, *Hindi Literature from Its Beginnings*, pp. 107–8.

[59] Cf. McGregor, 'The *Dhyān-mañjarī*', pp. 238–40 and Varmā, *Hindī sāhitya koś*, vol. 2, p. 275.

[60] Varmā, ibid.

[61] Yama (*yām*(*a*)) – a watch of the day or night, equal to three hours, thus eight yamas designate the twenty-four hours of a day (a word *pahar* is its synonym in modern Hindi).

[62] B. Siṁh mentions his two *aṣṭayāms* in Braj – one in verse, the other in prose; Siṁh, *Rāmbhakti*, p. 384.

played in Rasik Sampradāy, as well as because of their influence on further developments in the cult of Rām, it seems worthwhile to devote a few words to them, with special respect to the work of Nābhādās that initiated this tradition in the Hindi language.[64]

Aṣṭayām works, which are a description of God's day, originate from Krishnaite tradition. A daily ritual routine is in keeping with Indian traditional measurement of time. Not going into too many details, suffice it to say here that the entire twenty-four hours of a day are divided into eight units of three hours, each called *yām(a)*; a day commences at six o'clock in the morning. These texts in fact describe not only the daily routine of God and his beloved but also refer to the attitude that should be adopted by a worshipper at a given moment.

The description of the day begins with a splendid portrayal of Ayodhya, called here Saket, and of Kanak Bhavan, i.e. the Golden Palace of Sītā and Rām. Sītā and Rām get up after the night and perform purificatory acts. Then Rām goes to meet his brothers and companions, while Sītā meets her sisters and attendants, and later joins her husband. They both take a bath, after which Sītā's companions adorn them and Rām retires for *pūjā*. The couple take their meal and after dallying for a while they withdraw to their bedroom. Later Rām attends the court council meeting, where he also meets his father, and Sītā goes to meet her mothers-in-law. At his brothers' request, Rām makes an inspection of the royal stables. When it is over, he takes a stroll in Ayodhya and meets its inhabitants, and thus reaches groves planted by him and his brothers. From there, they go to the bank of the Sarayu, where for some time they play polo (*caugān*). In the afternoon, while Rām is returning home, young females of Ayodhya feast their eyes on his beauty. At home he meets his mothers, takes his meal and for sometime flies kites[65] with his companions. During this time, Sītā meets the women of Ayodhya and then devotes her time to her mothers-in-law. In the evening, when Rām with his brothers come back home, they sit down to dinner. When the meal is over,

---

[63] R. Pāṇḍey mentions six other important *aṣṭayām*s by different authors; Pāṇḍey, *Tulsīdāsottar*, p. 58.

[64] The two existing published versions of this text differ significantly; Varmā, *Hindī sāhitya koś*, vol. 2, p. 29. Cf. Siṁh, *Rāmbhakti*, p. 384.

[65] Flying kites was one of the favourite pastimes at Indian courts; it is well attested not only in literature but also in miniature paintings.

Sītā and Rām return to Kanak Bhavan. Her companions perform *ārtī*[66] and later dance, sing and entertain them in different ways. At midnight, the time for the love sports of Sītā and Rām comes; when attendants (*sakhīs*) see fatigue in the eyes of the couple, they bid farewell to them and depart – Rām draws the curtains over their bed.[67]

Another important author of Rasik Sampradāy is Bālkṛṣṇa, aka Bālalī,[68] the successor to Agradās at Raivāsā. He wrote in Braj the *Dhyānmañjarī* and the *Nehprakāś*[69] (The Light of Love).[70] Bālalī was not only one of the most important gurus of the sect but also its most accomplished poet in the seventeenth century. His *Dhyānmañjarī* contains descriptions of the extraordinary beauty of Rām and Sītā, and the splendour of Ayodhya. It is based on the contention that without realizing them, especially the beauty of the royal couple, any meditation is a meaningless, empty act. The *Nehprakāś* is a highly valued work of the sect, serving as one more of its manuals. The author mentions the names of Sītā's attendants and the functions they perform, stressing at the same time their exceptionally privileged position resulting from the fact that they can serve their mistress, Sītā. A description of the splendid beauty of Sītā that also indicates her greatness closes the poem.[71]

Substantial growth of Rasik Sampradāy took place at the turn of the eighteenth and nineteenth century and to a large extent was influenced by the activity of Rāmcaraṇdās (*c.*1760–1835[72]) who is an author of more than twenty works. The most important among them is a literarily accomplished, first commentary on the *Rāmcaritmānas* (1821[73]). In his works, Rāmcaraṇdās skilfully com-

---

[66] *Ārtī* is the most common ceremony performed in worshipping a god – a dish containing votive lamps and incense, flowers and/or other articles is moved in a circular movement, from the left to right side, in front of the idol. It is also performed during certain rituals or on festive occasions in front of people as a sign of respect.

[67] Varmā, *Hindī sāhitya koś*, vol. 2, p. 29.

[68] Siṁh, *Rāmbhakti*, pp. 385–6.

[69] Also known as the *Nehprakāśikā dhyānmañjarī*; ibid., p. 9.

[70] Eight works are ascribed to him altogether; ibid., p. 387 and Siṁh, *Rāmkāvyadhārā*, pp. 70–1.

[71] Miśra, *Rāmbhakti*, p. 199. Also see Varmā, *Hindī sāhitya koś*, vol. 2, pp. 377–8 and McGregor, *Hindi Literature from Its Beginnings*, p. 168.

[72] Varmā, *Hindī sāhitya koś*, vol. 2, p. 509.

[73] Siṁh, *Rāmkāvyadhārā*, p. 280.

bined the attitude of *dāsyabhakti* dominant among the majority of Rām's devotees with *mādhuryabhakti* practised by Rasiks. This interesting blend of the orthodox Ramaite Bhakti with the theology of Rasik Sampradāy resulted, on the one hand, in the flowering of Rasik literature, and, on the other hand, contributed to the further popularization of the *Rāmcaritmānas* and its vision of Rām.[74]

CONCLUSIONS

It is commonly maintained that the seventeenth and eighteenth centuries practically provided no new, important tellings of Rāmkathā. This is connected with the success of Tulsīdās and his poem that are supposed to have suppressed the ambitions of other potential authors of Hindi Rāmāyaṇas.[75] The foregoing discussion, however, seems to question the credibility of such a contention. It appears more plausible to view the role of Tulsīdās's poem, not only during that period, in terms of an accomplished and very influential expression of the type of devotion dominant among Rāmbhaktas. However, its characteristic features such as fervent devotion and ever present spiritual readiness to serve God, on the one hand, and the stress laid on following the rules of propriety (*maryādā*), on the other hand, did not harmonize with the atmosphere of courts and the character of Rīti court poetry that was interested in a decidedly this-worldly life full of miscellaneous pleasures. Poets were attracted to the secular and not spiritual dimension of the world with which the reference to Rām was inevitably connected after Tulsīdās. Thus, the majority of Hindi authors, having in mind the *Rāmcaritmānas*, did not consider the story of Rām a source of their inspiration. Composing a work that would simultaneously comply with the requirements of Rīti poetry and the complex image of Rām presented by Tulsī called for an outstanding author such as Keśavdās. His *Rāmcandrikā* is a display of poetic skills and its message stands in harmony with an attitude worthy of a Rām devotee. Therefore, it seems much more justified to consider Keśavdās as a point of departure for

---

[74] Varmā, *Hindī sāhitya koś*, vol. 2, p. 509; McGregor, *Hindi Literature from Its Beginnings*, p. 170 and Pāṇḍey, *Tulsīdāsottar*, p. 73.

[75] E.g. Siṁh, *Rāmbhakti*, pp. 122–3 and Bulke, *Rāmkathā*, pp. 199–200.

other Rīti authors who, aiming at narrating the story of Rām, would have to cope with his treatment of Rāmkathā and his poetical craft first of all. Apart from this, during the entire period the literature influenced by Rasiks flourished,[76] although due to its esoteric character it was not known to wider audiences. As I have already mentioned, the authors of these works did not deal with the entire story, being preoccupied mostly with the period of happy life Rām and Sītā led in Ayodhya-Saket. However, very interestingly, the court atmosphere that permeated all these works went hand in hand with the court culture of those days. This very feature of Rasik literature seems to have attracted, especially somewhat later – in the nineteenth century, a number of rajas, maharajas and their milieux; it is corroborated by the names of a number of authors who in one way or another referred to Rāmkathā. The fact that the first commentary on the *Rāmcarimānas* by Rāmcaraṇdās hails from the bosom of Rasik Sampradāy is also very significant. This exegesis, containing the numerous theological and philosophical concepts of the Rasiks, proved attractive to other bhaktas and enhanced interest in the poem itself. The synthesis of the esoteric current and mainstream of Ramaite Bhakti proposed by Rāmcaraṇdās was soon to bear fruit and result in many works in the nineteenth century.

[76] Gopināth Kavirāj in his introduction to Siṁh's work stresses that Siṁh quotes around a thousand titles of works related to Rasiks and about 800 of them are works in Hindi; Kavirāj, 'Bhūmikā', in Siṁh, *Rāmbhakti*, pp. IV-V.

CHAPTER FOUR

On the Threshold of Modernity: Rāmkathās in the Nineteenth Century

TRANSFORMATION OF LANGUAGE AND FORM

In the discussion of the nineteenth-century developments in the Hindi Rāmāyaṇa tradition, it is essential to pay attention to fundamental changes that took place in the sphere of language and genre in Hindi literature in general. Thus, untill the nineteenth century Hindi literature was composed in a number of cognate dialects, among which Avadhi and Braj played the most important role. The latter, especially in the seventeenth and eighteenth centuries, became the most common medium of literary expression in north India, gaining thus the status of the most important literary language in the Hindi-speaking area.

It is noteworthy that literary works in their majority were in the form of poetry – prose compositions are very few and they are mainly non-literary pieces, such as treatises or commentaries. In the second half of the eighteenth century, a slight change in this regard can be noticed when a few specimens of prose works in Hindi based on the Khariboli dialect appeared. This is a trait that seems to reveal the increasing role of this form of speech and anticipates the developments that flourished in the second half of the nineteenth century.[1] This also makes one reconsider the widespread opinion that the language and literature in Khariboli Hindi owe their beginnings to the institutionalized activity of the British[2] as it does not seem to fully comply with the actual state of things. Extant literary evidence indicates that the beginnings of Khariboli Hindi were independent of the presence of the British and they date, as has been already mentioned, at least to the end

---

[1] It is worth noting here that Khariboli Hindi had an unprecedented career as the language of nineteenth-century prose but as far as Hindi poetry is concerned it made a triumphant entry into it only as late as the beginning of the twentieth century.

[2] First of all the activity of Fort William College is referred to. It was founded in 1800 in order to educate East India Company officers, providing them with a knowledge of Indian languages and culture.

of the eighteenth century.[3] However, it is also true that, as in the case of other prose works, the majority of them are of a non-literary character, though the examples of the earliest examples of relatively well-formed prose in Khariboli Hindi can be found among them. Despite the fact that its very beginnings were independent of the British activity, however, there is no doubt that its flowering in the nineteenth century, as well as the beginning of such modern genres as the novel and the short story, owe much to the activities and influence of the British. All these changes were inseparable from the process of the formation of the modern standard of Hindi that is based on the Khariboli dialect.

The growth of European influences, more and more pronounced with the expansion of colonial power, and the deeper and deeper penetration of new ideas in north India resulted, among other things, in new linguistic requirements. On the one hand, Persian, Urdu/Hindustani (understood here as that form of north Indian speech of the turn of the eighteenth and ninteenth centuries which was dominated by a Perso-Arabic lexis and written in Arabic script) as well as English did not seem to satisfy fully the purposes of the East India Company as in fact they ignored the linguistic practices of the Hindu majority. On the other hand, Braj, though it prevailed in the literature of those times, did not achieve the staus of an extra-regional medium of communication and it was also strongly associated with the passing epoch. Thus, especially with the passage of time, the speech based on Khariboli but written in Devanagari and drawing on Sanskrit vocabulary, must have appeared close to Sanskrit and therefore to the Hindu tradition, and at the same time far from Persian and Urdu and therefore from the Muslim tradition. From the beginning of the nineteenth century, its presence became more and more pronounced and its position more and more siginficant vis-à-vis Urdu/Hindustani common in speech and Brajbhasha

[3] Shardadevi Vedalankar, *The Development of Hindi Prose Literature in the Early Nineteenth Century (1800–1856 A.D.)*, Allahabad: Lokbharati Publications, 1969, pp. 20–7, HSI, pp. 277–8, 419–23 and R.S. McGregor, *Hindi Literature of the Nineteenth and Early Twentieth Centuries*, Wiesbaden: Otto Harrassowitz, 1974, p. 62. Cf. G.A. Zograf, *Chindustani na rubeže XVIII i XIX vv.*, Moskva: Izdatel'stvo vostočnoj literatury, 1961, pp. 29–30.

used in literature. With the passage of time it was more and more consitenly called Hindi[4] and its role grew parallel to the expansion of education, printing and the press, as well as the rise of the socio-cultural consciousness and identity of the Hindus. During the nineteenth century, it became not only a convenient medium in the sphere of everyday as well as public communication but also a convenient literary vehicle. It is worth noting that it owes a lot to Urdu and English due to the constant competition with them especially in such spheres as administration, law and politics. It also drew from the numerous dialects used by its speakers over a vast territory, benefitting from their literary traditions and, mainly indirectly via Bengali, from Western traditons. As a result, in the second decade of the twentieth century, it acquired the position of the fully established language of Hindi literature. And because the literature written in Braj was regarded as a continuation, if not a relic, of a bygone epoch, it ceased to be an object of interest to historians and critics of Hindi literature. Therefore, especially from the mid nineteenth century, which is considered to be the beginning of the modern period (*ādhunikkāl*), the history of Hindi literature is almost exclusively concerned with works written in Khariboli Hindi.[5] However, it should also be remembered that many works, especially those that were written in the first half of the nineteenth century, although composed in Khariboli Hindi, continued the preceding literary traditions as far as their form, contents and language are concerned, which is also true in the case of the works that belong to the Rāmāyaṇa tradition. Many of them are related to the esoteric current and most of them are short compositions in the

---

[4] For more on the intricate history of Hindi see McGregor, *Hindi Literature of the Nineteenth and Early Twentieth Centuries*, esp. pp. 62–9; Amrit Rai, *A House Divided: The Origin and Development of Hindi/Hindavi*, Delhi: Oxford University Press, 1984; Christopher Shackle and Rupert Snell, *Hindi and Urdu since 1800: A Common Reader*, London: School of Otriental and African Studies, 1990, pp. 1–23; Christopher King, *One Language, Two Scripts: The Hindi Movement in Nineteenth Century North India*, Bombay: Oxford University Press, 1994 and Alok Rai, *Hindi Nationalism*, Delhi: Orient Longman, 2001.

[5] Vedalankar, *The Development of Hindi Prose*, pp. 20–7 and McGregor, *Hindi Literature of the Nineteenth and Early Twentieth Centuries*, pp. 62–9.

form of independent stanzas. One can also find longer works, among which the works of the *aṣṭayām* type prevail; there are also dramas and one among them is considered to be the first drama in Hindi (see below).

While the nineteenth century in the entire history of Hindi literature should be treated as a transitional period during which older forms coexisted with newer ones, with regard to the works related to Rāmkathā, as I will try to demonstrate, one still remains in the circle of traditional concerns.

Hindi Rāmāyaṇas as the Earliest Examples of Hindi Prose

Before discussing the new developments in the nineteenth-century Rāmāyaṇa tradition in Hindi, one should pay attention to two works that are considered to be the oldest specimens of relatively mature literary prose in Khariboli Hindi, i.e. Daulatrām's *Padma purāṇa* (*c.*1765) and Rāmprasād 'Nirañjanī's *Yogavāsiṣṭha* (1798).[6]

Daulatrām's[7] work is an adaptation of the Jaina *Padma purāṇa*. It was written sometime in the 1760s, and in 1801 it was, most probably, re-edited and its language modernized.[8] It is a voluminous work of around seven hundred pages and its language is under the evident influence of Rajasthani and Braj.[9]

Rāmprasād 'Nirañjanī's *Yogavāsiṣṭha* is an adaptation of the *Yogavāsiṣṭha* in Sanskrit. Its date, i.e. 1798 (1855 of the Vikram era)

---

[6] For the excerpts from both these works see Vedalankar, *The Development of Hindi Prose*, pp. 22–5 and Śukla, *Hindī sāhitya kā itihās*, pp. 390–1. For more on the pre-nineteenth prose in Khariboli Hindi see McGregor, *Hindi Literature from Its Beginnings*, pp. 213–14.

[7] For more on Daulatrām see Kastūrcand Kāsalīvāl, *Mahākavi Daulatrām Kāsalīvāl: vyaktitva aur kṛtitva*, Jaypur: Sāhitya Śodh Vibhāg, 1974.

[8] Śukla and McGregor date it in 1761 (McGregor also gives the year 1764); Śukla, *Hindī sāhitya kā itihās*, p. 391 and McGregor, *Hindi Literature from Its Beginnings*, p. 214. Varmā dates it in 1766; Varmā, *Hindī sāhitya koś*, vol. 2, p. 268 and idem, *Hindī sāhitya*, vol. 2, p. 497; cf. Vedalankar, *The Development of Hindi Prose*, p. 22.

[9] Ibid. and Vedalankar, *The Development of Hindi Prose*, p. 22.

is given by Sh. Vedalankar who convincingly argues that the year 1741 that can be found in R. Śukla's work is in fact an error resulting from his acceptance of the year 1798 being the year of the Vikram era.[10] One may add here that its author, Rāmprasād, was an ascetic from the *nirañjanī* sect[11] from which his name is derived. The laguage of Rāmprasād is full of influences of other languages and dialects, mainly of Panjabi and Braj.[12]

Somewhat later comes *Rāmcaritra* (1805) by Sadal Miśra (?1767–1848[13]), an employee of the famous Fort William College in Calcutta and the author of another work in Khariboli Hindi, i.e. *Candrāvatī athavā Nāsiketopākhyān* (1803). The *Rāmcaritra* is a translation of the *Adhyātma rāmāyaṇa*, written by Miśra at the request of his superior, John Borthwick Gilchrist. Miśra mentions it at the beginning of his work, adding that he wrote it for the purpose of the school, which had been opened in Calcutta for the British,[14] avoiding Persian and Arabic [lexis]. He also adds that he omitted fragments with 'difficult *vedānta*'.[15] Miśra's text is a quite faithful translation of the *Adyātma rāmāyaṇa*. It is noteworthy that it was the *Rāmagītā* that meant for him 'difficult *vedānta*' and he simply

---

[10] Cf. Vedalankar, *The Development of Hindi Prose*, pp. 22–5 and Śukla, *Hindī sāhitya kā itihās*, pp. 390–1. Also see Premprakāś Gautam, 'Bhāṣā Yogavāsiṣṭha aur uskā lekhak', *Hindustānī*, vol. 34, no. 2, 1973 (April–June), pp. 106, 108. It is noteworthy that many authors rely on the date given by Śukla and thus consider Rāmprasād 'Nirañjanī' as the author of the first work written in mature Khariboli prose; e.g. see Varmā, *Hindī sāhitya koś*, vol. 2, p. 519.

[11] A group in the *nirguṇ* current of Bhakti; David N. Lorenzen, *Kabir Legends and Anantadas's Kabir Parachai*, Albany: State University of New York Press, 1991, p. 82.

[12] Vedalankar, *The Development of Hindi Prose*, p. 24 and McGregor, *Hindi Literature from Its Beginnings*, p. 214.

[13] *Sadal Miśra granthāvalī*, ed. Nalinvilocan Śarmā; Paṭnā: Bihār Rāṣṭrabhāṣā Pariṣad, 1960, p. VIII and Śyamsundardās, 'Bhūmikā', in Sadal Miśra, *Candrāvatī athavā Nasiketopākhyān*, 6th edn, Kāśī: NPS, 1950, p. III.

[14] *pāṭhśālā* (...) *jo sāhab logõ ke liye kalkattā mẽ hūī*; *Sadal Miśra granthāvalī*, p. 33.

[15] *jahā̃ kahī̃ kaṭhin vedānt thā maine deṣā ki iskī bhāṣā sav koī samajh na śakegā is kāraṇ vuse choṛ diyā*; ibid.

omitted it. It may appear especially surprising in view of the significance of this part of the original text but taking into consideration that it was meant for the European students of the college such a decision may appear as justified. The text of the *Rāmcaritra* seems not to raise any doubts that it was Gilchrist who had chosen it.[16] However, one may wonder about the reasons for his choice as well as about whose was the decision to omitt the *Rāmagītā* and why?

The language of Miśra deserves special attention as it is rich in similes, metaphors and alliteration. His style is considered to be very natural and comprehensible, sentences short and not as ornate as in the works of Lallū Lāl (*c.*1763–1825[17]), Miśra's colleague from the college. However, although both *Candrāvatī* and *Rāmcaritra*, for the reasons just given, are valued higher than the works of Lallū Lāl, nevertheless they have not become so popular as Lallū's compositions, what is more, they were not even published in Miśra's life time.[18] It is noteworthy that the 1960 edition of the *Rāmcaritra* was prepared on the basis of a manuscript from the collection of the India Office Library.[19] Its text was only slightly edited, some punctuation marks (in brackets) were introduced and the arrangement of the original verses was specially marked. Apart from this the text was kept as in the original and only some clarifying notes were added in footnotes. The parts of the work are not differentiated in any way, the continuous arrangement of the manuscript has been retained. This edition includes colophons of particular books and chapters but because they are not typographically differentiated working with it reminds one of working with a manuscript. It must be said that although *Rāmcaritra* does not contribute much to the development of the Rāmāyaṇa tradition itself, it is very interesting evidence of its epoch that speaks a lot about Hindi prose at the beginning of the nineteenth century.

---

[16] *ek din ājñā kī ki ādhyātma rāmāyaṇa ko aisī bolī mẽ karo jīsme phārsī ārbī na āve* (orthography as in the original); ibid.

[17] Śukla, *Hindī sāhitya kā itihās*, p. 398.

[18] Vedalankar, *The Development of Hindi Prose*, p. 76.

[19] *Sadal Miśra granthāvalī*, p. 15.

ESOTERIC INFLUENCES

I have mentioned earlier that many nineteenth-century works are influenced by Rasik Sampradāy. However, out of the large number of compositions[20] the majority is in fact not the story of Rām but either only of a fragment of it or a description of Rām and Sītā or of their day; many of them have never been published. The following discussion is concerened chiefly with two of the most important authors – Viśvanāth Siṁh (1789–1854)[21] and Banādās (1821–92); the compositions of Raghurāj Siṁh (1833–79),[22] the son of Viśvanāth Siṁh, will also be mentioned at the end of the following section.

ĀNAND RAGHUNANDAN: THE FIRST MODERN HINDI DRAMA?[23]

INTRODUCTORY REMARKS

The foregoing presentation proves that Rāmkathā was also an interesting subject for those who were creatively active in the second half of the eighteenth century and the first half of the nineteenth century. The oldest specimens of relatively mature literary Hindi prose, i.e. Daulatrām's *Padma purāṇa* and Rāmprasād 'Nirañjanī's' *Yogavāsiṣṭha*, as well as a somewhat later

---

[20] See Siṁh, *Rāmbhakti*, pp. 379–547 and R. Pāṇḍey, pp. 79–88.

[21] Cf. Siṁh, *Rāmbhakti*, p. 431; Viśvanāth Siṁh, *Ānand raghunandan*, ed. Dīpcand Jain et al., Rīvā: Vindhyā Prādeśik Hindi Sāhitya Sammelan, 1960, p. II; Miśra, *Hindī sāhitya kā bṛhat itihās*, p. 282 and Śukla, *Hindī sāhitya kā itihās*, p. 327. Śukla, dating the reign of Viśvanāth Siṁh as 1778–97, most probably makes the same mistake as in the case of the date of Rāmprasād's *Yogavāsiṣṭha*, i.e. he confuses the AD years with the years of the Vikram era (*saṁvat*); also see Vedalankar, *The Development of Hindi Prose*, pp. 22–5 and Stasik, *Opowieść*, pp. 208–9.

[22] Siṁh, *Rāmbhakti*, pp. 470-1; McGregor, *Hindi Literature from Its Beginnings*, p. 171 and Varmā, *Hindī sāhitya koś*, vol. 2, p. 468. Cf. Śukla, *Hindī sāhitya kā itihās*, p. 554.

[23] An earlier version of this section was first published as 'On the Threshold of Modern Hindi Drama? A Few Remarks on *Ānand Raghunandan*', in Monika Nowakowska and Jacek Woźniak, ed., *Theatrum Mirabiliorum Indiae Orientalis: A Volume to Celebrate the 70th Birthday of Professor Maria Krzysztof Byrski* (*Rocznik Orientalistyczny*, vol. 60, no. 2), Warszawa: Dom Wydawniczy Elipsa, 2007, pp. 362–7.

Rāmcaritra by Sadal Miśra can serve as the best example of this. The interest in the Rāmkathā as a source or even the basis of subject matter also holds true in the case of drama, where most often Viśvanāth Siṁh's work *Ānand raghunandan* [*nāṭak*] is referred to as the first Hindi drama (*hindī pratham nāṭak*).[24] In view of the relatively small amount of attention devoted to this work and its seemingly important place in the history of Hindi literature, it is worthwhile investigating how well-founded such contentions are.

Viśvanāth Siṁh was the maharaja of Rewa, a princely state not far from Chitrakut, which became an important pilgrimage centre for the Rām cult in the nineteenth century. He was a prolific writer and an ardent Rāmbhakta, initiated into esoteric Rāmbhakti, i.e. Rāmrasik Sampradāy, which he supported generously, thus promoting its development.[25] Viśvanāth Siṁh wrote in Hindi (mainly in Braj with admixtures of Bagheli[26]) but he is also recognized, much the same as, somewhat later, his son, Raghurāj Siṁh, as one of the most important authors of his own times writing in Sanskrit. Many works are ascribed to Viśvanāth Siṁh[27] but the most important of them in the annals of Hindi

---

[24] Śukla, *Hindī sāhitya kā itihās*, pp. 310, 328, 439; the title page of *Ānand Raghunandan*. Also see Siṁh, *Ānand Raghunandan*, pp. I, II, IX, XII; Vijayendra Snātak, *Hindī sāhitya kā itihās*, Dillī: Sāhitya Akādemī, 1996, p. 172; Bhagīrath Miśra, ed., *Hindī sāhitya kā bṛhat itihās*, vol. 7, Vārāṇasī: NPS, 1972, p. 282. Cf. McGregor, *Hindi Literature from Its Beginnings*, p. 170 and Varmā, *Hindī sāhitya koś*, vol. 2, pp. 34. For more on the discussion of other works sometimes referred to as the earliest Hindi dramas see e.g. Somnāth Gupta, *Pūrva-Bhāratendu nāṭak sāhitya*, Jālandhar–Ilāhābād: Hindī Bhavan, 1958, pp. 15–45, 50–1; Gopīnāth Tivārī, *Bhāratendu kālīn nāṭak sāhitya (1850–1900 ī.)*, Jālandhar–Ilāhābād: Hindī Bhavan, 1959, pp. 11–91; Vinaymohan Śarmā, ed., *Hindī sāhitya kā bṛhat itihās*, vol. 8, Vārāṇasī: NPS, 1972, pp. 167–8, 315–16; cf. Devaṛṣi Sanāḍhya, *Hindī paurāṇik nāṭak*, Vārāṇasī: Caukhambā Vidyābhavan, 1961, pp. 97–9, 113.

[25] Varmā, *Hindī sāhitya kā ālocnātmak itihās*, p. 476; Siṁh, *Rāmbhakti*, pp. 431–3 and Śarmā, *Hindī sāhitya kā bṛhat itihās*, p. 41.

[26] Siṁh, *Rāmbhakti*, p. 434.

[27] Different sources enumerate up to 40 titles; see e.g. Siṁh, *Ānand Raghunandan*, p. III; Siṁh, *Rāmbhakti*, pp. 434–5; Miśra, *Hindī sāhitya kā bṛhat itihās*, p. 283 and Śarmā, *Hindī sāhitya kā bṛhat itihās*, p. 40.

literature is his above-mentioned drama in prose and verse in Braj *Ānand Raghunandan* (Blissful Raghunandan; ?1830). Thanks to this work, Viśvanāth Siṁh is referred to as the first author in Hindi literature who introduced prose to drama and divided his work into acts. Although in so doing he was referring to the tradition of Sanskrit drama, one should remember that it was a new step in the field of Hindi literature, where – due to different reasons – drama was not cultivated as a literary genre, practically till the nineteenth century. Therefore, *Ānand Raghunandan* is often considered to be the first drama in the Hindi language.

THE PLOT, THE STRUCTURE AND DRAMATIS PERSONAE

The exact date of *Ānand Raghunandan*, published for the first time in 1871 in Banaras by Lāyḍ Yantraṇālay,[28] is not known. According to some authors, it was written in the last decade of Viśvanāth Siṁh's life,[29] but according to others, it was composed some fifteen to twenty-five years before his death.[30] However, U.P. Śāh mentions a manuscript of 1830, which seems to be the earliest-known copy of this text, and, thus, 1830 appears to be the *terminus ante quem* of *Ānand Raghunandan*.[31]

The drama is divided into seven acts; six of them retell the deeds of Rām as known from tradition. The seventh, the last of them, depicts the life at his court; especially here the influence of the Rasik Sampradāy ideology is apparent – the act is full of dancing, singing and impressive descriptions of different types of heroines (*nāyikā bhed*).[32] The plot has a very interesting ending complying with the spirit of Rasik Sampradāy – Rām hands down his duties to his brothers, entrusting Bharat with the admin-

---

[28] See Siṁh, *Ānand Raghu-nandan*, p. I; Tivārī, *Bhāratendu kālīn nāṭak*, p. 44; Daśarath Ojhā, *Hindī nāṭak-koś*, Dillī: Neśanal Pabliśiṅg Hāus, 1975, p. 283 and McGregor, *Hindi Literature from Its Beginnings*, p. 170.

[29] Siṁh, *Ānand Raghunandan*, p. V.

[30] Miśra, *Hindī sāhitya kā bṛhat itihās*, p. 555 but also see p. 545.

[31] Umākānt Premānand Śāh, 'Ma. Viśvanāth Siṁh praṇīt "Saṅgīt Raghunandan"', in Ṛṣi Jaiminī Kauśik 'Baruā', ed., *Rāṣṭrakavi Maithilīśaraṇ Gupta abhinandangranth*, Kalkattā: M.G. Abhinandan Samiti, 1959, p. 734.

[32] Siṁh, *Ānand Raghunandan*, pp. 140–51.

istration of the kingdom, Lakṣmaṇ with its finances and giving Śatrughna command of the army. He does this with the intention of enjoying himself at his court.[33]

It is usually said that the basic story follows the *Rāmcaritmānas* but it seems more appropriate to see in it one of many tellings of the traditional story, in which – when compared with Tulsīdās' work – some episodes have been omitted, others shortened, still others extended, and some unconventional solutions introduced. The drama clearly betrays an interest in different episodes than its great predecessor. For example, Viśvanāth Siṁh does not mention the sacrifice of Daśarath at all; to the birth of Rām and his brothers and to their childhood he devotes only one verse. The events relating to Rām's investiture as Crown Prince and the intrigue, which prevented it and led to his banishment, is fashioned as a dialogue between two rivers, the Ganga and Yamuna. At the same time, a lot of attention and space have been devoted to the episode of Rām's stay in Chitrakut and, even to a greater extent, to the war on Lanka. The author also introduced into his drama the voice from heaven (*ākāśvāṇī*; indicated in the text as *ākāśe*), a traditional device that is used to foretell some events and complement others.[34]

Rām, the protagonist of *Ānand Raghunandan*, received the name Hitkārī, meaning literally 'Benefactor' (from Latin *bene facere* 'to do good'). He is portrayed as God, the Supreme Being, who shows, first of all, his human countenance; he is God who has descended to earth in order to change it into heaven.[35] It should be noted that this very interesting trait of the character of Rām anticipates the direction in which it evolved in the first half of the twentieth century in such works as Maithiliśaraṇ Gupta's *Sāket* (1932).[36]

Ānand Raghunandan may be viewed as a product of diversified sources and a relatively late culture. This is evident especially

---

[33] *Ḍahḍah Jagakārī tum rājya kī tatbīr karo. Ḍīl Dharādhar, tum koṣ kī tatbīr karo. Ḍimbhīdar tum senā kī tatbīr karo. Haũ gṛh bāg bihār karan jāv hõ*; Siṁh, *Ānand Raghunandan*, p. 152.

[34] Gupta, *Pūrva-Bhāratendu nāṭak*; p. 89.

[35] *Digsir daran, ran karan, sarvabhūt hitakārī, param puruṣ avatare*; Siṁh, *Ānand Raghunandan*, p. 40; cf. pp. XXXIX–XLIII.

[36] For more on this see Chapter Five in this study.

in the form of peculiar, allegoric names, such as: Hitkārī (Rām), Digjān (Daśarath), Ḍīl Dharādhar (Lakṣmaṇ), Ḍahḍah Jagakārī (Bharat), Jagadyonij (Vasiṣṭha), Bhuvan Hit (Viśvāmitra), Sugal (Hanumān), Dikśir (Rāvaṇ), or Bhayānak (Vibhīṣaṇ). These names, although in principle related to the most typical features of Rāmkathā characters or their deeds,[37] make it difficult to follow the plot easily; they have even been criticized as a futile and tasteless effort.[38]

It can be safely acknowledged that the major flaws in the construction of *Ānand Raghunandan* stem, firstly, from the accumulation of events – in a relatively small work of 153 pages, the entire story of Rām's deeds has been told – and, secondly, from the plethora of characters – there are thirty-two main male characters and eight female characters. The plot, therefore, appears to be very tangled and confusing and is additionally complicated by the unusual names of the characters. The audience, be they readers or the potential theatre public, would also have to face the use of different stylistic language registers.[39] Rather scanty stage directions in Sanskrit and Sanskritized solemn phrases are mixed with Braj, the predominant language of this work, and elements of other dialects and languages, e.g. Khariboli, Persian, and even Arabic and English (Act 7) are included.[40] Taking all this into consider-ation, a tough critic may say that *Ānand Raghunandan* is more interesting as a linguistic testimony of its own times than as a piece of belles lettres. However, Siṁh's drama also contains interesting material from the point of view of the development of the Rāmāyaṇa tradition, as it anticipates the direction of the evolution of the figure of Rām in the twentieth century. Above all, it prepared the ground for the further development of Hindi drama.

---

[37] Tivārī, *Bhāratendu kālīn nāṭak*, p. 38.

[38] Sanāḍhya, *Hindī paurāṇik nāṭak*, pp. 105–6; Gupta, *Pūrva-Bhāratendu nāṭak*, p. 87.

[39] Cf. Gupta, *Pūrva-Bhāratendu nāṭak*, pp. 87–8, 90 and Varmā, *Hindī sāhitya koś*, vol. 2, p. 34.

[40] E.g. Siṁh, *Ānand Raghunandan*, p. 151; cf. ibid., p. LXXIII and McGregor, *Hindi Literature from Its Beginnings*, pp. 170–1.

ĀNAND RAGHUNANDAN *AS THE FIRST HINDI DRAMA: AN APPRAISAL*

Different authors are almost unanimous that *Ānand Raghunandan* is the first Hindi work, in which the tradition of Sanskrit drama was revived, though some of them are in favour of the opinion that was first voiced by Bhāratendu Hariścandra. He maintained that the first attempt of that kind was made by Gopālcandra alias Giridhardās, i.e. Bhāratendu's father, in his drama entitled *Nahuṣ*, written in Braj probably some time between 1840 and 1859.[41] According to Hariścandra, the division into acts and other devices introduced in *Ānand Raghunandan* cannot compensate for the fact that its language is dominated by verse, and therefore this work cannot be considered as a drama.[42] Such an opinion betrays two facts. Firstly, thinking about the arrangement into acts and the dramatic devices implemented in Viśvanāth Siṁh's work, Bhāratendu meant exclusively the tradition of Sanskrit drama, dispensing with different indigenous forms of religious or popular drama such as Rāmlīlā, Rāslīlā, *nauṭaṅkī* or *svā̃g*. Secondly, stressing the necessity of the use of prose, he seems to be much under the influence of European, i.e. English, drama and even theatre of those times, which he had certainly become familiar with.[43] However, his opinion does not seem to give sufficient credit to the author of *Ānand Raghunandan*.

It is commonly known and repeated that Viśvanāth Siṁh divided his work into acts. However, a close investigation of the text proves that using such stage directions as *iti niṣkrāntaḥ sarve* ('all leave') followed with *saparikara devī praveśaḥ* ('entry of the chief queen with attendants')[44] he actually subdivided the acts into scenes.[45] Furthermore, he also regularly introduced other Sanskrit *didaskalía* and such scenic devices as off-stage lines, e.g. in order to inform the audience about the birth of Rām and his

---

[41] Tivārī, *Bhāratendu kālīn nāṭak*, pp. 121–2; Sanāḍhya, *Hindī paurāṇik nāṭak*, p. 97; Śukla, *Hindī sāhitya kā itihās*, pp. 375, 439 and Śarmā, *Hindī sāhitya kā bṛhat itihās*, pp. 168–70; cf. Siṁh, *Ānand Raghunandan*, p. III.

[42] After Śarmā, *Hindī sāhitya kā bṛhat itihās*, pp. 168–9.

[43] Ibid., p. 167.

[44] Siṁh, *Ānand Raghunandan*, p. 8.

[45] Ibid., p. XXXI.

brothers,[46] or a voice/voices from heaven (*ākāśe*). The drama also begins in a very conventional way with invocatory verses addressed to deities (*nāndī*), after which the stage-manager (*sūtradhār*) and his assistants (*māriṣ* and *paripārśvak*) enter the stage. Thus, it becomes obvious that Viśvanāth Siṁh followed more than only one aspect of the tradition of Sanskrit drama.[47] His work also draws one's attention to some other performing traditions. It seems probable that the (explicit) lack of the division of the text into scenes might be influenced by Rāmlīlā and Rāslīlā performances, in which the change of place and time is announced by means of dialogue.[48]

As far as the use of prose and verse in *Ānand Raghunandan* is concerned, one cannot deny that Viśvanāth Siṁh made ample use of verse in it, but also it cannot be denied that the dialogues are almost entirely in prose.[49] Subsequent authors, including Bhāratendu Hariścandra himself, employed a similar combination!

CONCLUSIONS

The features of *Ānand Raghunandan* mentioned in the preceding discussion, i.e. the way it is built and how the plot is constructed, suggest that it is reasonable to consider Siṁh's work as the first drama written in the Hindi region, in which its author made ample use of the traditional rules of Sanskrit drama, laid out as early as the *Nāṭyaśāstra*. Neither can one overlook other influences, especially of folk theatre traditions, however scanty they may be. Apart from this, of great importance is the way in which Viśvanāth Siṁh moulded the character of Rām that was subsequently further developed in important literary works in Hindi, such as Gupta's *Sāket*. Considering this as a meaningful contribution of *Ānand Raghunandan* to the development of Hindi literature,[50] nevertheless, I would prefer to avoid calling it 'the first Hindi drama', a claim that may be, and often is, misunder-

---

[46] Ibid., p. 4.

[47] Cf. Tivārī, *Bhāratendu kālīn nāṭak*, p. 39.

[48] Siṁh, *Ānand Raghunandan*, p. XXXII.

[49] Cf. Varma, *Hindī sāhitya kā alocnātmak itihās*, p. 478.

[50] Cf. Sanāḍhya, *Hindī paurāṇik nāṭak*, p. 105.

stood as 'the first **modern** Hindi drama'. Both the time of its creation and, to an even greater extent, its major language, i.e. Braj, testify against such labelling. Some critics would also like to add here the subject matter of this work but that would evidently be a blunder, as in Hindi literature there are many decidedly modern works which use mythological/epic narratives.[51]

Finally, referring to the title of this chapter, I would like to stress that Maharaja Viśvanāth Siṁh's drama is an excellent example of the work that stands on the threshold of modern Hindi drama. *Āṇand Raghunandan* is a very interesting specimen of a pre-modern work, which highlights many traits taken up and developed by conscious and unconscious followers of Viśvanāth Siṁh. One fact in this context, however, cannot be denied – *Ānand Raghunandan* is the first drama in the Hindi Ramaite tradition.[52]

* * *

Maharaja Raghurāj Siṁh, the son of Viśvanāth Siṁh, ascended the throne of Rewa after his father's death in 1854. He became famous as a generous ruler, keen hunter and devout Rāmbhakta. It is said that every day he read the Childhood Book of Vālmīki's *Rāmāyaṇa* and repeated the mantra of Rām twenty-four thousand times.[53] However, first of all he was a highly-regarded poet who wrote in Hindi and Sanskrit and also knew Persian and English. He composed about thirty works, the majority of which are devoted to Rām and in which he combines the attitude of *dāsyabhakti* with *mādhuryabhakti*.[54] The most important among these works is *Rāmsvayaṁvar* (1875),[55] a poem written in Avadhi.

---

[51] Cf. e.g. Śarmā, *Hindī sāhitya kā bṛhat itihās*, p. 166.

[52] Cf. Siṁh, *Rāmbhakti*, p. 434.

[53] Ibid., p. 470; cf. Varmā, *Hindī sāhitya koś*, vol. 2, p. 469.

[54] Siṁh, *Rāmbhakti*, pp. 471–2.

[55] Raghurāj Siṁh, *Rāmsvayaṁvar (saṅkṣipta)*, ed. Brajratnadās, Kāśī: NPS, 1924. For its date see Siṁh, *Rāmbhakti*, p. 472; cf. Varmā, *Hindī sāhitya koś*, vol. 2, p. 469 and Pāṇḍey, *Tulsīdāsottar hindī rāmsāhitya*, pp. 51–3. In fact this title is incorrect, it should be either *Sītāsvayaṁvar* (Sītā's Choice of Her Groom) or *Rāmvivāh* (The Marriage of Rām); cf. Pāṇḍey, *Tulsīdāsottar hindī rāmsāhitya*, p. 52.

Rāmsvayaṁvar is comprised of twenty-three chapters that almost exclusively deal with events from the Childhood Book with special attention paid to the marriage of Rām and of his brothers. The only exception is the last chapter in which events from the remaining books are dealt with which make the proportions of its structure ill-balanced.

It is evident from the title itself that the author was interested in Rām and Sītā's marriage. Its description is very detailed and colourful, as well as deeply set in the reality of nineteenth-century court life.[56] All this makes *Rāmsvayaṁvar* an interesting contribution to the Rāmāyaṇa tradition despite its compositional shortcomings. The Sanskritized language of Raghurāj Siṁh draws attention by its lightness and elegance. It is also worth adding in this context that many of his verses, especially some taken from *Rāmrasikāvalī* (Collection of a Rāmrasik), another of his works, are charcterized by extraordinary rhythm and melodiousness, thanks to which they have entered the canon of the favourite songs of Rasik Sampradāy.[57]

BANĀDĀS: A NINETEENTH-CENTURY SINGER OF RĀM'S GLORY[58]

THE LIFE AND WORKS OF THE POET

The name of Banādās (1821–92), a pious Rām devotee and one of the most important nineteenth-century exponents of Rāmbhakti in Ḥindi literature, although not altogether unknown to Hindi scholars, does not figure prominently in the works on the history of Hindi literature.[59] However, a deeper insight into Banādās's

---

[56] Siṁh, *Rāmbhakti*, pp. 472–3.

[57] Cf. ibid., p. 473.

[58] An earlier version of this section was published in *Cracow Indological Studies*, vols 4/5, 2004, pp. 517–25.

[59] Cf. McGregor, *Hindi Literature from Its Beginnings*, p. 171; Varmā, *Hindī sāhitya koś*, vol. 2, pp. 368–9; Varmā, *Hindī sāhitya kā alocnātmak itihās*, p. 481 and Dhīrendra Varmā et al., *Hindī sāhitya*, vol. 3, Prayāg: Bhāratīy Hindī Pariṣad, 1969, p. 12. Bhagavatīprasād Siṁh did remarkable work on Banādās; he, among other things, edited the works of Banādās; see Banādās, *Ubhay prabodhak rāmāyaṇ*, Ilāhābād: Lokbhāratī Prakāśan, 1980; idem, *Banādās bacanāmṛt*, Gorakhpur: Avadh Sāhitya

works and the way in which he combined in his devotional practice (*sādhanā*) different currents of Bhakti tradition, i.e. the predominantly *saguṇī* Rāmbhakti of his great sixteenth-century predecessor Tulsīdās, as well as elements of *nirguṇī sant* tradition and of the tradition of Rasik Sampradāy, proves that he deserves much more attention, especially in view of the opinion prevalent in most works on Hindi literature about the decidedly *saguṇī* character of north Indian Rāmbhakti.

Banādās[60] was born as Banāsiṁh, most probably in 1821, in a small village of Ashokpur, not far from Ayodhya. His family were Kshatriyas who made a living as farmers. Banādās is said to have already been inclined towards the world of religious practices in his childhood. However, due to his family background – learning was not a part of their tradition – and because of their very meagre means, Banādās could receive only a rudimentary education which he often regretted later in his life.[61] The situation of his family made him serve in the army of a local state for seven years. He returned home when he was about thirty-years old and not long after that his twelve-year-old son died. Grieving for the loss, Banādās set off to Ayodhya with the dead body of his only child. He settled there, first on Svargdvār Ghāṭ and then on Rām Ghāṭ. After some time he went on a pilgrimage to important north Indian religious centres (such as Kashi, Prayag, Chitrakut and Mithila)[62] and then he returned to Rām Ghāṭ, where for fourteen years (1856–69[63]) he practiced severe austerities, in which he identified himself with Bharat[64] (an ideal of bhakta for him), desiring to obtain a sight of his

---

Mandir, 1990 (including nine short works by Banādās, also fragmentary) and idem, *Bismaran samhār*, 2nd edn, Ayodhyā: Mahātmā Banādās Āśram, 1998 (1st published 1990). Siṁh is also the author of the already-quoted Banādās's literary biography: Siṁh, *Mahātmā Banādās*.

[60] For more details on the life of Banādās see Siṁh, *Mahātmā Banādās*, pp. 3–62; cf. Banādās, *Ubhay prabodhak rāmāyaṇ* (henceforth abbreviated in references as UPR), pp. XXXI–XL; Siṁh, *Rāmbhakti*, pp. 481–4; idem, *Bismaran samhār*, pp. 6–15, and Varmā, *Hindī sāhitya koś*, vol. 2, pp. 368–9.

[61] Siṁh, *Mahātmā Banādās*, p. 5 and idem, 'Mahātmā Banādās: jīvan paricay', in Banādās, *Bismaran samhār*, p. 6; cf. e.g. UPR, 1.2.29, p. 29.

[62] Siṁh, 'Mahātmā Banādās: jīvan paricay', p. 9.

[63] Ibid., pp. 9–10 and Siṁh, *Mahātmā Banādās*, p. 36.

[64] Cf. UPR, *Mūlkhaṇḍ* (46), p. 16.

beloved God (*iṣṭdev kā darśan*) in which he finally succeeded.[65] Then he settled on a small plot of land near the then Victoria Park (present Tulsī Udyān, i.e. Tulsi Park), which became the place of his ashram called Bhavharaṇ Kuñj. After some time (*c*.1882[66]) a temple dedicated to Rām was built there thanks to a donation by the already-mentioned Maharaja Raghurāj Siṁh. Banādās lived in his ashram till the end of his life and he died there in 1892, i.e. in the year of the publication of his *Ubhay prabodhak rāmāyaṇ*.[67]

Banādās began his literary activity in 1851 just before renouncing the world. He began his first work, *Arzpatrikā* (1851), when he still lived at home but finished it in Ayodhya. It was also during that time, as it appears from his works, that he acquired his new name, Banādās.[68] Tradition holds that he wrote sixty-four works and Bhagavatīprasād Siṁh managed to identify sixty-two of them.[69] Among them, there are also two versions of the Rāmāyaṇa, i.e. the *Anurāg vivardhak rāmāyaṇ* (Devotion Increasing Rāmāyaṇ; ?1858[70]) and the *Ubhay prabodhak rāmāyaṇ* (Doubly Illuminating Rāmāyaṇ; 1874[71]). However, up till the present only

---

[65] Siṁh, *Rāmbhakti mẽ rasik sampradāy*, p. 483 and idem, *Mahātmā Banādās*, pp. 35–6.

[66] Idem, *Mahātmā Banādās*, p. 39.

[67] Ibid., pp. 1–62, 110 and idem, *Rāmbhakti*, pp. 481–4.

[68] Idem, *Mahātmā Banādās*, pp. XVI and 31; see also note 124 below.

[69] Sixty-four may be either the number of works actually written by Banādās or a symbolic number often encountered in Indian tradition. Idem, *Mahātmā Banādās*, pp. V–X, XVI, XVIII, 63–7. Cf. idem, *Rāmbhakti*, pp. 484–5; idem, *Bismaran samhār*, p. 119 and Aniruddh Siṁh, 'Mahātmā Banādās', in Uday Pratāp Siṁh, ed., *Rām bhakti sāhitya: anveṣak aur rāhī (Pro. Bhagavatī Siṁh jīvan aur darśan)*, Mahātmā Banādās Sevā Samiti: Ayodhyā, 1999, p. 319.

[70] According to Siṁh (idem, *Mahātmā Banādās*, pp. 74–6), fragments of the Beautiful Book as well as the entire Later Book were available to him. However, the collected works of Banādās, i.e. *Banādās bacanāmṛt* edited by Siṁh and published in 1990, include only the Later Book with minor fragments missing from it.

[71] *sambata sahasra navasa (..) ekatīsa*; UPR, 2.2.36, p. 66. It should be noted that stanzas within the respective books of UPR are usually counted only up to one hundred and then the numbering starts from the beginning (but see e.g. pp. 39–40). Therefore, it is necessary (unlike in the most popular editions of the *Rāmcaritmānas*) to give a page number also. In the notation employed in the present analysis, numerals given as first

eleven of his works were published: *Ubhay prabodhak rāmāyaṇ* and *Bismaran samhār* have been published separately, and nine works, i.e. *Arzpatrikā, Nām nirūpaṇ, Rāmpañcāṅg, Surasari pañca ratna* (only five stanzas on one page), *Vivekmuktāvalī, Rām chaṭā, Garaj patrī, Mohinī aṣṭak* and *Anurāg vivardhak rāmāyaṇ* (only the Later Book) are included in *Banādās bacanāmṛt*, a collection edited by Bhagavatīprasād Siṁh.

Ubhay prabodhak rāmāyaṇ, a sizable poem in Avadhi,[72] is the most important of Banādās's works. Its author employed in it different metres among which *ghanākṣarī, chappay* and *savaiyā* predominate. The contents of the poem conveys several layers of Banādās's message in which he expounded the twofold nature of his chosen God Rām – the *nirguṇ*, unqualified Ultimate Being, and the *saguṇ*, qualified Lord – along with the significance of his Name, mediating between these two aspects of Rām's nature. *Ubhay prabodhak rāmāyaṇ* represents an important current in Rāmbhakti that is said to be especially common among the holy men (*sādhus*) of Ayodhya. However, to limit its influence only to them seems to be obscuring the fact that it has also become part and parcel of the commonly practiced Rāmbhakti. It can be best realized from the already-mentioned fact of the widespread popularity of Rāmbhakti in north India that does almost without temples dedicated exclusively to Rām – being practically limited to the sacred places of Rāmbhakti – and from a strong belief, expressed on a number of occasions by Rāmbhaktas, that Rām is contained, enshrined in his name which is inscribed on their souls, minds, hearts (*man*).[73]

In *Ubhay prabodhak rāmāyaṇ* Banādās, like his many predecessors, narrated the story of Rām's deeds. And like most of them, he did it not just for the sake of retelling it – he made it an occasion

---

refer to a book, numerals given as second and third refer to the number of a verse and a stanza, respectively. If only one numeral follows the number of a book it designates the number of a stanza.

[72] For more on the language of Banādās's see Siṁh, *Mahātmā Banādās*, pp. 295–317.

[73] Our attention may be drawn to popular chromolithograph representations of Hanumān, an accomplished Rāmbhakta, where he is shown with Rām's name (or with his image or the image of the couple Sītā-Rām) visible inside his, torn open, chest.

to deal with the nature of Rām, simultaneously unmanifested, impersonal, all-pervading, unqualified (*nirguṇ*), and manifested, personal, qualified (*saguṇ*). In order to achieve his aim, Banādās composed his poem in such a way that it can be interpreted in two ways: firstly, in terms of this world (*laukik*) with Rām in his *saguṇ* form and, secondly, in terms of the spiritual world (*ādhyātmik*) with Rām in his *nirguṇ* form. This intention is contained in the title of the poem, where 'double illumination' first of all refers to these two aspects of Rām's nature.[74] Of course, Banādās, having given such a title to his poem, framed its text deliberately.[75] He drew the inspiration from a fragment of Tulsīdās's *Rāmcarit-mānas*[76] that reconciles both these aspects and stresses the extra-ordinary role played by his name. The most crucial in this context is the *Rāmcaritmānas* verse saying:

> *The name is a glorious witness to the unqualified and the qualified;*
> *Like a skilful interpreter illuminating [the nature] of them both.*[77]

Bhagavatīprasād Siṁh in his preface to *Ubhay prabodhak rāmāyaṇ* points out[78] that Banādās in his understanding of Rām referred, among other things, to the *sant* tradition, namely to the type of Bhakti represented in Hindi literature by Kabīr. In this context, one should remember that much later in the sphere of Rāmbhakti itself it was practised by Tulsī Sāhib (?1763-1843[79]), who considered himself to be an avatār of Tulsīdās in his poem *Ghaṭ rāmāyaṇ*.[80] Even though its title may suggest that it narrates

---

[74] See Siṁh, *Mahātmā Banādās*, p. 215.

[75] Cf. Lutgendorf, *The Life of a Text*, esp. pp. 18ff.

[76] RCM 1.19.1–28.1; cf. Siṁh, *Mahātmā Banādās*, pp. 14–15.

[77] *aguna saguna bica nāma susākhī; ubhaya prabodhaka catura dubhāṣī*; RCM 1.21.4. Cf. e.g. UPR 2.1.70, p. 53: *aguna saguna doū rūpana ko bodha karai eka rāmanāma nahī̃ dūsare ko kāma jū.*

[78] UPR, p. XI; also see Siṁh, *Bismaran samhār*, p. 120.

[79] Tulsī Sāhib, *Ghaṭ rāmāyaṇ*, vol. 1, Ilāhābād: Belvīḍiyar Priṇṭiṅg Varks, 1997, p. III; cf. Harsvarūp Māthur, *Bhāratīy sādhanā aur Sant Tulsī*, Kānpur: Sāhitya Niketan, 1965, p. 104.

[80] The relationship between the theologies and practices of Tulsī Sāhib and Kabīr Panth, i.e. Kabīr's sect, is expounded in an extremely interesting dialogue between Tulsī Sāhib and a Kabīr Panthī saint

Rāmkathā, in fact it is structured as a series of dialogues in which Tulsī Sāhib discusses Rām's nature as the unqualified absolute (*nirguṇ brahman*) with different *sant*s. Although Tulsī Sāhib's work did not become popular and thus did not prove very successful, Banādās's poem bears witness to the continual search in this field of interest. At the same time, both Tulsī Sāhib's failure and Banādās's poem also testify to the importance ascribed by Rāmbhaktas to the qualified, personal form of Rām and therefore to the story of his life and deeds inseparably connected with it.[81]

UBHAY PRABODHAK RĀMĀYAṆ: *DOUBLE ILLUMINATION OF RĀMKATHĀ*

Banādās's poem is divided into seven books understood as subsequent steps on the path of devotional practice.[82] These books are preceded by an unnumbered *Mūl khaṇḍ* (Primary Book),[83] which forms a kind of a prologue common not only to many tellings of the story of Rām's deeds but, speaking more generally, to narratives rooted in oral tradition. Its aim is to prepare the reader/listener for the proper reception of the text as it places it within contexts that provide clues for understanding its message.[84] Therefore, after a short invocation to the Guru and the chosen deity, Banādās offers a short retelling of Rām's deeds pointing out the main ideals and objectives of his devotion. The seven following books, as has just been mentioned, can be interpreted in two ways – as a Rāmkathā, i.e. a retelling of the deeds of God Rām in his human form, and as a discourse on the nature of Rām as the unqualified Ultimate Being, understanding of which is essential in the spiritual practice of a bhakta striving towards liberation. Although, they are both in fact treated by Banādās as identical (see below), their specific hierarchy is alluded to elsewhere in a very apt way and refers to Banādās's spiritual progress as articulated in his works:

Phūldās; Tulsī Sāhib, *Ghaṭ rāmāyaṇ*, vol. 1, pp. 169–92 and idem, *Ghaṭ rāmāyaṇ*, vol. 2, Ilāhābād: Belvīḍiyar Prinṭiṅg Varks, 1981, pp. 1–28.

[81] Stasik, *Opowieść*, p. 215.

[82] Cf. UPR, pp. XVI–XIX.

[83] Ibid., pp. 1–22.

[84] Lutgendorf, *The Life of a Text*, pp. 18–23.

First I wrote 'Rāmāyaṇa', which is the book of devotion,
and then 'Brahmāyaṇa', which is the path of knowledge.[85]

In the first book of his poem, *Guru khaṇḍ* (Guru Book),[86] Banādās says that it was Tulsīdās, with whose works he had been familiar since childhood,[87] who had encouraged him to write the poem. Tulsīdās appeared in Banādās's dream and gave him his blessing.[88] Banādās considers his own poetry to be Tulsīdās's prasād (*kāvya banādāsa kī gosāī kī prasādī hai*).[89] Thus in this book, on the one hand, Banādās makes known whom he considers to be his guru and, on the other hand, he tells that a teacher's support is indispensable in devotional practice.[90]

Book 2, *Nām khaṇḍ* (Name Book),[91] reveals that repeating Rām's name (*rāmnāmjap*) was the basic principle of Banādās's devotional practice, thanks to which he was able to understand the nature of his God.[92] The author thus teaches that the Name is absolutely essential on the path of devotion; its chanting (*nāmajapa*) is the first step on this path.

Book 3, *Ayodhyā khaṇḍ* (Ayodhya Book),[93] opens with praising different gods and deities, *sant*s, the four Vedas, Rām and Sītā, Tulsīdās, the name of Rām, etc.[94] and after this Banādās's reflections on the nature of the Rāmāyaṇa tradition follow. He underlines its decidedly oral nature based on the interaction between

---

[85] *pahle rāmāyana bhayo jo hai upāsanā grantha; pīche brahmāyana bhayo jo hai jñāna ko pantha; Brahmāyandvār,* quoted in: UPR, p. XIII and Siṁh, *Mahātmā Banādās,* p. 75 (wordings of both quotations differ slightly).

[86] UPR, pp. 25–42. For unknown reasons B. Siṁh repeats in his publications (Siṁh, *Mahātmā Banādās,* pp. 112, 221 and UPR, p. XVII) that *Guru khaṇḍ* is the second book coming after *Nām khaṇḍ.* It stands in obvious contradiction both with the UPR edition prepared by Siṁh himself, where *Guru khaṇḍ* is printed on pages 25–40 and *Nām khaṇḍ* on pages 43–58, and the textual evidence of the poem itself: *prathamahī gurukhaṇḍa dūje nāmakhaṇḍa bhayo;* UPR, p. 66 (1.1.37).

[87] E.g. UPR, 1.3–4, p. 25; 1.32 and 34, p. 29.

[88] Ibid., 1.2.8–4.9, p. 26.

[89] Ibid., 1.1.3, p. 25; cf. Siṁh, *Mahātmā Banādās,* p. 210.

[90] UPR, 1.90–2, p. 37.

[91] Ibid., pp. 43–58.

[92] E.g. ibid., 2.2.2, 2.4.11, 2.38, 2.53–6, 2.70, 2.88–91, 2.104–6.

[93] Ibid., pp. 61–190.

[94] Ibid., 3.1.15, pp. 4–8.

the narrator and the listener[95] (*vaktā-śrotā paramparā*) and also introduces his own telling, giving the date of its creation and presenting its contents in brief.[96] Then the narrative proper follows, and in the main outline agrees with the *Rāmcaritmānas*.[97] It begins with Rām's birth[98] leading up to Sītā's *svayaṁvar*, their marriage[99] and life in Ayodhya.[100] Numerous passages encountered in this book, such as the descriptions of Rām, his capital, his companions and their joyful life,[101] are typical of the works of Rasik Sampradāy. In terms of *sādhanā*, this book teaches that living up to one's dharma is a precondition for any kind of advancement on the path of Bhakti.[102]

Book 4, *Vipin khaṇḍ* (Forest Book),[103] is the longest and it comprises well over a third of the whole poem. It narrates the events starting from the preparations for the ceremony of Rām's investiture as Crown Prince (*abhiṣeka*; 4.3ff[104]), Mantharā and Kaikeyī's plot leading to his fourteen-year banishment to the forest (4.3.13ff),[105] the kidnapping of Sītā by Rāvaṇ (4.67ff[106]), Rām's victory over Rāvaṇ (4.6ff[107]) and his winning Sītā back (4.13–16), up to his triumphant return to Ayodhya (4.72[108]). The focus of this book is on the fourteen years of the forest exile, which in terms of the devotional practice should be seen as fourteen years of ascetic renouncement, essential for a bhakta eager to understand the nature of his God. Here Banādās clearly refers to his own experience.

---

[95] Ibid., 3.26–35, pp. 64–6.

[96] Ibid., 3.36, p. 66.

[97] Siṁh, *Mahātmā Banādās*, p. 216.

[98] UPR, 3.15.94, p. 90.

[99] Ibid., 3.86ff, p. 143ff.

[100] Ibid., 3.52–4, pp. 187–8.

[101] E.g. ibid., pp. 98–101, 103–4, 154–7.

[102] Cf. ibid., p. XVIII.

[103] Ibid., pp. 193–441.

[104] Ibid., pp. 193–4.

[105] Kaikeyī expresses her wish with the following words: *rāja bharata ko dījie prathamai yaha baradāna; barṣa cāridasa rāma bana dūjo puni paramāna*; ibid., 4.1–2.53, p. 201

[106] Ibid., pp. 297ff.

[107] Ibid., pp. 412ff.

[108] Ibid., p. 424.

Book 5, *Vihār khaṇḍ* (Wander Book),[109] is considered with later events in Rām's life. It opens with praise of the greatness of Rāmrājya,[110] which is so glorious thanks to, among other things, Sītā being always present at her husband's side (5.1–28[111]). Then Rām, disturbed by the lack of news from Vibhīṣaṇ, decides to go to Lanka (5.29). He leaves with Bharat and Hanumān. On their way, they visit the most important places of his fourteen-year exile such as Shringaverapura, Bharadvāja's ashram in Prayag, Agastya's ashram, Chitrakut, Panchavati, Kishkindha, Mithila, and Kashi. This journey, during which he teaches Bharat, Vibhīṣaṇ (who joins Rām during his journey) and others about the nature of Bhakti (e.g. 5.5–32 and 38–44[112]), brings to mind Rām's journey in the *Ānanda rāmāyaṇa*.[113] The difference between them is that the version of Banādās takes the main interest in the pilgrimage centres concerned with Rām and not in the sacred places of Hinduism in general, the only exception being Śiv's city, i.e. Kashi. After Rām's return to Ayodhya the ritual of *aśvamedha* is performed (the text mentions 'innumerable *aśvamedhas*'[114]) what seems to refer symbolically to the triumph of Rāmbhakti. This book is meant to illuminate the real nature of things and to attain the highest truth about Rām.

Book 6, *Jñān khaṇḍ* (Knowledge Book),[115] opens with Rām's account of the greatness of Rāmbhakti.[116] Then he proceeds to explain the meaning of the path of renouncement (*vairāgya*) essential for all living creatures/souls caught in the snares of existence. Next, a series of instructions given by him to his brothers and Hanumān follow. First Hanumān wants to learn about the meaning of *jñān*, i.e. the knowledge of the identity of the self with

---

[109] Ibid., pp. 445–516.

[110] A short description of Rām's rule also comes at the end of this book; ibid., 5.45, p. 513.

[111] Ibid., pp. 445–50.

[112] Ibid., pp. 465–70, 492–3.

[113] The earliest accounts of Rām's journeys are found in the Purāṇas (e.g. *Nṛsiṁha, Skanda* and *Padma*). They also form the core of *Yātrākāṇḍa*, the second book of *Ānanda rāmāyaṇa*. See Introduction in this study and Bulke, *Rāmkathā*, pp. 497–9. Cf. Siṁh, *Mahātmā Banādās*, p. 224.

[114] *asvamedha aganita kiye*; UPR, p. 513.

[115] Ibid., pp. 519–600.

[116] *merī bhakti*; ibid., 6.2.2, p. 519.

the Ultimate Being. Rām teaches him that the individual soul (*jīva*) free from sensual enjoyment becomes aware of this unity.[117] Then Śatrughna asks Rām to enlighten him as to the nature of higher consciousness (*vijñān*; 6.37–47.2[118]) necessary in order to become one with the Ultimate Being (*kaivalya*), Lakṣmaṇ wants Rām to teach them about the nature of *kaivalya* (6.47.3–56.2) and Bharat asks him to unfold the essence of ultimate Bhakti (*parābhakti*; 6.56.3–67). Finally, Rām sums up his teachings. In this book, Banādās conveys the fundamental message of his teachings – the identity of ultimate Bhakti (*parābhakti*) attained by means of *saguṇsādhanā* with *kaivalya* reached as a result of *nirguṇsādhanā*, thus he teaches the identity of knowledge (*jñān*) with devotion, i.e. Bhakti, as well as the identity of *nirguṇ* with *saguṇ*.[119]

In Book 7, *Śānti khaṇḍ* (Quiet Book),[120] Rām instructs his brothers and Hanumān in the meaning of *śānti*, understood both as the fundamental ground for devotional practices and their real aim that is more important than liberation (*mukti*).[121] From the point of view of *sādhanā*, these teachings reveal that ultimate tranquility (*paramviśrām*) is identical with *jīvanmukti*, i.e. the release while living.[122]

The analysis of *Ubhay prabodhak rāmāyaṇ* seems to substantiate the contention that Banādās's telling of Rāmkathā is, first and

---

[117] *viṣaya bāsanārahita jīva jaba bhayo saceta;/ pāyo merā jñāna tabai advai ko betā;/ doū bhaye abheda* (…); ibid., 6.3–5.33, p. 525.

[118] Ibid., pp. 526–8.

[119] Cf. ibid., p. XIX.

[120] Ibid., pp. 603–43.

[121] See e.g. *sānti sādhu sṛṅgāra sānti bina santa na hoī;/ (…) jaise saritā nīra bina sānti binā sādhū ahai*, 7.7, pp. 604; *mṛgana māhī mṛgarāja jimi timi muktina mẽ sānti hai*, 7.12.7, p. 605; *saba sādhana kī mahā sidhi nahī̃ sānti te mukti hai*, 7.16.5, p. 606; *sānti siromani hai sabko jehi āye kachū nahī aur suhāī*, 7.88.1, p. 639; *sādhana nakhata sāre bhānu se prakāsa sānti muktina me mukhya mukti jānata sujāna hai*, 7.89.1, p. 639; *bhakti dūdha jñāna dadhi mākhana bijñāna jānau sānti sudha sarapi sukhada saba kāla hai*, 7.2.1, p. 641; *banādāsa jaise rāma nāma saba nāmana mẽ yāhī bhā̃ti muktina mẽ sānti mere jāna hai*, 7.4.4, p. 641; *sānti sama koū sidhi na pramāna hai*, 7.7.4, p. 641; *sānti binā nahī jīvana mukta bhalī bidhi beda purāna picāno*, 7.9.3, p. 642; *…jo na sānti lahe sakalau srama ko phala tau nahī pāye*, 7.10.4, p. 642 (repeated in 7.11.4, 12.4 and 13.4).

[122] Cf. ibid., p. XIX.

foremost, a splendid occasion for its author to expound his own understanding of Bhakti theory and practice. On the one hand, according to him Bhakti and knowledge, which are in fact one, are the means thanks to which a bhakta can reach the state of quiet (*śānti*) that he understands as the release during lifetime. On the other hand, the concepts of the unqualified and the qualified God must yield finally to the significance of the Name, which unifies them both.[123] It may be noted that Banādās in his interpretation of the nature of Rām as the Absolute 'dual in its unity' (*dvaitādvaita*) did not create a new concept but referred to the doctrine of *bhedābheda,* i.e. 'difference in non-difference', developed by Nimbarka. However, he was a pioneer of such an interpretation in relation to Rām in Hindi literature.[124]

The fact that in his *Anurāg vivardhak rāmāyaṇ* Banādās calls himself a 'sweet servant by the grace of Sītā and Rām' (*siyā rāma kṛpā te madhura dāsa*)[125] is also of great interest. Thus, he assumes the attitude of their most faithful 'sweet' servant and propagates *madhur dāsya bhāv,* another attitude towards Rām which combines *mādhurya bhāv,* i.e. that is the attitude towards God typical for Rasik Sampradāy, with *dāsya bhāv,* i.e. the attitude prevalent among the majority of Rāmbhaktas and the expounder of which was Tulsīdās. This is the reason why in *Ubhay prabodhak rāmāyaṇ,* evidently inspired by Tulsīdās's poem,[126] in addition to the already-mentioned descriptions[127] one can find a detailed account of Sītā's birth, her childhood and youth, as well as of the mutual affection of Sītā and Rām.[128]

It can be said that various elements of Banādās's teachings that are a mixture of different Bhakti traditions coalesce into a whole that at times appears to be rather eclectic which by itself

---

[123] Cf. McGregor, *Hindi Literature from Its Beginnings,* p. 171.

[124] Siṁh, *Mahātmā Banādās,* p. 209; also see Varmā, *Hindī sāhitya kā alocnātmak itihās,* p. 481.

[125] Banādās, 'Anurāg vivardhak rāmāyaṇ', *chand* 178, in idem, *Banādās bacanāmṛt,* p. 33. Cf. Siṁh, *Mahātmā Banādās,* pp. 203–4 and idem, *Rāmbhakti,* p. 484 where he adds that Banādās (lit. 'bridegroom's servant') was given this name by Rām himself, when on the occasion of his marriage Banādās accompanied him to Mithila.

[126] Siṁh, *Mahātmā Banādās,* p. 216 and UPR, p. XX.

[127] Cf. note 101 above and Siṁh, *Mahātmā Banādās,* pp. 218–20.

[128] UPR, pp. 105–7 (3.10.69–87).

should not be surprising in view of the poet's difficult and long journey to learning. It must also be admitted that it is not a great accomplishment as a literary work, although it cannot be denied features of originality. However, there is no doubt that *Ubhay prabodhak rāmāyaṇ* deserves more attention from literary and religious scholars not only for the reasons given in the foregoing discussion but also for at least two more reasons. First of all, its importance as revealing evidence of the Rāmbhakti of the latter part of the nineteenth century is unquestionable. Second, and it is maybe even more important, almost the same views as those expressed by Banādās in his *Ubhay prabodhak rāmāyaṇ* are still alive among practising Rāmbhaktas and the evidence found in the text of the already-mentioned *Mānas pīyūṣ*, the most influential and commonly used commentary on the *Rāmcaritmānas*, also corroborates this. Summing up this discussion, I would like to stress that, taking into consideration the way in which Banādās presented the story of Rām as well as its philosophical and theological contents, his *Ubhay prabodhak rāmāyaṇ* undoubtedly appears as the most interesting testimony of Rāmbhakti in the second half of the nineteenth century.

CONCLUSIONS

Considering Rāmkathās of the nineteenth century in their entirety, especially those written in Khariboli Hindi, the new literary vehicle of north India, one should remember that original works (with minor exceptions) started appearing in the second half of the nineteenth century. Earlier works in Khariboli Hindi in the majority were adaptations and translations, written mainly as teaching materials for foreigners. With Khariboli Hindi acquiring the role of a convenient literary medium and the growing belief in the potential of literature and its role in educating modern society, authors started to call for progress, enlightenment of society and stressed the achievements of contemporary (Western) science and culture. In their admiration for modernity not much space was left for narrating stories of such traditional heroes as Rām or Kṛṣṇa. Making them objects of interest of literary works for a long time was considered not only to be against the spirit of the time but also a repetition of what had already been said a long time ago. Even Rāmcandra Śukla (1884–1941), one of the most eminent historians and critics of Hindi literature, referred to earlier in this study, maintained that 'it is sheer stupidity to transform ancient characters or events to suit the spirit of the modern age'.[129] Thus, it should not be surprising that works turning for inspiration to the Rāmāyaṇa tradition for some time remained outside the scope of transformations taking place in the literature of those days and it had took a long time before works offering a new approach to Rāmkathā started appearing (novels were last ones in this regard).

However, the growing national awareness of the Indians and an attempt, related to this, at defining Indian identity were important factors adding to this change at the turn of the nineteenth and twentieth centuries. It was a period when referring to one's own tradition, of which Rām and Kṛṣṇa were part and parcel, seemed required. This was also the challenge with which authors looking for inspiration in Rāmkathā were to face soon.

[129] Quoted after Rāma Dhārī Singh 'Dinkara', 'Maithilīśaraṇa Gupta as a Poet of the Renaissance', in Nagendra, ed., *Maithilīśaraṇa Gupta: An Anthology*, Delhi: Bansal & Co., 1981, p. 99.

CHAPTER FIVE

Modernizing the Tradition: Rāmkathās of the First Half of the Twentieth Century

INTRODUCTION: CONTEXTUALIZING RĀMKATHĀS

As I have already mentioned, the turn of the nineteenth and twentieth centuries in India were characterized by the growing importance of the national movement. It was inseparable from the change in the attitude of Indians towards their history and cultural heritage which they began to view as an excellent vehicle helpful in defining and consolidating the identity of the Indian nation on its way to progress. In the literature of that period, an intensive search for patterns suitable for this purpose is apparent and towards the end of the nineteenth century the growing interest in India's past and its traditional values and heroes becomes more and more evident.

The year 1903, when Mahāvīrprasād Dvivedī (1864–1938[1]) became the editor of *Sarasvatī*[2] (one of the most important Hindi journals of those times), marks the beginning of a new period in Hindi literature. Dvivedī continued to be the editor of *Sarasvatī* until 1920 and during all those years, in its pages, he exerted an immense influence on the development of the standards of modern Hindi and on the literature written in it. Many of his contemporaries considered him a great authority and the fact that the first two decades of the twentieth century in Hindi literature are referred to as the Dvivedī period (*dvivedīkāl*) testifies to the extent of his influence.

He was an advocate of the kind of literature that can be viewed as engagé, meant to serve the strengthening of national feelings and social responsibility. The suitable vehicles for such ideas were, for example, epic characters and mythological heroes endowed with explicit human features. On the one hand, they

---

[1] Varmā, *Hindī sāhitya koś*, vol. 2, p. 438 and Peter Gaeffke, *Hindi Literature in the Twentieth Century*, Wiesbaden: Otto Harrassowitz, 1978, p. 16; cf. Śukla, *Hindī sāhitya*, p. 485.

[2] The publication of *Sarasvatī* was started in 1900 under the aegis of NPS; Varmā, *Hindī sāhitya koś*, vol. 2, p. 619.

personified the magnificence of India's past and served to contrast the golden period of Indian culture with a very imperfect present-day. On the other hand, these characters were transferred, to a greater or smaller degree, into modern times in which they were to act for the benefit of reviving the glory of the past. Descending from heaven of such mythical heroes whose human characteristics became very marked and the naïve trust that the glorious past of Hindu India could be restored to life thanks to social reform and earnest patriotism were the most characteristic features of this period. They found their fullest expression in national poetry, referring to the indigenous cultural heritage (*rāṣṭrīy[-sāṁskṛtik] kāvya*), that emerged during those times. Some time later the socio-political thought of Gandhi that is strongly rooted, among other things, in the Rāmāyaṇa tradition, as far as his ideas about the state and the ruler with the important role of Rāmrājya are concerned, also exerted a significant influence on the authors of that period.

Works inspired by the story of the deeds of Rām, who was then regarded not only as God but, primarily, as the leader of his people, their benefactor and protector, were appearing during the entire period. The focus of the discussion in this chapter will be these works of the first half of the twentieth century that constitute the most interesting contribution to the Rāmāyaṇa tradition. Thus, special attention will be paid to Maithilīśaraṇ Gupta's (1886–1964) poem *Sāket* (1932), which is considered to be one of the most important works in Hindi literature. It also seems to best exemplify, in the most accomplished form, the attitude to the Rāmāyaṇa of the authors active during that time.

TRANSFORMING POETICAL UTTERANCE

Opening this survey with a discussion of poetical works seems most natural in view of the fact that the majority of works dealing with Rāmkathā of the period under consideration are in verse.

One of the most important examples in this regard is Rāmcarit Upādhyāy's (1872–1938[3]) *Rāmcaritcintāmaṇi* (Miraculous

---

[3] Śukla, *Hindī sāhitya kā itihās*, p. 591 and Varmā, *Hindī sāhitya koś*, vol. 2, p. 509.

Jewel of Rām's Deeds; *c.*1913[4]) considered to be the first narrative poem (*prabandhkāvya*) in Khariboli Hindi that deals with Rāmkathā.[5] Upādhyāy, regularly published his poems loaded with a reformist and patriotic message in *Sarasvatī*, was under the great influence of Dvivedī.

His *Rāmcaritcintāmaṇi* consists of twenty-five untitled chapters (*sarga*) of uneven length that narrate the story following the tradition of Vālmīki[6] and not Tulsīdās. Conse-quently, it deals with the episode of the banishment of Sītā, the birth of Lav and Kuś at Vālmīki's ashram, the killing of Śambūk, a Shudra ascetic, as well as the *aśvamedha* performed by Rām which was interrupted by his sons. Upādhyāy attempted to adapt the traditional story for modern reality, first of all investing its hero, Rām, with more human features. His effort, however, proved unsuccessful as his telling does not add much to what was known from tradition. The language of the poem is noteworthy for its simple and lucid style and lively dialogues. Therefore, although the work as a whole is not innovative from the point of view of its contents, it managed to win some, however short-lived, popularity thanks to its skilful form.[7]

Upādhyāy is also the author of a collection of poems entitled *Rāmcaritcandrikā*[8] that is concerned, as its subtitle clearly indicates, with delineating the character of the protagonists of Rāmkathā. For example, Rām is dealt with in twenty-eight quatrains as a traditional paragon of all the virtues, god giving happiness to people and their teacher.[9] Upādhyāy uses the past tense in relation to Rām which may seem striking at first reading. A close reading, however, proves that it is an interesting device that helps to build a distance between the modern author and the past to which Rām evidently belongs. Nevertheless, belonging to the

---

[4] Pāṇḍey, *Tulsīdāsottar hindī rāmsāhitya*, p. 91. Rāmcarit Upādhyāy, *Rāmcaritcintāmaṇi. Khaṛībolī kā ek kāvya*, 2nd edn, Bākīpur: Granthmālā Kāryālay, 1929.

[5] Pāṇḍey, ibid.

[6] Rāmdahin Miśra, 'Prastāvnā', in Upādhyāy, *Rāmcaritcintāmaṇi*, p. I.

[7] Varmā, *Hindī sāhitya koś*, vol. 2, p. 509; Śukla, *Hindī sāhitya*, pp. 593–4 and Pāṇḍey, *Tulsīdāsottar hindī rāmsāhitya*, pp. 93–6.

[8] Rāmcarit Upādyāy, *Rāmcaritcandrikā arthāt rāmāyaṇ ke pradhān pātr kā caritra-citraṇātmak ek sphuṭ kāvya*, Bākīpur: Granthmālā Kāryālay, 1919.

[9] Ibid., pp. 16–22.

past, he does not cease to be the guide of people through the medium of his deeds.[10]

An early poetic attempt by Jayaśaṅkar Prasād (1889–1937), one of the most eminent Hindi poets, a short poem *Citrakūṭ*, is worth noting here, though it does not deal with the entire Rāmkathā. This work, included in Prasād's collection *Kānan kusum* (Wild Flowers),[11] depicts the beauty of Chitrakut and the happy life of Rām and Sītā there, interrupted by Lakṣmaṇ's anger and the dilemma raised in him at the sight of Bharat approaching their abode. The episode, as in all traditional Rāmkathās, ends well. Bharat, unable to contain himself with brotherly love, rushes towards Rām to greet him and pay him his obeisance. A characteristic feature of Prasād's poem, shared by many works of that period, is the presentation of Rāmkathā characters, Lakṣmaṇ, Rām and Sītā, as common people with their virtues and faults.[12]

Baldevprasād Miśra (1898–?) in the period under consideration wrote two poems related to Rāmkathā, i.e. *Kośalkiśor* (Youth from Koshal; 1934) and *Sāketsant* (Saint from Saket; 1946); much later he also published a poem on the just rule of Rām entitled *Rāmrājya* (1960).[13] The work on the first of these poems commenced in 1916. Miśra was inspired by the poem *Priyapravās* (The Exile of Beloved [Krishna]; 1914) by Ayodhyāsiṁh Upādhyāy 'Hariaudh' (1865–1947[14]), based on the story of Kṛṣṇa's life and

---

[10] Cf. *śikṣā dī hai mano āpne sab ke man mẽ*; ibid., p. 22.

[11] The collection was first published in 1912; its second, changed and enlarged edition, in which *Citrakūṭ* was included, was published in 1918. The contents of the collection, finally established in the third edition of 1929, appears in the same form till the present day; Varmā, *Hindī sāhitya koś*, vol. 2, pp. 81, 209. For the text see Jayaśaṅkar Prasād, 'Citrakūṭ', in idem, *Kānan kusum*, 8th edn, Ilāhābād: Bhāratī Bhaṇḍār, 1966, pp. 101–9.

[12] Cf. Pāṇḍey, *Tulsīdāsottar hindī rāmsāhitya*, p. 110.

[13] Baldevprasād Miśra, *Kośalkiśor*, Ilāhābād: Paṇḍit Kālīcaraṇ Trivedī, 1934 and idem, *Sāketsant*, Dillī: Vidyā Mandir, 1946; cf. Pāṇḍey, *Tulsīdāsottar hindī rāmsāhitya*, p. 134. Both poems were published in a changed, shorter version in 1954; Baldevprasād Miśra, *Rāmrājya*, Lakhnaū: Hindī Sāhitya Bhaṇḍār, 1960, p. VIII. It is noteworthy that Baldevprasād Miśra is also the author of a critical study of Tulsīdās; idem, *Tulsīdarśaṇ*, Prayāg: Hindī Sāhitya Sammelan, 1948.

[14] Śukla, *Hindī sāhitya kā itihās*, p. 506 and Varmā, *Hindī sāhitya koś*, vol. 2, pp. 22, 355; cf. Varmā, *Hindī sāhitya koś*, vol. 2, p. 583 and Gaeffke, *Hindi Literature*, p. 13.

considered to be the first mature, narrative poem in Khariboli Hindi. Miśra commenced his work as *Sītāsvayaṁvar* (Sītā's Choice of Her Bridegroom) but published it a few years later in the journal *Sukavi* as *Maithilīpariṇay* (Maithili's Marriage). It was noticed by Mahāvīrprasād Dvivedī who in a letter to Miśra encouraged him to write a poem entitled *Rāmrājya* (with a fictitious character) that would prove conducive to the well-being of Indian people.[15] At that time Miśra did not respond to Dvivedī's suggestion and after another several years a new version of *Maithilīpariṇay* appeared in book form as *Kośalkiśor*.[16]

Kośalkiśor is based on the traditional Childhood Book. It narrates the life of Rām from his birth up to his marriage with Sītā and their return to Ayodhya in eighteen chapters. The numerous descriptions, employing both the tradition of classical Indian poetics and the tradition of Rāmāyaṇa, are a characteristic feature of this poem. For example, in Chapter 3 Miśra describes Rām from top-nail to top-knot (*nakh-śikh*) and also offers a portrayal of the beauty of sunset and dawn; Chapter 10 shows a garden in Janak's capital where Sītā and Rām meet and are enchanted by each other (Chapter 12). The most magnificent is, however, the description of their marriage and nuptial rites (Chapter 16) that from the very beginning attracted Miśra's attention. His rendering follows the story as known from tradition, basically as told in the *Rāmcaritmānas,* and does not have much original in the way of content; an exception is allusions referring to the unity of India and India's independence.[17]

Miśra's second work, *Sāketsant*, testifies to his continual and many-sided interest in Rāmkathā. This poem, consisting of fourteen chapters, a prologue (*upakram*) and epilogue (*upasaṁhār*), is considered more mature than *Kośalkiśor* not only as far as its narrative and language are concerned but also because of the treatment of Rāmkathā. It encapsulates almost the entire story but the focus of it is the eponymous character of the poem, i.e. Bharat shown as a saint from Saket. He is the most loyal devotee of Rām who is made by the circumstances to take, against his own will,

---

15 Miśra, *Rāmrājya*, p. VII. For Miśra it was obvious that Rāmrājya is inseparable from Rāmkathā which found its expression in his poem under the same title published in the already independent India.

16 Ibid.

17 Cf. Pāṇḍey, *Tulsīdāsottar hindī rāmsāhitya*, pp. 125–7.

the burden of rule in Ayodhya during the fourteen years of his brother's exile. Chapter 14 is especially interesting – it shows Bharat as Rām's regent spending his days according to the schedule echoing the scheme of *aṣṭayāms*, disclosing his real nature as the most devoted servant of his people. In *Sāketsant*, Miśra provided not only a novel, interesting approach to the traditional story but also raised in it the question of the responsibility of rulers to their subjects (which Miśra once again undertook in his later, already-mentioned work *Rāmrājya*).

Despite their considerable originality and skilful handling of language, especially in the case of *Sāketsant*, Miśra's works have neither gained much popularity nor survived the trial of time – they often do not even feature in the histories of Hindi literature.

One of the most popular of Rāmkathās of the first half of the twentieth century (it is popular till the present day) is *Rāmāyaṇ* by Rādheśyām Kathāvācak (1890–1963),[18] commonly known after his name as *Rādheśyām rāmāyaṇ*. It was written probably in the 1920s; of its twenty-five parts twenty-one were composed by Rādheśyām, the last four of them, which are authored by his younger brother, Madanmohan Lāl Śarmā, were added to the rest around 1924.[19] However, neither the circumstances nor the reason for this co-authorship are clear.

---

[18] B.S. Kesavan and Y.M. Mulay, *The National Bibliography of Indian Literature 1903–1953 (comprising Hindi, Kannada, Kashmiri, Malayalam)*, Delhi: Sahitya Akademi, 1966, p. 134; cf. Anuradha Kapur, 'Deity to Crusader: The Changing Iconography of Ram', in Gyanendra Pandey, ed., *Hindus and Others: The Question of Identity in India Today*, Delhi: Viking, 1993, p. 99 and Gaeffke, *Hindi Literature*, p. 93.

[19] Pāṇḍey, *Tulsīdāsottar hindī rāmsāhitya*, p. 95; cf. Erndl, 'The Mutilation of Śūrpaṇakhā', pp. 78–81, esp. p. 87 n. 34. Interestingly, on the title pages of parts 22 and 23 both Rādheśyām and Madanmohan Lāl Śarmā figure as the authors (*lekhak*) and their names are given separately, while the title pages of the two last parts, i.e. parts 24 and 25, claim M.L. Śarmā as the author and Rādheśyām as the editor (*sampādak*). See Rādheśyām, *Rāmāyaṇ*, Barelī: Śrī Rādheśyām Pustakālay, n.d. (all references to the text of Rādheśyām's *Rāmāyaṇ* are to this edition); cf. Pāṇḍey, *Tulsīdāsottar hindī rāmsāhitya*, p. 95. In a bibliography of Hindi works up to 1964, the earliest work of Rādheśyām under the title *Rāmāyaṇ*, published in Barelī (Śrī Rādheśyām Pustakālay), is dated 1932, while the year 1921 follows the title *Śrī rāmkathā* (6th edn, Barelī, published by the author); Nārāyaṇ and Nāyar, *Hindī-sāhitya-sāriṇī*, p. 132.

The entire poem consists of eight books, subdivided into twenty-five parts. Seven books are entitled after the mode of the *Rāmcaritmānas* and Book 8, the Lav and Kush Book (*Lavkuśkāṇḍ*), is named in the same way as the interpolated book commonly added in popular editions of Tulsīdās's poem (it is this book that consists of four parts – 22 to 25 – written by (co-written with?) Rādheśyām's brother).[20]

The story narrated in the seven books is close to Tulsīdās but it neither follows it blindly nor lacks originality. Rādheśyām's telling is in tune with the spirit of its times, giving its protagonists a chance to educate their audience and act for their well-being. As a result, one of its most prominent features is the didacticism present in many places in the poem. However, it must be stressed that it does not make this work too dull or insipid, mainly because its contents are mostly conveyed through the medium of lively descriptions and dialogues, interspersed with songs in colloquial Hindi. Their character brings to mind the plays of the popular Parsi theatre for which Rādheśyām worked (The New Alfred Company).[21]

One of the most typical examples of *Rādheśyām rāmāyaṇ*'s didacticism concerns the episode of Rām and Sītā's marriage. The text of the poem, describing the course of the rites, more than once brings to mind a comparison with a 'marriage guide' (*vivāh-paddhati*). After the ceremony, when the time for the festal meal comes, Rādheśyām refers to it, using three words, i.e. *baṛhār*, *baṛhhār* and *varāhār*, belonging to different stylistic registers. The first of them is the most common (*tadbhav*) designation for the feast offered by the bride's party to the bridegroom's party, the second is its regional variant, and the last one is of Sanskrit origin. The text teaches that the three of them refer to one thing and outlines how, no matter what it is called, this meal should appear. Then the time for festive songs (lit. 'congratulatory'; *badhāiyā̃*) comes and after a song describing the appropriate behaviour of women towards their guests, the poem refers to the present-day situation and the author does not spare his criticism of it.

---

[20] Rādheśyām, *Rāmāyaṇ*, VIII.22–25.

[21] Kathryn Hansen, *Grounds for Play: The Nauṭaṅkī Theatre of North India*, Delhi: Manohar, 1993, p. 80 and Varmā, *Hindī sāhitya koś*, vol. 2, p. 497; also see Gaeffke, *Hindi Literature*, p. 93.

Today the custom of singing these songs has deteriorated;
Now during a wedding, it's customary to sing gali-*songs.*
(...)
Now women singing abusive song, make others feel shame for fun;
They make a laughing stock of themselves and of their own homes.
How uncouth! How filthy! How impure this custom is!
Who knows why such an indecent amusement has crept into homes?[22]

Another example of this type is concerned with the episode in Panchavati, when Śūrpaṇakhā, exemplifying a licentious woman, before being punished for her unseemly behaviour, has to face Lakṣmaṇ's moralizing sermon, opening with the following words:

Aren't you ashamed at all saying such words?
Why doesn't a sinful woman die before uttering them?[23]

Kathleen M. Erndl in her study devoted to the episode of the mutilation of Śūrpaṇakhā as presented by various authors,[24] commenting on Rādheśyām's rendering, very aptly observes: 'There is a very modern tone to this passage, reflecting the concern of conservatives in a rapidly changing twentieth century India. The poet seems to be telling his audience that he does not approve of the recent fashion of "love marriages", lest someone think they are permissible as the modern equivalent of the ancient *gandharva* rite'.[25] Judging from the above-quoted illustrations, one may be prone to see Rādheśyām as a reactionary conservative as far as women and their place in society are concerned but it is not that obvious. In the episode of the visit of the three exiles to the ashram of the sage Atri,[26] his wife, Anasūyā, as in many other Rāmkathās teaches Sītā the duties of a virtuous wife (*strīdharm*)

---

[22] *bigaṛ gaī hai ājkal in gītõ kī rīt;/ ab to gārī-gān hī hai byāhõ kī rīt./ (...) ab nārīyā̃ sīṭhne gā – utsav ke lie lajātī haĩ;/ apnī bhī hā̃sī karātī haĩ, ghar kī bhī hā̃sī karātī haĩ./ kitnī bhaddī! kitnī gandī! kitnī apavitr prathā hai yah!/ kyā jāne kyõ ghar ke bhītar, aślīl vinod calā hai yah*; Rādheśyām, *Rāmāyaṇ*, I.4, pp. 19–20.

[23] *yah* [sic!] *bātẽ karte mẽ tujhko kuch lāj na ātī hai?/ mukh se yah kahne ke pahle – pāpini* [sic!] *kyõ mar nahī̃ jātī hai?*; ibid., III.10, p. 20.

[24] Erndl, 'The Mutilation of Śūrpaṇakhā'.

[25] Ibid., p. 79.

[26] Rādheśyām, *Rāmāyaṇ*, III.10, pp. 5–11. In Rādheśyām's text this name appears in the form 'Atrī'; ibid.

but this time her instructions are placed in an evidently modern setting and end with an interesting counterpoint. It opens with a critique of selfish wives who in pursuit of their own well-being do not take proper care of their husbands. She distinguishes four kinds of women (*ati uttam, uttam, madhyam, nīc*) and proceeds to characterize each type. In her teaching Anasūyā makes it clear that home is the domain of a virtuous woman, where she should take care not only of her husband and the members of his family but also of children. Then a sudden turn takes place when Atri teaches Rām the duties of a man (*puruṣdharm*)![27] The sage is very critical observing that men treat their wives as their own property and consider them inferior instead of treating them as men's equals. The entire passage ends with an unexpectedly radical song.

> *A man imprisoned a woman in a cage; calling her a darling, he closed her in a cage.*
> *When the first man settled in this world, he made rights equal for all.*
> *A man showed his own manliness, deciding that his status is high and theirs [women's] low.*
> *They closed innocent birds in cages; calling them darlings, they closed them in cages (...).*[28]

Thus, as it can be seen, Rādheśyām through the medium of the sage Atri's wife, in a very simple, colloquial Hindi, reaffirms the traditional roles of both sexes in Indian society only to contrast them with a modern outlook. The message of the song that sums up this new approach, voicing the reformist sentiments prevalent at the time of the creation of this poem, evidently clashes with the traditional view expounded by Anasūyā.

The last four parts, constituting Book 8, open with a short description of Rāmrājya[29] where Rām treats his subjects as his own children, being for them their own father, and where every class of society performs their prescribed duties.

---

[27] Ibid., p. 10.

[28] *nar nārī ko phā̃s liyā piñjre mẽ; pyārī ko kah kah kar ḍāl diyā piñjre mẽ;/ jab ādi puruṣ ne yah saṁsār basāyā; adhikār sab kā ek samān banāya;/ puruṣ ne yah apnā puruṣārth dikhāyā; apne ko ū̃cā nīc unhẽ ṭhahrāyā;/ bholī ciṛiyõ ko band kiyā piñjre mẽ; pyārī kah kah kar ḍāl diyā piñjre mẽ*; ibid., p. 11.

[29] Ibid., VIII.22, pp. 3–7.

There is no doubt that the artistic value of many fragments of Rādheśyām's poem is disputable (meaning – does not have much artistic value). Its many passages are stylistically monotonous which, among other things, results from the repetitive chains of identical rhymes. Nevertheless, Rādheśyām proved his great talent for the use of colloquial language – though sometimes considered too coarse[30] – for the purpose of building the dramatic dimension of his telling. He achieved this aim also due to skilful, continual direct references to the life experiences and common sense of his audience. These features of his work have won him a great popularity. Till the present day, his *Rāmāyaṇ* is well-known and its subsequent editions are readily available almost everywhere in the Hindi-speaking area and used during devotional gatherings organized at private homes and other places.[31] It is also used in Rāmlīlā performances and parts of the poem were recorded and widely circulated.[32] One of the best proofs of its popularity are the works of other authors' imitating the style of Rādheśyām and its pirated editions against which information printed on the editions published by Śrī Rādheśyām Pustakālay warns.[33] Its most important contribution to Hindi literature is the fact that its popularity added significantly to the stabilization of the standard form of modern Hindi.[34] However, it seems that despite its unquestionable popularity, considering it one of the most important literary achievements of the Hindi Rāmāyaṇ tradition and placing it just after the *Rāmcaritmānas* and the *Rāmcandrikā*,[35] seems an exaggeration.

In the discussion of modern Hindi works based on Rāmkathā, one cannot overlook Sūryakānt Tripāṭhī 'Nirālā' (1896[36]–1961), one

---

[30] Pāṇḍey, *Tulsīdāsottar hindī rāmsāhitya*, p. 95.

[31] See e.g. advertisements of other Rādheśyām's works in the edition of his *Rāmāyaṇ*.

[32] Ibid., p. 93; Varmā, *Hindī sāhitya koś*, vol. 2, p. 497 and Erndl, 'The Mutilation of Śūrpaṇakhā', p. 78.

[33] See the back cover of Rādheśyām, *Rāmāyaṇ*; cf. Pāṇḍey, *Tulsīdāsottar hindī rāmsāhitya*, p. 94. Also see Govinddās 'Vinīt', *Rāmāyaṇ lay-rādheśyām*, Banāras: Baijnāth Prasād Bukselar, 1939.

[34] Pāṇḍey, ibid., pp. 98–100.

[35] E.g. ibid.

[36] See Varmā, *Hindī sāhitya koś*, vol. 2, p. 651 and *Nirālā granthāvalī*, ed. Omkār Śarad, Lakhnaū: Prakāśan Kendra, 1973, p. IX. Cf. the argument

of the most eminent Hindi poets of all times, who based two of his works – *Rām kī śakti pūjā* (Ram's Adoration of Shakti; 1936) and *Pañcavaṭī prasaṅg* (The Episode of Panchavati) – on the motifs of the story of Rām's deeds. It is also worth noting here that Nirālā is the author of a longer biographical poem *Tulsīdās* (1938).[37]

Rām kī śakti pūjā is one of the most important works of Nirālā. Written in 1936, it was published in 1938 in a collection *Anāmikā* (Nameless [Woman]/The Ring Finger). The author turned in it to the motif of the sacrifice offered by Rām to the Goddess that is known from Puranic tradition, most probably, of Shakta origin,[38] though the direct inspiration for Nirālā was most probably the Bengali *Rāmāyaṇa* of Kṛttivās.[39]

The poem opens with very meaningful words:

> *The sun set. The eternal, invincible war between Rām and Rāvaṇ,*
> *Written on the pages of the daytime light, stopped.*[40]

These verses are concerned with the suspension of military action for night. The armies of Rām and Rāvaṇ leave behind the horrifying battlefield, the arena of violence and the atrocities of war that are referred to in the later part of the poem. At the dark night of the new moon, Rām is overcome by a fit of very human despair and becomes doubtful if he is able to defeat Rāvaṇ. The only light dispelling the darkness of his thoughts seems to be his memories of Sītā. Rām, for a long while, is lost in his meditations. It is only Vibhīṣaṇ who shakes him out of them, making him realize that they head towards defeat as their foe has

---

of Rāmvilās Śarmā dating Nirālā's birth as 1899 in idem, *Nirālā kī sāhitya sādhanā*, Dillī: Rājkamal Prakāśan, 1969–72, vol. 1, pp. 490–7.

[37] It was written in 1934 and in 1935 it was published in the subsequent issues (February, March, April, May and July) of the journal *Sudhā*; Sūryakant Tripāṭhī Nirālā, *Tulsīdās*, Dillī: Rājkamal Prakāśan, 1993, p. 44.

[38] Mainly from such later Purāṇas as the *Mahābhāgavata*, the *Kālikā* and the *Devībhāgavata*; Bulke, *Rāmkathā*, p. 737.

[39] Śarmā, *Nirālā kī sāhitya sādhanā*, vol. 2, p. 515; cf. Haricaraṇ Śarmā, *Nirālā aur Rām kī śakti-pūjā*, Jaypur: The Students' Book Company, 1965, p. 139.

[40] *ravi huā ast; jyoti ke patr par likhā amar/ rah gayā rām-rāvaṇ kā aparājey samar*; Sūryakānt Tripāṭhī Nirālā, *Rām kī śakti pūjā*, in *Aparā*, 17th edn, Rājkamal Prakāśan: Dillī, 1993, p. 41.

the Goddess Śakti on his side. It is a shock for Rām who is not in a position to understand the decision of Śakti who sides with Rāvaṇ opposing dharm.[41] At one moment Jāmbavān gives advice to Rām to worship the Goddess and thus to let her know his true nature and convince her of himself. Rām realizes that he participates in a kind of game, a kind of test by Śakti. He decides to worship her, bestowing on her his highest devotion, and requests Hanumān to bring him a hundred and eight lotus flowers. Then he proceeds to offer them, one by one, to the Goddess.

After the eighth day of continuous adoration only one flower is left but Śakti takes it, unnoticed, under the cover of night's darkness. Rām, when he discovers it is missing, first panics but then recalls that his mother called him affectionally the 'Lotus-Eyed' (*rājīv-nayan*). Thus, he composes himself and decides to finish the offer-ing, sacrificing one of his eyes instead of the missing lotus flower.[42] He is just about to poke out his right eye with an arrow, when Śakti intervenes and stops him from doing it, saying the following words:

> *Oh, righteous, righteous, resolute devotee, the pride of dharm, blessings on you, Rām! (...)*
> *You will win, will win. Oh, the novel Best of Men!*[43]

Nirālā in *Rām kī śakti pūjā*, abounding with devotion and reverence, shows Rām in an innovative way. He is full of genuine doubts, in great pain, desperately looking for the right solutions. As usually, he is righteous, upholding dharma, and at the same time he is an incarnation of an ideal man but for the new times. He does not break down when it practically comes to a deadlock and instead is ready for a self-sacrifice in the name of a better future.

Such a perspective, very original in Hindi literature, also thanks to its strong Shakta flavour, has won genuine recognition despite, or maybe because of (?), a very difficult sanskritized lan-

---

[41] *āyā na samajh mẽ, yah daivī vidhān; rāvaṇ, adharmrat bhī, apnā, maĩ huā apar*; ibid., p. 48.

[42] *kahtī thī̃ mātā mujhe sadā rājīv-nayan!/ do nīl-kamal haĩ śeṣ abhī, yah puraścaraṇ/ pūrā kartā hū̃ dekar mātaḥ ek nayan!*; ibid., p. 52.

[43] *sādhu, sādhu, sādhak dhīr, darm-dhan dhanya rām!/ (...) hogī jay, hogī jay, he puruṣottam navīn!*; ibid., p. 53.

guage. By common consent, it is considered to be one of the best works in Nirālā's oeuvre. Separate editions of *Rām kī śakti pūjā* may additionally testify to its established literary position.

Nirālā is also the author of a poem *Pañcavaṭī prasaṅg* from the collection *Parimal* (Aroma) published in 1929. It is one of the most ambitious early works of Nirālā, however, not as highly valued as *Rām kī śakti pūjā*. It has an interesting form, a dramatized dialogue (*nāṭakīy saṁvād*),[44] divided into five scenes dealing with five different motifs, related to the peaceful life of the exiles in the forest of Panchavati that is brutally interrupted by the coming of Śūrpaṇakhā.

The poem opens with the portrayal of Sītā's enjoyment of the forest life that seems better than life in a palace. Then Nirālā proceeds to the description of Lakṣmaṇ's utmost dedication to Sītā and his concern for her as the Mother Goddess, Śakti. The third part provides an account of the beauty of Śūrpaṇakhā and then Rām gives his philosophical precepts to Lakṣmaṇ and Sītā. His teachings contain many elements of Advaitavedānta that Nirālā had an occasion to study in the years 1922–3, when he was working for the Mission of Rāmakṛṣṇa Paramahaṁsa (1834–86) in Calcutta.[45] The two last parts deal with the indecent advances of Śūrpaṇakhā and the severing of her nose and ears by Lakṣmaṇ.

In this work of Nirālā too, Shakta influences are evident. Nevertheless, while in *Rām kī śakti pūjā* the reverence for the Goddess was mediated by Rām, in *Pañcavaṭī prasaṅg* it is shown through the medium of Lakṣmaṇ.[46] This poem does not make for easy reading because of its philosophical charge as well as because of the fact that Nirālā experimented in it with the form of free verse.[47]

---

[44] Pāṇḍey, *Tulsīdāsottar hindī rāmsāhitya*, p. 107; cf. Surya Kant Tripathi Nirala, *A Season on the Earth: Selected Poems of Nirala*, trans. David Rubin, New York: Columbia University Press, 1976, p. 131.

[45] *Nirālā granthāvalī*, vol. 1, pp. 9–10; Varmā, *Hindī sāhitya koś*, vol. 2, p. 651 and Nirala, *A Season on the Earth*, pp. 128, 131.

[46] Cf. Pāṇḍey, *Tulsīdāsottar hindī rāmsāhitya*, p. 108. Also see Śarmā, *Nirālā kī sāhitya sādhanā*, vol. 2, pp. 509–17.

[47] For his ideas on free verse see e.g. his introduction in the collection *Parimal*; Sūryakānt Tripāṭhī Nirālā, *Parimal*, Dillī: Rājkamal Prakāśan, 1993, pp. 5–15.

Ayodhyāsiṁh Upādhyāy 'Hariaudh', the already-mentioned author of *Priyapravās*, in 1940[48] published the poem *Vaidehī vanvās* (The Forest Life of Vaidehi), dealing in its eighteen chapters with the events that, as the poem's title suggests, took place after Rām had banished Sītā. However, this work of Hariaudh not only failed to win as much recognition as his earlier poem *Priyapravās* but is in fact considered a flop.[49]

In the conclusion of this survey, it should be added that in the same way as at the end of the nineteenth century so also in the beginning of the twentieth century many works in the Bhakti mode were written. However, in most cases they are of a very traditional character thus as such do not enrich the Hindi Rāmāyaṇ tradition.

Other older inspirations and conventions are also apparent during this period. With regard to this, one of the most important examples is *Rāmcandroday kāvya* (Poem on the Rise of Rām the Moon; 1936) by Rāmnāth Jyotiṣī (1874–1953), the poem written in Braj and modelled after Keśavdās's *Rāmcandrikā*. In 1937, this work was awarded the Third Dev Prize (Dev Puraskār) established by the Raja of Tikamgarh.[50] However, it should also be noted that the authorship of *Rāmcandroday kāvya* by Jyotiṣī is doubted.[51] Another author, Bihārīlāl Viśvakarmā Pañcāl 'Kautuk' was influenced by the works of Tulsīdās, especially the *Rāmcaritmānas* and the *Kavitāvalī*, in his poem *Kauśalendra kautuk* (Spectacle[52] of the Lord of Kośala; 1936).[53]

---

[48] Varmā, *Hindī sāhitya koś*, vol. 2, pp. 22, 583; cf. Pāṇḍey, *Tulsīdāsottar hindī rāmsāhitya*, p. 111.

[49] Pāṇḍey, *Tulsīdāsottar hindī rāmsāhitya*, p. 114.

[50] Ātmārām Śarmā 'Aruṇ', *Śrī rāmcandroday kāvya: Ek satyānveṣaṇparak ākalan*, Dillī: Bhāgyavanti Prakāśan, 2002, p. 22.

[51] For more on this work and its doubtful authorship see ibid., pp. 51 and *passim*. Also see Ātmārām Śarmā 'Aruṇ', 'Śrīrāmcandroday kāvya: samīkṣātmak viśleṣaṇ', *Hindustānī*, vol. 43, no. 3, 1982, pp. 3–10 and idem, 'Śrīrāmcandroday kāvya: samīkṣātmak viśleṣaṇ' [*sic*!], *Hindustānī*, vol. 48, no. 4, 1987, pp. 29–36 and and Pāṇḍey, *Tulsīdāsottar hindī rāmsāhitya*, p. 57.

[52] It is a pun – the pen-name of the author lit. means 'spectacle; wonder; amazement'.

[53] Bihārīlāl Viśvakarmā Pañcāl 'Kautuk', *Kauśalendra kautuk*, Vārāṇasī: by the author, 1936; cf. Pāṇḍey, *Tulsīdāsottar hindī rāmsāhitya*, pp. 57–8.

MAITHILĪŚARAṆ GUPTA'S *SĀKET*[54]

INTRODUCTION

'National poet' (*rāṣṭrakavi*) – Maithilīśaraṇ Gupta – is the author of *Sāket*, one of the most important works in Hindi literature and not only in the Rāmāyaṇa tradition. The history of its creation is very interesting, especially in that it seems to graphically testify to Gupta's problems with transforming a traditional story into a novel, modern garb.

On the title page of the poem, one can find a couplet saying:

> *Rām, the tale of your life is a poem in itself,*
> *it is only natural that someone becomes a poet.*[55]

However, an investigation into the circumstances of *Sāket*'s genesis reveals that the poem was born as a result of a very long process, which was neither simple nor spontaneous. The analysis of *Sāket* and of other sources bear out the thesis that the long years of Gupta's work on the poem are, among other things, expressive not only of the author's changing view of it but also of his problems with several traditions that he wanted to incorporate in it. Apart from this, it also appears that responsibility for Gupta's troubles rests with Ūrmilā,[56] Lakṣmaṇ's wife and a minor character in Rāmkathā who for many years attracted the poet's attention. The result is, as I will try to demonstrate, that *Sāket* consists of two vividly distinct parts – Canto 9 of the poem and, to

---

[54] Earlier versions of parts of this chapter were published as Danuta Stasik, 'Modernising the Rāmāyaṇa Tradition: M. Gupta's *Sāket*', in idem and John Brockington, eds, *Indian Epic Traditions: Past and Present*, Warszawa: Wydawnictwo Naukowe PWN, 2002 (*Rocznik Orientalistyczny*, vol. 54, no. 1), pp. 159–72 and idem, 'Sāket: Maithilīśaraṇ Gupta's Version of Rām-kathā', in Piotr Balcerowicz and Marek Mejor, eds, *Essays in Indian Philosophy, Religion and Literature*, Delhi: Motilal Banarsidass, 2004, pp. 251–7.

[55] *Rām, tumhārā vṛtta svayam hī kāvya hai,/ koī kavi ban jay, sahaj sambhāvya hai*. Vālmīki addressed these words to Rām when they met in Chitrakut (Canto 5); Maithilīśaraṇ Gupta, *Sāket*, Cirgā̃v: Sāhitya Sadan, 1961, the title page and p. 156 (all the following references to the text of *Sāket* are to this edition).

[56] This name is also spelt Urmilā. With regard to *Sāket* I use the form Ūrmilā, as this is the spelling employed in Gupta's poem.

a somewhat lesser degree, Canto 10 do not seem to fit with the rest of the work.[57] Paradoxically, they are so distinct that it even seems justified to view *Sāket* not as one poem but as two poems within one. However, before this issue is dealt with in greater detail, first I would like to concentrate on other related questions – the sources of inspiration for Gupta's poem, the process of its creation and its results.

It is noteworthy that two of Gupta's other poems, i.e. *Pañcavaṭī* (Panchavati; 1925) and much later *Pradakṣiṇā* (Circumambulation; 1950), are also based on Rāmkathā. The first of them is mainly concerned with Lakṣmaṇ's life full of devotion for Rām and Sītā. The second is a short rendering of the story of Rām's life, in which Gupta referred to the tradition of oral narration in such a way that it could be told during one session.[58]

HOW *SĀKET* WAS WRITTEN

Initially *Sāket* was intended as a poem concerned with Ūrmilā, which Gupta began in response to Mahāvīrprasād Dvivedī's article 'Kaviyõ kī Ūrmilā-viṣayak udāsīntā' (Poets' Indifference to Ūrmilā) published in 1908 in the July issue of *Sarasvatī*.[59] Drawing inspiration from an article by Ravīndranāth Ṭhākur, Dvivedī became interested in Ūrmilā as an exemplification of female characters neglected by Indian authors of all epochs. He wrote: 'What a pity that even poets have kept concealing such a radiant character portrait as that of Ūrmilā in this way till the present

[57] See e.g. one of the most telling of Indian reactions to *Sāket*, i.e. Gāndhī's letter to Gupta, dated 5 April 1932, quoted in Ṛṣi Jaiminī Kauśik 'Baruā', ed., *Rāṣṭrakavi Maithilīśaraṇ Gupta abhinandangranth*, Kalkattā: Jaiminī Prakāśan, 1959, pp. 198–9; cf. Kamlākānt Pāṭhak, *Maithilīśaraṇ Gupta: vyakti aur kāvya*, Dillī: Raṇjīt Priṇṭars & Pabliśars, 1960, pp. 32–3, 398–400.

[58] Pāṇḍey, *Tulsīdāsottar hindī rāmsāhitya*, pp. 102–3; cf. Varmā, *Hindī sāhitya koś*, vol. 2, pp. 311–12.

[59] Dvivedī wrote this essay under a pen name Bhujaṅgbhūṣan Bhaṭṭācārya. At that time, Dvivedī was the editor of *Sarasvatī* and M. Gupta was emerging as a poet. See Kauśik, *Rāṣṭrakavi Maithilīśaraṇ Gupta*, pp. 49–50, 86–7 and Pāṭhak, *Maithilīśaraṇ Gupta*, p. 393. Cf. Jagdīśprasād Caturvedī, *Maithilīśaraṇ Gupta kī kāvya yātrā*, Ilāhābād: Sāhitya Saṅgam, 1986, pp. 25–7, 32.

day'.[60] He also held that such a situation should be changed. The twenty-two-year-old Gupta, who especially at that time, was under the great influence of Dvivedī, felt it his natural obligation to try to satisfy his guru's wish and started writing a poem entitled *Ūrmilā*.

It is worth noting here that it was not only Gupta who responded to Dvivedī's essay. In June 1914, Ayodhyāsiṁh Upādhyāy 'Hariaudh' published a poem *Urmilā* in *Sarasvatī*, and much later, in 1936, Bālkṛṣṇa Śarmā 'Navīn' (1897–1960) published the opening section of Canto 3 of his poem *Urmilā* under the title *Vangaman* (Departure for the Forest) in an annual issue of the journal *Pratāp*.[61]

Apart from Dvivedī's encouragement, at a somewhat later period, Gupta was also stimulated and advised by Choṭelāl Bārhaspatya, an erudite contributor to *Sarasvatī*.[62] From their correspondence, one learns that between 1909 and 1910 Gupta managed to complete a little more than two cantos (out of an intended four) and left his work unfinished.[63] Though in September 1915 he attempted to resume writing, up till November the work was not proceeding. He complained: 'I'm feeling sad and ashamed not being able now to write anything about Devī Ūrmilā'.[64] Finally, in the beginning of 1916, Gupta overcame his creative impasse and also started to refer to his work as *Sāket*, though he continued to use the older title as well. All that time he kept on consulting, among others, Dvivedī and Bārhaspatya and discussed the form of his work with them. In the following few months, the begin-

---

[60] *kaise khed kī bāt hai ki ūrmilā kā ujjval carit-citra kaviyõ ke dvārā bhī āj tak isī tarah ḍhãktā āyā*; cited after Kauśik, *Rāṣṭrakavi Maithilīśaraṇ*, p. 88; cf. Pāṭhak, *Maithilīśaraṇ Gupta*, p. 393.

[61] Navīn began his work around 1921 but the poem was published as late as 1957. This vast time gap made it outdated at the moment of its publication; it could consequently not meet the needs and literary tastes of the new epoch. Kauśik, *Rāṣṭrakavi Maithilīśaraṇ Gupta*, p. 86; cf. Varmā, *Hindī sāhitya koś*, vol. 2, p. 380.

[62] Bārhaspatya also advised Gupta on how the poem should be written. See his letter to Gupta, dated 1 January 1911 in Kauśik, *Rāṣṭrakavi Maithilīśaraṇ*, pp. 86–7 and Caturvedī, *Maithilīśaraṇ Gupta*, pp. 39, 128.

[63] Gupta's letter to Bārhaspatya, dated 4 January 1911; ibid., pp. 88, 89, 194 and Pāṭhak, *Maithilīśaraṇ Gupta*, p. 394.

[64] *ūrmilā (...) ke viṣay mẽ abhī kuch na likhne ke kāraṇ duḥkhit aur lajjit hū̃*; quoted after Kauśik, *Rāṣṭrakavi Maithilīśaraṇ Gupta*, p. 194.

ning cantos were ready and the first of them came out in *Sarasvatī* in June 1916 under the title *Sāket* and was followed by four other cantos soon.[65]

Nevertheless, it took sixteen years more before the poem was finally published in 1932. In his preface to *Sāket*, Gupta admitted that his work had been ready two years earlier[66] but then he had not been satisfied with its Canto 9: 'at that time something was unfinished in Canto 9 and, according to my perception, even today it is still incomplete'.[67]

HOW *SĀKET* IS WRITTEN

Sāket is a full-length poem divided into twelve cantos (*sarga*), composed in over sixty different meters.[68] Hindi critics often term it as *mahākāvya*[69] and Peter Gaeffke, following their example, calls it 'a huge epic on the Rāma story'.[70] Its language, although sanskritized, is not as difficult as it is in the case of many works of the *Chāyāvād* period.[71] This holds especially true when its syntax is considered – long nominal appositions, so typical of the Hindi poetry of that period, are relatively rare in Gupta's poem.

Before proceeding to an analysis of *Sāket*'s structure, it seems desirable to summarize the plot of the poem. It will not only make the ensuing argument easier to follow but will also allow for an

---

[65] Canto 2 in July 1916, Canto 3 in January 1917, Canto 4 in May 1917, and Canto 5 in July 1918. Also see ibid., pp. 194–5 and Pāṭhak, *Maithilīśaraṇ Gupta*, pp. 177–8, 395.

[66] The date given at the end of *Sāket* is '*Dīpāvalī 1986* (November 1929)'; Gupta, *Sāket*, p. 501.

[67] *kuch śeṣ rah gayā thā aur merī bhāvnā ke anusār āj bhī yah adhūrā hai*; ibid., p. III.

[68] The figure calculated on the basis of the listing of *Sāket* metres made by Pāṭhak, *Maithilīśaraṇ Gupta*, pp. 695–6.

[69] E.g. ibid., see esp. pp. 510–19, where the discussion of different authors' opinions is also included on pp. 517–19.

[70] Gaeffke, *Hindi Literature*, p. 81.

[71] This period is usually referred to in English as Romanticism. See e.g. Karine Schomer, *Mahadevi Varma and the Chhayavad Age of Modern Hindi Poetry*, Delhi: Oxford University Press, 1998 (1st published 1983), esp. pp. 19–65.

insight into *Sāket*'s narrative strategies, considered to be the most original and innovative feature of Gupta's retelling.

Canto 1 opens up with clarifying the reasons of Rām's *avatār* in this world. Rām was born, according to Gupta's own words, in order to:

> *To show the path to the world,*
> *To deliver the earth from the burden of [sin],*
> *To fulfil the expectations of the people* (...).[72]

After a very brief introduction to Rām's family, the poet proceeds to describe the prosperity of Saket-Ayodhya[73] and then concentrates on a lively dialogue between Lakṣmaṇ and Ūrmilā that is first and foremost expressive of their happy married life. It also refers to the investiture of Rām as Crown Prince[74] and Bharat's absence from Ayodhya[75] (Canto 1). Then the dialogue between Kaikeyī and her shrewd maid, Mantharā, follows. Mantharā succeeds in convincing her mistress that holding the ceremony during her son's absence is undoubtedly a conspiracy and makes Kaikeyī demand two boons from Daśarath, i.e. the crown for Bharat, and the fourteen-year exile for Rām (Canto 2). When Rām learns about his fate, he not only accepts it quietly but also tries to console a terribly distressed Daśarath as well as to appease Lakṣmaṇ's burst of rage. Eventually, Lakṣmaṇ, without much deliberation, decides to join Rām in his exile (Canto 3). Sītā, having learnt about everything, has no doubts what she should do and thinks of the forest exile as of her paradise to be.[76] Ūrmilā, deep in her heart, also wants to accompany her husband but she fears that her presence will prevent him from being always ready to serve Rām and Sītā with intense devotion and therefore she decides to stay behind (Canto 4). Rām and his companions, dressed as ascetics, are ready to set off from Saket. Crowds of citizens for whom Rām is their favoured king surround them and

---

[72] *path dikhāne ke lie saṁsār ko, dūr karne ke lie bhū-bhār ko, saphal karne ke lie jan-dṛṣṭiyā̃*; Gupta, *Sāket*, p. 18.

[73] Although the name Saket is more often used than Ayodhya, at some places Gupta uses them interchangeably; see e.g. ibid., pp. 19–20.

[74] Ibid., p. 33.

[75] Ibid., p. 37.

[76] Ibid., p. 105.

for quite a long time they do not want to let him go.[77] At last, the trio leave the city and after some time they reach the kingdom of the Niṣads whose king, Guh, helps them to cross the river Ganges. They proceed to Prayag to meet the sage Bharadvāj. Following his advice, they go to Chitrakut and on their way they meet Vālmīki. They decide to stay in Chitrakut (Canto 5).

In Canto 6, Gupta for some time reverts to Saket, where all wait for the return of Sumantra, Daśarath's minister, who was accompanying Rām up to the Ganges. The anguish of Daśarath is so great that he dies after hearing from Sumantra the news about his beloved son, Rām. Bharat and Śatrughṇa, who at that time were paying a visit to Kaikeyī's paternal home, are promptly recalled to Saket by the family priest, Vasiṣṭha (Canto 6). On coming home and learning the awful truth, Bharat treats his mother with great contempt. He is very disturbed but Kausalyā and Vasiṣṭha eventually manage to pacify him and the funeral rites of Daśarath can be duly performed (Canto 7).

In Canto 8, the poet goes back to Chitrakut and depicts the joyful life that Sītā and Rām lead there. Their peace is interrupted by the tumultuous advent of Bharat with the army, the queens and the retinue together with the citizens of Saket. Bharat's aim is to bring Rām back home and restore the kingdom to him. Nevertheless, despite his brother's most earnest persuasion Rām stays in the forest and Bharat returns to the capital to reign as regent with his brother's sandals, a symbol of Rām's royal power. Before the whole retinue sets out for Saket, Sītā arranges a secret meeting of Ūrmilā and Lakṣmaṇ (Canto 8).

In Canto 9, the narrative comes to a standstill; this section is entirely devoted to the description of Ūrmilā as a *virahiṇī*, i.e. suffering from the pangs of separation from her beloved Lakṣmaṇ. This theme is continued in Canto 10, in which Ūrmilā's thoughts flash back to her own and her sisters' childhood and adolescence, and to the bow tournament that was followed by her and her sisters' marriage with Daśarath's sons. She confides all her memories to the river Sarayu.

The beginning of Canto 11 introduces the reader to Bharat's hermitage with a golden temple, in the vicinity of the royal palace. There he leads a renouncer's life worshipping Rām's sandals en-

[77] Ibid., pp. 128–32.

throned on a magnificent jewelled footstool (*maṇimay pād-pīṭh*).[78] After a while, Māṇḍavī, Bharat's wife, joins him and, later still, Śatrughṇa, who repeats to them what he has heard about Rām from a certain merchant visiting their city.[79] He tells them about Rām's departure from Chitrakut for the Dandak forest where the incident of the severing of Śūrpaṇakhā's ears and nose took place and was followed up with a battle in which Rām killed Khar and Dūṣaṇ. While Māṇḍavī, Bharat and Śatrughṇa are still wondering about Rām's victory, Bharat notices a dark object in the sky. Considering it to be a demon, he hurriedly aims his arrow at it and actually wounds Hanumān flying for *sañjīvanī*, a life-saving herb, for Lakṣmaṇ. Luckily, Hanumān recovers very quickly, thanks to some amount of *sañjīvanī* that Bharat was given earlier by a *yogī*,[80] and narrates how Śūrpaṇakhā persuaded her brother Rāvaṇ to take revenge on Rām and kidnap his wife Sītā. He also tells how finally Rām, assisted by Sugrīv's monkey-troops, invaded Lanka to recover Sītā. Many brave warriors were killed on both sides during that war; Lakṣmaṇ, seriously wounded, was waiting for *sañjīvanī* that could save his life. Therefore, Hanumān – eager to fulfil his mission – leaves Saket immediately after finishing his lengthy[81] story (Canto 11).

The last Canto 12 opens with the description of great agitation that seized the city at the news of the war and the critical state of Lakṣmaṇ. Bharat – at the instigation of Māṇḍavī – orders Śatrughṇa to get the troops ready to attack Lanka. Almost all the citizens of Ayodhya, with Kaikeyī and Ūrmilā among them, are prepared for the battle. Then Vasiṣṭha intervenes and persuades them to calm down and to look at the sky where, thanks to his inner powers, they can see what is happening in Lanka (one could say it was 'a live broadcast from Lanka'!).[82] Thus, they learn about the fate of Lakṣmaṇ, the final victory of Rām over Rāvaṇ, and the release of Sītā. After Rām's return to Saket, everyone rejoices and

---

[78] Ibid., p. 389.

[79] Ibid., pp. 410–15.

[80] Ibid., p. 417–19.

[81] Ibid., pp. 418–49.

[82] Ibid., pp. 477ff. It is very interesting to note that Gupta uses here the word *dūrdṛṣṭi*, lit. 'far-off vision'. In fact, he employed here, in an original way, the traditional literary device (*divyacakṣus*, *divyadṛṣṭi*). I would like to thank Dr. Anna Trynkowska for bringing to my attention the concept of *divyacakṣus*.

especially Ūrmilā, reunited with Lakṣmaṇ, is unable to contain her happiness.

Looking at the poem's plot from the point of view of its narrative strategies, up to Canto 8 one is made aware of the events covering roughly the story of the traditional Ayodhya Book. In most cases they are presented through the medium of dialogues between different characters or by means of the poet's descriptions. Then follow Canto 9 with the monologue of Ūrmilā as a *virahiṇī* and Canto 10 in which her memories go back to the events of the traditional Childhood Book. The two last Cantos – 11 and 12 – cover the story of the conventional Books 3 to 6, though most of the events are narrated in an unconventional manner. Firstly, Śatrughṇa repeats what he heard from a merchant, secondly, Hanumān shot down by Bharat narrates what happened in Lanka, and, thirdly, the final war events are visualised and projected onto the sky by Vasiṣṭha. Thus it becomes obvious that the narration in Gupta's poem is constituted in such a way that almost the whole of the story is told at one place, i.e. Saket. One minor exception seems to occur in Canto 8 when the action moves to Chitrakut. Indian critics, however, do not treat it as a departure from the rule of the unity of place and, referring to the poem itself,[83] point to the fact that the whole society of Saket was present in Chitrakut. However, it should be noted that before Bharat with others reach Chitrakut, Gupta for quite a long while relishes its quiet atmosphere.[84] What is more, the rule of the unity of place, otherwise consistently obeyed by Gupta, is broken once more but critics seem to overlook this fact. In Canto 5, Rām with his brother and wife leave Saket and, having crossed the river Ganges, proceed on their way to the wilderness.[85]

WHY *SĀKET*?

With the problem of Saket as the place from which the major part of the poem's narration is carried out, one touches on one of the most intriguing questions connected with Gupta's telling: why

---

[83] *samprati sāket-samāj vahī̃ hai sārā*; Gupta, *Sāket*, p. 222. See e.g. Pāṭhak, *Maithilīśaraṇ Gupta*, p. 412.

[84] Gupta, *Sāket*, pp. 220–36.

[85] Ibid., pp. 144–58.

was it given this name – *Sāket*? In Rāmcandra Śukla's influential history of Hindi literature, one can read that Gupta's poem was entitled *Sāket* because 'it is preoccupied mostly with the account of the events and circumstances happening in Ayodhya' (!).[86] Similar explanations can be found in other works on the poem,[87] if their authors take the trouble to give one at all. Nevertheless, there can be no doubt that it cannot be called a real explanation, as in fact the word 'Saket' opens the realm of the diverse sources of Gupta's inspiration.

In this context, it is important to note that his family were devout Vaishnavas. His father practised *sakhībhāv upāsanā*, one of the modes of Rāmbhakti typical of Rasik Sampradāy, into which Gupta was also initiated.[88] This is not to say that Gupta aimed at creating a devotional poem in an esoteric mood, which *Sāket* is not by any means. However, naming it in such a way, he made use of the tradition, which looks at Rām's life from the perspective of the heavenly Saket, the abode of his divine play. At the same time, this device enabled the poet to narrate the story of his favoured deity and to devote his attention to Ūrmilā, a female character belonging to the circle of people close to Rām who, nevertheless, did not accompany him during the time of his exile.[89] Gupta used it in order to present his vision of the world that he sees as the stage on which Rām performs the drama of humanity (*manuṣyatva kā nāṭya*)[90] and Saket is the symbol of heaven on earth.

ŪRMILĀ, *SĀKET* AND RĀMKATHĀ

As has been noted in the foregoing discussion, the work on the poem took Gupta more than twenty years from its inception or sixteen years from the publication of its first canto in *Sarasvatī*. It is worth noting in this context, however, that it was not just that

---

[86] *ayodhyā mẽ honevālī ghaṭnāõ aur paristhitiyõ kā hī varṇan pradhān hai;* Śukla, *Hindī sāhitya*, p. 587.

[87] Cf. Pāṭhak, *Maithilīśaraṇ Gupta*, p. 412.

[88] Kauśik, *Rāṣṭrakavi Maithilīśaraṇ Gupta*, p. 18; Pāṭhak, ibid., pp. 408–9 and Caturvedī, *Maithilīśaraṇ Gupta*, pp. 18–19, 24–5.

[89] Cf. Gupta's letter to Gandhi (dated rāmnavamī 1989, i.e. AD 1932) in Kauśik, *Rāṣṭrakavi Maithilīśaraṇ Gupta*, p. 199.

[90] For more on Gupta's Rām see below in Chapter Eight, Part Two.

single work which engaged his attention – during all those years Gupta was very active and published a lot.[91] But as far as *Sāket* is concerned, Gupta kept postponing its writing, then he had problems with working on it and yet, after all those years – as is known from his preface and what does not look like a token expression of a poet's modesty – he was not satisfied with the final effect, i.e. with Canto 9. Although Gupta did not give the actual reasons for his dissatisfaction, an analysis of *Sāket*'s contents indicates that Canto 9 and 10[92] are a jarring note in an otherwise traditional story, which is not only an integral part of *Sāket*'s narrative but also forms its core – these two cantos, 9 and 10, disrupt the poem's natural flow. What is more, while the major focus of the poem is Rām and Sītā,[93] Canto 9 and, to a lesser degree, also Canto 10 are monopolized by Ūrmilā who is otherwise not of much significance in the rest of the poem. Although, it must be acknowledged, Gupta treated her with plenty of attention and more sympathy than anyone before him in Hindi literature.

As a result, the overall impression of *Sāket* is that one is dealing practically with two autonomous works. Moreover, such a notion is corroborated in the tradition of *Sāket* criticism where authors very often concentrate either on Gupta's treatment of Rāmkathā with its leading characters Rām and Sītā or view this work as a poem of which Ūrmilā is the heroine.[94]

It is also not uncommon to view *Sāket* as a poem on separation from one's beloved (*virah-kāvya*),[95] which convincingly verifies the interpretation of Canto 9, together with Canto 10, as a poem within a poem – they do originate from *Sāket*'s main

---

[91] E.g. *Raṅg mẽ bhaṅg* (1910), *Jayadrathvadh* (1910), *Bhāratbhāratī* (1914), *Pañcavaṭī* (1925) or *Jhaṅkār* (1929).

[92] It may be interesting to note here that Canto 9 constitutes about 20 per cent of the poem and Canto 10 about 10 per cent; Cantos 1 to 8 constitute about 50 per cent and Cantos 11 and 12 about 20 per cent.

[93] More accurately – Sītā-Rām, as Gupta put it in his letter to Gāndhī: 'In *Sāket*, Sītā-Rām are celebrated as the leaders of the leaders and the teachers or the rulers of all' (*sītā-rām 'Sāket' mẽ nāyakõ ke nāyak aur sabke śikṣak athavā śāsak ke rūp mẽ pratiṣṭhit haĩ*); Kauśik, *Rāṣṭrakavi Maithilīśaraṇ Gupta*, p. 200. It can be noted here that the word *nāyak* used by Gupta, translated here as 'leader', also means 'leading character, hero'.

[94] E.g. Pāṭhak, *Maithilīśaraṇ Gupta*, p. 444.

[95] E.g. Dham, *Maithilīśaraṇ Gupta* or Bhāṭī, *Sāket kā navam sarg*.

narrative but neither develop it nor enrich it, living their own lives washed down with Ūrmilā's tears.[96]

Considering the reasons for the form of Gupta's work, it is important to remember that originally Gupta had intended to compose a poem concerned with Ūrmilā but after some time he changed his initial idea and began to conceive it on a wider scale.

The time when Gupta began his work was witnessing the rising tide of the Indian national movement and Hindi poetry of the first decades of this century served its cause by drawing inspiration from the lost ideal of the traditions of India's past, in order to promote pride in it (*atīt gaurav*), and interpreting it anew. For example, poets were looking for the characters and motifs known from the tradition but neglected by it, as was the case with Ūrmilā. In their reinterpretations, they were willing to enhance the awareness of Indian society (*janjāgraṇ*), to educate it, and to evoke patriotic feelings.

Here a very important question arises – was the potential of Ūrmilā's character powerful enough to meet such a challenge? The evidence that can be found in the present form of *Sāket* itself as well as in Gupta's correspondence of that time suggests a negative answer to this question and indicates the reason why Gupta decided to narrate the story of Ūrmilā against the background of the entire story of Rām.[97] However, composing a poem conceived in such a way took him many years and it seems that this long haul should be seen first of all in terms of an, as it seems, insoluble dilemma – how to reconcile the status of Ūrmilā as a heroine (*nāyikā*) with Rāmkathā? It is noteworthy that according to some critics Gupta's problems were caused by the fact that the idea to write about Ūrmilā was imposed on him by his mentor (*kāvya-guru*) Dvivedī and Gupta actually never made this conception his own.[98]

It is very revealing to refer in this context to Gupta's answer to a question considering the reasons for writing *Sāket*. Many years after the publication of his poem, Gupta revealed in one

[96] Cf. B.H. Rājūrkar, *Rāmkathā ke patr (Vālmīki, Tulsī evam Maithilīśaraṇ Gupta ke sandarbh mẽ)*, Kānpur: Grantham, 1972, p. 98.

[97] Cf. Nagendra, *Sāket: ek adhyayan*, Āgrā: Sāhityaratna Bhaṇḍār, 1960, p. 13.

[98] Ibid., p. 2 and Saksenā, *Sāket mẽ kāvya*, p. 50.

interview: 'I had to write about my favoured deity. I wrote *Sāket*'.[99] No mention of Ūrmilā!

SĀKET'S APPRAISAL

Gupta's poem is undoubtedly an interesting piece of evidence of the period of Indian national and social awakening when modern Hindi authors turned their attention to the well-known epic and mythological sources. It seems thus natural that the very popular story of Rām – who, at least from the times of Tulsīdās, functions in the Hindi speaking region as God-King protecting his devotees-subjects – proved to be ideal material for the poem. Suffice it to say here that Gupta, far from being silent about Rām's divinity, first and foremost tried to reveal his human nature and to make him a true leader of his people for whom, thanks to his righteous deeds and steadfastness, he could bring well-being and peace.[100] It is justified to say that although Gupta created a modern poem, having retained both aspects of the nature of Rām (with the indisputable dominance of the human aspect), he situated its hero between tradition and modernity.

Sāket, like other modern tellings of Rāmkathā,[101] reveals a multilayered approach to the story, which by its nature is a repository of myth. Gupta built his retelling on the original myth of Rām. However, he interpreted it by means of rationalizing, demythologizing and introducing new original elements. The most vital of them, which determines the interpretative frames of the poem already indicated by its title, was the choice of Saket as the site of its narration. It intermingled with other elements of this telling and as a result Gupta's Rām appears to be not only a master of the hearts and minds of his subjects but also their most devoted servant willing to provide them with all that was his lot, i.e. with all that was the embodiment of his very self and of his abode, Saket.

Gupta was one of the first really successful poets who looked for inspiration from Indian tradition and believed that interpret-

---

[99] *iṣṭdev ke viṣay mẽ kuch likhnā hī thā. 'sāket' likh gayā'*; quoted after Bhāṭī, *Sāket kā navam sarg*, p. 5.

[100] Cf. Rājūrkar, *Rāmkathā ke patr*, p. 99.

[101] For more see below Chapter 6.

ing it anew could serve the cause of the national movement and social change. As a result his story evolved into another myth – a myth of heaven on earth, which is to come soon due to the divine nature of humankind brought out in them under the leadership of Rām. Therefore the choice of the poem's title seems clear. *Sāket* is a symbol of heaven on earth, where nothing is mundane and all is divine – as long as the faithful have faith, the drama of existence takes place in Saket. Gupta's novel approach to Rāmkathā and its hero, who will be discussed later in this study, as well as the poem's artistic values made *Sāket* count among the classics of modern Hindi literature.

DRAMA AND NOVEL

Far less accomplished realizations of this period than the poetical works are the dramas and novels based on Rāmkathā. There is no doubt that the entire story, because of its scope may not be an exceptionally suitable material for a play, especially a play meant to be staged in a theatre. However, talking about modern Hindi drama, one should remember that for a long time its existence was almost exclusively limited to the domain of literature – Hindi dramas were rather intended to be read and not necessarily, if ever, to be staged.[102]

The non-stageable character of some plays results from the ideas adopted by their authors. More often, however, it is an outcome of their authors' lack of knowledge of theatrical conventions. This is also valid in relation to the plays inspired by the Rāmāyaṇa tradition. At that time, they usually dealt not with the entire story but with one or more of its motifs. It is also true that despite the significant number of this type of works, the majority of them not only did not become a theatrical event but they also failed as literary works, nor did they contribute much to the development of the tradition. However, there are a few works that are worth noting and undoubtedly a drama *Kartavya* (Duty;

---

[102] For a general introduction into the problems of the modern Indian theatre see Farley P. Richmond, 'Characteristics of the Modern Theatre', in idem et al., eds, *Indian Theatre: Traditions of Performance*, 1st Indian edn, Delhi: Motilal Banarsidass, 1993, pp. 387–406.

1935?[103]) by Seṭh Govinddās (1896–1974[104]) is one of them as it is the first thought-provoking modern Hindi play concerned with the life of Rām. Its author undertakes in it the question of the duty resting with everyone, and especially with those who have authority, and of the choices that have to be made in order to perform it. Govinddās made an interesting exercise, juxtaposing and contracting two important culture figures – Rām and Kṛṣṇa whom he attempted to dress in a real man's garb.

This drama consists of two self-contained parts, each consisting of five acts, subdivided further into scenes; the first part of the drama is concerned with Rām, the second one – with Kṛṣṇa. The part devoted to Rām opens with the presentation of the preparations for his coronation that are interrupted by Daśarath's decision about his exile. Rām's heart is filled with different, contradictory feelings. However, his sense of duty wins over though it does not appease his mind completely (Act 1). In Act 2, the action moves to Panchavati and the kidnapping of Sītā. In the search for her, Rām befriends Sugrīv and in the name of their friendship he helps him to regain the throne of Kishkindha by killing his brother Bāli. This evokes in Rām an inner conflict, the sense of wrong-doing and guilt. Act 3 moves the action to Lanka and deals with Rām's victory over Rāvaṇ after which Rām tests Sītā's purity with fire, tormented by inner turmoil. Act 4 concentrates on the dramatic decisions made by Rām after ascending the throne of Ayodhya, i.e. the banishment of Sītā as a result of people's gossip and the killing of Śambūk whose ascetic practices caused the death of a Brahmin youth. Interestingly, the real focus of this act is the dilemma about the killing of Śambūk. The last act depicts the distress of Rām who witnesses the departure from this world of his guru, wife and brother, and finally his own death ensues.[105]

---

[103] Gaeffke, *Hindi Literature*, p. 100 and Pāṇḍey, *Tulsīdāsottar hindī rāmsāhitya*, p. 142; cf. Varmā, *Hindī sāhitya koś*, vol. 2, p. 156. The text consulted by me in 1999 in the library of Hindī Sāhitya Sammelan (Allahabad), unfortunately, had no title page.

[104] Vijayendra Snātak, *Hindī sāhitya kā itihās*, Dillī: Sāhitya Akādemī, 1996, p. 314.

[105] Cf. Rāmcaraṇ Mahendra, *Seṭh Govinddās: nāṭya, kalā tathā kṛtiyā̃*, Dillī: Bhāratī Sāhitya Mandir, n.d. (1956?), esp. pp. 49–54 and Pāṇḍey, *Tulsīdāsottar hindī rāmsāhitya*, pp. 142–4.

Kartavya in the part concerned with Rām depicts him as an ideal man who time after time has to choose between his duty and conscience, and his decisions make him experience strong moral objections. However, his guru, Vasiṣṭha, makes him realize that one life is not enough to achieve internal peace and tranquillity from the due performance of one's duties and it has to take more lives.[106] This seems a convenient departure point for the understanding of the composition of this drama – the deeds of Kṛṣṇa and his character supplement that which was lacking in Rām's life.[107] This drama of Seṭh Govinddās is differently assessed[108] but as far as the part dealing with Rām is concerned, it is said that it does not form a true expression of the deeds of Rām.[109]

The Miśra brothers, Śyāmbihārī Miśra (1873–1947) and Śukdevbihārī Miśra (1878–1951),[110] co-authored the drama *Rāmcaritra* (Deeds of Rām; 1941).[111] In the introduction published with the text of the play, the authors clearly expressed their attitude to the events presented in it, as well as to their participants, calling them 'historical'.[112] Thus, Rām is not God but

---

[106] *āp kahte haĩ na ki karttavya-pālan se anant sukh kī prāpti ek janm mẽ na hokar anek janm mẽ hotī hai; āp kahte haĩ na ki karm ke suphal aur kuphal ke prabhāv kā hṛday par paṛnā ek janm mẽ nahī̃, anek janm ke paścāt miṭtā hai;* quoted after Mahendra, *Seṭh Govinddās*, p. 50.

[107] Ibid., p. 53.

[108] See e.g. ibid., pp. 51–4.

[109] *(…) na hī rāmcarit kī saccī abhivyakti hai;* Pāṇḍey, *Tulsīdāsottar hindī rāmsāhitya*, p. 144.

[110] Varmā, *Hindī sāhitya koś*, vol. 2, p. 446, cf. Gaeffke, *Hindi Literature*, p. 20. It is worth noting here that Gaṇeśbihārī (1865–?), Śyāmbihārī and Śukdevbihārī Miśras are the authors of the first history of Hindi literature written by Indians published in 1913 in three volumes with the title *Miśrabandhuvinod athavā hindī sāhitya kā itihās tathā kavi-kīrttan;* Miśrabandhu, *Miśrabandhu vinod*, rev. & corr. edn, Lakhnaū: Gaṅgā Pustak Mālā, 1972, vol. 1, pp. 1–2 and vol. 2, pp. 310–11, 337–9, 341.

[111] Śyāmbihārī Miśra and Śukdevbihārī Miśra (Miśrabandhu), *Rāmcaritra*, Lakhnaū: Avadh Priṇṭiṅg Varks, n.d. (Introduction dated 1941) and Pāṇḍey, *Tulsīdāsottar hindī rāmsāhitya*, p. 148. According to Nārāyaṇ and Nāyar (*Hindī-sāhitya-sāriṇī*, p. 241) *Rāmcaritra* was published in 1944.

[112] *jo ghaṭnāẽ kahī gaī haĩ ve prāyaḥ sabkī sab aitihāsik haĩ, keval vibhīṣaṇ aur rāvaṇ kā yuddhkṣetr mẽ mel nāṭakatva ke lie likhā gayā hai;* Miśra

an ideal man. Rāvaṇ is a civilized ruler of the Dravid(ian) people, whose culture, however, has significantly deteriorated. The conflict between Rām and Rāvaṇ is conceived as a confrontation between the Aryan and non-Aryan people of India.[113]

Rāmcaritra consists of three acts, subdivided into scenes. Dialogues dominate in it but there are also songs to be performed by dancing female singers (*gāyikā*) which brings to mind the popular Parsi theatre and/or (?) folk theatrical forms of the *nauṭaṅkī* type.[114] The plot of *Rāmcaritra* covers the events starting from Rām's childhood up to his victory over Rāvaṇ (interestingly, the war on Lanka is not actually shown up to its culmination) and his return to Ayodhya where Bharat transfers power to him. The authors attempted in it to rationalize and modify the original mythological contents. This experiment, however, did not prove a real success. The main characters ceased to be gods and demons but, one can say, the authors of the play have not endowed them with enough abilities to cope with their human condition. Essentially, *Rāmcaritra* is neither accomplished in the sphere of its structure nor in the sphere of style.[115]

The first half of the twentieth century did not witness the publication of any major novel dealing with the Rāmāyaṇa. In fact, one of the first novels, if not – the first novel, referring to Rāmkathā is *Rāvaṇrājya* (Rule of Rāvaṇ; 1923) by Śrī Kṛṣṇa Hasrat. However, because its protagonist, the focus of it is Rāvaṇ, an eternal foe of Rām, it should rather be referred to as anti-Rāmkathā or 'Rāvaṇkathā'. Hasrat attempted in it to offer an objective portrayal of Rāvaṇ who, according to the author, was depicted by Vālmīki as void of faults and it was only Tulsīdās who made his character vile in each and every aspect.[116]

A prose rendering of the story of Rām is authored by Premcand (1881–1936), one of the most eminent prose writers in Hindi

---

(Miśrabandhu), *Rāmcaritra,* p. III. It is obvious that 'historical' is used here as 'belonging to/known from the Rāmāyaṇa tradition'.

[113] Miśra (Miśrabandhu), *Rāmcaritra*, pp. I–II and VI.

[114] For more on their mutual relations see Hansen, *Grounds for Play*, pp. 79–85.

[115] Cf. Pāṇḍey, *Tulsīdāsottar hindī rāmsāhitya*, p. 148.

[116] *...vālmīki ne rāvaṇ ke carit citraṇ mẽ koī kamī nahī̃ rakhī kintu iske uparānt bhāṣā kāvya mẽ kavivar tulsīdās ādi ne rāvaṇ ko har tarah se nīcā dikhāyā;* quoted after ibid., p. 191.

literature, 'the emperor of the novel' (*upanyās samrāṭ*). His telling is simply entitled *Rāmkathā*, with a subtitle *Rāmcarcā* added in brackets.[117] It was published in 1938[118] and is referred to as 'a Rāmāyaṇa in simple prose'.[119] Actually, it is not a novel but a kind of story, performed by a story-teller who addresses his audience – children, teenagers and their elders. Premcand recreates in it a traditional form of story-telling, communicating with his audience directly in a lively, effortless style, using at times very colloquial language. He is not concerned with repetition, on the contrary – he resorts to it in order to imprint on his audience a particular word or phrase. This 'oral form' of Premcand's *Rāmkathā* is its most interesting feature, while its story is traditional and not innovative, which most probably was not even intended by its author.

It is traditionally divided into seven books, named as in Vālmīki. They are subdivided into episodes – each is given its own title – that also follows the system of Vālmīki. Of course, because of the size of this work (131 pages) many details of the traditional story are omitted, especially that, as it seems, Premcand retold it with a special aim, which becomes absolutely clear in the last passage of *Rāmkathā*.

> *It is an abridged story of the life of Ramchandra. The sense of his life is just one word and it is 'duty'. He always considered duty as the principal thing. In his whole life he never moved aside, even a bit, from the path of duty. (...) Children! You also consider duty as the principal thing. Never turn your face from duty. It is a very difficult path. In order to do your duty, you will have to challenge great difficulties but the pleasure you will achieve after fulfilling it will be your prize.*[120]

---

[117] Premcand, *Rāmkathā (Rāmcarcā)*, Jaypur: Sāhityāgār, 1992.

[118] Pāṇḍey, *Tulsīdāsottar hindī rāmsāhitya*, p. 161.

[119] Kesavan and Mulay, *The National Bibliography*, pp. 175–6.

[120] *yah hai rāmcandr ke jīvan kī saṅkṣipt kahānī. unke jīvan kā arth keval ek śabd hai, aur uskā nām hai 'karttavya'. unhõne sadaiv karttavya ko pradhān samjhā. jīvan bhar karttavya ke rāste se jau bhar bhī nahī̃ haṭe. (...) bacco! tum bhī karttavya ko pradhān samjho. karttavya se kabhī mũh na moṛo. yah rāstā baṛā kaṭhin hai. karttavya pūrā karne mẽ tumhẽ baṛī-baṛī kaṭhinaiyõ kā sāmnā karnā paṛegā, kintu karttavya pūrā karne ke bād tumhẽ jo prasanntā prāpt hogī, vah tumhārā puraskār hogā*; ibid., p. 131.

CONCLUSIONS

Considering the developments of the first half of the twentieth century, and especially of the Dvivedī period, one first of all should remember that it was the time when Khariboli Hindi superseded Braj and became a fully-fledged medium of poetical expression. It was also the time when authors turned for inspiration to their own history and tradition, hoping to make them a helpful tool in social reforms and forming patriotic attitudes (not infrequently this reformist approach aimed in fact at strengthening the Hindu traditionalist outlook). Thus after an earlier, nineteenth-century initial state of euphoria and interest in all that was modern, old motifs ceased to be unfashionable and making them a source of literary inspiration became for authors a touchstone of their creative imagination and skills. This turn of Hindi writers to India's past proved inseminating, especially in poetry, and the poets debuting in the 1920s and 1930s prove that it was a topical move with a lot of potential for the future.

As I have noted in the foregoing discussion, the majority of works are in the form of poetry and among them one can find a few really accomplished poems. There are plenty of dramas that are much less satisfying and the novel is represented very poorly. Considering the reason for this situation, it seems that the novel that was dominated by social and historical themes, because of its Western late provenance for long was not considered to be the right vehicle for traditional mythological motifs. One can also presume that the tradition of oral transmission and performance so strong in the Rāmāyaṇa tradition could contribute to this. Hindi poetry, though written and published, has always really lived thanks to its public performances (*kavitāpāṭh, kavi sammelan*, etc.) and not only thanks to the reading of it by individuals, whereas the novel undoubtedly belongs to the realm of reading. Maybe these were the factors that were responsible for such a dearth of, especially, novels related to the story of Rām in the period under consideration?

Another trait worth noting here, especially as it was continued in later times, is the interest of the authors concerned with Rāmkathā not only in Rām and Sītā (who with time also began to receive more attention) but also in other Rāmāyaṇa characters such as Bharat, Lakṣmaṇ, Urmilā or Kaikeyī. That is why modern writers augmented and supplemented what had been 'untold by tradition' and often did not deal with the entire story. This was also a time, when authors, even if they considered Rām as God, did not underline his divine status; they were interested in his human potential and the reformist capacities dormant in the story of his deeds.

CHAPTER SIX

Rāmkathās of the Second Half of the Twentieth Century

INTRODUCTION

1947 as the year of India's Independence and thus an unquestionable turning point in India's history is also commonly accepted as a convenient dividing line in discussions on modern Hindi, and, in general – Indian – literature. Nevertheless, one should remember that India's freedom with its far-reaching implications for the country and its people, did not mean immediate changes in all spheres of Indian life and this also concerns literature. Authors of the pre-Independence period were still active, and in fact it was they who set the tone of the Hindi literary scene before the newer trends were set by the younger generation of writers. Generally, this is also true of Hindi works referring to the Rāmāyaṇa tradition. In this chapter, I will try to demonstrate that their authors could not remain indifferent to the transformations taking place in the reality surrounding them. As it appears, forming their tellings of Rāmkathā, they approached the story in different ways but treating it, to a much larger extent than ever before, as an account of real events which seems to be the most characteristic feature of the works published during the period under consideration.

However, it is important to note that not many authors dealt with the full story of Rām's deeds which is especially relevant with regard to poets. It is worth noting here that, beginning with the 1940s, i.e. with the period which is called in Hindi literature Experimentalism (*prayogvād*), and then in the 1950s, i.e. during the period of New Poetry (*naī kavitā*), Hindi poetry underwent radical transformations, as a result of which it preferred shorter forms, rather avoiding longer narratives. It is mainly the novel that by that time had become a well-established genre and had managed to win a loyal audience – which emerges as the most favourable form for large-scale literary utterances dealing with the entire story of Rām.

RĀMKATHĀ IN CONTEMPORARY HINDI POETRY AND DRAMA

After 1947, Hindi poets have not produced significant, artistically accomplished works that deal with the entire Rāmkathā. In the works that are better-known and most highly valued, authors focus on particular characters or certain motifs. Also quite popular are female characters of the Rāmāyaṇa, serving as a medium through which different problems related to women and their role in Indian society are raised.

Thus, for example, Kedārnāth Miśra 'Prabhāt' (1907–84) is the author of the poem *Kaikeyī* (1950?[1]), in which he tries to portray the character of Kaikeyī in a new light. Miśra focuses on her role in the intrigue leading to Rām's exile, traditionally presented as a result of her wicked plotting. In this work, it is viewed rather as a consequence of Kaikeyī's understanding of the complicated situation in Ayodhya, threatened by non-Aryan foes. She knew that only Rām could defend the Aryan culture, and, therefore, she did not let him ascend the throne of Ayodhya, making him instead go to the forest and face the enemies.[2]

Almost at the same time, in 1952, Śeṣmaṇi Śarmā 'Maṇirāypurī' published his poem under the same title as the previous work, i.e. *Kaikeyī*.[3] Focusing on the title character and referring to the contemporary socio-political situation, the author argues that it was Rām's exile that enabled Rāmrājya, his just rule, to become accomplished.[4] Though this poem was actually published ten years after it had been written, its narrative and its message are considered to exceed the work of 'Prabhāt'. However, its language and style are criticized as lifeless.[5]

A few works deal with the character of Sītā, among them are Candraprakāś Varmā's poem *Sītā* (1958),[6] viewing the later events

---

[1] Kedārnāth Miśra 'Prabhāt', *Kaikeyī (mahākāvya)*, Paṭnā: Śrī Ajantā Pres, n.d.; cf. Nārāyaṇ and Nāyar, *Hindī-sāhitya-sāriṇī*, p. 22 and Sureś Candra, *Bīsvī̃ sadī kā rāmkāvya aur mūlyabodh*, Dillī: Anaṅg Prakāśan, 2002, p. 30.

[2] Cf. Varmā, *Hindī sāhitya koś*, vol. 2, pp. 106–7, 112 and Pāṇḍey, *Tulsīdāsottar hindī rāmsāhitya*, pp. 133–5.

[3] Śeṣmaṇi Śarmā 'Maṇirāypurī', *Kaikeyī (rājnaitik khaṇḍ kāvya)*, Ilāhābād: Rāmnārāyaṇ Lāl, 1952.

[4] *rām ban na jāte to kaise/ rāmrājya sārthak hotā*; ibid., p. 36.

[5] Pāṇḍey, *Tulsīdāsottar hindī rāmsāhitya*, p. 133.

[6] Candraprakāś Varmā, *Sītā*, Ilāhābād: Hind Prakāśan, 1958

in her life from the perspective of the awakening of women in contemporary India, the poem *Bhūmijā* (Earth-born; 1961[7]) by Raghuvīr Śaraṇ 'Mitra' and the controversial *Agniparīkṣā* (Ordeal by Fire; 1961[8]) by Ācārya Tulsī (1914–97), a famous Jaina teacher. The latter of these works, based on Jaina Rāmāyaṇas, and especially on Vimalasūri's *Paümacariya,* sympathizing with Sītā as the epitome of rejected, downtrodden women let down by their men and society, in 1970 was interpreted by Hindu traditionalists as an insulting attack on their beliefs and ethos and as a result it was banned by the state government of Madhya Pradesh.[9] However, thanks to the popularity of the poem and its inherent poetical values, as well as because of the person of its author, *Agniparīkṣā* was published for the second time in 1972[10] in a revised version. Ācārya Tulsī, considering himself first of all as a man of religion and only then as a poet, never intended to insult anyone's feelings. Nevertheless, it is noteworthy that the agitation provoked by *Agniparīkṣā* is expressive of the influences of traditionalist, conservative circles in contemporary Indian society.

Of interest to contemporary authors has also been Śambūk, a Shudra who broke the rules of dharma by practising asceticism, leading thus to the death of a Brahmin boy, for which Rām punished Śambūk with death. To this character, Jagdīś Gupta (b. 1926) devoted his poem *Śambūk* (1977),[11] in which its title hero serves as an embodiment of the oppressed classes and is considered a genuine 'son of [Indian] soil' (*bhūmiputra*).[12] Gupta says about his hero:

> *Wherever a human being will be hurt, silent,*
> *There Śambūk will become his voice.*[13]

---

[7] Raghuvīr Śaraṇ 'Mitra', *Bhūmijā,* 4th edn, Meraṭh: Bhāratīy Sāhitya Prakāśan, 1973. Also see Candra, *Bīsvī̃ sadī kā rāmkāvya,* pp. 38–41 and Pāṇḍey, *Tulsīdāsottar hindī rāmsāhitya,* pp. 135–7.

[8] Ācārya Tulsī, *Agniparīkṣā: jain rāmāyaṇ ke ādhār par racit,* 2nd edn, Cūru: Ādarś Sāhitya Saṅgh Prakāśan, 1972, p. xvii; Candra, *Bīsvī̃ sadī kā rāmkāvya,* p. 171; Nārāyaṇ and Nāyar, *Hindī-sāhitya-sāriṇī,* p. 48 and Śivāśaṅkar Trivedī, *Ācārya Śrī Tulsī kṛt 'Agniparīkṣā' kī agniparīkṣā,* Sardāśahar: Śivāśaṅkar Trivedī, Sṛjancetnā, 1970.

[9] Trivedī, *Ācārya Śrī Tulsī,* the first unnumbered page.

[10] Cf. Pāṇḍey, *Tulsīdāsottar hindī rāmsāhitya,* p. 139.

[11] Jagdīś Gupta, *Śambūk,* Ilāhābād: Lokbhāratī Prakāśan, 1977.

[12] Ibid., p. XIV.

[13] *manujatā ho jahā̃ āhat, mūk,/ vahī̃ uskā svar bane śambūk;* ibid., p. 2.

Baldevprasād Miśra, known from the previous period as the author of *Kośalkiśor* and *Sāketsant,* in 1960, as has already been mentioned, published a poem *Rāmrājya*. It is devoted to the just rule of Rām that in fact for Miśra is a synonym of the cultural unification of India, a glorification of Aryan dominance over non-Aryan people. It has been criticized for its pronounced, at times even bombastic, patriotic note.[14] However, one should also point out Miśra's approach to the question of Indian unity in terms of the polarity between the Aryas and the non-Aryas and his propagating the superiority of the culture of the former that is highly objectionable to many people not only in India.

Nareś Mehtā (1922–2000), a renowned Hindi poet, is the author of a well-known, important poem *Saṁśay kī ek rāt* (A Night of Doubt; 1962)[15] that shows Rām lost in deep thought during the night preceding his entry into Lanka, when almost everything is ready for the war with Rāvaṇ. This episode from Rām's life allows Mehtā to elucidate the problem of thoughtful, righteous people who, like Rām, become entangled in responsibilities towards others and live in a world engulfed by conflict as well as struggle that cannot be avoided.[16] On the one hand, they, like Rām, are fully conscious that their decisions have far-reaching implications for the life of other people but, on the other hand, they are not even able to foresee the direct or indirect consequences of these decisions.[17] The emotional and mental upheaval caused by this dilemma is best exemplified in the following words of Rām:

> *Instead of becoming an arrow*
> *in the hands of history, it will be better*
> *if we ourselves*
> *are lost,*
> *wandering in the dark...*[18]

Once Rām makes up his mind and is ready to fight, he utters very significant words:

---

[14] Pāṇḍey, *Tulsīdāsottar hindī rāmsāhitya*, p. 129; cf. ibid., p. 131.

[15] Nareś Mehtā, *Saṁśay kī ek rāt*, Ilāhābād: Lokbhāratī Prakāśan, 1962.

[16] Cf. Janārdan, 'Prajñapuruṣ Rām ke antarjagat kī dvandva-kathā "Saṁśay kī ek rāt"', *Hindustānī*, vol. 41, no. 2, 1980, pp. 46–51.

[17] Cf. ibid., pp. V–XIV and Pāṇḍey, *Tulsīdāsottar hindī rāmsāhitya*, pp. 199–206.

[18] *itihās ke hāthõ/ bāṇ banne se adhik acchā hai/ svayam ham/ ādherõ mẽ yātrā karte hue/ kho jāẽ*; Mehtā, *Saṁśay kī ek rāt*, p. 10.

Now, I am the decision
of all,
not mine own.

Don't ask me,
oh, my reason!
Don't ask me...

Neither the heaven,
nor its gods
and the gods of gods,
no one,
yes, no one
knows answers to questions.[19]

In his poem, Mehtā was the first Hindi author to deal with the extraordinary loneliness of Rām and the people like him who in situations of crisis have to make big decisions on behalf of others, only hoping that the future will prove they were right.

It is worth noting here that Nareś Mehtā also became interested in other themes of the Rāmāyaṇa. Firstly, he turned to the character of Śabarī who became the title figure of his poem *Śabarī* (1977),[20] and, secondly, he undertook the episode of the questioning of Sītā's purity by one washerman that leads to her banishment by Rām and dealt with it in the poem *Pravād parva* (Time of Gossip; 1977).[21] However, these poems did not receive as much attention as *Saṁśay kī ek rāt*.

The least accomplished in the entire period seem to be the dramas drawing on the Rāmāyaṇa tradition, most probably because of the fact that the entire Rāmkathā is very demanding material for a modern play. Thus, one can rather talk about works inspired by the traditional motifs or characters, or referring to the Rāmāyaṇa lore and its message without actually dealing with the story itself. One can mention here, for example, a one-act play *Aśokvan* (The Ashok Grove; 1950) and a drama *Citrakūṭ* (1960) by Lakṣmīnārāyaṇ Miśra (1903–87); a monodrama *Śabarī* (1959) by

---

[19] *ab maĩ nirṇay hū̃/ sabkā/ apnā nahī̃./ mujhse mat praśna karo/ o mere vivek!/ mujhse mat praśna karo,/ na ākāś/ na uske devtā aur/ na devtāõ ke devtā/ kisī ke pās/ hā̃ kisī ke pās/ praśnõ ke uttar nahī̃*; ibid., pp. 88–9.

[20] Nareś Mehtā, *Śabarī*, Ilāhābād: Lokbhāratī Prakāśan, 1977.

[21] Idem, *Pravād parva*, Ilāhābād: Lokbhāratī Prakāśan, 1977.

Seṭh Govinddās, known from the previous period; *Śambūk kī hatya* (The Killing of Shambuk; 1975) by Narendra Kohlī (b. 1940), whose Rāmkathā novel cycle will be discussed further in this chapter; *Rām kī laṛāī* (Ram's War; 1979), an interesting allegory of independence and freedom, built on, among other things, the traditional Rāmkathā, by a well-known playwright Lakṣmīnārāyaṇ Lāl (1927–87), or a play focusing on Śabarī – *Yah rakt sarovar kyõ* (Why This Lake of Blood?; 1987) by Rameścandra Miśra.[22] However, these works became neither major literary nor theatrical events. Such a situation is most probably one of the results of the actual, rather pitiful, state of Hindi drama and theatre but it may also be related to the unprecedented popularity of Rāmlīlā performances, presenting the entire Rāmkathā. It seems plausible that, on the one hand, they fulfil the requirements of the potential audience and, on the other hand, their popularity discourages potential authors from undertaking Rāmkathā in their works.

One such exception that deals with the entire story of Rām's life is a drama, simply entitled *Rāmkathā* (1987),[23] by Gopāl Upādhyāy (b. 1940). It may be added here that in 1980 and 1981 fragments of it were broadcast by different radio stations, in 1981 it was awarded Lālit Sāhitya Puraskār by Mānas Saṅgam (Kanpur), and finally published for the first time in 1987.[24] It is a bulky work of more than 450 pages that is definitely not a stageable play. The author views the protagonist of the story, Rām, as a character that has a long history behind him as well as ahead of him and thus is ever present. Upādhyāy compares Rām to water, seemingly the same in all the places where it can be found, which, however, is drawn and made use of in different ways by different people.[25] In Upādhyāy's play Rāmkathā becomes a convenient tool to express his opposition to any kind of exploitation, and especially

---

[22] Rameścandra Miśra, *Yah rakt sarovar kyõ*, Dillī: Anubhūti Prakāśan, 1987; Śrī Lalit Śukla, 'Śabarī āj bhī sārthak hai', *Hindustānī*, vol. 50, no. 1, 1989, pp. 77–9.

[23] Gopāl Upādhyāy, *Rāmkathā*, Dillī: Sāmayik Prakāśan, 1992.

[24] See ibid. for the information on the jacket of its 1992 edition and ibid., p. 455.

[25] Ibid., pp. IX–X. In this context, the title of Bhagvān Siṁh's novel – *Apne apne Rām* (To Each His Own Rām) – that will be discussed further in this chapter, also comes to mind.

feudalism.[26] The author voices his belief in, on the one hand, humanistic values and, on the other hand, the unity of India, which means for him Hindu India.[27] This brew of Marxist and Maoist ideology[28] as well as Hindu traditionalism, plus the volume of the work, results in a quite explosive mixture that more than once tries its readers' patience.

Rāmkathā in the Contemporary Novel

Introductory Notes on Myth in Literature[29]

As has already been mentioned, it is the novel that in most recent times has proved to be most favourable for the treatment of the entire story of Rām's life and the most important contemporary Hindi Rāmkathās, such as *Apne apne Rām* (To Each His Own Ram; 1992) by Bhagvān Siṁh,[30] belong to this genre. This work is referred to here as it stirred the world of Hindi critics who have raised many questions with regard to it and a significant number of them deal with the author's approach to myth[31] which is not surprising in the case of a work based on a story that by its nature is a repository of myth. Thus, before proceeding with the discussion, it seems necessary to ask a few interrelated questions concerning the relationship between myth and modern literature and to attempt to answer them.

---

[26] Ibid., pp. XII–XV.

[27] Ibid., pp. XXXVIII–XXXIX.

[28] Ibid., p. XL.

[29] An earlier version of this section is included in Danuta Stasik, 'On Modern Retellings of Rām-kathā in Hindi Literature: Bhagvān Siṁh's Novel "Apne apne Rām"', *Berliner Indologische Studien*, nos 11/12, 1998, pp. 259–62.

[30] Bhagvān Siṁh, *Apne apne Rām*, Dillī: Mānak Pablikeśans, 1992, pp. 130–1.

[31] E.g. Naṁvar Siṁh, 'Rāmkathā kī udheṛ-bun', *Haṁs*, no. 8, 1992, pp. 67–71; Rajendra Śarmā, 'Vāh! Rām – āh! Rām', ibid., pp. 71–2; Gopāl Rāy, 'Sāhitya mẽ lālūvād', *Samīkṣā*, January–March 1992, pp. 2–4; Rajeev Saxena, 'Hero Rama and Villain Vasishta', *Indian Literature*, vol. 155, 1993, pp. 193–6; Vimal Varmā, 'Khoe hue kāl kī khoj', *Sāmayik paridṛśya*, nos 4–5, 1995, pp. 175–85 and Nanda Bhāradvāj, 'Rāmkathā kā mithak aur Apne apne Rām', *Antardṛṣṭi*, no. 7, 1995, pp. 44–7.

Firstly, one should consider what method – or methods? – can prove useful when examining a definitely modern literary genre, which serves as a vehicle for myth that has an established tradition behind it; secondly, how to reconcile myth with the modern outlook of an author; thirdly, to question what the role assigned to myth by a contemporary artist is.

In order to answer these and other related questions, it seems very useful to turn to Eleazar Meletinsky's approach to myth in twentieth-century literature, which he expounded in his book *Poėtika mifa* (The Poetics of Myth).[32] It should be noted that the choice of Meletinsky's work has been chiefly influenced by the relevance of his concepts with regard to Hindi tellings of Rām-kathā, as well as by the fact that it differs widely from the attitude of other Western authors (no indigenous works on the subject have been published, as far as I am aware) and above all from the attitude of Northrop Frye whose works, especially his *Anatomy of Criticism* and *Fables of Identity*, paved the way for the school of myth criticism.[33] Frye's approach provoked various questions and weighty objections have been raised against it.[34] Many critics not belonging to this school, while investigating literary texts, made efforts to find permanent structures and motifs which could be related to structures of mythical narration and known mythical motifs. Their attitude can be best described by the words of Walter Jens, quoted by Weimann,[35] as 'coming from myth, returning to myth'. Nevertheless, it is easy to observe that such an approach certainly does not refer to 'living in myth' and therefore

---

[32] Eleazar M. Meletinsky, *Poėtika mifa*, Moskva: Nauka, 1976. All the references to his text in this study are to the Russian original. For its English translation see Eleazar M. Meletinsky, *The Poetics of Myth* (Series 'Theorists of Myth', ed. Robert A. Segal), tr. Guy Lanoue and Alexandre Sadetsky, New York and London: Garland Publishing, 1998.

[33] Northrop Frye, *Anatomy of Criticism: Four Essays*, Princeton: Princeton University Press, 1957; idem, *Fables of Identity: Studies in Poetic Mythology*, New York: Harcourt, Brace & World, 1963; also see idem, *Spiritus Mundi: Essays on Literature, Myth, and Society*, Bloomington: Indiana University Press, 1976.

[34] E.g. John J. White, *Mythology in the Modern Novel: A Study of Prefigurative Techniques*, Princeton: Princeton University Press, 1971, pp. 33–4.

[35] Robert Weimann, *Literaturgeschichte und Mythologie: methodologische und historische Studien*, Berlin: Aufbau-Verlag, 1971, p. 365.

as a method does not *a priori* seem appropriate for the analysis of modern tellings of a story with a long but still living tradition, such as the Rāmāyaṇa tradition. On the other hand, there is Meletinsky's proposal, in which myth is understood as an intentional means of literary creation, through which an author experiences and expresses the world he lives in. In other words, myth as a form of thought and a powerful creative instrument with its multiple functions in prose narration, in Meletinsky's opinion, opens up new possibilities of dealing with the concerns of contemporary man, as well as of interpreting different aspects of a particular cultural and social order.

Eleazar M. Meletinsky in his erudite work compares classical forms of myth with their scientific and artistic interpretations in the twentieth century basically within the framework of the modernist renaissance of myth. Myth as a form of thinking and a product of the poetic imagination is viewed by Meletinsky predominantly in terms of the prehistory of literature and hence the title of his book.[36] The term 'poetics of myth', when applied to twentieth-century literature and then used interchangeably with the term 'poetics of mythologizing' (*poėtika mifologizirovanija*),[37] receives a new meaning because of the conscious shift of some writers towards mythology. These authors saw myth as an instrument of artistic organization of literary material and a way of expressing certain 'eternal' psychological elements or lasting patterns of culture.[38] According to Meletinsky, '"mythologism" (*mifologizm*) is a phenomenon characteristic of twentieth-century literature, both as an artistic method and as a means of experiencing the world expressed through this method'.[39] Mythologism not only offered new possibilities for unmasking the process of the degradation of man or the crisis of the spiritual culture. Perhaps even more important was its potential to reveal the unchanging positive and negative elements of empirical existence

---

[36] Meletinsky, *Poėtika mifa*, p. 399.

[37] I prefer to use in this study terms derived from the noun 'mythologism' and the verb 'to mythologize'. However, see the English translation of Meletinsky's text where the noun 'mythification' and the verb 'mythicize' and their derivatives are used.

[38] Meletinsky, *Poėtika mifa*, p. 7.

[39] Ibid., p. 295.

and historical changes, reaching beyond the socio-historical limits and the limits of time and space.[40]

According to Meletinsky, this literary development came as a result of two important processes expressive of the changing role of myth in Western culture – the process of 'demythologization' (*demifologizacija*) followed by the process of 'remythologization' (*remifologizacija*). The first of these began during the Renaissance and was marked by a radical withdrawal from the total symbolism of culture and a shift towards a deep interest in the world of nature subjected to the activity of man.[41] Meletinsky agrees with Leonid Batkin who observes that: 'The Renaissance is the last closed system of culture built on archetypes, i.e. on myth (...). The Renaissance myth with its anthropocentrism, inclination to historicism and critical attitude of mind, interest in reality – is a precondition for demythologization'. Batkin also observes that 'until the "use" of mythology (with all the consequences of the fact that it is being "made use of" and not "lived in") is a common and widespread feature of literature, the temperature of myth has not yet fallen completely'.[42] Thus from the fifteenth to seventeenth centuries images and motifs of ancient and later of Biblical mythology became repositories of poetic imagery, the source of plot, and a special formalized 'language' of art.

From the eighteenth century onwards, two types of mutual relationship between literature and myth can be observed. The first of them continues the Renaissance developments (the demythologization pattern), i.e. the conscious resignation from the traditional plot and *topoi* (*loci communes*), which signifies a passage from medieval symbolism to mirroring reality in different forms. The second type of relationship, the above-mentioned 'remythologization', is a conscious attempt at an entirely informal, non-traditional use of myth, which quite often becomes individual mythologizing. In the first decades of the twentieth century, the remythologization, the 'renaissance' of myth, becomes a dynamic process spreading to different spheres of European culture. Acknowledging the fact that myth is an eternal source of inspi-

---

[40] Ibid., pp. 295–6.

[41] Ibid., pp. 277–80.

[42] Leonid Batkin, 'Renessansnyj mif o čeloveke', *Voprosy literatury*, no. 9, 1971, pp. 116–18.

ration and also plays a practical role in modern society was a common element in the unfolding of this process.[43]

Meletinsky observes that the poetics of mythologizing presupposes certain oppositions between universal psychology and history, mythological syncretism and pluralism, as well as the use of elements of irony and travesty. It serves as one of the ways of organizing of narration and creates an independent 'mythological' plot, which structures both people's consciousness and common history. It is also a medium for a metaphorical description of a contemporary society realized through the parallels to traditional myths belonging to a different stage of historical development. In the case of such authors as James Joyce or Thomas Mann, the poetics of mythologizing is not an intuitive return to mytho-poetic thinking but one of the aspects of the intellectual, even 'philosophical' novel, based on deep, erudite knowledge of ancient culture, history of religion and modern scientific theories.[44]

Mythologizing appears to be internally connected with the aesthetics of modernism. However, the poetics of mythologizing has become a definite artistic method and may be employed differently by writers of different outlooks, as well as of different creative methods. Meletinsky observes that the poetics of mythologizing penetrates the literatures of Latin America, Africa and Asia where it takes roots in the soil of local folklore and in the living mythological consciousness. As a result, these literatures (and cultures, in general) are of a multilayered character where one deals with the coexistence and interpenetration of elements of historicism and mythologism, social realism and authentic folklore.[45]

CATURSEN ŚĀSTRĪ'S *VAYAṀ RAKṢĀMAḤ*

Catursen Śāstrī (1891–1960), who is first of all known as the author of historical novels, in one of his later works, the novel *Vayaṁ rakṣāmaḥ* (We Protect; 1955), made use of the Rāmāyaṇa plot in order to portray the pre-Vedic (*prāgvedkālīn*) times.[46] The title page of this work claims it proudly to be 'a great, original

---

[43] Meletinsky, *Poėtika mifa*, p. 280.

[44] Ibid., p. 339.

[45] Ibid., p. 365.

[46] Ācārya Catursen, *Vayaṁ rakṣāmaḥ*, Dillī: Rājpāl eṇḍ Sanz, 1995, p. 7.

[novel], set in the context of ancient time'.[47] In a short opening address (*pūrva nivedan*), Śāstrī writes that in his work he included sketches from the lives of different peoples of the pre-Vedic times, depicting as humans also those who were traditionally treated as gods or demons. Śāstrī's novel, according to himself, is a result of his research on, among other things, Vedic literature, the Puranas, as well as foreign historical sources.[48] It is very difficult to say which sources he used but one of the authorities he refers to is one Genesis (*sic*!), introduced as an English historian (*sic*!).[49] If it is taken into consideration that according to Śāstrī, quite rightly, the historical novel does not have to follow strictly historical facts because it is not an account of a real life,[50] then one should not be surprised by the pseudohistorical revelations that take his work to absurd levels! For example, the Asurs[51] originate from Assyria.[52] Rudra-Śiva was worshipped throughout the entire world,[53] and the Mayas of Mexico are related by Śāstrī to the demon Maya, known in Hindu mythology as a great, accomplished architect. What is more, an old name for Africa was 'Śivdān' which is reflected in the name of contemporary Sudan.[54] Such 'facts', no matter how odd they may seem, are, however, an essential feature of *Vayaṁ rakṣāmaḥ*.

The novel consists of 127 chapters (each of them with its own title) and an epilogue. It first introduces the character of Rāvaṇ who is depicted as the founder of a new culture – the culture of the Rākṣasas that combined Vedic and non-Vedic traditions.[55]

---

[47] *prācīn yug kī pṛṣthbhūmi par ādhārit ek mahān maulik upanyās*; ibid., title page.

[48] Ibid., p. 9.

[49] See ibid., pp. 27, 29 and 30.

[50] *sāhitya jīvan ka itivṛtt nahī̃ hai*; ibid., p. 8; cf. Dhīrendra Varmā et al., *Hindī sāhitya*, vol. 3, Prayāg: Bhāratīy Hindī Pariṣad, 1969, pp. 313–14.

[51] *Asur*(*a*)s are known in Hindu mythology as the opponents of the gods (*sur*(*a*)s), commonly recognized as demons or sinful spirits. Śāstrī uses this noun as the name of one of the ancient non-Aryan peoples of India.

[52] Catursen, *Vayaṁ rakṣāmaḥ*, pp. 102–4.

[53] Ibid., pp. 124–6, 133–40.

[54] Ibid., p. 125.

[55] The lack of consistency between the message contained in the introduction as well as the subtitle of the novel and its actual contents is noteworthy.

It was Rāvaṇ who made use of the Veda, taking into consideration the traditions of the Daityas and the Dānavas.[56] His aim was to eliminate the differences between the Aryas and the non-Aryas and to unite all the peoples in the name of the oneness of the human race. The war cry of the Rākṣasas was 'We protect!' (in Sanskrit: *vayaṁ rakṣāmaḥ*), and hence the title of the novel.[57] This phrase meant that the Rākṣasas, as the guardians of this new culture, not only protected all those who represented it or were ready to adopt it, but, primarily, they stood guard over the Veda that was the focus of their culture.[58] Rāvaṇ, having extended his territory in the South, finally set off to the North (chapter 52).

Soon Śāstrī introduces Rām[59] who earlier was merely mentioned (after over seventy pages of the novel[60]) in a brief note included in connection with the genealogy of the Solar royal family, i.e. the lineage of Rām, hostile to the Rākṣasas. Rāvaṇ and Rām meet for the first time on the occasion of a bow tournament organized by king Janak. Then Rām is once again referred to by Śūrpaṇakhā after her mutilation by Lakṣmaṇ in the forest of Panchavati.[61] From this moment on (chapter 72), the plot, generally, narrates the events known from the traditional story but they are arranged according to Śāstrī's vision. A lot of space is devoted to the war between Rām and Rāvaṇ.[62] The novel ends with the epilogue that deals with Rām's return to Ayodhya and the following expansion of his rule, famous throughout the whole world.[63]

In fact, Śāstrī's novel lacks a plot that would form a logical whole. It is rather a collection of different sorts of pseudohistorical as well as pseudogeographical deliberations and unrelated events. In addition, the whole structure is out of balance which exposes

---

[56] *Daitya*s and *dānavas*, in Hindu mythology, classes of *asura*s.

[57] The author refers here to the traditional etymology of the word 'rākṣas', relating it to the Sanskrit verbal root 'rakṣ', i.e. 'guard; defend; protect'; cf. John Dowson, *A Classical Dictionary of Hindu Mythology and Religion*, Delhi: Manu Publications, 1987 (rpt), p. 255.

[58] *(...) ved hī hamārā sāṁskṛtik kendrbindu ho*; Catursen, *Vayaṁ rakṣāmaḥ*, p. 196, also see pp. 66–8, 131–2, 196–9.

[59] Ibid., p. 201.

[60] Ibid., p. 75.

[61] Ibid., pp. 224ff.

[62] Ibid., pp. 353–420.

[63] Ibid., pp. 423–7.

the lack of inner logic of the work. Rāvaṇ – portrayed as a mighty ruler with, as it seems, noble intentions – who occupies the attention of the author for the greater part of his work, is defeated – for unknown reasons – by Rām, an ill-defined character who appears in the middle of the novel but finally emerges to influence the life of the entire world. Even if one tried to understand this as Śāstrī's reliance on the Rāmāyaṇa tradition, i.e. his presumption of its common knowledge among his readers, it would not make his novel a convincing piece of well-balanced literary structure. Leaving aside the plot and composition of *Vayaṁ rakṣāmaḥ*, one should also pay attention to the language of this work, in which Śāstrī, more than once, uses Sanskrit not only in single phrases or sentences (as in the title of the work) but also in longer passages.[64] Of course, making the novel sound very solemn and learned, it adds authority to it but certainly also makes the reading as well as understanding of these passages very difficult, if not impossible. This is consequently another reason that makes one feel constrained to reconsider these opinions that ascribe considerable popularity to Śāstrī's work[65], term it the most important Hindi novel dealing with Rāmkathā and hold it in high esteem just after the *Rāmcaritmānas*.[66] Very symptomatically, Indranāth Madān, a contemporary Hindi critic, in his discussion of Hindi novels based on the Rāmāyaṇa, referring to *Dīkṣā* (Initiation; 1975[67]) by the already-mentioned Narendra Kohlī, does not spare a word for Śāstrī's *Vayaṁ rakṣāmaḥ*.[68]

THE RĀMKATHĀ CYCLE BY NARENDRA KOHLĪ

It was the just-mentioned novel *Dīkṣā* that opened Narendra Kohlī's tetralogy, or – in fact – a pentalogy, published under the

---

[64] Ibid., e.g. pp. 132–3, 204–6, 403–5.

[65] Varmā, *Hindī sāhitya koś*, vol. 2, p. 181.

[66] *rāmcaritmānas ke bād hindī mẽ rāmkathā par itnī mahattvapūrṇ kṛti kadācit dūsrī nahī̃ hai*; Pāṇḍey, *Tulsīdāsottar hindī rāmsāhitya*, p. 183 also see pp. 181–5; cf. Varmā, *Hindī sāhitya*, vol. 3, p. 314.

[67] Narendra Kohlī, *Dīkṣā*, 4th edn, Dillī: Parāg Prakāśan, 1980.

[68] Indranāth Madān, *Samkālīn sāhitya: ek naī dṛṣṭi*, Dillī: Lipi Prakāśan, 1977, p. 143.

title *Abhyuday* (The Rise; 1989[69]) that apart from *Dīkṣā*, consists of *Avasar* (An Occasion; 1976[70]), *Saṅgharṣ kī or* (Towards the Conflict; 1978[71]) and *Yuddh* (The War; 1979[72]) in two parts. It is worth adding here that Kohlī is known for his long novel cycles, based on epic and Puranic themes, such as his *Mahāsamar*,[73] dealing with the *Mahābhārata*, or the much shorter *Abhijñān*,[74] concerning the story of Kṛṣṇa.

The moment of the creation of *Dīkṣā*, the first part of the Rāmāyaṇ cycle, is worth mentioning here. Kohlī, giving the background of his work, writes that the story of Rām and his victory over Rāvaṇ, became an irresistible source of inspiration during the war between India and Pakistan in 1971, as a result of the birth of a new state, i.e. Bangladesh.[75] Very symptomatically, this preface is absent from the edition of the entire cycle.

Dīkṣā opens with Viśvāmitra's preparations for a sacrifice at his ashram. The sacrifice is destroyed by the Rākṣasas, a people hostile to the Aryas. They are powerful and rich but uncivilized, violent and cruel – some of them are even cannibals. They spread terror and destruction and exploit those who are less powerful. Viśvāmitra is in possession of a miraculous weapon that is the object of desire for the Rākṣasas who demand it from the sage. However, he fears that with this weapon, they could rise further in power. The Rākṣasas harass Viśvāmitra who makes every effort

---

[69] Narendra Kohlī, *Abhyuday*, vol. 1 (*Dīkṣā, Avasar, Saṅgharṣ kī or*), Dillī: Parāg Prakāśan, 1992 and vol. 2 (*Yuddh 1, Yuddh 2*), Dillī: Abhiruci Prakāśan, 1994. It is noteworthy that *Abhyuday* is advertised, contrary to the actual facts, as 'the first, important Hindi novel based on Rāmkathā' (*'Abhyuday' rāmkathā par adhṛt hindī kā pahlā aur mahattvapūrṇ upanyās hai*); see ibid., the jackets of both volumes.

[70] Idem, *Avasar*, Dillī: Parāg Prakāśan, 1976.

[71] Idem, *Saṅgharṣ kī or*, Dillī: Parāg Prakāśan, 1978.

[72] Idem, *Yuddh*, Dillī: Parāg Prakāśan, 1979.

[73] Narendra Kohlī, *Mahāsamar – 1 (Bandhan)*, Dillī: Vāṇī Prakāśan, 1988; idem, *Mahāsamar – 2 (Adhikār)*, Dillī: Vāṇī Prakāśan, 1990; idem, *Mahāsamar – 3 (Karm)*, Dillī: Vāṇī Prakāśan, 1991; idem, *Mahāsamar – 4 (Dharm)*, Dillī: Vāṇī Prakāśan, 1993; idem, *Mahāsamar – 5 (Antarāl)*, Dillī: Vāṇī Prakāśan, 1995; idem, *Mahāsamar – 6 (Pracchanna)*, Dillī: Vāṇī Prakāśan, 1997; idem, *Mahāsamar – 7 (Pratyakṣ)*, Dillī: Vāṇī Prakāśan, 1998; idem, *Mahāsamar – 8 (Nirbandh)*, Dillī: Vāṇī Prakāśan, 2000.

[74] Idem, *Abhijñān*, Dillī: Rājpāl eṇḍ Sanz, 1981.

[75] Idem, *Dīkṣā*, the first unnumbered page of 'Ādhārbhūmi'.

not to yield to them and, therefore, decides to seek help from Daśarath. However, Daśarath is reluctant to do anything against the Rāksasas, as it could provoke the anger of their ruler, Rāvaṇ, who is a terror to the whole world. Thus, the sage asks Daśarath to let him take with him his eldest, twenty-five-year-old son, Rām, about whom he has heard a lot of good things. When Daśarath is reluctant to do what is asked of him, Viśvāmitra reminds him that his consent is not just his good will, that helping him is his kingly duty.[76]

Daśarath finally agrees and soon the sage leaves Ayodhya not only with Rām but also with Lakṣmaṇ who idolizes his elder brother. What is important is that Rām grew up without his father's love. However, Daśarath, seeing Rām's many virtues, takes to his first-born son and with time begins to entrust him with more and more responsible tasks. In fact, Rām has ruled in Ayodhya for the last few years, taking great care of the subjects who like him very much.[77]

Viśvāmitra takes Rām from Ayodhya in order to prepare him for the future struggle. He treats Rām as his pupil on whom he will be able to bestow his weapon and entrust the task of crushing the Rākṣasas. Anticipating Rām's future, Viśvāmitra asks him to promise that he will never become an arrogant ruler, uninterested in the lives of his subjects and that he will not wait for the attack of Rāvaṇ but will be the first to set on him.[78] The sage prepares Rām for his future tasks and Rām introduces peace and order in the ashram and its surroundings.

Viśvāmitra decides to take both brothers back to Ayodhya, also intending to show them Mithila. On the way, he tells them the story of Ahalyā, seduced by Indra, the chief of the people named Devas. This very long narrative in Kohlī's novel[79] serves the author as a pretext to deal with the situation of a woman hurt by a man and rejected by the society. Rām appears here as the protector of Ahalyā who symbolizes such women.

After reaching Mithila, they meet Janak and his daughter, Sītā. Rām and Lakṣmaṇ learn that Janak found her as a baby abandoned in a field. He took her in and brought her up as his

---

[76] Idem, *Abhyuday*, vol. 1, p. 22.
[77] Ibid., pp. 33–4.
[78] Ibid., pp. 45–7, 82.
[79] Ibid., pp. 88–143.

own daughter. When she grew up and was ready for marriage, her unknown descent became an obstacle in finding a suitable match for Sītā – those who could have been taken into consideration would not even think of marrying her and those willing to marry her could not be considered by Sītā's parents. Therefore, Janak found a solution in order to justify her imminent spinsterhood. All potential candidates for the hand of Sītā had to raise the giant bow of Śiv that for generations had been kept in his family. Rām guesses that Viśvāmitra wants him to marry Sītā and because he liked the girl himself, he is only worried how he will manage with the bow that in order to be raised has to be handled by many people. However, the task proves to be not so difficult. The sage tells Rām the secret – the bow has an invisible, self-acting mechanism and discharging it properly, makes the bow fall into parts. Of course, Rām emerges victorious from this trial[80] and Sītā becomes his wife.

The second part of the cycle, *Avasar*, focuses on the events that traditionally constitute the core of the Ayodhya Book. Daśarath feels very old and exploited by Kaikeyī and her brother. Appreciating Rām's rare virtues that predispose him to become his heir, he decides to make over the throne to him.[81] Daśarath, however, fears the reaction of Kaikeyī, to whose family he promised that her son would ascend the throne of Ayodhya, therefore, he orders the preparations for Rām's installation to be made secretly. However, Kaikeyī learns about them from servants and despite the fact that she feels real affection for Rām, treating him as her son, she demands from her husband the throne for Bharat and fourteen years of forest exile for Rām. Kaikeyī hopes that these fourteen years of Rām's exile will allow Bharat to strengthen his position as a ruler while, at the same time, the citizens of Ayodhya will forget about their favourite. It is also Kaikeyī who names Dandak forest as the final destination for the exile. Rām is only glad to learn about such turn of events, as he understands it as an excellent opportunity to fulfil the wish of Viśvāmitra, eager to see him as the guardian of ascetics, sages and other people living in Dandak.[82] First, the exiles live in Chitrakut, where they meet many individuals, mainly the representatives of dif-

[80] Ibid., p. 180.
[81] Ibid., pp. 207–9.
[82] Ibid., pp. 239–40.

ferent less civilized communities (these characters are an invention of Kohlī). Rām tries to enlighten them and teach them how they can withstand the attacks of Rākṣasas. Very little space, less than one page,[83] is devoted to the episode of Bharat's unsuccessful attempt to bring Rām back to Ayodhya that is so important in the traditional story.

The third part of the cycle, *Saṅgharṣ kī or*, depicts the sojourn of the exiles in Dandak where besides the sages and ascetics different, socially and culturally backward, communities also live. Rām, Sītā and Lakṣmaṇ teach them all how to live a life worthy of human beings, treating this task as their mission because they know that 'first of all, the awareness of being human should be awakened in them, [as] although they are human beings, they live like animals'.[84]

Rām does not tire of building a new society, as well as educating it, and because he is against any kind of exploitation of people, he makes over their workspace to them.[85] He also organizes a kind of people's militia (*janvāhinī*). They farm the land given in their charge and continually practice their combat skills in order to fight against Rākṣasas.[86] Actually, it is not an exaggeration to call Dandak a big training camp.[87] After their first victorious battles with Rākṣasas, Rām can leave his new friends on their own.

Rām departs for Panchavati where, after some time, he meets Śūrpaṇakhā. Kohlī devotes a lot of space to this motif.[88] Śūrpaṇakhā is first shown in her palace as a woman who is past her prime. She is merciless, with a whip at her side that she does not spare on her servants and is fond of alcohol. The fame of Rām has reached her and she is very eager to meet him. A few times, she goes close by his abode and watches him from behind trees and finally, one day, dressed up, she approaches him. Introducing herself with a false name, she tells him that she is being persecuted and asks for his protection. Rām, seeing in the middle of the forest a dressed-up woman in garish make-up, becomes doubt-

[83] Ibid., pp. 370–1.

[84] *sabse pahle un mẽ mānav-cetnā jagānī hogī. ve manuṣya hokar bhī paśuõ ke samān jī rahe haĩ*; ibid., p. 425; cf. p. 440.

[85] Ibid., e.g. pp. 443ff, esp. 454–5, 457, 458–9, 460–1.

[86] Ibid., p. 464.

[87] Cf. ibid., p. 501.

[88] Ibid., pp. 593–688.

ful about her words. When he asks who her persecutor is, Śūrpaṇakhā mentions the name of Kāmdev, the god of love. This time Rām manages to reject her advances[89] but they are repeated by Śūrpaṇakhā the next day. Desperate, Rām has no idea how to free himself of her and, without thinking much, says that he is married but his younger brother is a bachelor. (It is worth noting here that in Kohlī's telling this is true, because after the bow tournament in Mithila, only Rām was married.) In the end, Śūrpaṇakhā, infuriated with Lakṣmaṇ's indifference to her charms, goes to Rām to complain and meets on her way the young Sītā of exceptional beauty. Realizing that she cannot be a rival for such an exquisite woman, she attacks Sītā with a dagger. Lakṣmaṇ intervenes and in the end punishes her for her uncontrolled passions, cutting the skin of her nose and ears. It is noteworthy that during the battle with Khar and Dūṣaṇ, following this incident and won by Rām and his allies, Rām sustains numerous wounds![90] As in the traditional story, Śūrpaṇakhā looks for Rāvaṇ's help. He becomes so intrigued by the depiction of Sītā's beauty that he decides to kidnap her. Rāvaṇ also cursorily adds that in case he does not take a fancy to Sītā, he can always feast on her meat.[91]

His cousin, Mārīc, assists him in the abduction of Sītā. Mārīc, dressed as an ascetic, arrives at Rām's ashram, allegedly in order to tell him about his problems. He takes out of his bundle an extraordinary deerskin, shining gold and blue, spreads it on the ground and with the greatest ease sits on it. When Sītā catches sight of it, she is instantly overwhelmed with a desire to have an identical deerskin. Rām asks Mārīc where he could obtain it and learns that although such deer are more typical of the South, their guest saw such a deer in the vicinity of Rām's ashram.[92] They both go searching for it, while Sītā stays in the company of Lakṣmaṇ and two other men.

However, as soon as Lakṣmaṇ hears, as it seems to him, the despairing cry of Rām, he rushes to the forest. Then Rāvaṇ, who till that moment had stayed in hiding, enters the ashram and after a short fight kidnaps Sītā. When he arrives with her in Lanka,

---

[89] Ibid., pp. 625–7.
[90] Ibid., p. 675.
[91] Ibid., p. 703.
[92] Ibid., p. 708–12.

Mandodarī expresses her dissatisfaction with his act, trying to convince him of the senselessness of it, and tells him how he can still remedy this situation.[93]

The last part of the cycle, divided into two parts, although entitled 'The War', is based on episodes not only from the traditional War Book but also from the Kishkindha and the Beautiful Books. It opens with a detailed introduction to the reality of the life of the poor Vānar people, the history of their royal family and the circumstances how Sugrīv ascended the throne of Kishkindha. Sugrīv is depicted as a wise, just ruler, for whom the well-being of his subjects, exposed to the bad influences of the Rākṣasas, is the highest good. Thus, when he meets Rām, they become allies in their fight against their common foe. Taking into consideration the fact that in comparison with other episodes Kohlī does not elaborate much on the course of events concerning the war on Lanka,[94] one can presume that the title war means not so much the climax of the conflict between Rām and Rāvaṇ but rather the constant struggle of Rām and his allies with the people of Rāvaṇ.

The final combat on Lanka is very fierce and so balanced that it is not obvious who will win. Indra, the king of the Devas, upset with such a situation, decides to intervene in order to prevent the possible victory of Rāvaṇ, the enemy of the Devas.[95] Indra manages to bring to his cause Durgā, the wife of Śiv who sides with Rāvaṇ. Durgā reassures him that Śiv will no longer support the unrighteous evil-doer.[96] Thanks to Indra's help, the scales turn in Rām's favour and finally Rāvaṇ falls dead on the battlefield.[97] When after Rām's victory, Hanumān and Vibhīṣaṇ bring Sītā to him, he accepts her and addresses her with the following words:

> *Come, Sita! Now don't stay away from your Rām any more! You have passed a year-long fire-test. Now you should also have some comfort.*[98]

Sītā is not in a position to believe all that has happened to her and Rām.

---

[93] Ibid., pp. 723–7.

[94] Kohlī, *Abhyuday*, vol. 2, pp. 539–621.

[95] Ibid., pp. 593ff.

[96] Ibid., p. 607. Cf. Nirālā's *Rām kī śakti pūjā*.

[97] Ibid., p. 621.

[98] *āo, sīte! (...) apne rām se ab aur dūr nahī̃ raho. ek varṣ kī dīrgh agniparīkṣā dī hai tumne. ab tumhẽ kuch sukh bhī milnā cāhie...*; ibid.

In the end, Vibhīṣaṇ, the new ruler of Lanka, meets Rām and assures him that:

> *Now in Lanka no Śurpanakhas will be born. And those who are already here will have to change their ways. The new society is not cruel but it will either transform the symptoms of transgression [into something positive] or otherwise destroy them.*[99]

These words from Vibhīṣaṇ at the very end of the novel, and thus of, the entire cycle are very symptomatic and surprising. They seem to oversimplify the meaning of Rām's mission and make it shallow, suggesting that it was not so much the evil embodied in Rāvaṇ but the evil embodied in Śūrpaṇakhā that was the real threat to human civilization. It is especially unexpected in view of the fact that this apparently contradicts the message of the overwhelming part of the cycle.

The foregoing discussion reveals that Kohlī, in general, quite closely follows the layout of the traditional narrative. However, he also introduces many new situations and characters whom he treats in a rational way, i.e. demythologizes them. As in the works of other modern authors, Kohlī depicts people and not gods, demons or monkeys and that is why the Devas, the Rākṣasas and the Vānars are as human as the Aryas, although they all have their distinct cultures and these differences lead sometimes to conflicts.

Rām is portrayed as a person sensitive to any kind of injustice, righteous, dutiful, striving for the betterment of other people's lives and providing them with education.[100] It is important to note here that Kohlī's social justice is evidently of a Marxist provenance and one should not be misled with the label of 'democratism' (*janvād*) commonly used in Hindi in such contexts.[101] Its spirit permeates the whole cycle but it is most evident in the passage that treats with the exploitation of the workers of the coal mine in Dandak. As has already been mentioned, Rām finally makes the workers take possession of the mine, thus transferring power to the people.[102] In India, and for that matter anywhere in

---

[99] *ab laṅkā mẽ śūrpaṇakhāẽ utpann na hõgī. jo haĩ bhī, unhẽ apnā mārg badalnā hogā. nayā samāj krūr nahī̃ hai, kintu atyācār ke pratīkõ ko yā to badal degā, anyathā naṣṭ kar degā*; ibid., p. 629.

[100] Kohlī, *Abhyuday*, vol. 1, e.g. pp. 33–4, 44, 252 and 455–7.

[101] Madān, *Samkālīn sāhitya*, p. 143.

[102] Kohlī, *Abhyuday*, vol. 1, pp. 443–54.

the world, such views have numerous supporters as well as opponents but it is also a fact that *Abhyuday* at times becomes heavy with the ideological charge.

Although, in general, the style and plot of the cycle are interesting, a number of its parts are too diffuse. This is especially apparent when Kohlī attempts to provide a suitably modernized, rational context for traditional events. However, because he resorts to it fairly often, the result is a voluminous work, at least twice as big as Tulsīdās's *Rāmcaritmānas*!

Summing up the discussion of Kohlī's Rāmkathā cycle, one can say that, despite the above-mentioned shortcomings, it is an interesting proposal that can be considered not only as a new interpretation of Rām's story but also as an allegory of the condition of contemporary India and the world in general.[103] However, the author's predilection to say too much is its major flaw that, more than once, makes the reading of his work a tiresome task.

BHAGVĀN SIṀH'S *APNE APNE RĀM*[104]

Bhagvān Siṁh's novel was claimed as one of the most controversial and/or the best prose works of the independent era.[105] While some attacked Siṁh's inventiveness and accused him of betraying the ideals of tradition, others treated these very features as strong points of the novel and praised the author for his original treatment of the Rāmāyaṇa. It should also be noted that *Apne apne Rām* appeared in the beginning of 1992, i.e. during the more and more intense agitation of Hindu fundamentalists for, as they used to put it, the 'liberation' of Rām's birthplace from the domination of Muslim rule. This means that the novel was published before the tragic aftermath of this campaign, the demolition of Babri Masjid in Ayodhya on 6th December 1992. It can be as-

[103] Cf. Madān, *Samkālīn sāhitya*, pp. 143–4 and the jackets of both volumes of *Abhyuday*.

[104] For an earlier version of this section see Stasik, 'On Modern Retellings of Rām-kathā', pp. 259–68.

[105] See e.g. Siṁh, 'Rāmkathā kī udheṛ-bun', pp. 67–71; Śarmā, 'Vāh! Rām – āh! Rām', pp. 71–2; Saxena, 'Hero Rama and Villain Vasishta', pp. 193–6; Rāy, 'Sāhitya mẽ lālūvād', pp. 2–4; Varmā, 'Khoe hue kāl kī khoj', pp. 175–85 and Bhāradvāj, 'Rāmkathā kā mithak aur Apne apne Rām', pp. 44–7.

sumed that Siṁh's choice of the theme and contents of his novel are a meaningful reaction to the times in which he was writing. No doubt, it is an important and interesting voice in the discussion on the nature of the Rāmāyaṇa and its hero Rām.

SIṀH'S RĀMKATHĀ

Apne apne Rām is a full-length novel of 306 pages divided into 36 untitled chapters of different length. The main events that form its plot are taken from the story well-established in the Rāmāyaṇa tradition but their causes, the circumstances under which they happen, are utterly different – the most dramatic events in Rām's life are an outcome of a number of court intrigues designed by Kaikeyī and Vasiṣṭha as a logical consequence of their striving to seize power in Ayodhya. It is worth noting here that a renowned Hindi critic, Naṁvar Siṁh, even calls this novel 'a story of a widespread conspiracy' (*viśāl ṣaḍyantr kathā*),[106] and in fact it contains the elements of a skilfully structured political thriller. Moreover, Daśarath's family in *Apne apne Rām* is portrayed not as the very epitome of an ideal family, where – paternal, maternal, fraternal or marital – love and loyalty are the fundamental values. Instead, it is ambition, envy and greed that are the basic motives for the actions undertaken by many characters in the novel.

The narration in Siṁh's telling is not linear – it opens with the events that take place at the court of Ayodhya before Rām sends Sītā away to Vālmīki's ashram and then it regresses and progresses through the medium of the narrator (in the third person narration) and the dialogues as well as interior monologues of the characters of the story (both in the first person narration and the third person narration). The core of the imaginative narrative in Siṁh's novel arranged in chronological order may be summarized as follows.

Daśarath, despite his advanced age still very passionate for women,[107] becomes attracted to Kaikeyī and wants to marry her. Her parents agree to this marriage (this is the third marriage of Daśarath) on condition that their future grandson will ascend the throne of Ayodhya. Kaikeyī comes to Daśarath's capital as his

[106] Siṁh, 'Rāmkathā kī udheṛ-bun', p. 68.
[107] Siṁh, *Apne apne Rām*, pp. 130–1.

wife with her family priest Vasiṣṭha who soon, thanks to her efforts, becomes the court priest of Ayodhya. She is also accompanied by lots of soldiers (among them is also her own brother who becomes the commander of Ayodhya's army) and many servants. Before long, Kaikeyī – continually counselled by Vasiṣṭha – manages to dominate the weak, spineless Daśarath and gains control of Ayodhya. She becomes the mother of Bharat.

Seventeen years after his third marriage, Daśarath launches preparations for the installation of his eldest son Rām as his heir apparent. Thus, it proves that he was not serious when he promised the throne to the son of Kaikeyī. She, greatly upset at such a move by her husband, demands from him the throne for Bharat and a fourteen-year exile for Rām and his wife Sītā. At that time, Bharat together with Śatrughna and the army are proceeding to their mother's family home. (It is worth noting here that the inseparability of Bharat and Śatrughna, on the one hand, and Rām and Lakṣmaṇ, on the other, result from the cool calculations of Sumitrā. She was aware of Kaikeyī and Vasiṣṭha's machinations taking place in Ayodhya and wanted to secure her own future and thus the future of her sons in the best possible way.[108]) Kaikeyī threatens Daśarath that if he does not consent to her demands, the army will turn back home and take up arms against him. He gives in and Vasiṣṭha fabricates the story of two boons that Daśarath allegedly granted to Kaikeyī long ago. This story is supposed to justify the king's decision about Rām's exile, implying that he is forced to act in such a manner in order to be true to his word.[109]

Rām, Sītā and Lakṣmaṇ set off on their journey to the forest. From the very beginning, the spies of Kaikeyī follow them and there are several attempts on their lives.[110] Daśarath dies soon after their departure. The actual cause of his death is poison he was advised to take in order to withdraw from this world with honour in the eyes of his people.[111] After some time Bharat with a huge retinue sets off to fetch Rām back. However, Rām, willing to carry out his dead father's wish, does not want to return to Ayodhya. Therefore, he is asked to touch a golden sandal, which

---

[108] Ibid., p. 61.
[109] Ibid., pp. 136, 144, 162–3.
[110] Ibid., pp. 187, 194–9.
[111] Ibid., p. 78.

will be put on the throne of Ayodhya. It is another scheme designed by Kaikeyī, with Vasiṣṭha's help, meant to prevent Bharat – a vain, unintelligent youth, addicted to alcohol (!) – from ascending the throne officially and thus giving her full freedom to rule the kingdom.[112]

During the exile, Rām and his companions meet different people living in the forest. The longest time they spend in Panchavati, in the neighbourhood of a very primitive tribe nicknamed by them 'Vultures' (*gīdh*) after the way they eat raw meat. Their chief sends to Rām Suparṇā (lit. 'The One Having Beautiful Wings') – afterwards nicknamed by Sītā as Sūrpaṇakhā – one of the most attractive girls of the tribe as a token of their friendship. Rām, not willing to consummate this relationship, rejects the girl who feels greatly insulted and abuses Sītā, pointing out to her her childlessness. In such a way, Sūrpaṇakhā questions Sītā's womanhood which provokes Lakṣmaṇ who, as a punishment, hits her with the wood of his bow.[113]

After some time, Rāvaṇ – helped by Kaikeyī's spy Mārīc, disguised as a deer – kidnaps Sītā. Her abduction is an element of Kaikeyī's scheming. She offers Rāvaṇ, the king of Lanka and a slave trader, a thousand slaves for Sītā. Rāvaṇ, driven by greed, sure that Rām and Lakṣmaṇ will come to her rescue, includes in his own plan also the two brothers. Thus, instead of bringing Sītā to Ayodhya, he takes her to his kingdom where he decides to wait for an occasion to seize the brothers.[114] However, Rāvaṇ's plan fails completely when Rām, supported by the army of the forest people (*narvānar*) led by Hanumān and Aṅgad, attacks Lanka. Their invasion coincides with a revolt of the suppressed subjects of Rāvaṇ against their ruler. When finally Rāvaṇ is killed, Vibhīṣaṇ, a respectable citizen of Lanka, is appointed as the new king. Rām, Sītā and Lakṣmaṇ can return to Ayodhya, as the fourteen years of the exile have expired.[115]

Bharat fears Rām's return, so do Kaikeyī and Vasiṣṭha, as their plans to seize power in Ayodhya as well as to dispose of Rām and Sītā have proved a total failure. First, they want to fight against Rām but then Vasiṣṭha suggests preparing such a lavish

[112] Ibid., pp. 134, 176–7, 181–2.
[113] Ibid., pp. 207–10.
[114] Ibid., pp. 217–26, 230–4.
[115] Ibid., pp. 255–64.

welcome for Rām that admittedly he will get the kingdom back but with an empty treasury. Of course, this is supposed to end his career as king very soon. Indeed, after his installation, Rām has great problems with the administration of his kingdom but after some time he manages to overcome the severe financial crisis.[116] When the kingdom prospers under his rule, slanderous gossip questioning Sītā's virtue during her imprisonment by Rāvaṇ makes Rām send his pregnant wife to Vālmīki's ashram. He does this reluctantly and in secret, acting on Viśvāmitra's advice, in order to protect the unborn heir to the throne of Ayodhya.[117]

At Vālmīki's hermitage, Sītā gives birth to their twin sons, Lav and Kuś. Vālmīki learns from Sītā the story of her and Rām's life. Moved deeply by it, the sage composes a poem which he later teaches the boys. They leave the ashram and perform the poem in public. They finally reach Ayodhya. When Rām hears them sing, he recognizes in them his sons. He sends his brothers, Lakṣmaṇ and Śatrughna, to Vālmīki's ashram with a mission to bring Sītā back. However, she refuses to go with them. Therefore, Rām goes himself as a humble suppliant. Neither Rām nor Sītā utter a single word, she just joins him on the way back to Ayodhya.[118]

TOWARDS A NEW MYTH?

It is apparent that the basic source for Siṁh is the Rāmāyaṇa tradition but he does not always refer to its mainstream. Such fundamental concepts of the Hindu ethos as, e.g. dharma or varṇa, also play an important role in this telling. They are usually used when the author intends to expose the, in his opinion, negative sides of Hindu culture. This is especially evident in these, quite frequent, situations, in which Brahmins and their privileged position or, formulating it in more general terms, the caste society based on the purity of birth are attacked (in these contexts the decidedly leftist outlook of Siṁh is manifest).[119] A good example of such a censorious attitude towards Brahmins is, among other things, a very unsympathetic portrayal of Vasiṣṭha who is virtually behind all the actions against Rām. Therefore, in *Apne apne*

[116] Ibid., pp. 2–3, 242–3, 249–53.
[117] Ibid., pp. 8, 25–33, 114.
[118] Ibid., p. 306.
[119] See e.g. ibid., pp. 4–5, 21, 42, 46, 69–70, 74, 84–5, 127.

Rām it is not Rāvaṇ but Vasiṣṭha who is the real antagonist of Rām. It can be said that Siṁh uses the well-known story of Rām's deeds as a special kind of ready-made symbolic language for his novel, offering his own artistic interpretation of it. He demythologizes this story-myth and is quite successful in bringing it down to rational, realistic dimensions.[120]

One of the most important constituent elements in Siṁh's rationalization is in introducing conflict into Daśarath's family that makes his telling so different from the story known from the tradition. Siṁh's idea departs radically from the concept of the epic poets who, as Robert Goldman observed 'are at pains to minimize and diffuse, if not totally eliminate, conflict within the heroic family. (...) In the world of the *Rāmāyaṇa* struggle must always be directed outward'.[121] However, in *Apne apne Rām* conflict is within the family of Rām which is most obviously introduced as a device meant to make the narrative more probable and to bring the characters of the story closer to common man.

Thus, the characters of the novel are depicted as flesh and blood persons, acting in a world where there is no place for demons, demigods or animals behaving like humans. Therefore, while the traditional story is commonly interpreted in terms of the conflict between good and evil, or dharma–adharma, in Siṁh's novel the ultimate good is found in human beings as well as the progress of human civilization and all that obstructs it is evil. As a result, it can be understood as human striving for development and justice (in the widest sense of this word) and that is why Rām has to struggle with the problems of this world and not with mythical beasts. Putting it differently, *Apne apne Rām* offers a metaphorical exposition of Indian society and civilization expressed through the medium of the acts and words of the characters of Rāmkathā.

One of the most important structural elements of the traditional story, which Siṁh has made use of, is the character of Rām, interpreted in such a way as to express the historical experience of Indian society on its way to progress.[122]

---

[120] Meletinsky, *Poėtika mifa*, pp. 345ff.

[121] Goldman, 'Introduction', p. 53; also see Introduction above, esp. pp. 9–10.

[122] For a more detailed discussion of Rām's character in *Apne apne Rām* see Chapter Nine below.

Siṁh, demythologizing the traditional story, uses it as a tool in his own mythologizing in which an important role is played by history, understood as a source of human experience affecting the present and future of humanity.[123] Rām's understanding of the role of history and the historical experience of mankind is, apparently, of Marxist provenance, and it is best expressed in his own words:

> *(...) for a wise person history is a high and a very firm rock; a highly risen peak, stratified with thousands, hundreds of thousands of years of human experiences, standing on which one can look far away towards the future and can take the precaution of not repeating the mistakes made earlier.*[124]

Does this not mean that *Apne apne Rām*, thanks to Siṁh's poetics, leans towards a new myth that is built both on Rāmkathā and a belief in an intelligent, educated human being, always alert to potential dangers awaiting him in life, able to discern what is beneficial for him?

Undoubtedly, *Apne apne Rām* does not leave its reader indifferent to it – its style is vivid and the skilfully structured plot is absorbing, keeping the reader in suspense till the very end of the novel. A new, original approach to the characters and episodes of the traditional story fully justify the opinion that it is not only one of the best Rāmkathās in Hindi but also one of the best Hindi novels in the last few decades.

CONCLUSIONS

The foregoing analysis of Hindi Rāmkathās of the second half of the twentieth century has revealed their multilayered approach to myth that can be easily related to the discussion of Meletinsky's concepts presented above. Such an approach is especially strongly

---

[123] E.g. Siṁh, *Apne apne Rām*, pp. 54, 258; cf. Meletinsky, *Poėtika mifa*, pp. 366–9 and 417.

[124] *(...) sudhī vyakti ke lie itihās ek ũcī aur sudṛṛh caṭṭān hotā hai. hazārõ, lākhõ varṣ ke mānavīy anubhavõ ke starībhūt hone se ũcā uṭhā śikhar jis par khaṛā hokar vah bhaviṣya kī or dūr tak dekh saktā hai aur is bāt kī sāvadhanī barat saktā hai ki pahle huī bhūlẽ punaḥ duhrāī na jāẽ;* Siṁh, *Apne apne Rām*, p. 54.

pronounced in the novels by Siṁh and, to a lesser degree, by Kohlī, but is also discernible in works by other authors. Three elements structuring the poetics of such authors become notably apparent. Firstly, it is the preservation of the constituent elements of the original myth, i.e. the archetypal myth of Rām as the ideal king and man. Secondly, it is the interpretation of the original myth, through the medium of rationalizing and demythologizing. Thirdly, the introduction of an author's original 'mythological' plot, i.e. individual mythologizing, should be noted here. Such mythologizing manifests itself in the use of mythological designs and motifs as a means to interpret both Indian society and universal human nature.[125] It is based on the elements of the myth of Rām transmitted through the channels of the Rāmāyaṇa tradition, so there is no question of a complete dissociation with the classical myth. However, the story of Rām as retold by Siṁh due to demythologizing and rationalizing, drawing from many other, not only literary, sources (among them very apparent is, e.g. Marxist dialectics) evolves into another myth, a myth of egalitarian society, which has its roots in open access to education, with a human being as the focus of a new cosmos. In other words, it is the Rāmrājya, the ideal rule of Rām, of our times. Thanks to such poetics, these works, and especially *Apne apne Rām,* appear to be a very good example of the intermingling influences, which express the changing modern outlook through the eternal language of Indian tradition.

Summing up this discussion, I also want to note that the multilayered character of these works is apparent not only in their plots but can also be discerned in their titles understood thus as their interpretive frame which is best exemplified by the title of Siṁh's novel that is very revealing as far as the nature of the story of Rām's deeds is concerned. *Apne apne Rām* – 'To Each His Own Ram' – means that no one has the monopoly on Rām and the story of his life and acts,[126] there is no single Rāmkathā and no single interpretation of it. This attitude is, in turn, best expressed in Sītā's words addressed to her sons singing about her and Rām's life: 'It is the poet's truth' (*vah kavi kā satya hai*).[127]

---

[125] Cf. Meletinsky, *Poėtika mifa*, p. 326.

[126] Cf. Siṁh, 'Rāmkathā kī udheṛ-bun', p. 67.

[127] Siṁh, *Apne apne Rām*, p. 301.

PART TWO

THE PROTAGONIST OF THE STORY

CHAPTER SEVEN

On the Nature of Tulsīdās's Rām[1]

INTRODUCTION

As set out above,[2] in the oldest extant form of the story of Rām's life and deeds, i.e. in the *Rāmāyaṇa* ascribed to the sage Vālmīki, Rām figures as the ideal man, the son who without the slightest hesitation acquiesces in his father's will and at the same time is a paragon of brotherly and marital love; he has become known to the world as the 'best of men' (*puruṣottama*). Rām's steadfastness in striving for his people's well-being, true concern for their opinion, as well as his just rule to this day are famous and serve as an epitome of a state, in which all goes according to the prescribed order. Rām is such an ideal character that in India he has become the most important and at the same time the clearest example of a perfect human being. His perfection actually means that, both emotionally and morally, he surpasses the average mortal. Tranquillity, restraint and absolute esteem for the rules of dharma characterize him almost all the time and two moments especially graphically display his character: firstly, his acquiescence in the fourteen-year exile depriving him of the right to the throne of Ayodhya and, secondly, his abstention from defending his beloved wife, Sītā, against the slanderous gossip which spread among his subjects in Ayodhya. They prove that

[1] Parts of this chapter, in their earlier version, were published as Danuta Stasik, 'On the Nature of Rāma in Tulsīdās's Rāmcaritmāṇas', in Dirk W. Lönne, ed., *Toḥfa-e-dil: Festschrift Helmut Nespital*, Reinbek: Dr. Inge Wezler Verlag für Orientalistische Fachpublikationen, 2001, pp. 487–500; idem, 'He Who Dwells in the Hearts of All: Notes on the Nature of Rām in Hindi Literature', *Archiv orientální/Oriental Archive*, vol. 75, no. 3, 2007, pp. 305–27; idem, 'Gniew boży w hinduizmie – na przykładzie poematu Ramćaritmanas' (in Polish), in Anna Duszak and Nina Pawlak, eds., *Anatomia gniewu. Emocje negatywne w językach i kulturach świata*, Warszawa: Wydawnictwa Uniwersytetu Warszawskiego, 2003, pp. 75–83 and idem, 'God's Anger: Notes on the Nature of Tulsīdās's Rām', in Horstmann, *Bhakti in Current Research*, pp. 295–304.

[2] See Introduction above, esp. pp. 8–10.

in the name of the set rules, which are aimed at maintaining law and order, Rām is capable of renouncing his own rights and suppressing his emotions – thus in both situations he is true to the traditional concept of *puruṣārthas*.[3]

Rām's consistent line of conduct and his perfect control of his emotions are the basic reason for the enormous esteem in which he is held in India,[4] despite the oft-overlooked fact that in certain situations he is portrayed as losing control over himself.[5] These situations, among other things, seem to picture him as a character so humanly ambivalent that countless generations of Indians, for different reasons, refer to the story of his life and deeds. One should also not forget that being the ideal man, Rām is also, what seems even more important in this context, the very epitome of kingly virtues.

As I have noted in the preceding discussion, with the passage of time the divinity of Rām became more and more prominent and finally he was equated with the absolute being – God who is always content and infinite in his love and mercy, one of the best expressions of this attitude being found in Tulsīdās's *Rāmcaritmānas*. Drawing upon the most important traditions, the poem has become the embodiment of an ideal of society, state and its ruler. Describing the story of Rām's deeds, the poet set a pattern of behaviour for every Hindu and because his vision has perfectly met the needs of Hindu society, the poem, being a clear exposition of rules governing different spheres of life, has become an authority.

The *Rāmcaritmānas* is one of the best, most complete and most interesting expressions of Bhakti devotion, not only in Hindi literature, but also in Indian literature in general. It gained unprecedented popularity soon after its creation and acted as a stimulus to both the development of the cult of Rām and its stabilization in north India. Above all, it exerted a significant influence on socio-cultural life in the Hindi-speaking region, having become an important component of the north Indian ethos. To seek the causes of the *Rāmcaritmānas*'s success, one has inevitably to turn to its protagonist, the God Rām, who – worshipped and revered – has also become an important cultural

---

[3] See ibid. and Das, 'Kāma in the Scheme of Puruṣārthas'.

[4] Goldman, 'Introduction', pp. 49–50.

[5] For more see below and Stasik, 'God's Anger'.

figure. Such an attitude towards Rām is visible not only in numerous aspects of religious, social and political life[6] but also found a very telling expression in the tragic aftermath of the Ayodhya events of December 1992, when *karsevaks* 'liberated' the Rāmjanmabhūmi, the place commonly believed to have been the birthplace of Rām, demolishing Babri Masjid. There is no doubt that our better understanding of many developments in the religious and socio-political life in today's India is determined, among other things, by our understanding of the protagonist of Tulsīdās's poem. Therefore, I put foreward here an analysis of the character of Rām in his complete manifestation, i.e. as an earthly – or more precisely, kingly – manifestation of the Ultimate Being.

One should remember that while Tulsīdās's Rām epitomizes the most characteristic features of north Indian Bhakti, he is also a product of the long-lived Rāmāyaṇa tradition, which over centuries has been influenced by various religious, mythological, theological and philosophical concepts and ideas. But although a number of important passages of the *Rāmcaritmānas* (and among them those which are concerned with the figure of Rām) contain more or less developed notions of a philosophical nature, it should be stressed that Tulsīdās was first and foremost not a philosopher but a bhakta, who in his poetry worshipped Rām as his chosen deity (*iṣṭa-devatā*) and contemplated his nature.[7] It may be added here that Ramaite sects descending from Rāmānanda – like Rāmānanda himself – did not formulate a cohesive philosophical system; their discourse is, however, based on Rāmānuja's *viśiṣṭādvaita* coloured strongly by the teachings of other schools.[8] As a result, the image produced by Tulsīdās is not homogenous and Rām appears as a God whose nature is composite. First of all, he is God infinite in his mercy who in his non-

---

[6] For more on this subject see, e.g. Philip Lutgendorf, 'Interpreting Rāmrāj: Reflections on the *Rāmāyaṇa*. Bhakti, and Hindu Nationalism', in Lorenzen, *Bhakti Religion in North*, pp. 253–87 and Peter van der Veer, 'The Politics of Devotion to Rāma', ibid., pp. 288–305.

[7] Cf. Whaling, *The Rise*, p. 239. This very useful study is of much interest to all concerned with the nature of Rām, and especially in its theological implications.

[8] Cf. Farquhar, *An Outline of the Religious Literature of India*, p. 326.

manifested form is a *nirguṇ Brahman* – the Absolute, the unqualified Ultimate Being and in his manifested form is a *saguṇ Brahman* – the qualified, personal Ultimate Being. At the same time, Rām did not cease to be an avatāra of Viṣṇu known from the Purāṇas and the Rāmāyaṇa tradition and Viṣṇu himself, although he is both distinct from and superior to him – in the *Rāmcaritmānas,* he is the Supreme Being who, having become incarnate as a human being, has to overcome numerous adversities.

The intertwining elements of Rām's nature are very difficult, often impossible, to separate, but at least in one respect Tulsīdās's poem leaves no doubt – whatever Rām does in this world, having appeared in the form of Daśarath's son, it is a divine drama or *līlā*.[9] In the *Rāmcaritmānas* the divinity of Rām dominates.

In the following analysis, I seek to explore the composite character of Rām, viewing him not only as a literary figure but also as a cultural hero, the one who shows others what the proper life should look like.

The Incarnate Absolute

Divine Aspect

On a number of occasions, Tulsīdās stresses that it is not easy to penetrate the nature of Rām. Even gods and sages find it difficult, which is clearly expressed in one of the passages in Book 1. It forms a fragment of the dialogue between Śiv and Parvatī, who – having problems with the understanding of Rām's nature – turns for help to her spouse:

> *O Ananga, the Enemy of Kam!*
> *Day and night you reverently repeat: 'Ram! Ram!'*
> *[Is] this Ram the son of the King of Ayodhya,*
> *[or] some other unborn, unqualified, invisible [being]?*
> *If he [is] the king's son, how [can] he [also be] the Absolute*
> *and losehis senses [because of] the separation from [his] wife? (...)*

[9] E.g. RCM 1.36.3, 1.105.1, 1.113.4 or 1.110.4, 1.141.3, 6.61.9 and 6.73.6. Cf. K.P. Bahadur, *Rāmacharitamānasa: A Study in Perspective*, Delhi: Ess Ess Publications, 1976, pp. 160–1.

And [what] if someone else [is] the desireless, all-pervading, omnipresent [Absolute]? O Lord, explain it to me! (1.108.4–109.1)[10]

Śiv utters the following words almost at the beginning of his reply to Parvatī:

With qualities [or] without – there is no difference,
so sing munis, Puranas, wise men and the Veda.
The unqualified, formless, invisible, unborn,
out of love for devotees becomes the qualified (1.116.1).[11]

Book 2 contains one more telling exemplification of the composite nature of Rām underlying its most important constituent elements. It refers to the moment when Rām, at the beginning of his exile, reaches Vālmīki's abode. Rām turns to the sage for advice and asks where he could find a place to stay with Sītā and Lakṣmaṇ. Vālmīki does not answer immediately, as he is aware of how complicated it is to give advice to someone who inhabits the whole world, permeates it – who is the whole world![12] Before expressing his opinion, he addresses Rām with the following words:

Ram, you are the guardian of the bounds of propriety
set by the Veda and Janaki is your power that
according to your will, O Store of Mercy,
creates, preserves or destroys the world. (...)
On account of the gods you have assumed the body of a human king
and set out to crush the army of vile demons.

Ram! Your nature transcends speech and goes beyond understanding. It is ubiquitous, ineffable, infinite; the Veda always calls it 'not this, not this'.

---

[10] *tumha puni rāma rāma dina rātī; sādara japahū anãga ārātī./ rāmu so avadha nṛpati suta soī; kī aja aguna alakha gati koī./ jaũ nṛpa tanaya ta brahma kimi nāri birahã mati bhori; (...) jaũ anīha byāpaka bibhu koū; kahahu bujhāi nātha mohi soū.*

[11] *sagunahi agunahi nahĩ kachu bhedā; gāvahĩ muni purāna budha bedā./ aguna arūpa alakha aja joī;/ bhagata prema basa saguna so hoī.*

[12] Cf. e.g. the epithets: *bisvarūpa raghubaṁsa mani* (RCM 6.14) or *jagamaya prabhu* (7.15.4).

The world is a spectacle and you are [its] spectator;
making Brahma, Vishnu and Shiv dance [at your will] (2.126 chand – 127.1).[13]

These passages stress the most essential elements of the divine nature of Rām. He is *Brahman*, the unqualified, unknowable Absolute, who elsewhere in the poem is also said to be: 'without beginning' (*anādi/anādī*; 1.21.1, 1.108.3),[14] 'without form' (*arūpa*; 1.13.2), 'without shape' (*nirākāra*; 7.72.3), 'eternal' (*nitya*; 7.72.3). Rām is 'the cause of the whole world' (*akhila bisva kārana*; 1.208), which at his request is created, preserved and destroyed by Sītā, said to be his creative power (*māyā jānakī*);[15] he is the foundation and soul of the world (*jagadādhārā*; 6.77.2; *jagadātma*; 6.35.3) and pervades it, dwelling in 'the city of the hearts of all' (*saba ura pura*; 1.120.3).[16]

It should be stressed that Rām in the *Rāmcaritmānas* is not simply one of many gods – he is the Supreme Being who makes Brahmā, Viṣṇu and Śiv, the Hindu Holy Trinity (*trimūrti*), do whatever he wants them to do. It is symptomatic that he acts not only as the guardian of the Veda,[17] protecting the bounds of propriety set by it, but he is also its vital breath (*beda prāna*; 1.19.1), its summit (*śrutimāthā*; 1.128.2) and his name is 'the essence of śruti' (*śruti sārā*; 1.10.1). What is more, the Vedas that,

---

[13] *śruti setu pālaka rāma tumha jagadīsa māyā jānakī;/ jo sṛjati jagu pālati harati rukha pāi kṛpānidhāna kī./ (...) sura kāja dhari nararāja tanu cale dalana khala nisicara ani./ rāma sarūpa tumhāra bacana agocara buddhipara;/ abigata akatha apāra neti neti nita nigama kaha./ jagu pekhana tumha dekhanihāre; bidhi hari sambhu nacāvanihāre.*

[14] Most of these epithets occur in the poem more than once; therefore, I refer only to their first occurrence and/or their most characteristic usage. Of great help to me has been an extremely useful RCM word index by Winand M. Callewaert and Philip Lutgendorf, *Rāmcaritmānas Word Index*, Delhi: Manohar, 1997. Cf. also Suryakant, *Index Verborum to Tulasīdāsa's Rāmāyaṇa*, Delhi: Meharchand Lachhmandas, 1973 (1st published in 1937).

[15] For more about the goddess as God's creative power (*māyā*) see Hawley and Wulff, *The Divine Consort*, esp. pp. 67–9, 154–6 and 375.

[16] Cf. RCM 1.259.3 and 7.72.4.

[17] Cf. *beda* (...) *racchaka* (RCM 5.39.2) or *setu śruti racchaka* (7.35.4).

in many points in the poem, sing Rām's praises,[18] assume the human form of Brahmins[19] and royal bards[20] in order to be able to worship and extol him 'in person'.[21] It should be noted here that a fairly frequent occurrence of the word Veda[22] in the text of the *Rāmcaritmānas* is by no means coincidental; the authority of the Veda is, among other things, evoked in order to sanction the sacredness of Rām himself.[23] A point made by F. Whaling is worth mentioning in this context. According to him, Rām and his Bhakti complete the Veda, which otherwise would be like the Holy Bible consisting only of the Old Testament.[24]

Rām in his manifested form, acquired by him – according to the textual evidence – at the request of the gods in order to destroy demons and to protect the world from imminent danger, is the most dear to Tulsīdās's heart. The reasons for Rām's appearing in the world in human form are given many times and in different ways, which seems to be justified, e.g. by Śiv's words: 'there are many causes of Rām's birth and each one [is] stranger than the other.[25] Their analysis, however, proves that they are not much different from the well-known causes of Viṣṇu's becoming an avatāra and basically should be viewed as their development. It is clear from one of the most extensive formulations, in which Śiv explains this question to Parvatī. He tells her that any time dharma is threatened by the growing power of demons who resort to unimaginable violence against Brahmins, cows, gods and Earth, the Lord (*prabhu*), having assumed different forms, appears in the world and delivers the earth from danger, killing demons, restoring gods to the places due to them and protecting the Veda of which he is the essence (1.121.3–121).

---

[18] E.g. RCM 1.12, 1.51 chand, 1.108.3, 2.105, 6.48.4, 7.12kha–13ka, 7.34.3.

[19] RCM 1.323.

[20] RCM 2.105 and 7.12ka.

[21] Cf. Whaling, *The Rise*, p. 272.

[22] The word Veda (separately, not in compounds) occurs in the poem 174 times (93 – *beda* and 81 – *śruti*); Callewaert and Lutgendorf, *Rāmcaritmānas Word Index*, pp. 224 and 284.

[23] Cf. Macfie, *The Ramayan of Tulsidas*, p. 156.

[24] Whaling, *The Rise*, p. 273. P.A. Grincer expresses similar thought, likening the Veda to the Old Testament and the *Mahābhārata* and *Rāmāyaṇa* to the New Testament; idem, *Drevneindijskij ėpos*, p. 7.

[25] *rāma janama ke hetu anekā; parama bicitra eka tē̃ ekā*; RCM 1.122.1.

As noted above, Rām assumes human form and thus becomes a personal god out of his love for devotees (1.116.1).[26] This view is corroborated and developed in different parts of the poem. For example, Bṛhaspati, the preceptor of the gods, reveals to Indra that the 'unqualified, spotless, immeasurable, unchanging Rām has become qualified out of love for his devotees' (2.219.3).[27] Śiv explains (1.122.1) that 'the Ocean[28] of Mercy assumes a body for the well-being of people'.[29] In the same book (1.192), there is a passage elaborating on this, in which Kausalyā addresses Rām after his birth: 'You assumed a human body for the well-being of Brahmins, cows, gods and saints'.[30] All such passages deal with a God who is compassionate and brimming with infinite love for his devotees.

This image constitutes the most characteristic feature of Bhakti devotion, in which all who offer loyalty and love to their Lord can rest assured that the Lord will reciprocate these feelings. This is the mutual bond of Bhakti, which really matters to Rām. He expresses this attitude, e.g. during his meeting with Śabarī, a woman of low caste who wonders whether she could praise him:

> *I acknowledge no relationship save Bhakti.*
> *Caste, lineage, righteous way of life, status,*
> *wealth, power, family, virtue, ability –*
> *how splendid is a man [with all these but] without Bhakti?*
> *He is as splendid as a cloud without water!* (3.35.2–3)[31]

The love of Rām rises above all divisions, as they do not matter in the world of Bhakti. It is nicely depicted in another situation in which Hanumān and Rām meet for the first time.

---

[26] It should be remembered that in Bhakti it is both the love of devotees and the love for devotees. See below.

[27] *aguna alepa amāna ekarasa; rāmu saguna bhae bhagata pema basa.*

[28] The word 'ocean' (*sāgara, sindhu, ambunidhi*) is a very frequent constituent in the epithets of Rām.

[29] *kṛpāsindhu jana hita tanu dharahī̃.*

[30] *bipra dhenu sura santa hita līnha manuja avatāra.*

[31] (…) *mānaū̃ eka bhagati kara nātā./ jāti pā̃ti kula dharma baṛāī; dhana bala parijana guna caturāī./ bhagati hīna nara sohai kaisā; binu jala bārida dekhia jaisā.*

Hanumān, like Śabarī, is doubtful whether he deserves the honour of worshipping Rām. Rām assures him that he is twice as dear to him as Lakṣmaṇ (*lachimana te dūnā*) and then adds – maybe not in much consistency with it – that although everyone calls him 'viewing all equally' (*samadarasī*; 4.3.4), his devotees, seeing in him their only resort, are especially dear to him. Therefore, it is not surprising that Rām is regarded as the Abode of Love (*saneha nidhāna*; 2.66), the Ocean of Mercy (*kṛpāsindhu*; 1.122.1 or *kṛpā ambunidhi*; 2.267.1) and his grace as infinite. He is compassionate (*karunāmaya*; 2.40.2) not only to bhaktas sincerely devoted to him but even to those who (albeit demons) incidentally utter his name and, having done so, become released from the wheel of births (6.45.1–3). The whole of existence depends on Rām (6.6.5), because being the 'father and the mother of the world' (*jagata pitu mātā*; 1.200.1), Lord of the World (*bhuvanesvara*), he is the Death of Death (*kālahu kara kālā*; 5.39.1). He is also pictured as a true supporter or cherisher of the poor (*garība nevājū*; 1.13.4), compassionate for the suffering (*dīnadayāla*; 1.16, 2.102.4) and as 'the refuge of the helpless, the supporter of the suffering'[32] and, therefore, he is regarded as the Ultimate Well-Being (*parama hita*; 2.298.1).

Rām is 'the Lord of the inanimate and the animate', i.e. of creation in its entirety (*aga jaga nātha*; 7.2 chand), 'the Lord of vital breath' (*prānanātha*; 2.64), the 'sun [dissipating] the darkness of sin' (*pātaka tama taranī*; 2.248.1) and he delivers people from ignorance and vice (1.285.1, 3.4.2). He carries them across the 'ocean of existence' (*bhava sāgara*) and releases them from rebirth (1.2.1, 3.10.5). All this makes him a true 'giver of all happiness' (*sakala sukha dāyaka*; 1.146.1).

This analysis of the divine aspect of the character of Rām, reveals that Tulsīdās pictures him as a God who is ready to protect anyone irrespective of their status and morals. Moreover, it is not difficult to secure his compassion – one's readiness to yield to him and the repetition of his name are enough, though, as the textual evidence proves, even this is not indispensable.[33]

---

[32] *asarana sarana dīna jana gāhaka*; RCM 7.51.2.

[33] Cf. Whaling, *The Rise*, p. 306.

HUMAN ASPECT

Rām was known in the world as 'Daśarath's son, kind to bhaktas, the lord of Kosala, God [incarnate]' (1.118).[34] In this very form he performs his memorable exploits, which are dear to the hearts of those who love him. Yet his earthly existence viewed from the perspective of his divine self is nothing other than a play, in which he himself participates both as actor (*naṭa iva kapaṭa carita kara nānā*; 6.73.6) and as spectator (*jagu pekhana tumha dekhanihāre*; 2.127.1). Thus, portraying Rām's humanity, Tulsīdās does not let one forget that one is dealing with God. What is more, even if Rām just plays the role of a man, he has not only to play it according to the expectations of the people who surround him but also, most probably, not against their nature.[35]

In the *Rāmcaritmānas*, as in Vālmīki's *Rāmāyaṇa*, it is righteousness that, above all, characterizes Rām – his steadfast devotion to truth and dharma are testified to in a number of the poem's passages. One of the most telling of them forms a part of Rām's answer given to Sumantra, Daśarath's minister, who tries to persuade him to come back to Ayodhya:

> *There is no dharma equal to truth.*
> *so preach the Agamas, Nigamas and Puranas*
> *I have acquired it naturally*
> *had I abandoned it, the three worlds would have been disgraced.*
>
> *[And] disgrace to a man of honour*
> *is like a fearful fire of myriads of deaths* (2.95.3–4).[36]

The question of dharma, and of following its path, is very important for Tulsīdās, which seems to be a natural consequence of the reasons for Rām's avatāra – 'he descends to earth for the sake of dharma' (*dharama hetu avatarehu*; 4.9.3).[37] There are many

---

[34] *dasaratha suta bhagata hita kosalapati bhagavāna.*

[35] Interesting remarks concerning this thesis can be found in Pollock, 'Introduction', vol. 3, pp. 63–4.

[36] *dharamu na dūsaṛa satya samānā; āgama nigama purāna bakhāna./ maĩ soi dharamu sulabha kari pāva; tajẽ tihũ pura apajasu chāvā./ sambhāvit kahũ apajasa lāhū; marana koṭi sama dāruna dāhū.*

[37] Cf. RCM 1.121.3–121 and above.

passages in the *Rāmcaritmānas* which refer to dharma directly[38] and most of them are related to Rām. Tulsīdās depicts him as the 'guardian of the bounds of dharma' (*dharama setu pālaka*; 1.218.4) or simply the 'guardian of dharma' (*dharama racchaka*; 5.39.2), as well as a 'mighty upholder of dharma' (*dharama dhurandhara*;[39] 2.78.1) and the 'armour of dharma' (*dharma varma*; 3.11.8). In the culminating stage of the battle, before the decisive encounter with Rāvaṇ, Rām sets off to the battle on foot, declaring that dharma is his chariot (*dharmamaya ratha*); thanks to this, he is able to defeat the most potent of foes – the cycle of births, i.e. life and death (6.80.2–80).

The essential feature of Rām's nature, as has already been mentioned, is his devotion to truthfulness (*satyabrata*; 2.207.2, 292) and being true to his (and not only to his) word (*satyasandha*; 2.82.1, 254.2). His acquiescence to a fourteen-year exile, which enabled his father's word given to Kaikeyī to be fulfilled, is the best example of this. In this context, Rām expresses very meaningful words, presenting him as an ideal son. He says that blessed (*baṛbhāgī*) is the son who is devoted to his parents' words (2.41.4). Somewhat later, he adds that blessed is the life (*dhanya janamu*) of a man whose father is pleased with his deeds and that the four goals of life are attained by those to whom their parents are as dear as their own lives (*priya pitu mātā prāna sama*; 2.46.1). It is worth remembering that Rām is a man of his word, no matter at what cost, because he knows that the well-being of all depends on it (7.41.1). At the same time, he is the epitome of virtuous nature – the 'Ocean of Virtue' (*sīlasindhu*; 2.243.1), thus setting an example to others.

Rām in the *Rāmcaritmānas* is as uncompromising as in Vālmīki's *Rāmāyaṇa*, yet one can note that Tulsīdās diminished, to a certain degree, the steadfastness of Rām's character by structuring his telling in a different way. He achieved this making Rām avoid situations resulting in dramatic decisions.

---

[38] Their exact number is 172; Callewaert and Lutgendorf, *Rāmcaritmānas Word Index*, pp. 147–9; cf. Suryakant, *Index Verborum*, pp. 265–6 and 268.

[39] It is also an epithet of other characters', e.g. of Daśarath and Bharat; see e.g. RCM 1.143.3, 1.153.2, 1.188.4 and 2.30.

The most obvious example of this is the episode concerned with the banishment of Sītā, which in the Rāmāyaṇa tradition has become a source of many controversies and which for centuries has been attracted different authors. Many of them, including Tulsīdās, in one way or another have tried to solve this dilemma in the life of a hero considered to be the ideal man. Therefore, although Tulsīdās makes Rām test Sītā's faithfulness in the ordeal by fire (6.108.6–109), his poem leaves no doubt that he does it for the sake of tradition and that in fact it is an element of the divine play, *līlā*. It is aimed at destroying an 'illusory Sītā' and restoring the real one who (as in the *Adhyātma rāmāyaṇa*), acting under the orders of Rām, entered the fire, having left outside only her shadow or reflection (*pratibimba*; 3.24.1–3). In consequence, in the *Rāmcarit-mānas* Rāvaṇ kidnapped the illusory Sītā and there was no reason for her later banishment.

Another important innovation is the episode of the killing of Śambūk, a Shudra practising ascetic austerities and thus breaking the prescribed order of things – Tuslsīdās simply skips this incident. This omission can be explained when one refers to Bhakti[40] as an ideology which is an expression of the orthodoxy's attempt to open itself to all classes of Hindu society. One should not, however, be misled by a number of passages in the *Rāmcarit-mānas* that testify to Shudras' low position and even express derogatory opinions of them and thus seem to contradict this attitude.[41] Bhakti meant an opening of the way to God, opening of the doors to salvation[42] and not, as is sometimes believed, a social reform aimed at the abolition of caste system.[43] That is why Tulsīdās saw nothing wrong in referring to the ideal picture of a social hierarchy, although it is also true that he chose to save Rām, the Ocean of Mercy, from staining his hands with Śambūk's blood. Such a solution provokes a question whether it was not also designed to attract new devotees of Rām from among the

[40] Meaning *saguṇī* Bhakti here; for more see Lorenzen, 'Introduction. The Historical Vicissitudes of Bhakti Religion', pp. 13–21.

[41] E.g.: RCM 3.34.1, 5.59.3, 7.99.1, 99kha and 100.5.

[42] Lorenzen, 'Introduction. The Historical Vicissitudes of Bhakti Religion', p. 15.

[43] David Lorenzen rightly notes that *saguṇī* Bhakti has served to justify *varṇāśrama* dharma; cf. ibid., p. 20.

Shudras? Whatever the correct answer to this question is, one can see how a small episode, or rather its absence, becomes an important testimony to Tulsīdās's beliefs, which were in accordance with his own times and his social milieu.

Considering the human aspect of Rām's nature in the *Rāmcaritmānas,* one may have the impression that though one is dealing with the same character as depicted by Vālmīki, Tulsīdās's Rām is, in certain aspects, much closer and more familiar to an average member of the *Rāmcaritmānas*'s audience. Tusīdās achieved such a result by devoting more attention to important moments in the life of his protagonist.[44] First one sees Rām as a child trying to utter his first words, inclined, as most children are, to being playful and mischievous. His loving parents, Kausalyā and Daśarath, fondle and pamper him.[45] As a youth he is brave, wise, full of respect for his elders (1.205.1–4). When the right time comes, he undergoes the prescribed rites, Hindu sacraments (*saṁskāra*), such as: the name-giving ceremony (1.197.1–198.1), the first shaving of his head (203.2), the initiation, i.e. the investiture with the sacred thread (1.204.2), and later the marriage ceremony (1.286–361). It is very meaningful that while Tulsīdās introduced the first three rituals, so to speak, for the sake of presenting the scheme of an ideal life, in his depiction of the nuptial rites he did not restrict himself to presenting a mere scheme but also filled it with splendid contents. Judging by the length of this presentation, one may contend that Tulsī ascribed a special significance to that event in Rām's life, which can be related to the fact that *vivāha* is considered to be the most important Hindu sacrament – 'it is the origin and centre of all domestic sacrifices'.[46]

Tulsīdās, offering accomplished descriptions of the magnificence of Rām and Sītā's nuptials, skilfully disclaims his own poetical skills:

---

[44] Cf. Whaling, *The Rise*, p. 253.

[45] RCM 1.198.4–198, 199.5, 200.4–200, 203.1, 203–204.1.

[46] Raj Bali Pandey, *Hindu Saṁskāras: Socio-religious Study of the Hindu Sacraments*, Delhi: Motilal Banarsidass, 1969, p. 153; cf. Stasik, 'The Divine Marriage', p. 246.

It can be told neither by hundreds of Sharadas,[47]
Sheshas, the Vedas, Viranchis,[48] *Maheshas nor Ganeshas;*
so how could I tell?
Can an earthworm support the Earth on its head? (1.355.3)[49]

Tulsī knows very well that these are the very moments that Rām is being born as a *gṛhastha,* a householder, the master of his hearth and home (although one should not forget that soon he will have to abandon it for a long time).

To this day, the passages describing the nuptial rites of Rām and Sītā are very popular and they are often recited or sung, giving much pleasure to the listening audience. They function as a pattern deserving of imitation, which is also testified to by the number of wedding songs (not infrequently they are a closer or more distant echo of the poem), in which the names of Rām and Sītā often serve as synonyms of a bride and a groom.[50] One can sum up by bringing to our attention an opinion of F. Whaling who rightly observes that in these long descriptions of moving marriage scenes Tulsī 'supplies what must have been a long-felt need in the Rāma tradition for a fully adequate treatment of this important event. (...) In the process we gain a clearer view of Rāma the man who married Sītā, the woman'.[51]

Although the human aspect of Rām's nature is easily seen in all books, it plays the most prominent role in Book 2, the Book of Ayodhya. Nevertheless, even here one cannot forget that Rām is the Supreme Being, the all-pervading Absolute.[52] In this context, an interesting observation made by F. Whaling is worth recalling. He noted that in the narrative of Book 2 Tulsīdās does not use the term *līlā,* the divine play, 'which brings out the reality of Rāma's manhood in a more systematic way than the rest of the work'.[53]

---

[47] Sharada (Śāradā) – an epithet of Sarasvatī.

[48] Viranchi (Virañci) – an epithet of Brahmā.

[49] *kahi na sakahī̃ sata sārada sesū; beda birañci mahesa ganesū./ so maĩ kahaū̃ kavana bidhi baranī; bhūmināgu sira dharai ki dharani.*

[50] Cf. Agarwala, 'Marriage Songs in Harauti', e.g. pp. 151–2 and 175–7; Archer, *Songs for the Bride,* e.g. pp. 58, 60, 90, 101–5 and 114.

[51] Whaling, *The Rise,* p. 243.

[52] Cf. Macfie, *The Ramayan of Tulsidas,* pp. 107 and 110.

[53] Whaling, *The Rise,* p. 313; cf. Callewaert and Lutgendorf, *Rāmcaritmānas Word Index,* p. 280.

RĀM THE KING

In one of the above quoted passages, one reads:

> *On account of gods you have assumed the body of a human king and set out to crush the army of vile demons.*

These words are expressive of the fact that Tulsīdās's Rām is not just a human – he is born into the royal family of Ayodhya and in due time Daśarath intends to appoint him to become his heir, the Young King (*yuva rājā*) of Ayodhya. However, the fulfilment of his father's wish is postponed by Kaikeyī who demands a fourteen-year exile for Rām and the throne for her son, Bharat. Rām does not show any sign of distress when he hears the decision concerning his future that has been forced upon his father. What is more, he accepts it gladly, considering that the time spent in the forest in the company of sages and ascetics will contribute in every way to his well-being (2.41).

As known from the Rāmāyaṇa tradition and indicated in the above-quoted verses, the period of Rām's life (especially in exile) served the purpose of eliminating the forces of evil personified by demons (and by Rāvaṇ in particular) and all that was in accordance with the plan designed by the gods. However, in the *Rāmcaritmānas*, unlike in Vālmīki's *Rāmāyaṇa*, Rām is aware of this plan – he is the all-knowing actor-spectator. Although there can be no doubt that the victory over Rāvaṇ is a crucial point in the *Rāmcaritmānas*'s narrative, it seems – especially in view of the later developments in the Rāmāyaṇa tradition – that in itself it is not the ultimate end of Rām's mission. His victory should rather be viewed as a factor determining the achievement of his ultimate objective, i.e. the re-establishment of an ideal order in the world. Such a moment comes when the victorious Rām ascends the throne of Ayodhya and Rāmrājya, his famous just rule, the culmination of his earthly existence as Rām, ensues.[54]

---

[54] Or rather, can be continued without any impediment. In the opinion of Rāmkiṅkar Upādhyāy, a renown RCM expounder: 'Rāmrāj itself must be reckoned to begin not from the moment of Rām's installation on the throne of Ayodhya, but paradoxically, from the moment when he steps across its borders into exile'; quoted in Lutgendorf, 'Interpreting

Tulsīdās, like Vālmīki,[55] devoted relatively little space to the account of Rāmrājya – it occupies about two and a half strophes (i.e. thirty-seven verses) in the opening part of Book 7 (7.20.3–23). It should be noted that the numbers of the verses describing Rāmrājya given here are in accordance both with Indian commentarial tradition and with the opinion of most Western scholars.[56] Nevertheless, at least one different opinion should also be noted here. A.G. Menon and G.H. Schokker,[57] in their article devoted to Rām's rule, maintain that only verses 7.20.4–22.3 contain Tulsīdās's original vision of Rāmrājya, viewing the rest, i.e. 7.22.4–23, as a mere tribute paid to the tradition of classical Indian descriptions of the golden age. Such a contention seems quite controversial. Firstly, A.G. Menon and G.H. Schokker assume that the latter part of the description can be safely omitted, because, accordingly to them, it does not express Tulsīdās's own views. Therefore, they exclude it from their analysis as if it did not exist. Secondly, the way they divide the whole passage is astonishing, because, in fact, this more stereotyped description – but nevertheless still forming a part of the *Rāmcaritmānas* – consists only of the verses 7.23.1–23. It seems that the authors' decision to omit this fragment cannot be justified by the tradition and is also groundless. What is more, it impoverishes the picture created by Tulsīdās.

Thus, the description of Rāmrājya in the *Rāmcaritmānas* begins just after the presentation of the ceremony of Rām's consecration as king (7.20.3). It is said that the three worlds rejoiced seeing Rām seated on the throne.

All griefs were gone, no one felt hostility (*bayaru*) towards others, thanks to Rām's power all inequality (*biṣamatā*)

Rāmrāj', p. 258. The analysis of different Hindi tellings of the Rāmāyaṇa, put forward in Part One, corroborates this opinion.

[55] See 6.116.83–90 in *Vālmīki Rāmāyaṇa: Text as Constituted in Its Critical Edition*, Vadodara: M.S. University of Baroda, 1992.

[56] See e.g. Śaraṇ, *Mānaspīyūṣ*, vol. 7, pp. 162–3 and Lutgendorf, 'Interpreting Rāmrāj', pp. 262–3.

[57] A.G. Menon and G.H. Schokker, 'The Conception of Rāma-rājya in South and North Indian Literature', in A.W. van den Hoek et al., eds, *Ritual, State and History in South Asia: Essays in Honour of J.C. Heesterman*, Leiden: E.J. Brill, 1992, pp. 612 and 625.

disappeared. All people were devoted to their own duties resulting from their social status and stage of life (*baranāśrama*) and followed the path of the Veda (*beda patha*), which was the cause of their happiness. No one was affected with any sort of suffering (neither bodily, nor caused by divine forces or worldly existence; *daihika daivika bhautika tāpa*). All lived in accordance with their dharma (*svadharma*) and the rules of moral conduct expounded by the Veda (*śruti nīti*); sin (*agha*) did not appear even in dreams. Men and women were engrossed in devotion to Rām (*rāma bhagati rata*) and all deserved to attain the ultimate state (*paramagati ke adhikārī*). No one died young (*alpmṛtyu*), no one suffered from any disease and their bodies were beautiful; no one was poor (*daridra*), distressed or wretched (*kou dukhī na dīna*).[58] In short, it can be said that the rule of Rām was the source of his people's well-being and their high morals, e.g. there were no hypocrites (*nirdambha*), nobody who would know how to cheat or deceive (*nahī̃ kapaṭa sayānī*); just the opposite – all of them were not only clever, wise, learned, virtuous and full of merit (*catura; gyānī; paṇḍita; gunī; punī*), but they also knew how to recognize the merits of others (*gunagya*) and how to be grateful (*kṛtagya*).[59] All men and women were generous (*udāra*), extremely helpful (*para upakārī*) and full of reverence for Brahmins – they were the 'servants of Brahmins' feet' (*bipra caraṇa sevaka*). All men, like Rām, had only one wife (*ekanāri brata*), and wives, in their turn, were devoted to the well-being of their husbands (*pati hitakārī*) with their hearts and thoughts (*mana*), words (*bacana*) and deeds (*krama*).[60]

Under Rām's rule the entire creation (*sacarācara*) was free from suffering[61] and his kingdom was safe from any sign of violence or imminent danger. In his realm, which encompassed the whole Earth, girdled by the belt of the seven oceans (*bhūmi sapta sāgara mekhalā*[62]), trees were always in blossom and fruit, animals lived in harmony; the entire Nature was favourable to men – it

---

[58] RCM 7.20.4–21.3.
[59] RCM 7.21.3–4.
[60] RCM 7.22.4.
[61] RCM 7.21.
[62] RCM 7.22.1.

was a land of milk and honey.[63] Thanks to Rām's rule, which took place in the *tretayuga*, the *kṛtayuga*, the golden age, returned.[64]

It is worth noting here that Tulsīdās begins his description of Rāmrājya just after the enthronement ceremony. And although, for obvious reasons, there is no discussion of his rule, the picture created by the poet presents us immediately with an ideal state of all things. It seems to be a logical consequence of the structure of the *Rāmcaritmānas*'s narrative. There was no need for Tulsīdās to go on at length about the protagonist of his story and about his rule at that particular moment, because the whole poem had given evidence of his ideal nature! No wonder that its exemplary hero became an ideal king of the realm of universal happiness (often termed as a utopia) in such a natural way. It should be noted, however, that considering Rām's kingdom as a utopia is justified only when one does not forget to add that it is a utopia by the standards of Hindu tradition and its hierarchical order,[65] which is clearly stated not only at the beginning of the description of Rāmrājya (7.20; cf. also 7.22.4) but also in a number of other passages of the *Rāmcaritmānas*.[66] However, there is one essential innovation – thanks to Rāmbhakti all can hope to attain the realm of their chosen God who, in a more explicit way than in the preceding Rāmāyaṇa tradition, functions as the Divine King, Lord of Heaven and Earth,[67] embodying the features of both these worlds. Thus in this context, the fundamental feature of Rām's character becomes apparent. Putting to death his opponent, Rāvaṇ, Rām did what for certain reasons neither gods nor humans were able to do. He thus proved his true nature, the nature of man-god, or more precisely of a divine king,[68] who is a real support to his subjects, saves them from any imminent danger and at the same time is the embodiment of virtues essential for the harmonious existence of any society. These features of Rām's

---

[63] Ph. Lutgendorf noted that under Rām's rule even 'elemental limitations were transcended'. Lutgendorf, 'Interpreting Rāmrāj', p. 262.

[64] RCM 7.22–23.

[65] Cf. Lutgendorf, 'Interpreting Rāmrāj', p. 267.

[66] One of the best expressions is RCM 2.172.2–3.

[67] Cf. Lutgendorf, 'Interpreting Rāmrāj', p. 257.

[68] For more on this subject see Pollock, 'The Divine King in the Indian Epic' and idem, 'Introduction', vol. 3.

nature, and especially his divinity, portrayed by Vālmīki rather symbolically,[69] were taken up and developed in the later tradition. The culmination of this process was the rise and lively growth of Rām's cult (Rāmbhakti), in which an important role was played by the *Rāmcaritmānas*.

One more aspect of Rām's character should be acknowledged here. As I have pointed out elsewhere,[70] some authors, with Anuradha Kapur among them,[71] maintain that in recent times the above-mentioned image of Rām has undergone a radical transformation – from compassionate, benign and graceful into angry and fierce God (*ugra*). They view it as a result of the Hindu-Muslim conflict in Ayodhya over his legendary birthplace, i.e. Rāmjanmabhūmi or Babri Masjid.[72] However, this opinion, seems to be only partly right, since the *Rāmcaritmānas* as well as other texts belonging to the Rāmāyaṇa tradition prove that Rām's anger forms an integral feature of his nature and should not be viewed as a contemporary addition to it. It manifested itself whenever his welfare or, especially, the welfare of people dear to him – his relatives, subjects, devotees etc. – was directly threatened or violated and it is testified to by the plethora of texts belonging to this tradition.[73] Although it is an entirely different matter, it must also be admitted that it has been relatively rarely used in the iconography of Rām.

While Vālmīki pictured Rām's anger in three different situations, Tulsīdās chose to depict the angry countenance of his protagonist in two of them. In the first of these, Rām tries to persuade the ocean to subdue its waters and let his army cross over to Lanka. The ocean, however, does not give in to his persuasion. Finally, Rām concludes angrily that the ocean will not be of help to him until it experiences the feeling of fear (*bole rāmu sakopa taba bhaya binu hoi na prīti*; 5.57). Therefore, he takes his bow and fits to it a frightful arrow of fire, which – still on the bowstring – emits blazing fire straight onto the ocean. As this poses a terrible threat

[69] Cf. Whaling, *The Rise*, p. 92.

[70] Stasik, 'God's Anger'.

[71] Kapur, 'Deity to Crusader'. Also see Dāmodar Agarvāl, 'Sattā kī rājnīti mẽ Rām kā badaltā svarūp', *Dharmyug*, 1.01.1993, pp. 32–3.

[72] Kapur, 'Deity to Crusader', p. 74.

[73] For more on this subject also see Stasik, 'God's Anger', pp. 295–304.

to its existence, the frightened ocean asks Rām to forgive him. Rām, himself the Ocean of Mercy, smiles, as if nothing has happened, and wants to learn about the way in which the monkey host could cross over to Lanka (5.51.3–4, 56.1–3, 57–60.4).

Angry Rām also appears in battle scenes, i.e. in a few interventions during the war on Lanka, and when it comes to its climax, i.e. in his duel with Rāvaṇ (6.69.3, 71.2, 87.4, 91.4, 91 chand, 92.3, 93.3 and 101 chand). It is symptomatic that in all these scenes the comments on Rām's emotions are limited to, so to say, a symbolic minimum. Whenever his anger is referred to, it is synonymous with the uplifting of his bow ready for a shot (e.g. 6.71.2, 87.4, 91.3 and 101 chand), sometimes it is accompanied with his smile or laugh. It is so, because these terrifying moments are a real threat but for others, not for Rām, because it is others, and not him, who are filled with fear. What is significant, fear is familiar not only to the soldiers of the two armies but also to the gods observing the battle (cf. e.g. 6.71.2.).

Taking into consideration the fact that in the entire poem Rām is pictured as the one who eradicates every fault (*doṣa*) and sin (*pāpa*) and anger is one of their sources, a question essential for the understanding of Rām's nature arises. How to reconcile his anger, the anger that annihilates dharma (4.15.2), with the fact that Rām is the one who upholds dharma?

The analysis of the appropriate passages of the *Rāmcaritmānas* proves that Rām's behaviour, reduced almost to a symbol, sets the standard of the modes of conduct that are culturally best justified and thus most acceptable. The poem also clearly indicates that anger as such is not proper and is an emotion which should earnestly be avoided, because unrestrained leads almost straight to violence which may lead to annihilation. What is very symptomatic Rām grows angry in situations in which the well-being of persons dear to him – his relatives, devotees and subjects – has been threatened in the course of someone's vicious, hostile actions. In such circumstances, Rām has to intervene which can take the form of either his direct persuasion or a mediation on his behalf. However, if his efforts fail, anger accumulates in Rām and is demonstrated by him in order to evoke fear in the person concerned. Out of this fear an evildoer either withdraws from his course of action, which means his pleading with Rām for his forgiveness that is instantly granted, or a flight, i.e. a physical withdrawal. However, if such a demonstration does not bring the desired effect, the whole situation results in the death of everyone infatuated with conceit and stubbornness. They have to end their lives in such a way, because being elements of chaos and anarchy they pose a threat to society. And because from the very beginnings of the Rāmāyaṇa tradition it is known that Rām, in the name of dharma, is able to subdue his emotions, his outbursts of anger can only signify that maintaining order or upholding dharma is otherwise impossible. They can be understood, using Sheldon Pollock's words, as 'a "natural" manifestation of those violent and destructive capacities inherent in him as king, which have hitherto lain dormant and (...) are above (or a part of superordinate) dharma'.[74]

In such a way, the divine king Rām teaches his subjects-devotees what dharma is, as he knows very well that:

> *Lamentable is a king, who does not understand statecraft, and to whom his subjects [are] not as dear as his life* (2.172.2).[75]

* * *

Tulsīdās's vision of an ideal society, in which there is no place for evil in whatever form, undoubtedly is an expression of human eternal longing for the land of true happiness and prosperity. No matter how disputable its realization in this world may seem to us, all sorts of evidence leave no doubt about the main cause of the unprecedented success of the *Rāmcaritmānas*. Tulsīdās in his poem presented his audiences (past and present) with a vision of the cosmos – an orderly, harmonious whole – continuously watched over by Rām who is omnipotent and will determinedly eliminate any symptoms of chaos if they happen to occur anywhere. As a result, the *Rāmcaritmānas* has become a clear exposition of the rules governing different spheres of life. To the present day, their clarity and unchangeability have attracted many Hindus in north India, encouraging the implementation of these rules in their own lives, in one way or another.

---

[74] Pollock, 'Introduction', vol. 3, p. 66.

[75] *socia nṛpati jo nīti na jānā; jehi na prajā prana samāna.*

CHAPTER EIGHT

The Heaven on Earth Builder: Rām in Gupta's *Sāket*[1]

In the preceding chapters, I have noted that Maithilīśaraṇ Gupta's *Sāket* is an interesting piece of literary work written on the rising tide of the period of Indian national and social awakening when the well-known epic and mythological sources were extensively used by modern Hindi authors. Gupta, himself a Vaishnav bhakta, in his poem did not deny the divinity of Rām but first and foremost concentrated on his human nature, portraying him as a true leader of his people.[2]

The aim of the present analysis is to substantiate the opinion expressed in Chapter Five of this book that although Gupta created a modern poem, by retaining both aspects of the nature of Rām (with the indisputable dominance of the human aspect), he positioned its hero[3] between tradition and modernity. Therefore, I propose to analyse *Sāket* from the point of view of the impact of the traditions that express themselves in the different layers of the poem, by concentrating on the figure of its protagonist, as his character is expressive of the traditions, ideologies and influences, which served Gupta as the means of constructing his own telling.

A stanza preceding Gupta's poem (printed on a separate page) is very revealing. At first glance, it seems to express the perplexity of a modern man living in the rational world who, pressed by reality, is confronted with the question of the existence of God.

> *Ram, are you a man, not God,*
> *who dwells in every corner of this world?*

---

[1] An earlier version of some parts of this chapter was published in Stasik, 'Modernising the Rāmāyaṇa Tradition' and idem, 'He Who Dwells in the Hearts of All'.

[2] Cf. Rājūrkar, *Rāmkathā ke patr*, p. 161.

[3] Nevertheless, it should be noted here that some authors consider Rām neither as the protagonist nor as the main male character of *Sāket*, giving precedence in this regard to Ūrmilā and Lakṣmaṇ respectively. See e.g. Pāṭhak, *Maithilīśaraṇ Gupta*, pp. 444–5.

So I am Godless, God forgive me!
And if you do not dwell [here], mind will dwell upon you.[4]

The very personal tone of these words makes one treat them as Gupta's profession of a lack of faith, allowing him to treat Rām merely as a human being. However, as a further reading of the poem indicates, this is not so – this stanza seems to be rather a reaction of a tradition-loving man to contemporary reality, in which reason tends to take over faith.[5] The poet seems to seek an answer just in case had Rām turned out to be not God but just a human being. Such an interpretation can be inferred from the words in which Gupta first expresses his seeming atheism, declaring that he has no God but then immediately adds his apology: 'God forgive me!'

This attitude is also corroborated in a number of other passages expressive of the nature of Rām, two of which are especially important as far as their immediate impact on Gupta's audience is concerned.

The first of these significant passages comes almost at the beginning of the poem.

He who is without qualities has got a form with qualities,
The Lord of All has become incarnate.
For what reason has the Lord played this game?
Having become a human being drank milk of a woman?
He has done it out of love[6] *for his devotees,*
He, [who] is the Lord of Universe, the Abode of Play.
In order to show the way to the world,
to deliver earth from the burden of [sin],
to fulfil people's expectations,
why wouldn't he bring into existence his own creations?
[Now] it's the cold winter of the demons' rule
but very near is the spring of Ram's reign.[7]

---

[4] *rām, tum mānav ho? īśvar nahī̃ ho kyā?/ viśv mẽ rame hue nahī̃ sabhī kahī̃ ho kyā?/ tab maĩ nirīśvar hū̃, īśvar kṣamā kare;/ tum na ramo to man tummẽ ramā kare;* Gupta, *Sāket*, unnumbered page.

[5] Pāṭhak, *Maithilīśaraṇ Gupta*, p. 459.

[6] Lit. 'it (i.e. its reason) is called [parental] affection'.

[7] *ho gayā nirguṇ saguṇ-sākār hai,/ le liyā akhileś ne avatār hai./ kislie yah khel prabhu ne kiyā?/ manuj bankar mānavī kā pay piyā?/ bhakt-vatsaltā isīkā nām hai,/ aur vah lokeś līlā-dhām hai./ path dikhāne ke lie saṁsār ko,/ dūr karne*

The second passage comes from Canto 8 that describes the life of the exiles in Chitrakut. The poet, in a very thorough way, develops the characteristics of Rām and clearly states the reasons for his appearance in this world. This passage forms the core of Rām's answer to Sītā's queries about, among other things, the meaning of existence. He explains to her that the forest exile, which means suffering, is in fact his individual sacrifice for the well-being of the rest of society (*samaṣṭi ke lie vyaṣṭi-balidānī*).[8] His aim is to change people and to build a new society by means of spreading the Aryan culture among those who are either not familiar with it or, for certain reasons, deprived of it.[9] One may add here that elsewhere in the poem Gupta also makes Rām speak about every man's right to self-determination and practically creates the vision of the welfare state responsible for its citizens.[10] Below follows an extensive fragment of Rām's speech:

I came to tell about the ideal for Aryans,
I came to explain that riches mean nothing as against a man.
I came to bring about the revolution for happiness and peace,
I came to protect the faith of the faithful.
I came for those who are suffering,
who are helpless, distressed, weak, wretched, cursed.
[I came] so that they, whose fear is manifest,
who in silence endure the rule of demons, can become fearless.
I came so that propriety lasts,
pure and simple life is not fated to be extinguished.
I came to give happiness and to experience pain,
I came to play in the drama of humanity.
I came here to bring support,
I came to build, not to destroy.
I came here not to amass but to share,
I came to trim the thickets of the garden of the world.
I came not to enjoy rule myself but to make others enjoy it,
I came to feed the pearls of freedom to those who are virtuous like swans.
I came to spread new grandeur in the world,

---

ke lie bhū-bhār ko,/ saphal karne ke lie jan-dṛṣṭiyā̃,/ kyõ na kartā vah svayaṁ nij sṛṣṭiyā̃?/ asur-śāsan śiśir-may hemanṭ hai,/ par nikaṭ hī rām-rājya-vasant hai. Gupta, *Sāket*, p. 18.

[8] Ibid., p. 233.

[9] Cf. ibid., pp. 411–12, 414, 470 and 475.

[10] *nij rakṣā kā adhikār rahe jan jan ko,/ sabkī suvidhā kā bhār kintu śāsan ko;* ibid., p. 233.

I came to cause people to obtain divine nature!
I didn't bring here the message of heaven,
I came to make this very earth heaven. (...)
Those who will remember just my name,
they will cross the ocean of existence without any effort.
But those who will assume my virtues, works and nature,
they will also take others across.[11]

The contents of this and the two other fragments of the poem quoted above are expressive of the fact that Gupta's image of Rām is characterized by traditional features stemming directly from the Rāmāyaṇa tradition, established in the Hindi-speaking area mainly on the basis of Tulsīdās's *Rāmcaritmānas*. These features are combined with modern traits which are substantially the poet's original contribution to the image of Rām. In other words, the traditional image is intertwined with ideas expressive of later developments that took place both inside and outside the tradition and the four main sources of Gupta's inspiration become clear: 1. Tulsīdās's Bhakti; 2. the tradition of Rasik Sampradāy; 3. Gandhi's socio-political philosophy and other ideologies prevalent in Gupta's times[12] and, especially 4. the Indian national movement drawing inspiration from the ideal of India's past.

Thus, Rām in *Sāket* is the Ultimate Being, *Brahman* without qualities who has manifested himself to the world as God, Lord of All (*akhileśvar*). He has descended from heaven, assuming the form of a man out of love for his devotees and for their well-being. He is compassionate, full of support for all those who need any kind of help, especially those who are weak and down-

---

[11] *maĩ āryõ kā ādarś batāne āyā./ jan-sammukh dhan ko tucch jatāne āyā./ sukh-śānti-hetu maĩ krānti macāne āyā, viśvāsī kā viśvās bacāne āyā./ maĩ āyā unke hetu ki jo tāpit haĩ,/ jo vivaś, vikal, bal-hīn, dīn, śāpit haĩ./ ho jāyā abhay ve jinhẽ ki bhay bhāsit haĩ,/ jo kauṇap-kul se mūk-sadṛś śāsit haĩ./ maĩ āyā, jismẽ banī rahai maryādā,/ bac jāy pralay se, miṭai na jīvan sādā./ sukh dene āyā, duḥkh jhelne āyā,/ maĩ manuṣyatva kā nāṭya khelne āyā./ maĩ yahā̃ ek avalamb choṛne āyā,/ gaṛhne āyā hū̃, nahī̃ toṛne āyā./ maĩ yahā̃ joṛne nahī̃, bā̃ṭne āyā,/ jagadupavan ke jhaṅkhāṛ chā̃ṭne āyā./ maĩ rājya bhogne nahī̃, bhugāne āyā,/ haṁsõ ko muktā-mukti cugāne āyā./ bhav mẽ nav vaibhav vyāpt karāne āyā,/ nar ko īśvartā prāpt karāne āyā!/ sandeś yahā̃ maĩ nahī̃ svarg kā lāyā,/ is bhūtal ko hī svarg banāne āyā./ (...) jo nām mātr hī smaraṇ madīy karẽge,/ ve bhī bhavsāgar binā prayās tarẽge./ par jo merā guṇ, karm, svabhāv dharẽge,/ ve aurõ ko bhī tār, pār utrẽge;* ibid., pp. 234–5.

[12] See e.g. Nagendra, *Sāket: ek adhyayan*, pp. 97–8.

trodden. Such an image, typical of Bhakti expounded in the *Rāmcaritmānas*, is strengthened by the lines beginning with the words 'those who will remember just my name'. Being in the form of a traditional *phalaśruti*, they are expressive of the power of Rām and his name. At the same time, as other passages of the poem indicate, Rām retains the features known from the tradition – he is 'the best among men' (*puruṣottam*), the Abode of Steadfastness (*dhṛti-dhām*) as well as 'an embodiment of Eternal Truth' (*cirsatya-mūrti*).[13]

In this context, I would like to express my conviction, which is contrary to the opinion of some critics. Interpreting the stanza preceding the poem, they tend to see in Gupta's Rām a human being only.[14] However, from the point of view of the above-quoted passages there is no doubt that for the author of *Sāket*, Rām is the Ultimate Being and God incarnate. Although it is also true that having so openly acknowledged Rām's divinity once (in the stanza that begins with: 'He who is without qualities…'), Gupta does not develop this trait later in the poem but concentrates on the earthly exploits of his protagonist. For Gupta the divinity of Rām symbolizes an ideal of humanity, an exemplar to be imitated by all people in order to bring out the divine in them.[15]

Secondly, Rām, who is portrayed by Gupta as the Abode of Play (*līlā-dhām*), like an actor, has entered the stage of the world in Saket to act out the drama of humanity. Such a treatment draws our attention to the tradition of Rasik Sampradāy that looks at Rām's life from the perspective of the heavenly Saket. As has been noted earlier in this study, Saket is the main place from which the poem's narration is conducted. Thus it becomes a point of reference for the entire reality in which Rām carries out his mission aimed at transforming the whole earth into heaven.

Thirdly, this vision is evidently filtered through the poet's modern outlook and especially by the Gandhian thought that significantly influenced Gupta. It finds its expression in thinking about heaven on earth in very worldly terms, i.e. in terms of the betterment of people's existence and of the selfless service for

---

[13] Gupta, *Sāket*, p. 468.

[14] Cf. e.g. Varmā, *Hindī sāhitya*, vol. 3, pp. 159–60 and Rājūrkar, *Rāmkathā ke pātr*, pp. 98–9.

[15] Cf. Pāṭhak, *Maithilīśaraṇ Gupta*, p. 459.

the people. As a result it seems more proper to view Rām not so much as an ideal king known from the very beginnings of the Rāmāyaṇa tradition but rather as an ideal leader influenced by democratic ideals (coloured strongly by a Utopian concept of society) who wants to invest his people with power and who manifests his humanist belief in man. He also appears to be a resolute reformer ready for revolution who, by means of his mission, intends to change the world and the people living in it. Gupta believes that Rām's rule is as a safeguard to achieving these aims. How significant in this context Gandhi's opinion is, which is referred to by authors interested in the righteous reign of Rām: 'Rāmrāj means rule of the people. A person like Rām would never wish to rule'.[16] No wonder Rām in *Sāket* says: 'I came not to enjoy rule myself but to make others enjoy it'. Very meaningful are also Gandhi's words adding to our understanding of Gupta's Rām: 'God calls himself a servant of servants'. Their echo can also be found in the poem, verbalized by Bharat who says in one of the passages that a person appointed as a ruler is only a servant of the people (*niyat śāsak lok-sevak mātr*[17]).

Finally, the reference to the ideal for Aryans, which is to be taught by Rām, is also very revealing. On the one hand, it is indicative of Gupta's time when India was swept by the tide of the national movement. Looking back to India's glorious past, which for Gupta is synonymous with the Veda and Vedic tradition,[18] served, among other things, the purpose of building up a national identity and preparing the Indians for the struggle with the British. On the other hand, it is reminiscent of Svāmī Dayānanda Sarasvatī (1824–83), the founder of the Ārya Samāj (1875), who preached the revival of Hinduism according to the spirit of the Veda.[19]

---

[16] M.K. Gandhi, *The Collected Works of Mahatma Gandhi*, Delhi: Publications Division, Ministry of Information and Broadcasting, Govt. of India, 1972, p. 92. Cf. Menon and Schokker, 'The Conception of Rāmarājya in South and North Indian Literature', p. 623 and Lutgendorf, 'Interpreting Rāmrāj', p. 254.

[17] Gupta, *Sāket*, p. 93.

[18] E.g. ibid., pp. 235, 411–12, 415, 475; cf. Nagendra, *Sāket: ek adhyayan*, p. 83.

[19] Cf. 'Dinkara', 'Maithilīśaraṇa Gupta as a Poet of the Renaissance', pp. 102–3; also see J.N. Farquhar, *Modern Religious Movements in India*, Delhi: Munshiram Manoharlal, 1977 (1st published in 1914), pp. 102–29.

One should not overlook a very meaningful fact, namely, that Rām reveals the purpose of his coming to this world during his forest exile. Consequently, a very important question arises: why does the forest become the scene of Rām's mission? To seek an answer to this question, one should refer to the verse saying that Rām came 'to make this very earth heaven'. Saket, as his heavenly abode, symbolizes heaven, therefore Rām's mission has to be addressed to those who live in the forest, i.e. the natural antithesis of Saket[20] which is not only a symbol of heaven but also of civilization, Aryan civilization. Thus contact with demons, the culmination of which is the fight between Rām and Rāvaṇ, receives here a new dimension – it is viewed as a conflict between two civilizations and Rām's victory, of course, as the victory of Aryan civilization. It is evident from the words summing up his victorious battle with the demons Khar and Dūṣaṇ: 'Aryan civilization has been established, Aryan dharm has been confirmed'.[21] It is noteworthy that Rāmdhārī Siṁh 'Dinkar' (1908–74) – like Gupta a well-known representative of the national-patriotic poetry (*rāṣṭrīy kāvya*) and like him hailed as 'national poet' (*rāṣṭrakavi*) – considers *Sāket* to be the first work of the Rāmāyaṇa tradition (not only in Hindi), which interprets Rām's exile and his struggle with demons in terms of the conquest of (uncivilized) non-Aryan peoples.[22]

When Rām's mission comes to an end, the whole earth will be cleansed of demons. There is no doubt that for Gupta these demons, the epic enemies of Rām, also have a much more familiar countenance, that of the British who ruled his country. Rām's victory is an allegory of the imminent triumph of the Indians, the noble, civilized Aryans, over the British, the incarnate forces of evil.

It is very important to note that Gupta's poem provides us with one more interesting feature of Rām. He is portrayed very

---

For more on Svāmī Dayānanda see J.T.F. Jordens, *Dayānanda Sarasvatī: His Life and Ideas*, Delhi: Oxford University Press, 1978.

[20] For more on the connotations of the opposition between the forest and the city and the connotations of the nature of kingship in Indian tradition see Pollock, 'Introduction', vol. 3, pp. 12–54 and 68–84; cf. also Lutgendorf, 'Interpreting Rāmrāj', p. 259.

[21] Gupta, *Sāket*, p. 415; cf. Varmā, *Hindī sāhitya koś*, vol. 2, p. 622.

[22] 'Dinkara', 'Maithilīśaraṇa Gupta as a Poet of the Renaissance', p. 102.

graphically as a character to whom readiness for revenge is not entirely alien. This feature manifests itself vividly in the passage describing that moment during the war on Lanka when Lakṣmaṇ, wounded with Meghanād's spear, falls to the battlefield and Rām, driven by anxiety over his younger brother's life, sets off for the battle to take vengeance for his brother on Kumbhakarṇa, Rāvaṇ's brother. Gupta makes Rām say very striking words, which are, one would even say, unfit for Rām, the Lord of Mercy. He roars: 'A revenge for a brother is just a brother!'[23] In this scene, one deals with angry Rām, Rām as an avenger or, as Anuradha Kapur[24] puts it, with his fierce aspect (*ugra*).

Another interesting feature of Gupta's telling is his approach to Rām's rule. If one wants to analyse Rām's image from the point of view of Rāmrājya and looks for its description in its usual place, i.e. after the enthronement ceremony, one will face a basic problem. The poem is almost silent on the subject in this place as the poet merely mentions the name Rāmrājya in the line saying: 'Let this world extol the triumph of Rāmrājya'.[25] On the other hand, for example the opening passages of *Sāket* prove that the concept of Rāmrājya is not only present in the poem but also well-known to it.[26] A careful reading of the whole text indicates clearly that whereas traditionally Rāmrājya ensues after Rām's victory over Rāvaṇ, in Gupta's poem – much the same as in the *Rām-caritmānas*[27] – Rām already begins his famous rule during his exile. Although he has not formally been installed as king, from the moment of his exile, ceaselessly, Rām continues to build his new society. The closing verses of Canto 4, from which it is clear that Rām's departure to the forest was in fact meeting his folk[28] and entering the real human world (*nar-lok*), convincingly support this argument. It is also corroborated by the above-quoted passage in which Rām reveals to Sītā the purpose of his earthly mission, aimed at the communities living in the forest. In the context of his own words, it seems obvious that Rāmrājya, which in *Sāket* is

---

[23] *bhāī kā badlā bhāī hī*; Gupta, *Sāket*, p. 445.

[24] Kapur, 'Deity to Crusader'.

[25] *dharā-dhām ko rām-rājya kī jay gāne do*; Gupta, *Sāket*, p. 500.

[26] Ibid., pp. 18 and 33–4.

[27] Cf. footnote 54 in Chapter Seven.

[28] *prasthān – van kī or, yā lok-man kī or?/ (...) haĩ rām jan kī or*; Gupta, *Sāket*, p. 123.

synonymous with building on earth the state of almost heavenly happiness and justice, has to begin there. Therefore, Gupta, taking for granted the acquaintance of his audience with the motif of Rāmrājya, confines himself to a few allusions scattered all over the text and lacking in detail. Like many authors who preceded him, he feels no need to go on at length about it, as everyone knows what sort of ruler Rām is and what his rule is like.

At the end of his poem, Gupta once again gives a vivid expression of his attitude towards Rām. It can be termed as the attitude of a bhakta reformed in the spirit of modernity. The poet continues to worship Rām but basically, due to developing his human features, which are in keeping with a rational viewpoint, he makes him an exemplar of a fulfilled existence, saying that 'our master is our ideal' (*ādarś hī īśvar hai hamārā*).[29] In such a way, the image of Rām in *Sāket* combines the characteristics of tradition and modernity, of human and divine nature.

Sāket, like the novel *Apne apne Rām,* also reveals a multi-layered approach to a story that by its nature is a repository of myth. Gupta constructed his telling on the original myth of Rām but interpreted it by means of rationalizing, demythologizing and introducing new original elements.[30]

However, the most vital device, determining the interpretative frames of the poem already in its title, was the choice of Saket as the site of its narration. All the devices implemented by Gupta intermingle with one another and as a result his Rām appears to be not only a master of the hearts and minds of his subjects but also their most devoted servant, willing to provide them with all that was his lot, all that was the embodiment of his very self and of his abode – the heavenly Saket.

As N.C. Sehgal observed, referring to *Sāket* in his biographical sketch on Gupta: 'This poetic epitome of Indian culture enjoys a place of its own in Hindi literature'.[31]

---

[29] Gupta, *Sāket,* p. 500. It is worth noting here that the word *īśvar,* used in the original, denotes both the personal god and the earthly king.

[30] Cf. Chapter Six.

[31] N.C. Sehgal, 'Maithilīśaraṇa's Works: A Chronological Survey' in Nagendra, *Maithilīśaraṇa Gupta,* p. 54.

CHAPTER NINE

Creating New Mythological Spaces? On Tradition, Society and the Role of People in Bhagvān Siṁh's *Apne apne Rām*[1]

Bhagvān Siṁh's novel *Apne apne Rām* offers a very original telling of Rāmkathā abundant with new insights into the problem of understanding its nature and the nature of its protagonist. It seems even more interesting,. when one realizes that its author, while of an evidently modern outlook, dissociating himself from Rām as conceived by Tulsīdās and modern religious people, uses for his purpose the symbolic language of the Rāmāyaṇa.

There is no doubt that Siṁh's work, one of the most discussed contemporary Hindi novels, like many other Rāmkathās owes much to its portrayal of Rām. Therefore, in this chapter, I would like to concentrate on the figure of the novel's protagonist who appears to be the most important element in the structure of the story preserved from the archetype though, it should be once again said here,[2] reinterpreted by Siṁh to express the historical experience of Hindu society on its way towards progress.

Rām is the real protagonist of *Apne apne Rām*. He is almost omnipresent, being the focus of most of the passages, both in a direct and an indirect manner.

First of all he is pictured as an ideal ruler for whom the well-being of his subjects as well as the prosperity of his kingdom are the ultimate end. However, Siṁh's audience from the very beginning has no doubts that his Rām is different from the Rām known from the tradition. He is rendered as a human of flesh and blood who is no stranger to serious dilemmas. Apart from this, unlike in the already-discussed Rāmkathās, not all people think of him positively and some of them even question his virtue and try to discredit him. What is more, he is surrounded by enemies even in his closest circle, appearing to be a villain especially in the

---

[1] Sections of this chapter in an earlier version were published in Stasik, 'On Modern Retellings of Rām-kathā' and idem, 'He Who Dwells in the Hearts of All'.

[2] See Chapter Six, p. 221.

eyes of those for whom he is an obstacle on the way towards the realization of their (not always noble) plans. Thus, standing in Kaikeyī's way in seizing power in Ayodhya, he is a thorn in her side. Vasiṣṭha is her equal in negative feelings towards Rām. With time, he rises to the position of the main adversary of Rām in whom he sees a deadly threat to caste society and the priviledged status of Brahmins.

Vasiṣṭha's fears are not groundless as Rām is very critical of his own society which he considers to be sick (*rugṇa*) and immoral (*anaitik*); he suffers because of its decay.[3] According to him, one of the fundamental reasons for such a situation is social unequality, pushing some behind the margins of decent life and unjustly elevating others. For Rām all people are equal, therefore he always and everywhere acts against judging anyone according to his birth. It is best exemplified in his rebellious utterance:

> *How useless this boasting with the superiority of one's birth and blood is! How foolish these bounds of caste are!*[4]

Rām's critique of the hierarchical structure of Indian society goes parallel with his questioniong of many fundamental concepts of the traditional Indian ethos whenever he considers them to be against common sense as well as imposible to be logically proved and substantiated. He is also disinclined to trust the Veda and its tradition only because that is the way of the Brahmins who defend it at any cost. He is thus ready to reject it, and even to question the need to perfom sacrifices,[5] if logic and reason (*tark aur vivek*), which he considers to be fundamental on the journey towards attaining real humanity, do not substantiate them.[6] Logic and reason are for him the principal touchstones of man's progress on this journey.

This attitude is best exemplified in the answer given by him to Vasiṣṭha who plies Rām with questions in this regard. Rām says: 'Having acknowledged fossilized scriptures, I will myself

---

[3] Siṁh, *Apne apne Rām*, pp. 17 and 46.

[4] *kitnā vyarth hai janm aur rakt kī śreṣṭhtā kā dambh! kitnī mūrkhtāpūrṇ hai varṇõ kī yah sīmā!* Ibid., p. 21.

[5] Cf. ibid., pp. 3, 72 and 105–6.

[6] Cf. ibid., pp. 4, 89, 103–4 and 152.

become a scripture fossil!'[7] He says so because for him it is not the dead letter of any scripture but people and their wisdom as well as selfless reasoning (*svārth rahit vivek*) that detrmine the rules of conduct and say what is proper and what is improper (*ucit-anucit*).[8]

According to Rām, only rational thinking helps a human being to discern between good and evil. It is especially important in view of the fact that – as he thinks – there is no single truth and no single morality that could be applied in all epochs. It is due to the fact that all lives, in both individual and social dimensions, undergo historical changes related to newer and newer experiences. Thus, the teachings of the so far respected scriptures may lose their relevance and the same happens with dharma. In no case should they be accepted blindly – they should always be judged with one's common sense. Thanks to such an attitude, one is in a position to adjust one's conduct to the times in which one lives.[9] Rām is of the opinion that new scriptures including new teachings should be thought of in the case where it is felt that the old scriptures have not kept up with the times.[10] How radical such thinking is from the point of view of the tradition! However, Rām goes even further and propagates the need for education for all, considering that people, in order to be able to live their lives humanely, should be given access to education and thus to knowledge. According to him, this is the only way to pull people out of their lamentable condition.[11] Rām's outlook stems directly from his conviction that: 'a human being is above all the scriptures and humanity above all the classes',[12] thus equal chances for everyone are fundamental in his understanding of social justice.

---

[7] *jaṛībhūt śāstr ko mānne par maĩ bhī śāstrjaṛ ho jāū̃gā;* ibid., p. 4. It is worth noting here that the author very skilfully utilizes the semantic field of the adjective (with substantivized meanings) *jaṛ* 'lifeless, inert, numb' and 'senseless, stupid'.

[8] Ibid., p. 89.

[9] Cf. e.g. ibid., p. 4: *śāstr aur dharm to yug ke anurūp badalte rahte haĩ. (...). phir inkī antim kasauṭī kyā hai? tark aur vivek hī to!*

[10] Ibid., pp. 4–5.

[11] Ibid., pp. 55, 156, 245 and 246.

[12] *sabhī śāstrõ se ūpar manuṣya hai aur sabhī varṇõ se ūpar manuṣyatā;* ibid., p. 248.

Bearing in mind this attitude of Rām, one should not be surprized that mainly Brahmins, with Vasiṣṭha and the priestly circles close to him but not only them, consider him to be not only their enemy (*brahmadveṣī*, *brahmaghātī*)[13] but also the enemy of sacrifice (*yajñadveṣī*)[14] and dharma (*dharmadveṣī*).[15] At the same time, however, he is very popular with the majority of Ayodhya's citizens who show him such affection and respect that it is very difficult for his adversaries to accuse him of anything or attack him openly. Therefore, at the instigation of Vasiṣṭha, it was decided that Rām's position should be weakened by spreading allegations of his hostility to Brahmins.[16] In view of his popularity with the people, it is obvious that such measures were doomed to failure from the start.

Considering human dignity and social justice – the most valued ideals, Rām regards all divisions of society into classes and castes to be a curse and opposes them in the name of these ideals. Because so many times he has been tried in arduous and dangerous situations by his wily opponents, Rām is well aware how difficult it can be to live one's life as a human being, not losing one's self-respect.[17] However, he remains faithful to his ideals and is untiring in his efforts to make others appropriate them. He teaches how they can affect his people, sticking to his *idée fixe* because according to him:

> *A man can act only in one form (...) – in the form of a human being. It's not one's choice, one cannot help it.*[18]

As I have argued in Chapter Six in the discussion of the novel *Apne apne Rām*, history plays a very important role in Siṁh's mythologizing as a source of experience influencing the present and the future of society. Although Rām stresses that it is not possible to live the past in the present, at the same time he knows that one's experiences from the past are very important as they

---

[13] Ibid., pp. 5, 156 and 268.
[14] Ibid., p. 268.
[15] Ibid.
[16] Ibid., p. 5.
[17] Cf. ibid. e.g. pp. 202–3, 204, 207 and 253.
[18] *manuṣya keval ek hī rūp mẽ vyavahār kar saktā hai (...). manuṣya ke rūp mẽ. yah uskā cunāv nahī̃, uskī vivaśtā hai*; ibid., p. 204.

help one to avoid making the same mistake again. Therefore, he pays a lot of attention to the role of history and of the historical experience of mankind in human life.[19]

More than once various characters of the novel express the opinion that Rām differs from other people.[20] Siṁh achieves such a result, visualizing him as a character with a high sense of morality and deep sympathy for the disturbed and lowly, and these are the features that distinguish him from the common man. Thus, Rām as the archetypal king is himself an embodiment of moral merit. He also knows what human dignity and social justice mean and how his people can achieve them. In this regard he resembles the Rām created by Gupta. Having added to these features Rām's steadfastness and extraordinary composure in the face of different adversities, he appears to be the paragon of propriety, the *maryādā-puruṣottam*, i.e. the best among the righteous,[21] although it must be stressed that this designation does not figure in the novel itself.

The goodness of his heart and deep concern for others cause some kind of dismay in people who, in the first instance, are not fully aware of who they are dealing with. Therefore, those who meet him on their way often ask him: 'Who are you? Who?', and without waiting for his reply answer themselves: 'You cannot be an ordinary man'.[22] In the eyes of other people, he is too good to be just a human being and, therefore, they consider him none other than a god which is best exemplified by Lakṣmaṇ's words:

---

[19] Ibid., pp. 53–4 and 201.

[20] Cf. ibid. e.g. pp. 43–4, 46 and 90.

[21] It is one of the most commonly used epithets of Rām. Its rendering into non-Indian languages is difficult because of the wide semantic field of the noun *maryādā* (Sanskrit > Hindi), meaning among other things: 'boundary, limit; borderline, shoreline; [that what is within the] bounds of propriety / law / custom; honour, good reputation, dignity'. Thus, this designation highlights the fact that Rām is not only 'the best among men' (*puruṣottam*) but also acts within the bounds of the time-honoured custom. It should be noted here that from Vālmīki's *Rāmāyaṇa* onwards, he is the one who himself, as well as indirectly, determines the boundaries in this world (*maryādānāṃ ca lokasya kartā kārayitā ca saḥ*; 5.33.11). I am grateful to Prof. John Brockington for the localization of this quotation in the critical edition of Vālmīki's *Rāmāyaṇa*.

[22] *tum kaun ho? kaun ho tum?* as well as: *tum manuṣya nahī̃ ho sakte/tum sādhāraṇ manuṣya nahī̃ ho sakte*; Siṁh, *Apne apne Rām*, pp. 13 and 15; cf. pp. 43 and 46.

> *Brother, you aren't an ordinary man. You are a man by name only but [in fact] you are a god. (...) You don't bother about your own advantage, fame or life, and having sacrificed all that you want to protect this ideal which makes a man out of a man (...).*[23]

Addressing Rām or talking about him, more than once people use the word *bhagvān*, which designates a revered person but also the supreme being, Lord, God. The latter meanings are evidently evoked by such adjectives as *patitpāvan* 'purifying the fallen' and *kṛpālu* 'compassionate, merciful'.[24] All similar statements acquire proper meaning in the context of Bhakti, where they are the epithets of Rām in the *Rāmcaritmānas*.[25] However, while in the *Rāmcaritmānas* Rām is God, an object of devotion, in Siṁh's novel he is not God (nor a god), although he embodies important features of a god. Thus, his goodness is limitless, he is merciful, kind and cares for his people, and this makes the people who come into contact with such an outstanding personality as Rām ascribe to him supernatural features. It is apparent that Siṁh – a contemporary writer – tries to give his vision a rational form. Therefore, he treats Rām's divinity (in the *Rāmcaritmānas* understood literally) symbolically. That is why, when Lakṣmaṇ calls him 'god', he reacts very decisively to his brother's words. Rām is simply a human being – he has not come to this world in order to take part in a divine play (*līlā*). He lives his own real life and he cherishes it as the highest value. He is not a god and does not want to be a god. He does not want others to see a god in him either. He says to Lakṣmaṇ:

> *(...) there are two methods of killing a man – making him a god or an animal. The result of these two is just one – not letting him live as a human. The gods are not my ideals, nor do I want to live having become one.*[26]

---

[23] *bhaiyā, āp sādhāraṇ manuṣya nahī̃ haĩ. nām ke lie hī manuṣya haĩ, par haĩ devtā. (...) āp apne lābh aur kīrti aur jīvan kī cintā nahī̃ karte aur svayam in sabko utsarg karke bhī us ādarś kī rakṣā karnā cāhte haĩ jo manuṣya ko manuṣya banātā* (...); ibid., p. 203.

[24] Cf. ibid., pp. 13 and 52.

[25] *patitpāvan* – RCM 7.130.4 and 7.130 *chand* 1; *kṛpālu* RCM e.g. 1.28k and 2.110.2.

[26] (...) *lakṣmaṇ, kisī manuṣya kī hatyā karne ke do upāy haĩ – use devtā yā paśu banā denā. donõ kā pariṇām ek hī hai – use manuṣya na rahne denā. na to*

The foregoing discussion explicitly shows that in no case should Rām be considered an ordinary character, nor is he a traditional ruler. As is suggested in the text of the novel itself,[27] it may have been a result of the fact that during his childhood Rām was not brought up to take up this role – according to the promise given by Daśarath to Kaikeyī's parents, it was their grandson, i.e. Bharat, who was to succeed Daśarath on the throne of Ayodhya. Possibly, such an 'un-princely' upbringing resulted in Rām's decisively non-conformist outlook that was formed under the great influence of Viśvāmitra.

It is worth noting here that although Siṁh's novel propagates a vision of egalitarian society, Rām acts in it as a king and considering the matters of his state, refers to them, using the categories of kingdom. One could consider it a contradiction but it seems inapt in reaction to the work, in which the traditional story functions as a symbolic language helpful in diagnosing and interpreting the present. Thus Siṁh's Rām being the embodiment of the best ruler of his people does not cease to be an ideal king known through the ages.

Significantly, Rām is considered as the ideal leader before he formally ascends the throne of Ayodhya, in which he resembles Tulsīdās's and Gupta's Rām. In fact, he needs neither throne nor kingdom because the affection and respect he is entrusted with by most people means that he is everywhere treated as a real king. It is a direct outcome of the fact that the sufferings and joys of others become his own and that in the name of the well-being of his subjects he is ready for great sacrifices.[28] He is aware – like no other – that the greatest strength not only of a ruler but also of every man is the love and trust of others. In order not to lose this strength and one's humanity, one should always be with people and for people.[29] Rām tells Lakṣmaṇ that 'a king is always rooted in his people'.[30] Making them prosperous and satisfied, securing their access to law and education, showing them due respect, a ruler becomes so powerful that even the most potent

---

devtā mere ādarś haĩ na hī maĩ devtā bankar jīnā cāhtā hū̃; Siṁh, *Apne apne Rām*, p. 203.

[27] Ibid., pp. 69–71.

[28] Ibid., e.g. pp. 5, 111, 119 and 165–6.

[29] Ibid., p. 112.

[30] *rājā kī jaṛẽ apnī prajā ke bhītar hotī haĩ*; ibid., p. 262.

enemy cannot pose a real threat to him and his state.[31] What is more, having enemies is almost an indispensable element of any rule. However, a good ruler, i.e. the one who is motivated with common sense and the interest of his nation (*rāṣṭrahit*), will always be able to distinguish between his allies and his adversaries.[32]

The best exemplification of Rām's qualifications to be a ruler, as it is seen by his subjects, can be found in the passage concerned with the episode in which Daśarath begins his preparations to install Rām on the throne of Ayodhya. As has been said, it is against his earlier promise, given to the parents of Kaikeyī, that her son will become his successor.[33] One of the most important elements of Daśarath's plan is to summon the council of eminent citizens of his kingdom in order to know their opinion about his succession. The council is absolutely unanimous that it is Rām who should ascend the throne. They substantiate their opinion saying that Rām suffers and rejoices with his people, is brave and valiant, righteous and law-abiding, well-educated, has a placid nature and is in perfect control of himself.[34] Like the overwhelming majority of Ayodhya's citizens, none of them has any doubts pointing out Rām – capable and endowed with all qualities (*yogya aur sarvaguṇ sampann*).[35]

In keeping with tradition, Rām of *Apne apne Rām* finally assumes power in Ayodhya. However, unlike in tradition, Ayodhya's treasury is empty and the whole country is in the grip of terrifying drought and the famine resulting from it. Thus, at the beginning of his rule, he faces enormous problems, the culmination of which is the imminent threat of rebellion by his court and subjects. Soon it appears that Rām's devotion to and sacrifice for his people are reciprocated by them – they are ready to suffer a lot for him, knowing that he does all that is possible in order to put an end to their misery.[36] It is worth noting here that Brahmins, the only group not participating in the anti-crisis enterprises initiated by Rām, consider them to be anti-Brahmin.

---

[31] Ibid.
[32] Ibid., p. 54.
[33] Ibid., pp. 116–19.
[34] Ibid., p. 119.
[35] Ibid., p. 118.
[36] Cf. ibid. e.g., pp. 2 and 242–3.

They reason that these projects distract people, and thus their money, from the sacrifices and rituals forming the basis of their existence. It is an additional reason that they, led by Vasiṣṭha, try to spread among the citizens of Ayodhya an accusation of Rām's being their enemy.[37]

Relating Siṁh's image of Rām to Tulsīdās's and Gupta's concepts, one can easily see how far from them it departs. The protagonist of *Apne apne Rām* is in conflict with Brahmins for whom the protagonist of the *Rāmcaritmānas* has descended to the earth. Siṁh's Rām has not even the slightest intention to trust the Veda blindly, the Veda that Tulsīdās's Rām protects unconditionally. The same concerns the sacrifice, the propagation of which is one of the reasons of Rām's descending from heaven in Gupta's work. One can say, using the language of traditional Indian culture, that *Apne apne Rām* reflects a record of the decline of the eternal law – dharma – which at the same time can be seen as a classic example of the worst of eons in the history of creation (*kaliyug*). However, referring to the language of today's sociocultural studies or literary criticism, one would prefer to say that this novel forms an attempt to evaluate a number of the fundamental concepts of Indian culture in the spririt of the author's contemporary notions of state and society. His ideas are of a decidedly leftist character, in which both the conviction about the superiority of the material world over the world of the spirit and a typically postmodern questioning of universal ethics are apparent.

Rām's opinions, in which his attitude to his own heritage is expressed, more than once may strike one with a lack of distance to this heritage. This becomes especially clear in the contrast with the passages, in which Rām is almost blindly uncritical regarding the ideas and concepts introduced by Siṁh that are new for the Rāmāyaṇa tradition. Despite all this, however, he remains realistic in his appraisal of the actual condition of mankind. He is aware that his ideal, the fully-fledged man relying on himself, is still a thing of the future and until this goal is accomplished, mankind will have to turn for guidance to supernatural powers, because such is human nature.[38] In this context, it is worth adding

[37] Ibid., pp. 243–4.
[38] Ibid., p. 205.

that Rām notes that some people (and there can be no doubt that he means Brahmins) live continually increasing the pantheon of gods whose numbers have become so great that 'the society trails and creeps under their burden, crawling like worms'.[39] A specific blending of the terror of tradition and the psychological constitution of man reaching beyond the limits of history and society is evident in such thinking.

Summing up the foregoing discussion of the image of the protagonist of *Apne apne Rām*, one can say that Siṁh interprets the traditional character departing from a rational standpoint. It is evident that many features of the traditional Rām as well as of the world he lives in, Siṁh treats as not being subject to rational judgement. He considers them as a relic of a bygone age and, therefore, he demythologizes them. The most important of them seems to be the divinity of Rām who ceases to be God but still functions as his symbol. Structuring the vision of the state headed by Rām, Siṁh's Rāmkathā, due to the method employed by its author, in essence becomes a story of the struggle to attain human dignity and social justice.

However, despite the fact that the author attaches a lot of significance to the rational outlook, some of his proposals simply strike with their almost incurable idealism. As a result, a new myth – which, nevertheless, remains in close touch with the Rāmāyaṇa tradition – emerges out of Siṁh's text. It is a myth of a Utopian state of social equality and justice whose guarantor is Rām. It seems that a decisive role in the creation of such a vision has been played by the fact that the myth of Rām is still a living part of the north Indian ethos. As long as it holds true, different authors will resort to it, visualizing – in their own way – the ideal ruler and his state, in which his contented subjects live.

---

[39] *(...) samāj inke bojh ke nīce ghisaṭtā aur rẽgtā huā cal rahā hai (...) kīṛõ kī tarah rẽgtā huā*; ibid., p. 207.

THE INFINITE STORY?

Conclusions

In the light of the foregoing analysis, there should be no doubt that in order to comprehend the reasons for the phenomenon of the success of the Rāmāyaṇa story, one needs a deeper insight into the role of the figure of Rām in it as well as into the pattern of the development of his character.

From the times of Vālmīki, Rām has served as a paragon of humanity, an embodiment of eternal human longing for righteousness personifying the ideal ruler. However, with time Rām acquired more and more divinity finally elevating him to the status of the Supreme Being, God, and the culmination of this process can be seen in Tulsīdās's *Rāmcaritmānas*. Nonetheless, this does not mean that its author neglects the human aspects of the character of its protagonist. Tulsīdās skilfully blends Rām's divinity and humanity, i.e. the two constituent elements of his nature, although he does so in inverse proportion when compared with the vision presented in Vālmīki's *Rāmāyaṇa*. This strategy allowed the author of the *Rāmcaritmānas* to picture Rām as God who – as the omnipotent Lord – maintains order in the universe, teaches his subjects-devotees what dharma is, thus providing his people not only with a feeling of security but also with limitless love. Structuring the story of Rām's life in such a way, Tulsīdās set a clear pattern of respectful life for Hindu society, also bearing in mind a time of crisis and including in it both a king and a common man. As a result, his proposal to this day attracts many Hindus, and not only in north India. Therefore, considering the *Rāmcaritmānas* solely as a devotional text reduces, even falsifies, its message.

The image of Rām crystallized in the *Rāmcaritmānas,* which – once again referring to Philip Lutgendorf's observation[1] – 'has become (...) the archetypal Ramayan text for Hindi speakers', prevailed in Hindi literature for more than three centuries. It is still alive, especially in the religious as well as the ritual context and the traditional literature drawing upon it, and time and again it is also used, or misused, in the realm of politics. Nevertheless,

[1] See above Chapter One, p. 71.

it has lost its significance in modern writing which is best exemplified with such important Hindi Rāmkathās as Gupta's *Sāket* or Siṁh's *Apne apne Rām*.

In *Sāket*, created at the time of the rising tide of the national movement, Gupta acknowledges Rām to be God and thus pays him due respect. However, later in his poem, he concerns himself almost solely with Rām's human character, visualizing him as an ideal human being and a devoted servant of his people. There is no doubt that such a design in Gupta's poem owes a lot to modern times characterized with a multilayered approach to Rāmkathā, which – as has been said earlier in this study – by its nature is a repository of myth.

In this context, it seems noteworthy to draw an interesting analogy between the meanings of the noun *kathā*, i.e. 'story', and the noun 'myth' originating from Greek *mýthos* of the same meaning, i.e. 'story'. How expressive this analogy becomes when one, having in mind Meletinsky's concepts, refers, on the one hand, to the apostrophe preceding Gupta's poem: 'Ram, are you a man, not God (…)?',[2] and, on the other hand, to the words of the utterly contemporary author, Devdutt Pattanaik, who writing in connection with Rām observes:

> *(…) religion anchors itself in myth – subjective truth of the believer, which is falsehood for the non-believer. Mythology is the vehicle of that truth – the stories, symbols and rituals that communicate the idea to the people through the ages. Myth expressed through mythology constructs the context for religion and faith.*[3]

No matter how right Pattanaik's argument is in the context of religion, nevertheless it does not concern other spheres in which myth can also function, such as literature that fruitfully operates as a vehicle of myth. As I have already observed,[4] Gupta in *Sāket* does not dissociate himself from the original myth of Rām. However, adding to it his modern, rational outlook, he first rationalizes his Rāmkathā and its protagonist and thus demythologizes it; while his own individual mythologizing leads

---

[2] For the entire passage see Chapter Eight, pp. 248–9.

[3] Devdutt Pattanaik, *The Book of Ram*, Delhi: Penguin Books, 2008, p. 204.

[4] See Chapters Five and Eight.

him to a remythologized Rāmkathā that narrates a new myth – a myth of heaven on earth. Therefore, such authors as Nandadulāre Vājpeyī, a well-known Hindi critic, and Rāmdhārī Siṁh 'Diṅkar', who quotes his opinion, are substantially right to observe that while in the Rām of the *Rāmcaritmānas* Tulsīdās brought out the humanity of the divine, in the Rām of *Sāket* Gupta pictured the divinity of man.[5] Yet, Gupta's openly verbalized attitude towards Rām, i.e. the attitude of a Rām believer, situates his telling and its hero between tradition and modernity.

It is only in the second half of the twentieth century that Hindi authors offer tellings that daringly meet the challenge of the contemporary, more and more secular, world. One of the most significant examples of such Rāmkathās is Siṁh's novel *Apne apne Rām,* published almost at the end of the century. It pictures its protagonist as a human being. Nonetheless, Rām's exceptional character, his goodness and devotion to people make him such an uncommon person that others see a god in him. However, Siṁh, unlike Gupta, nowhere in his work appears to be a devotee of Rām. Firstly, this may simply result from the fact that he is not a devotee of Rām; secondly, even if he is one, he does not disclose it. No matter which of these cases applies to the author of *Apne apne Rām,* such silence is expressive of the author's dissociation from the religious context of Rāmkathā (though not from the original myth of Rām!). As a result, Siṁh goes a lot further in his own mythologizing than Gupta and many other authors. He does not hesitate to reinterpret Indian society as well as human nature, offering his audience a myth of egalitarian society, firmly rooted in the ideals of humanism, in which everyone has his own Rām and his own Rāmkathā.

Looking at these three images of Rām, as well as many others that have not been dealt with here, one may say that they are all constituted in agreement with the long-established 'Rāmāyaṇa recipe'. They are all blendings, in different proportions, of the two constituent elements of Rām's nature – humanity and divinity, while their proportion depends on the outlook and intentions of the individual author as well as the spirit and/or ideologies of his time. Thus, it appears that the several-hundred-year growth of the Rāmāyaṇa tradition in Hindi, which can also be advantage-

[5] Singh 'Dinkara', 'Maithilīśaraṇa Gupta', p. 100.

ously analysed from the perspective of the development of the figure of Rām, does not so much mean a gradual evolution from one form to another. Its pattern should rather be conceived as oscillating in the field determined by two poles in the form of two basic aspects of Rām's nature, which are not really opposed but complement each other.

Concluding this discussion of various aspects of Rāmkathā in Hindi and the image of its protagonist, one feels compelled to say that authors of all epochs and of different outlooks have always sought to redefine the archetypal Rāmkathā, i.e. the myth of Rām, to fit the changing values of the changing world.[6] Putting it another way and looking at it from a broader perspective, one can also say that the paradigm of the development of the Rāmāyaṇa as well as the character of its protagonist can be viewed as a reflection – on a reduced scale – of the evolution of traditional Indian culture.

Judging from the number of different, not only Hindi, works that to this day are regularly published, the story of Rām appears to be an endless source of inspiration for many generations of authors to come.[7]

Hari is infinite, his story is endless;
all pious people tell it and listen to it in many different ways.
The appealing deeds of Ramchandra
cannot be all sung even in myriads of aeons.[8]

---

[6] Cf. Ashis Nandy's opinion referring to Madhusūdan Datta's *Meghanādavadha kāvya* in Nandy, *The Intimate Enemy*, p. 18, quoted above in Introduction, p. 32, n. 166.

[7] Cf. the text of Vālmīki who says: 'This wondrous tale (...) is the great source of inspiration for poets' (*āścaryamīdamākhyānaṃ (...) paraṃ kavīnāmādhāraṃ*); English translation by Goldman in idem, *The Rāmāyaṇa of Vālmīki*, vol. 1, p. 133.

[8] *hari ananta harikathā anantā;/ kahahī sunahī bahu bidhi saba santā./ rāmacandra ke carita suhāe;/ kalapa koṭi lagi jāhī na gāe;* RCM 1.140.3.

APPENDICES

Appendix A: A Summary of the Story in Tulsīdās's *Rāmcaritmānas*

BOOK ONE: CHILDHOOD

Daśarath, a righteous, virtuous and wise king, a jewel of Raghu's family, lived in Ayodhya with his three wives: Kausalyā, Kaikeyī and Sumitrā. He felt very depressed because despite his advanced age, he had no son. Advised by his guru, the sage Vasiṣṭha, he performed a sacrifice in order to obtain a male issue (*putrakāmeṣṭi*). At the end of the sacrifice the god of fire, Agni, appeared in front of Daśarath with a sacrificial dish of milk and rice in his hand and gave it to him. Daśarath distributed the offering among his wives and they all became pregnant. After some time, on the ninth day of the light half of the month Caitra, the queens gave birth to their sons: Kausalyā to Rām, Kaikeyī to Bharat and Sumitrā to the twins Lakṣmaṇ and Śatrughna. From the earliest moments of his life, Rām proved himself to be the all-pervading Supreme Being. The family, the people of Ayodhya, as well as gods and the entire creation rejoiced over the birth of Daśarath's sons. The boys grew up, surrounded by affection and love, to the delight of their parents.

One day, the sage Viśvāmitra arrived at Daśarath's court. He told the king about demons tormenting him at his hermitage and disrupting his sacrifices. Viśvāmitra asked Daśarath to let his two sons, Rām and Lakṣmaṇ, go with him to his ashram in order to destroy the demons. At first, Daśarath's heart trembled at the thought of separation from his two young sons, especially because of such a dangerous mission, and refused the sage's request. However, Viśvāmitra pleaded much with him and succeeded in dispelling his doubts. Daśarath entrusted his sons to the sage and they departed from Ayodhya. On their way to the hermitage, Rām, at Viśvāmitra's behest, killed a demoness Tāḍakā with a single arrow. Although the sage was well aware of Rām's divine character, when they reached his ashram, he endowed him with extraordinary strength and bestowed on him divine weapons.

Soon Viśvāmitra and other sages of the hermitage set out to perform a sacrifice and Rām himself guarded it. The demons, Mārīc and Subahu with an army, wanted to interrupt it but Rām intervened. Assisted by Lakṣmaṇ, he slew them all.

After some time spent peacefully at the ashram, Viśvāmitra with the boys departed for Janakpur, the capital of Mithila, to witness a bow contest organized by King Janak. They reached Janakpur some time before the contest. One morning, Rām and Lakṣmaṇ left the sage to gather flowers for his sacrifice. They went to a beautiful royal garden in which they met Sītā, a daughter of Janak, who had come there with her female companions to worship the goddess Girijā at her temple. Rām and Sītā, enchanted with each other, fell in love.

Viśvāmitra arrived with Rām and Lakṣmaṇ at the tournament ground. Many princes and kings had already gathered there in the hope of winning Sītā's hand after having lifted Śiv's bow and thus defeating other contestants. One by one, they tried to lift the bow but to no avail. Even a group of ten thousand daring men did not succeed in doing it. It was Rām who not only raised the bow but also broke it, winning thus the hand of Sītā. She confirmed the result of the contest and invested Rām with a garland of victory, placing it around his neck much to the annoyance of the defeated princes. Amidst an uproar caused by those who were displeased, Paraśurām arrived on the spot. He became furious when he learnt that Rām had broken the bow of his guru, Śiv. After a verbal skirmish with Lakṣmaṇ, which only inflamed Paraśurām's anger, Rām succeeded in pacifying him. Paraśurām recognized the might of Rām and withdrew to the forest to do penance.

The preparations for the marriage of Sītā and Rām began and soon the ceremony was performed in a glorious way according to the family custom sanctioned by the Veda. Not only did Rām marry Sītā but his brothers also got married to Sītā's sister and her cousins. Thus, Bharat married Māṇḍavī, Lakṣmaṇ – Sītā's younger sister, Urmilā, and Śatrughna – Śrutakīrti. When all the nuptial ceremonies and feasts had finished, the newly-weds with Viśvāmitra and Daśarath heading the marriage party, which had come from Ayodhya to Janakpur for the wedding, returned to Ayodhya. They were all duly received in their capital and some time passed in a joyful atmosphere, while all rejoiced over the marriage of Rām and his brothers. Viśvāmitra left Ayodhya blessed by the marital happiness of Rām and Sītā.

BOOK TWO: AYODHYA

One day, Daśarath decided to install his eldest son, Rām, as his heir apparent to the great joy of his guru, ministers, family and dependants. However, all the preparations for the installation of Rām as Crown Prince had to be stopped because due to the scheming of gods, Sarasvatī, the goddess of speech, made Mantharā, a handmaid of Kaikeyī, influence her mistress to stand up to Daśarath's decision. At first Kaikeyī did not yield to her handmaid's instigations as Rām was as dear a son to her as Bharat, but eventually Mantharā succeeded. She reminded Kaikeyī that Daśarath had once granted her two boons. She also convinced her that it was the right time to claim the fulfilment of that promise from him. Kaikeyī demanded from her husband the throne for Bharat and exile to the forest for fourteen years for Rām. Daśarath was horrified when he heard her demands and especially when he realized that she would not withdraw them: as king he was bound by his word. The next morning, it was Kaikeyī who communicated that decision to Rām. Daśarath, who was also there, was so stricken with grief that he was practically unconscious and did not utter a single word. However, Rām was truly pleased to learn the news. Firstly, because he wanted to obey his father's commands, secondly, because he was looking forward to spending some time in the forest among the sages. Sītā, having learnt what had happened, decided to accompany her husband. Kauśalyā and Rām tried to dissuade her from that idea but to no avail. Lakṣmaṇ also decided to accompany his brother during the exile.

Soon, the three exiles clad in hermit's garb left the palace in the company of Daśarath's minister, Sumantra. For some time a crowd of the citizens of Ayodhya also followed them but they were left behind when, tired, they fell asleep and Rām with his companions went away in a chariot driven by Sumantra. They arrived at the outskirts of Shringaverapura, the capital of Guh, the chief of the Niṣāds. The exiles met him and rested at the bank of the river Ganges, having declined his invitation to his abode. Next morning Sumantra departed for Ayodhya and Rām with his wife and brother crossed the Ganges. Guh accompanied them during their wanderings through the woods and helped them a lot. Finally, they reached Sangam in Prayag and went to the hermitage of the sage Bharadvāj where they had some rest. Soon after they had left Bharadvāj's ashram, Rām asked Guh to return to his home.

Admired and praised by all those whomever they met on their way, Rām, Sītā and Lakṣmaṇ arrived at the hermitage of Vālmīki. Rām asked the sage where they should settle. Vālmīki, before he advised them to go to the hill of Chitrakut on the banks of the river Mandakini, had said that it was not easy to answer such a question, because in fact Rām was present everywhere, enshrined in the temple of people's hearts! Following his advice, the three exiles settled in the beautiful neighbourhood of Chitrakut where they led a peaceful, happy life.

In the meantime, Sumantra returned to Ayodhya. He met the extremely distressed Daśarath and the queens. After hearing the news about Rām, Daśarath's heart filled with such grief that he departed to the world of gods. Because at that time Bharat and Śatrughna were away from Ayodhya, visiting their uncle, they had been summoned to come back and the king's body was deposited in a vessel filled with oil (in order to prevent it from decaying until their return). When Bharat had learnt the cause of their early return, he was overwhelmed with grief and when he realized what was the cause of his father's death, his heart filled with a great contempt for his mother. Vasiṣṭha helped Bharat to compose himself and the cremation rites as well as other ceremonies could be duly performed. However, Bharat was very unhappy with that situation and accused himself of being the cause of Rām's exile. He decided to go to Chitrakut and meet Rām there in order to convince him to return and ascend the throne of Ayodhya.

Bharat set out on his way to Chitrakut in the company of Vasiṣṭha, hosts of Brahmins, the queens and Ayodhya's citizens. Having seen him approach with his entourage, Lakṣmaṇ was sure that Bharat wanted to eliminate them but Rām convinced him that he was wrong. Bharat made obeisance to Rām and there was no end to a warm welcome, persuasions and explanations. Even Sītā's father, King Janak, and her mother, Queen Sunayanā, arrived from Mithila. When Bharat asked Rām to return to Ayodhya, he refused to comply with his request and stuck to fulfilling his father's commands. He succeeded in convincing Bharat to go back and rule Ayodhya during the period of his exile. On leaving Chitrakut, Bharat received a pair of Rām's wooden sandals. He understood it as an act of symbolic support from Rām and Sītā, as if they had agreed to return to Ayodhya themselves. Back in Ayodhya, on an auspicious day, Bharat installed Rām's sandals on the throne and himself resolved to live a life of penance in Nandigram.

Book Three: The Forest

After some time, Rām with his companions left Chitrakut and proceeded to the hermitage of the sage Atri. During their stay there, Sītā met Atri's wife, Anasūyā, who taught her the duties of a virtuous wife. On their way from Atri's hermitage, they encountered the demon Virādh. Rām killed him and the demon instantly assumed a divinely beautiful form and ascended straight to Rām's heavenly abode. Proceeding on their way, they met the sage Śarabhaṅga whose desire was to meet Rām before his death. When the sage's wish came true, he built his funeral pyre and rose straight to Rām's heavenly abode, while many other sages witnessed that. Finally, the exiles reached the hermitage of the sage Agastya who advised them to make their home in Panchavati in the Dandak forest.

Rām's presence in Panchavati made that previously dangerous wilderness a peaceful place where hermits and the exiled could live happily and without fear. That was also the right time for Lakṣmaṇ to ask Rām to explain to him the doctrine of Bhakti. The tranquillity of Panchavati was disturbed by the arrival of Śūrpaṇakhā, the sister of Rāvaṇ, the ten-headed demon king of Lanka. When she saw two handsome brothers, she was so infatuated that she assumed a beautiful form and made advances to Rām. Having glanced at Sītā, he sent her to Lakṣmaṇ saying that he was a bachelor. When Lakṣmaṇ also rejected her advances, Śūrpaṇakhā returned to Rām. He once again sent her to his younger brother who again rejected her. Furious Śūrpaṇakhā, coming back to Rām, revealed her true form as a demoness. Rām noticed that she frightened Sītā and made a sign to Lakṣmaṇ who deprived her of her nose and ears. Mutilated Śūrpaṇakhā went sobbing to the demons Khar and Dūṣaṇ. They gathered an army and assisted by another demon, Triśirā, advanced to take revenge on the two princes but they lost their lives on the battlefield. However, because during the fight they shouted the name of their enemy (Rām, Rām!), they attained eternal bliss in a reunion with God Rām. After that lost battle, furious Śūrpaṇakhā went to Rāvaṇ and succeeded in provoking him to undertake action against Rām, for which he requested the help of the demon Mārīc.

Meanwhile, in Panchavati, when Lakṣmaṇ had gone to the forest to gather some food, Rām asked Sītā to enter fire and dwell in it until he destroyed all the demons. She did as asked by Rām, leaving only her reflection outside. Not even Lakṣmaṇ knew the secret.

Mārīc was a devotee of Rām and he knew that Rāvaṇ's plans would fail. He decided to help him in order to reap the fruit of his existence at the sight of his Lord. Mārīc assumed the form of a marvellous, golden deer. When Sītā saw that extremely captivating animal, she requested Rām to kill it and get its hide for her. Rām asked Lakṣmaṇ to take care of Sītā and set out on the deer hunt. Mārīc as a deer, showing and concealing himself, drew Rām away from the hermitage but finally Rām shot him with an arrow. Mārīc fell to the ground and mimicking Rām's voice called the name of Lakṣmaṇ. When Sītā heard his cry, she persuaded her brother-in-law to go and help Rām. Lakṣmaṇ left Sītā under the care of forest deities and the guardians of the quarters of the world and rushed to Rām. Rāvaṇ entered the deserted hermitage in the disguise of an ascetic and, having seized Sītā, seated her in his chariot and drove away from Panchavati. Jaṭāyu, the brave king of vultures, having heard Sītā crying and seeing Rāvaṇ carry her away, tried to rescue her but the king of Lanka cut off his wings and Jaṭāyu fell to the ground.

When Rām and Lakṣmaṇ returned to their hermitage, they realized that Sītā had disappeared from there. They immediately started searching for her and Rām especially was frantic with worry. Before his death, Jaṭāyu told them that it was the Ten-Headed who had kidnapped Sītā. Dying Jaṭāyu abandoned his vulture body and attaining Hari's form ascended his heavenly abode. Rām, with his own hands, performed the cremation rites for him. During their search for Sītā, they encountered the demon Kabandha. Rām killed him but before the demon's death, he instructed him in the doctrine of Bhakti and the demon went to heaven. The brothers also visited the ashram of Śabarī, an ascetic woman of low status. She reverently washed their feet, gave them seats and offered Rām very juicy and tasty bulbs, roots and fruit to eat.[1] Rām reciprocated her hospitality with his loving instructions in the nine kinds of devotion. Śabarī advised him to go to lake Pampa and to befriend Sugrīv there.

While the brothers were proceeding on their way, Rām lamented, suffering from the pangs of separation from his beloved Sītā. Finally, they reached the lovely lake Pampa, where all the gods and sages sang hymns of praise to Rām. The sage Nārad approached the brothers and asked a boon from Rām. He wanted Rām's name to be an exterminator of sin and to abide in the hearts of his devotees. Rām consented to the sage's request and extolled the virtues of saintly people.

Book Four: Kishkindha

Rām and Lakṣmaṇ reached the Rishyamuk hill where a monkey king, Sugrīv, lived. One of his ministers, Hanumān, was first to learn who they were and that they were searching for Rām's wife. Hanumān introduced the brothers to his master and acquainted them with the conflict they had with Sugrīv's brother, Bāli. Both parties decided to form an alliance in order to help each other solve their problems. Sugrīv consoled Rām that Sītā would be recovered and also gave him the garment she had dropped at his sight when Rāvaṇ had been carrying her away. He also told Rām how the discord with Bāli had started: the demon Māyāvī had arrived at the gates of their city and had put a challenge to Bāli, the then ruler of Kishkindha. Bāli met that challenge and rushed after the enemy, accompanied by Sugrīv, but the demon took to flight and entered a cave in a mountain. Bāli asked Sugrīv to wait for him at the entrance to the cave and followed his enemy. Sugrīv had waited there for his brother for a whole month but seeing a massive stream of blood coming out of the cave, he presumed that Bāli was dead. He closed the cave entrance with a rock and ran away. Hearing the news, the ministers pressed him to take up the rule of Kishkindha. However, after some time Bāli returned home. He realized what had happened during his absence,

---

[1] Despite the oft-repeated opinion, in the *Rāmcaritmānas* there is no mention of 'pre-testing' by Śabarī the sweetness of the berries she offered to Rām. For more on this see Śaraṇ, *Mānas-pīyūṣ*, vol. 5, pp. 349-51.

beat up his brother and deprived him of all that he possessed, including his wife, Tārā. Since then, Sugrīv had lived in the forest. Rām promised to restore him to the throne and kill Bāli with a single arrow. Soon he fulfilled his promise. Bāli was killed by him during the fight between both brothers and was then sent to Rām's heavenly abode. In due time, Sugrīv was installed on the throne and Aṅgad, Bāli's son, became Crown Prince. Because the rainy season had started, Rām settled on a hill, not far from Kishkindha.

When the season of rains was over, it seemed that Sugrīv with Tārā at his side had forgotten about his promise to Rām. Rām got annoyed with him and sent Lakṣmaṇ to remind him of his commitment. Sugrīv begged pardon from Rām and ordered his army – under command of Nīl, Aṅgad, Hanumān and Jāmbavān, the chief of bears – to go south to look for Sītā. On their way, they met Sampātī, Jaṭāyu's elder brother, who told them that Sītā was a captive in the city of Lanka across the ocean. Hanumān resolved to leap across the waters in order to confirm the news about Sītā.

Book Five: Beautiful

Hanumān leapt across the ocean and, having become as small as a mosquito, he entered Rāvaṇ's capital and made his way to his palace. On his way, he met Vibhīṣaṇ, the younger brother of Rāvaṇ, who proved to be Rām's devotee. Hanumān in the disguise of a Brahmin, having become sure of Vibhīṣaṇ's love for Rām, revealed to him the purpose of his visit to Lanka. Vibhīṣaṇ told him in detail about the life Sītā led there and explained to him how he could succeed in meeting her in the Ashok (*Aśok*(*a*); *Jonesia asoka*) grove. Hidden among the leaves of the trees, Hanumān became a witness to Rāvaṇ's attempts to convince Sītā to become his lady. After Sītā had rejected his advances, Rāvaṇ ordered demonesses to make her obey him within one month, otherwise he would kill her. His order, however, was not duly observed, because the demoness Trijaṭā, one of the demonesses attending Sītā, told the others her dream. She saw in it Rām's victory over Rāvaṇ who had lost the throne of Lanka during the war with Rām and his kingdom passed to Vibhīṣaṇ. When Sītā was left alone, Hanumān approached her as Rām's messenger with the ring he had been given by him and assured her of Rām's great love for her. He told Sītā that Rām would come with his troops after a few days and would take her home. Before his departure, Hanumān asked Sītā for her approval to eat the delicious fruit from the grove. After eating the fruit, he began to break trees and to fight with the guardians of the grove and then with the warriors sent by Rāvaṇ and later also with his younger son, Akṣay, but Hanumān killed them all. Hearing about the death of his son, Rāvaṇ sent his elder son, Meghnād, ordering him not to kill Hanumān but to bind him and bring him to the palace. The tied up Hanumān, escorted to the court by Meghnād, explained the purpose of his mission to Lanka and asked Rāvaṇ to surrender Sītā and praise Rām. Rāvaṇ did not want to listen to such counsels, became furious with Hanumān and wanted to put an end to his life. At that moment, Vibhīṣaṇ intervened, stating that an envoy should not be killed, and asked Rāvaṇ to punish him in some other way but to spare his life. Therefore, Rāvaṇ ordered them to soak cloth in oil and wrap it around the monkey's tail and then to set it on fire. The demons did as they had been ordered but when Hanumān saw his tail in flames, he diminished his size and escaped from his bonds. Then forty-nine winds began to blow, Hanumān grew in size so much that he touched the sky and started springing from one palace to another. Soon the entire Lanka was burnt except for Vibhīṣaṇ's house. Hanumān extinguished his tail in the ocean and went to Sītā to ask her for a token for Rām; she gave him a jewel from her hair. After completing his mission successfully, Hanumān returned to his fellows jumping across the ocean. When he met Rām, he gave him the jewel from Sītā and conveyed her loving message to him. Soon Rām's army of mighty bears and monkeys marched off to Lanka.

Meanwhile, in the capital of Rāvaṇ burnt by Hanumān, Mandodarī, the principal wife of Rāvaṇ, entreated him to give Sītā back to Rām and thus avert the extinction of the demons' race. Vibhīṣaṇ, supported by a senior minister Mālyavān, also tried to persuade his elder brother to restore Sītā to Rām who was not merely a king but the Lord of the world, the all-pervading Ultimate Being. Rāvaṇ kicked his brother, thus spurning his advice. Vibhīṣaṇ went over to Rām's side, seeing in Rām his Lord, and his services were accepted.

Rām went to the seashore to ask the Ocean to facilitate the passage of his army to Lanka. After spending three days there in vain, he finally threatened the Ocean with a terrifying fiery arrow and made him yield to cooperation with him.

Book Six: Lanka

Nal and Nīl, assisted by other monkeys and bears, constructed a causeway to Lanka, using for this purpose trees, huge mountains and hills. Rām with his army crossed the waters and pitched his camp at the seaside.

Mandodarī once again tried to make Rāvaṇ send Sītā back to Rām but to no avail. Rāvaṇ was counselled by his ministers and his son, Prahasta, but remained unyielding to all pleading. Rām also gave him one more chance to change his mind and sent Aṅgad to him as his emissary. Aṅgad, unafraid of Rāvaṇ, told him to surrender to Rām and then, with great cleverness and sarcasm, faced all his verbal assaults. When he could not stand Rāvaṇ's boasting any longer, he planted his foot firmly amidst Rāvaṇ's assembly, challenging him that if he could just only move his foot, Rām would go back without Sītā. Meghnād and other valiant demon warriors tried to lift it but Aṅgad's foot did not move a bit. When eventually Rāvaṇ rose from his seat and proceeded to him, Aṅgad told him that grasping his feet would not bring him salvation and instead he should embrace Rām's feet. Rāvaṇ, feeling ashamed, went back to his seat. In this way, Aṅgad, having crushed the pride of Rām's enemy, returned to his master. Mandodarī reminded Rāvaṇ that two of his sons had been killed and his capital had been burnt. She asked him to worship Rām and ask for his forgiveness, once again to no avail.

On his return, Aṅgad reported to Rām on the events in Lanka and Rām resolved to attack Rāvaṇ. The war broke out and military activity used to cease for the night only. After some battles and losses, Meghnād struck Lakṣmaṇ on his breast with a spear and Lakṣmaṇ lost consciousness. Hanumān brought him to their camp and Rām, seeing his brother senseless, was extremely worried. A doctor who was brought in, told Hanumān to go to a certain mountain and bring a special herb. When he reached the mountain, he had no idea which of many herbs growing on it he should take, therefore he rooted up the whole mountain and, taking it with him, rushed back. While he was passing over Ayodhya, Bharat, having noticed a huge shape in the sky, mistook it for a demon and shot it down with an arrow. The monkey fell to the ground with Rām's name on his lips. After regaining consciousness, he told Bharat briefly about all that had happened to Sītā and Rām. Realizing that Hanumān should get to Lanka as soon as possible, Bharat offered to despatch him instantly to Rām on his arrow but Hanumān, too proud to accept such a proposal, set forth himself. When he came back, the doctor quickly applied the medicine and Lakṣmaṇ got up joyfully. Rām embraced his brother and all the bears and monkeys rejoiced.

In the meantime, Rāvaṇ decided to awake his mighty brother, Kumbhakarṇa. When this huge demon learned what had happened, he reproached Rāvaṇ for kidnapping Sītā, the Mother of the world, and for fighting with Rām whom he should worship. On his way to the battlefield, he met Vibhīṣaṇ and was happy to learn that he was a devotee of Rām. Kumbhakarṇa fought fiercely with Rām's warriors and finally with Rām. He lost his life but his spirit was absorbed in the Lord's mouth.

At one stage of the war, Rām got involved in a combat with Meghnād who used his magic power. Well-familiar with the course of events in the Rāmāyaṇa, Rām complied with the tradition and let himself be bound by serpents into which Meghnād's arrows were turning. All were terrified at that sight until Garuḍ, the king of birds, relieved Rām, devouring all the serpents. Later, Lakṣmaṇ shot Meghnād dead. After much fighting and many losses on both sides, Rāvaṇ set out to perform a sacrifice to gain immortality. Rām, having learnt about it, sent his monkey warriors to Rāvaṇ's palace to interrupt his sacrifice. The monkeys got into the palace and assaulted not only Rāvaṇ but also his wives. Rāvaṇ, hearing their cries, became furious and started fighting with the monkeys, and thus his sacrifice was disrupted.

The war reached its climax – the battlefield, flowing with rivers of blood, was covered with dead bodies on which vultures, jackals, ghosts and the attendants of fearful goddesses feasted. When the scales seemed to turn in Rām's favour, Rāvaṇ used his magic power and created a multitude of Rāms and Lakṣmaṇs in the ranks of his army. Only Rām was not under the influence of that illusion but Lakṣmaṇ and all the bears and monkeys were paralyzed by fear and could not fight. Rām, laughing, dispelled the illusion with his arrow. Soon, the final combat between Rām and Rāvaṇ commenced. The opponents fought in great fury, using their all skills and later Rām was also assisted by his warriors but fighting stopped for the night. After the daybreak, both parties returned to the battlefield. Rām's army showed its courage and might, which Rāvaṇ tried to crush with magic. Rām attacked Rāvaṇ and his arrows kept on cutting off Rāvaṇ's ten heads and twenty arms but they were continually growing again. For the all-knowing Rām it was just a pastime but for others, including the gods watching the battle from heaven, that sight caused great distress. Vibhīṣaṇ told Rām that in Rāvaṇ's navel there was the nectar of immortality. Rām shot thirty-one arrows at once: one for the navel and the rest for his heads and arms. The headless and armless trunk of Rāvaṇ finally fell to the ground.

The whole universe rejoiced, gods were showered from heaven and cheered on the account of Rām's victory. Soon after performing Rāvaṇ's last rites, at Rām's order, Vibhīṣaṇ was crowned king in the presence of Lakṣmaṇ, Sugrīv, Aṅgad, Nal, Nīl, Jambāvan and Hanumān; Rām, true to the instructions of his father, did not enter the city.

Rām sent Hanumān to Sītā to inform her about all that had happened and then Vibhīṣaṇ, Aṅgad and Hanumān were sent to bring her back. The right moment to release the real Sītā hidden in the fire had come and Rām ordered Lakṣmaṇ to prepare a heap of firewood and to set it ablaze. The illusory Sītā entered the flames and was destroyed by them. Agni, having assumed a body, returned the real Sītā to Rām. All those gathered rejoiced, seeing Rām and Sītā reunited. Gods praised Rām, the all-pervading Lord. For a while Daśarath also joined them and bestowed with the knowledge of true nature of Rām as well as with his heart set on Bhakti, he returned to the abode of the gods.

Rām, accompanied by Sugrīv, Nīl, Jāmbavān, Aṅgad, Nal and Hanumān as well as, of course, by Lakṣmaṇ and Sītā, departed for Ayodhya in an aerial vehicle, Puṣpak, driven by Vibhīṣaṇ. On their way, they visited the places of their exile and the sages living there. On reaching Ayodhya, Rām told Hanumān to go to Bharat in the disguise of a Brahmin student and after telling him about his well-being to return with news about him.

Book Seven: Later

Only one day of the period of Rām's exile was left. All the citizens of Ayodhya waited impatiently for the end of their separation from Rām. When Hanumān saw Bharat in an ascetic garb, repeating Rām's name continually, his heart was filled with joy. He informed Bharat that Rām had safely returned. He also told him about the great deeds of Rām and returned to his master. Bharat set off for Ayodhya to tell all the people the news about Rām's return. Soon, together with a crowd of people whose bodies were emaciated with the grief caused by the separation from Rām, he went to meet him. A very touching scene of their meeting ensued. The queens also arrived and embraced Rām, Lakṣmaṇ and Sītā but Lakṣmaṇ still harboured a grudge against Kaikeyī.

After a warm welcome, Rām went to the palace. Vasiṣṭha summoned Brahmins and informed them that the time was auspicious for Rām's coronation. Appropriate preparations for the ceremony commenced. When Rām ascended the throne, the three worlds rejoiced and Rām's just rule – Rāmrājya – began. All the people were happy, healthy, well-off and full of devotion and love. Rām performed myriads of horse-sacrifices, was very generous to Brahmins, protected Vedic tradition and dharma. After some time Sītā gave birth to two beautiful sons – Lav and Kuś – and each of Rām's brothers also had two sons. The great happiness and prosperity of Ayodhya was beyond any description.

During that time, Rām spread his teachings among his people. One day, he gave instructions to his companions to dispel their all doubts – he answered a question of Hanumān who wanted to know the difference between the virtuous and the wicked (*santa asanta*). Another day, he summoned Vasiṣṭha, the Brahmins and all the citizens of Ayodhya and taught them Rāmbhakti which was an easy and happiness-giving remedy to cross the ocean of mundane existence. After listening to Rām's words, all the assembled praised him, seeing in him their mother and father, their guru and brother. At last, after meeting Vasiṣṭha, Rām took with him his brothers and Hanumān. They went outside the city where he distributed all he had among the people. Then, feeling fatigue, he retreated to a cool mango grove. Bharat spread his robe for Rām to sit. All the brothers attended Rām and Hanumān fanned him. The sage Nārad came with his *vīṇā* lute in his hands and sang hymns of praise to Rām, after which the sage returned to the abode of Brahmā.

Appendix B: Names of the Major Characters and Places in the *Rāmcaritmānas*

Ahalyā	wife of the sage Gautam, turned into stone as a result of the curse of her husband after she had been seduced by the god Indra; Rām restored her previous form with an incidental touch of his foot.
Anasūyā	wife of the sage Atri; she taught Sītā the duties of a virtuous wife.
Aṅgad	son of Bāli, Crown Prince during the reign of his uncle Sugrīv, a commander in Sugrīv's and Rām's armies.
Bāli	monkey king of Kishkindha, elder brother of Sugrīv, father of Aṅgad, killed by Rām.
Bharadvāj	a great sage who received Rām in his ashram in Prayag; he heard the story of Rām's deeds from the sage Yājñvalkya.
Bharat	son of Daśarath and Kaikeyī, younger brother of Rām.
Bhuśuṇḍi	a crow, a model devotee of Rām (especially the child Rām); he told the story of Rām to Garuḍ and other birds coming to his abode.
Chitrakut	(Citrakūṭ) hill where Rām and Sītā spent the beginning of their exile.
Daśarath	Rām's father, king of Ayodhya from the family of Raghu of the Solar Dynasty.
Dandak	(Daṇḍak) forest near the river Godavari; in one of its parts called Panchavati Rām with his companions spent most of their exile.

Dūṣaṇ	a demon who with his two brothers, Khar and Triśirā, tried to avenge the mutilation of their sister Śūrpaṇakhā; killed by Rām.
Garuḍ	the king of birds, delivered Rām from serpents' tangles.
Guh	chief of the Niṣāds, his capital was Shringavera (Śṛṅgavera) on the banks of the river Ganges; an ally of Rām.
Hanumān	the son of the god of wind (Vayu); played an important role in rescuing Sītā from the hands of Rāvaṇ; a model servant and devotee of Rām.
Hari	epithet of Viṣṇu, in the *Rāmcaritmānas* mostly used in reference to Rām.
Indrajit	lit. 'he who conquered Indra'; *see* Meghnād.
Jāmbavān	chief of bears who played an important role during Rām's war with Rāvaṇ.
Janak	king of Mithila, Sītā's father.
Jānakī	epithet of Sītā, a patronymic from the name of her father Janak.
Janakpur	the capital of Janak in Mithila.
Jaṭāyu	a vulture who tried to rescue Sītā from Rāvaṇ and was killed by him.
Kaikeyī	junior wife of Daśarath, mother of Bharat.
Kausalyā	senior wife of Daśarath, mother of Rām.
Khar	*see* Dūṣaṇ
Kumbhakarṇa	Rāvaṇ's gigantic brother who used to sleep for the half year and when awake had an insatiable appetite; killed by Rām.

Kuś	one of the twin sons of Rām and Sītā; in the Rāmāyaṇa tradition Kuś and his brother Lav are known as the first public performers of the epic.
Lakṣmaṇ	son of Daśarath and Sumitrā, twin brother of Śatrughna, Rām's younger brother and his constant companion.
Lanka	(Laṅkā) the capital of Rāvaṇ, where Sītā was kept captive by him.
Lav	*see* Kuś
Māṇḍavī	elder daughter of Janak's younger brother Kuśadhvaj, wife of Bharat.
Mandodarī	daughter of a demon Maya, the principal wife of Rāvaṇ.
Mantharā	a vicious handmaid of Kaikeyī, whose intrigue led to Rām's exile.
Mārīc	son of a demoness Tāḍakā who helped Rāvaṇ seize Sītā from Rām.
Meghnād	son of Rāvaṇ, valiant warrior, killed by Lakṣmaṇ; also known as Indrajit.
Maithilī	epithet of Sītā, lit. 'descending from Mithilā'.
Mithila	(Mithilā) Janak's kingdom, the birthplace of Sītā.
Nal and Nīl	monkey warriors of Sugrīv who fought against Rāvaṇ and built a causeway to Lanka.
Nandigram	(Nandigrām) Bharat's ashram where he led a life of penance during the fourteen-year exile of Rām, not far from Ayodhya.
Niṣād(s)	tribal people whose chief was Guh.

Pampa	(Pampā) lake where Rām and Lakṣmaṇ first met Hanumān and Sugrīv.
Panchavati	(Pañcavaṭī) part of the Dandak forest where Rām, Lakṣmaṇ and Sītā lived until Rāvaṇ seized Sītā from there.
Paraśurām	lit. 'Rām with an axe'; sixth incarnation of Viṣṇu, an ardent devotee of Śiv. He got furious when Rām broke Śiv's bow in Janakpur and wanted to punish him for it but abandoned his intention recognizing in Rām the true Lord.
Rāghava	epithet of Rām, a patronymic from Raghu.
Raghu	ancestor of Rām.
Raghubīr	epithet of Rām, lit. 'the hero of the Raghu [family].
Raghunāth	epithet of Rām, lit. 'the lord of the Raghu [family].
Rākṣasas	demons; their king was Rāvaṇ.
Rāvaṇ	ten-headed demon king of Lanka, main antagonist of Rām. He seized his wife, Sītā, and was eventually killed by Rām.
Rishyamuk	(Ṛṣyamūk) hill where Sugrīv lived banished from Kishkindha by his brother Bāli.
Śabarī	an ascetic woman of low status who aided Rām during his wanderings in the forest.
Sampātī	a vulture, Jaṭāyu's elder brother.
Sangam	(Saṅgam) lit. 'confluence', also called Triveni (Triveṇī), i.e. 'triple-braid'; the confluence of the rivers Ganges and Yamuna with a subterranean river Sarasvati in Prayag (modern Allahabad).
Śatrughna	son of Daśarath and Sumitrā, twin brother of Lakṣmaṇ, Rām's younger brother.

Sītā	daughter of Janak, beloved wife of Rām; according to the *Rāmcaritmānas* Rāvaṇ actually kidnapped an illusory Sītā, while the real Sītā was protected by Agni, the god of fire.
Śrutakīrti	wife of Śatrughna, younger daughter of Janak's younger brother Kuśadhvaj.
Sugrīv	the king of monkeys, younger brother of Bāli; ascended the throne of Kishkindha, thinking that his brother had died. However, Bāli returned and banished him. Rām helped him regain the throne in return for his help in recapturing Sītā.
Sumantra	charioteer and minister of Daśarath, accompanied Rām in the very beginning of his exile.
Sumitrā	junior wife of Daśarath, mother of Lakṣmaṇ and Śatrughna.
Sunayanā	lit. 'having beautiful eyes', wife of Janak, Sītā's mother.
Śūrpaṇakhā	the sister of Rāvaṇ; in Panchavati, infatuated with Rām, she tried to seduce him but at his behest was punished and mutilated by Lakṣmaṇ who cut her nose and ears. She took revenge on Rām bringing about the kidnapping of his beloved Sītā by Rāvaṇ.
Tāḍakā	a demoness killed by Rām at Viśvamitra's behest.
Trijaṭā	a demoness who in her dream saw Rāvaṇ's ignominious defeat in his war with Rām.
Triśirā	*see* Dūṣaṇ
Urmilā	younger sister of Sītā, wife of Lakṣmaṇ.
Vālin	*see* Bāli

Vālmīki	a great sage, in the Rāmāyaṇa tradition considered the composer of the epic; in the *Rāmcaritmānas* told Rām to settle in Chitrakut.
Vasiṣṭha	Daśarath's court priest and family preceptor.
Vibhīṣaṇ	brother of Rāvaṇ who in vain tried to prevent war between Rām and his brother. A true devotee of Rām joined him after Rāvaṇ had turned down all his counsels and after the defeat of his brother ascended the throne of Lanka.
Viśvāmitra	sage who took Rām from Daśarath in order to extinguish demons disrupting his sacrifice; he bestowed on Rām supernal might and weapons.

BIBLIOGRAPHY

ORIGINAL RĀMKATHĀ SOURCES

Ācārya Catursen, *Vayaṁ rakṣāmaḥ*, Dillī: Rājpāl eṇḍ Sanz, 1995.

Ācārya Tulsī, *Agniparīkṣā: jain rāmāyaṇ ke ādhār par racit*, 2nd edn, Cūru: Ādarś Sāhitya Saṅgh Prakāśan, 1972.

Ācārya Vimalasūri's Paumacariyam (with Hindi translation), ed. H. Jacobi, 2nd edn, Varanasi: Prakrit Text Society, 1962.

Adbhuta rāmāyaṇa, ed. Rām Kumār Rāy, Vārāṇasī: Prācya Prakāśan, 1982.

Agradās granthāvalī (Kuṇḍaliyā̃, Dhyan mañjarī, Sādhan gītāvalī), ed. Balbhadra Tivārī, Ilāhābād: Satyendra Prakāśan, 1985.

Agradās, *Dhyān mañjarī*, comment. Rāmvallabhāśaraṇ, Ayodhyā: Śrī Rāmkṛṣṇadās Utsavī, 1940.

Ānanda rāmāyaṇa, ed. and comment. Rāmtej Pāṇḍey and Yugal Kiśor Dvivedī, Kāśī: Paṇḍit Pustakālay, 1958.

Banādās, *Ubhay prabodhak rāmāyaṇ*, Ilāhābād: Lokbhāratī Prakāśan, 1980.

——, *Banādās bacanāmṛt*, Gorakhpur: Avadh Sāhitya Mandir, 1990.

——, *Bismaran samhār*, 2nd edn, Ayodhyā: Mahātmā Banādās Āśram, 1998 (1st published 1990).

Bhagvāndīn, Lālā, *Keśavkaumudī arthāt rāmcandrikā saṭīk*, 2 vols, 9th edn, Ilāhābād: Rāmnārāyaṇ Lāl Benī Mādhav, 1961.

Bhatt, G.H. and U.P. Shah, eds, *The Vālmīki Rāmāyaṇa, Critically Edited for the First Time*, Baroda: Oriental Institute, 1960–75.

Bhuśuṇḍi rāmāyaṇa: Dvitīya bhāg (dakṣiṇa khaṇḍa), ed. Bhagavatīprasād Siṁh, Gorakhpur: Avadh Sāhitya Mandir, n.d.

Bhuśuṇḍi rāmāyaṇa: Pūrva khaṇḍa, ed. Bhagavatīprasād Siṁh, Vārāṇasī: Viśvavidyālay Prakāśan, 1975.

Bhuśuṇḍi rāmāyaṇa: Tṛtīya bhāg (paścima-uttara khaṇḍa), ed. Bhagavatīprasād Siṁh, Gorakhpur: Avadh Sāhitya Mandir, n.d.

Caturvedī, Javāharlāl, ed., *Sūrsāgar*, Kalkattā: Śrīnand Mīnānī, 1965.

Dvivedī, Loknāth 'Silākārī', ed., *Viṣṇudāskṛt rāmāyaṇkathā*, Ilāhābād: Sāhitya Bhavan, n.d. [1972].

Govinddās 'Vinīt', *Rāmāyaṇ lay-rādheśyām*, Banāras: Baijnāth Prasād Bukselar, 1939.

Gupta, Jagdīś, *Śambūk*, Ilāhābād: Lokbhāratī Prakāśan, 1977.

Īśvardās, *Satyavatī tathā anya kṛtiyā̃*, ed. Śivgopāl Miśra, Gvāliyar: Vidyāmandir Prakāśan, 1958.

Īśvardāskṛt Aṅgad paij tathā Svargārohiṇī kathā, ed. Rāṁkumārī Miśra, Śivgopāl Miśra, Ilāhābād: Vijñān Pariṣad, 1979.

Keśav granthāvalī, ed. Viśvanāthprasād Miśra, 3 vols, Ilāhābād: Hindustānī Ekeḍemī, 1954–9.

Keśavdās, *Rāmcandrikā saṭīk*, comment. Jānakīprasād, Lakhnaū: Navalkiśor Pres, 1923.

Kohlī, Narendra, *Avasar*, Dillī: Parāg Prakāśan, 1976.

——, *Saṅgharṣ kī or*, Dillī: Parāg Prakāśan, 1978.

——, *Yuddh*, Dillī: Parāg Prakāśan, 1979.

——, *Dīkṣā*, 4th edn, Dillī: Parāg Prakāśan, 1980.

——, *Abhyuday*, vol. 1 (*Dīkṣā, Avasar, Saṅgharṣ kī or*), Dillī: Parāg Prakāśan, 1992.

——, *Abhyuday*, vol. 2 (*Yuddh 1, Yuddh 2*), Dillī: Abhiruci Prakāśan, 1994.

Kṛṣṇalāl, *Rāmcaritra*, ed. Manmohan Sahgal, Delhi: Sanmārg Prakāśan, 1978.

Mehtā, Nareś, *Pravād parva*, Ilāhābād: Lokbhāratī Prakāśan, 1977.

——, *Śabarī*, Ilāhābād: Lokbhāratī Prakāśan, 1977.

——, *Saṁśay kī ek rāt*, Ilāhābād: Lokbhāratī Prakāśan, 1962.

Miśra, Baldevprasād, *Kośalkiśor*, Ilāhābād: Paṇḍit Kālīcaraṇ Trivedī, 1934.

——, *Rāmrājya*, Lakhnaū: Hindī Sāhitya Bhaṇḍār, 1960.

——, *Sāketsant*, Dillī: Vidyā Mandir, 1946.

Miśra, Kedārnāth 'Prabhāt', *Kaikeyī (mahākāvya)*, Paṭnā: Śrī Ajantā Pres, n.d.

Miśra, Rameścandra, *Yah rakt sarovar kyõ*, Dillī: Anubhūti Prakāśan, 1987.

Miśra, Sadal, *Candrāvatī athavā Nasiketopākhyān*, 6th edn, Kāśī: NPS, 1950.

Miśra, Śyāmbihārī and Śukdevbihārī Miśra (Miśrabandhu), *Rāmcaritra*, Lakhnaū: Avadh Prinṭiṅg Varks, n.d. [1941?].

Miśrabandhu, *Miśrabandhu vinod*, rev. & corr. edn, 2 vols, Lakhnaū: Gaṅgā Pustak Mālā, 1972 (1st published 1913).

Nirālā granthāvalī, ed. Omkār Śarad, Lakhnaū: Prakāśan Kendra, 1973.

Padmākar granthāvalī, ed. Viśvanāthprasād Miśra, Vārāṇasī: NPS, 1956, p. 33.

Padmākar, *Rāmrasāyan*, Kāśī: Bhāratjīvan Pres, 1895.

Pañcāl, Bihārīlāl Viśvakarmā 'Kautuk', *Kauśalendra kautuk*, Vārāṇasī: by the author, 1936.

Prasād, Jayaśaṅkar, *Kānan kusum*, 8th edn, Ilāhābād: Bhāratī Bhaṇḍār, 1966.

Premcand, *Rāmkathā (Rāmcarcā)*, Jaypur: Sāhityāgār, 1992.

Pṛthvīrājrāso, ed. Mohanlāl Viṣṇulāl Pāṇḍya et al., 2 vols, 2nd new edn, Kāśī: NPS, 1994–5.

Rādheśyām, *Rāmāyaṇ*, Barelī: Śrī Rādheśyām Pustakālay, n.d.

Rāmājñāpraśna, comment. Sudarśan Siṁh, Gorakhpur: Gītā Pres, 1983.

Sadal Miśra granthāvalī, ed. Nalinvilocan Śarmā; Paṭnā: Bihār Rāṣṭrabhāṣā Pariṣad, 1960.

Śaraṇ, Añjanīnandan, *Mānaspīyūṣ*, vol. 1, 11th edn, Gorakhpur: Gītā Pres, 1998.

Śaraṇ, Raghuvīr 'Mitra', *Bhūmijā*, 4th edn, Meraṭh: Bhāratīy Sāhitya Prakāśan, 1973.

Śarmā, Śeṣmaṇi 'Maṇirāypurī', *Kaikeyī (rājnaitik khaṇḍ kāvya)*, Ilāhābād: Rāmnārāyaṇ Lāl, 1952.

Senāpati, *Kavittratnākar (bhūmikā, pāṭhāntar tathā ṭippaṇī sahit)*, ed. Umāśaṅkar Śukla, Ilāhābād: Hindī Pariṣad–Prayāg Viśvavidyālay, 1936.

Siṁh, Bhagvān, *Apne apne Rām*, Dillī: Mānak Pablikeśans, 1992.

Siṁh, Raghurāj, *Rāmsvayaṁvar (saṅkṣipta)*, ed. Brajratnadās, Kāśī: NPS, 1924.

Siṁh, Viśvanāth, *Ānand raghunandan*, ed. Dīpcand Jain et al., Rīvā: Vindhyā Prādeśik Hindi Sāhitya Sammelan, 1960.

Śrīrāmagītā (Adhyātma rāmāyaṇa), comment. Svāmī Cinmayānanda, Hindi tr. Rāv Raṇbahādur Siṁh, Kānpur: Sentral Cinmay Miśan Ṭrasṭ, 1994.

Śrīrāmgītā. Tulsīrāmāyaṇ par ādhārīt, Bambaī: Sentral Cinmay Miśan Ṭrasṭ, 1989.

Sūrsāgar, ed. Nanddulāre Vājpeyī, vol. 1 and 2, 3rd edn, Vārāṇasī: NPS, 1958.

The Kāshmīrī Rāmāyaṇa, Comprising the Śrīrāmāvatāracarita & the Lavakuśa-yuddhacarita of Divākara Prakāśa Bhaṭṭa, ed. George A. Grierson, Bibliotheca Indica no. 253, Calcutta: Asiatic Society of Bengal, 1930.

Tripāṭhī, Sūryakānt 'Nirālā', *Parimal*, Dillī: Rājkamal Prakāśan, 1993.

———, *Rām kī śakti pūjā*, in *Aparā*, 17th edn, Rājkamal Prakāśan: Dillī 1993.

———, *Tulsīdās*, Dillī: Rājkamal Prakāśan, 1993.

Tulsī granthāvalī, ed. Rāmcandra Śukla et al., Kaśī: NPS, 1974.

Tulsī Sāhib, *Ghaṭ rāmāyaṇ*, 2 vols, Ilāhābād: Belvīḍiyar Prinṭiṅg Varks, 2001–2.

Tulsīdās, *Rāmcaritmānas*, ed. Viśvanāthprasād Miśra, Vārāṇasī: Kāśirāj Nyās, n.d. [1962].

——, *Śrīrāmcaritmānas*, ed. and comment. Hanumānprasād Poddār, 19th edn, Gorakhpur: Gītā Pres, 1972.

——, *Vinaypatrikā (haritoṣiṇī ṭīkā sahit)*, ed. and comment. Viyogī Hari, Dillī: Sastā Sāhitya Maṇḍal Prakāśan, 1981.

——, *Vinaypatrikā (saral bhāvārth sahit)*, 30th edn, Gorakhpur: Gītā Pres, 1983.

Tulsīdāsgosvāmīkṛt saptakāṇḍa rāmāyaṇagranthaḥ, ed. (?) Tilakrām Nāth-rām, Kalikattā, 1839.

Tulsīkṛt rāmāyaṇ, ed. Rāmjasan, Benares: E. Lazarus & Co., 1869.

Tulsīkṛt rāmāyaṇ, ed. Sadal Miśra, Calcutta, 1810.

Tulsīkṛt rāmāyaṇ, ed. Sadāsukh Lāl, Ilāhābād: Nūrula Absār Pres, 1869.

Upādhyāy, Gopāl, *Rāmkathā*, Dillī: Sāmayik Prakāśan, 1992.

Upādhyāy, Rāmcarit, *Rāmcaritcandrikā arthāt rāmāyaṇ ke pradhān pātr kā caritracitraṇātmak ek sphuṭ kāvya*, Bā̃kīpur: Granthmālā Kāryālay, 1919.

——, *Rāmcaritcintāmaṇi: Khaṛībolī kā ek kāvya*, 2nd edn, Bā̃kīpur: Granthmālā Kāryālay, 1929.

Vālmīki Rāmāyana. Text as Constituted in Its Critical Edition, Vadodara: M.S. University of Baroda, 1992.

Varmā, Candraprakāś, *Sītā*, Ilāhābād: Hind Prakāśan, 1958.

Other Sources

Agarvāl, Dāmodar, 'Sattā kī rājnīti mẽ Rām kā badaltā svarūp', *Dharmyug*, 1.01.1993, pp. 32–3.

Agarwala, Atul Kumar, 'Marriage Songs in Harauti', Ph.D. dissertation, Kiel: Christian-Albrechts-Universität, 1982.

Archer, William G. and Barbara Stoler Miller, eds, *Songs for the Bride: Wedding Rites of Rural India*, New York: Columbia University Press, 1985.

Ārya, Rāmsvarūp and Girirājśāraṇ Agravāl, *Tulsī mānas sandarbh*, Sambhal: Mānas Catuśśatī Ayojan Samiti, 1974.

Avasthī, Baccūlāl, *Tulsī śabdakoś*, 2 vols, Dillī: Buks en' Buks, 1991.

Babineau, Edmour J., *Love of God and Social Duty in the Rāmcaritmānas*, Delhi: Motilal Banarsidass, 1979.

Bahadur, K.P., *Rāmacharitamānasa: A Study in Perspective*, Delhi: Ess Ess Publications, 1976.

Bahadur, S.P., tr., *Complete Works of Goswami Tulsidas: Minor Works*, vol. 6, Delhi: Munshiram Manoharlal, 1998.

Bāhrī, Hardev, *Prācīn bhāratīy saṁskṛti koś*, Dillī: Vidya Prakāśan Mandir, 1988.

Bakker, Hans, *Ayodhyā*, Groningen: Egbert Forsten, 1986.

——, 'The Rise of Ayodhyā as a Place of Pilgrimage', *Indo-Iranian Journal*, vol. 24, 1982, pp. 103–26.

——, 'Reflections on the Evolution of Rāma Devotion in the Light of Textual and Archaeological Evidence', *Wiener Zeitschrift für die Kunde Südasiens*, vol. 31, 1987, pp. 9–42.

Bālasubrahmaṇyam, P.K., 'Tamilnāḍu mẽ rāmsaṁskṛti', in Siṁh, *Śrī Rām viśvakoś*, pp. 530–42.

Balcerowicz, Piotr and Marek Mejor, eds, *Essays in Indian Philosophy, Religion and Literature*, Delhi: Motilal Banarsidass, 2004.

Banerjee, P., *Rama in Indian Literature, Art and Thought*, 2 vols, Delhi: Sundeep Prakashan, 1986.

Bangha, Imre, 'Dynamics of Textual Transmission in Premodern India: The *Kavitavali* of Tulsidas', *Comparative Studies of South Asia, Africa, and the Middle East*, vol. 24, no. 2, 2004, pp. 33–44.

Bartley, C.J., *The Theology of Rāmānuja: Realism and Religion*, London: RoutledgeCurzon, 2002.

'Baruā' *see* Kauśik, Ṛṣi Jaiminī 'Baruā'

Basham, A.L., *The Sacred Cow: The Evolution of Classical Hinduism*, ed. Kenneth G. Zysk, London: Rider, 1990.

Bhagīrath Miśra, ed., *Hindī sāhitya kā bṛhat itihās*, vol. 7, Vārāṇasī: NPS, 1972.

Bhandarkar, R.G., *Vaiṣṇavism, Śaivism and Minor Religious Systems*, Strassburg: Karl J. Trübner, 1913.

Bhāradvāj, Kauśalyā, *Hindī rāmkāvya mẽ svabhāvokti (san 1450 se 1650 tak)*, Rohtak: Manthan Pablikeśans, 1982.

Bhāradvāj, Nanda, 'Rāmkathā kā mithak aur *Apne apne Rām*', *Antardṛṣṭi*, no. 7, 1995, pp. 44–7.

Bhāradvaj, Rāmdatt, 'Tulsī kā janma sthān aur sorõ sāmagrī', in Ārya and Agravāl, *Tulsī mānas sandarbh*, pp. 12–39.

Bharatamuni, *The Nāṭyaśāstra (A Treatise on Ancient Indian Dramaturgy and Histrionics)*, ed. Manmohan Ghosh, vol. 1, 3rd edn, Calcutta: Manisha, 1995.

Bhāṭī, Deśrājsiṁh, *Keśavkāvyasudhā (keśav-sāhitya kā ālocnātmak tathā vyākhyātmak adhyayan)*, Dillī: Kalā Mandir, 1974.

Bhattacharji, Sukumari, *Indian Theogony: A Comparative Study of Indian Mythology from the Vedas to the Purāṇas*, [London]: Cambridge University Press, 1970.

Bhayani, H.C., 'The Prakrit and Apabhraṁśa Rāmāyaṇas', in Iyengar, *Asian Variations in Ramayana*, pp. 77–82.

Bose, Mandakranta, ed., *The Rāmāyaṇa Culture: Text, Performance and Iconography*, rpt, Delhi: D.K. Printworld, 2003.

Brockington, J.L., *The Sacred Thread: Hinduism in Its Continuity and Diversity*, Edinburgh: Edinburgh University Press, 1981.

——, *Righteous Rāma: The Evolution of an Epic*, Delhi: Oxford University Press, 1985.

——, *The Sanskrit Epics*, Leiden: E.J. Brill, 1998.

——, 'Sanskrit Epic Tradition I: Epic and Epitome (*Rāmāyaṇa* and *Rāmopākhyāna*)', *Indologica Taurinensia*, vol. 6, 1978, pp. 79–111.

——, 'The Rāmāyaṇa of Vālmīki: An Epic of Ancient India. Vol. III', *Orientalistische Literaturzeitung*, vol. 87, no. 6, 1992, p. 575.

——, 'The Rāmāyaṇa through the Centuries', *Utkal Historical Research Journal*, vol. 5, 1994, pp. 79–95.

——, 'Visual Epics', in Stasik and Brockington, *Indian Epic Traditions*.

Bryant, Kenneth E., *Poems to the Child-God: Structures and Strategies in the Poetry of Sūrdās*, Berkeley: University of California Press, 1978.

——, 'Toward a Critical Edition of the Sūrsāgar', in Callewaert, *Early Hindi Devotional Literature*, pp. 5–12.

——, 'The Fatehpur Manuscript and the Sūrsāgar Critical Edition Project', in Thiel-Horstmann, *Bhakti in Current Research, 1979–1982*, pp. 38–44.

——, 'The Bottom of the Page: Representing Variation in an Oral Tradition', in Entwistle, *Studies in Early Modern Indo-Aryan Languages, Literature and Culture*, pp. 87–100.

Bühnemann, Gudrun, *Budha-Kauśika's Rāmarakṣāstotra: A Contribution to the Study of Sanskrit Devotional Poetry*, Vienna: University of Vienna, 1983.

——, *Pūjā: A Study in Smārta Ritual*, Vienna: University of Vienna, 1988.

Bulcke, C[amille] *see* Bulke, Kāmil

Bulke, Kāmil, *Rāmkathā: utpatti aur vikās*, 6th rev. edn, Prayāg: Hindī Pariṣad, 1999.

——, '*Rāmacaritmānasa* and Its Relevance to Modern Age', in Raghavan, *The Ramayana Tradition*, pp. 58–75.

Busch, Allison, 'Questioning the Tropes about "*Bhakti*" and "*Rīti*" in Hindi Literary Historiography', in Horstman, *Bhakti in Current Research, 2001–2003*, pp. 33–47.

Callewaert, Winand M., ed., *Early Hindi Devotional Literature in Current Research*, Leuven: Katholieke Universiteit, 1980.

—— and Rupert Snell, *According to Tradition: Hagio-graphical Writing in India*, Wiesbaden: Otto Harrassowitz, 1994.

—— and Philip Lutgendorf, *Rāmcaritmānas Word Index*, Delhi: Manohar, 1997.

Candra, Sureś, *Bīsvī̃ sadī kā rāmkāvya aur mūlyabodh*, Dillī: Anaṅg Prakāśan, 2002.

Carman, John Braisted, *The Theology of Rāmānuja: An Essay in Inter-religious Understanding*, New Haven: Yale University Press, 1974.

Caturvedī, Paraśurām, 'Rāmopāsakõ kā "Rasik Sampradāy"', *Hindustānī*, vol. 19, no. 3, 1958, pp. 3–42.

Chaudhuri, Nirad C., *The Autobiography of an Unknown Indian*, 3rd impression, Bombay: Jaico Publishing House, 1969.

Choudary, D. Kiran Kranth and C. Udayalakshmi, *Rāmāyaṇa in Indian Art and Epigraphy*, Delhi: Harman, 2006.

Coburn, Thomas B., *Devī Māhātmya: The Crystallization of the Goddess Tradition*, Delhi: Motilal Banarsidass, 1997 (1st published 1984).

——, 'Consort of None, Śakti of All: The Vision of the Devī-māhātmya', in Hawley and Wulff, *The Divine Consort*, pp. 153–65.

Cvetkov, Yuriy V., *Surdas i ego poėzija*, Moskva: Nauka, 1979.

Das, Prabin Chandra, 'Durgavari: An Assamese Version of the Ramayana', in Singh and Datta, *Rama-katha*, pp. 139–52.

Das, Veena, 'Kāma in the Scheme of Puruṣārthas: the Story of Rāma', *Contributions to Indian Sociology* (n.s.), vol. 15, nos 1–2, 1981, pp. 183–203.

Datta, Birendranath, 'Rama-katha in Assam and its Neighbourhood: Popular and Folk Traditions', in Singh and Datta, *Rama-katha*, pp. 119–30.

de Tassy, Garcin, *Chrestomathie hindie et hindouie*, Paris: Imprimerie Nationale, 1849.

Dharwadker, Vinay, ed., *The Collected Essays of A.K. Ramanujan*, Delhi: Oxford University Press, 2004.

Diehl, Anita, *E.V. Ramaswami – Periyar: A Study of the Influence of a Personality in Contemporary South India*, Stockholm–Göteborg–Lund: Esselte Studium, 1977.

Dīkṣit, Hīrālāl, *Ācārya Keśavdās*, Lakhnaū: Lakhnaū Viśvavidyālay, 1954.

Dimock, Edward C., *The Place of the Hidden Moon: Erotic Mysticism in the Vaiṣṇava-sahajiya Cult of Bengal*, Chicago: University of Chicago Press, 1966.

——, 'Doctrine and Practice Among the Vaiṣṇavas of Bengal', in Singer, *Krishna: Myths, Rites and Attitudes*, pp. 47–63.

'Dinkara' *see* Singh, Rāma Dhārī 'Dinkara'

Dowson, John, *A Classical Dictionary of Hindu Mythology and Religion*, Delhi: Manu Publications, 1987 (rpt).

Duszak, Anna and Nina Pawlak, ed., *Anatomia gniewu: Emocje negatywne w językach i kulturach świata*, Warszawa: Wydawnictwa Uniwersytetu Warszawskiego, 2003, pp. 75–83.

Dvivedī, Hazārīprasād, *Hindī sāhitya kī bhūmikā*, 2nd edn, Dillī: Rājkamal Prakāśan, 1969.

Eck, Diana L. and Françoise Mallison, ed., *Devotion Divine: Bhakti Traditions from the Regions of India*, Groningen: Egbert Forsten, Paris: École Française d'Extrême-Orient, 1991.

Eliade, Mircea, *Yoga: Immortality and Freedom*, London: Routledge and Kegan Paul, 1969.

Entwistle, Alan W. et al., eds, *Studies in Early Modern Indo-Aryan Languages, Literature and Culture*, Delhi: Manohar, 1999.

Erndl, Kathleen M., 'The Mutilation of Śūrpaṇakhā', in Richman, *Many Rāmāyaṇas*, pp. 67–88.

Farquhar, J.N., *Modern Religious Movements in India*, Delhi: Munshiram Manoharlal, 1977 (1st published in 1914).

——, *An Outline of the Religious Literature of India*, Delhi: Motilal Banarsidass, 1984 (1st published 1920).

Frawley, David, comment., *The Oracle of Rama: An Adaptation of Rama Ajna Praśna of Goswami Tulsidas*, 2nd edn, Delhi: Motilal Banarsidass, 1999.

Frye, Northrop, *Anatomy of Criticism: Four Essays*, Princeton: Princeton University Press, 1957.

Frye, Northrop, *Fables of Identity: Studies in Poetic Mythology*, New York: Harcourt, Brace & World, 1963.

——, *Spiritus Mundi: Essays on Literature, Myth, and Society*, Bloomington: Indiana University Press, 1976.

Gaeffke, Peter, *Hindi Literature in the Twentieth Century*, Wiesbaden: Otto Harrassowitz, 1978.

Gandhi, M.K., *The Collected Works of Mahatma Gandhi*, Delhi: Publications Division, Ministry of Information and Broadcasting, Govt. of India, 1972.

Garg, Vedprakāś, 'Tulsī kī kṛtiyā̃', in Ārya and Agravāl, *Tulsī mānas sandarbh*, pp. 40–57.

Gautam, Premprakāś, 'Bhāṣā Yogavāsiṣṭha aur uskā lekhak', *Hindustānī*, vol. 34, no. 2, 1973 (April–June), pp. 106–11.

Ghosh, Sujit K., ed., *Rāmāyaṇa in the North-East India: Proceedings of the National Seminar Organised by Bharatiya Itihas Sankalan Samiti, Silchar*, Delhi: B.R. Publishing Corporation, 2002.

Giradhara Rāmāyaṇa, tr. Shanti Lal Nagar and Tripta Nagar, Delhi: Munshiram Manoharlal, 2003.

Goldman, Robert P., general ed., *The Rāmāyaṇa of Vālmīki: An Epic of Ancient India*, vols 1–, Princeton: Princeton University Press, 1984–.

——, 'Rāmaḥ Sahalakṣmaṇaḥ: Psychological and Literary Aspects of the Composite Hero of Vālmīki's Rāmāyaṇa', *Journal of Indian Philosophy*, vol. 8, 1980, pp. 149–89.

——, 'Introduction', in idem, general ed., vol. 1, *The Rāmāyaṇa of Vālmīki*, pp. 1–81.

Gombrich, Richard, 'The Vessantara Jātaka, the Rāmāyaṇa and the Daśaratha Jātaka', *Journal of American Oriental Society*, vol. 105, no. 3, 1985, pp. 427–37.

Gonda, Jan, *Ancient Indian Kingship from the Religious Point of View*, Leiden: E.J. Brill, 1969 (1st published 1966).

——, *Medieval Religious Literature in Sanskrit*, Wiesbaden: Otto Harrassowitz, 1977.

Goswami, Bhrigu Mohan, 'The Ramayana-based Ojapalis of Assam', in Singh and Datta, *Rama-katha*, pp. 153–60.

Grierson, George A., *The Modern Vernacular Literature of Hindustan*, Calcutta: Asiatic Society of Bengal, 1889.

——, 'Notes on Tul'sī Dās', *Indian Antiquary*, vol. 22, 1893, pp. 89–98, 122–9, 197–206, 225–36, 253–74.

Grincer, P.A., *Drevneindijskij ėpos: Genezis i tipologija*, Moskva: Nauka, 1974.

Gupta, Mātā Prasād, *Tulsīdās: Ek samālocnātmak adhyayan*, 5th edn, Prayāg: Hindi Pariṣad Prakāśan, 1972.

Gupta, Gargī, *Rāmcandrikā kā viśiṣṭ adhyayan*, Dillī: Bhāratī Sāhitya Mandir, 1964.

Gupta, Somnāth, *Pūrva-Bhāratendu nāṭak sāhitya*, Jālandhar–Ilāhābād: Hindī Bhavan, 1958.

Hacker, Paul, 'Zur Entwicklung der Avatārlehre', *Wiener Zeitschrift für die Kunde Südasiens*, vol. 4, 1960, pp. 47–70.

Hansen, Kathryn, *Grounds for Play: The Nauṭaṅkī Theatre of North India*, Delhi: Manohar, 1993.

Hawley, John Stratton, *Three Bhakti Voices: Mirabai, Surdas, and Kabir in Their Time and Ours*, Delhi: Oxford University Press, 2005.

—— and Donna Wulff, eds, *The Divine Consort: Rādhā and the Goddesses of India*, Boston: Beacon Press, 1982.

Heesterman, J.C., 'The Conundrum of the King's Authority', in Richards, *Kingship and Authority in South Asia*, pp. 13–40.

Hertel, Bradley R. and Cynthia Ann Humes, ed., *Living Banaras: Hindu Religion in Cultural Context*, 1st Indian edn, Delhi: Manohar.

Hess, Linda, 'Staring at Frames Till They Turn into Loops: An Excursion through Some Worlds of Tulsidas', in Hertel and Humes, *Living Banaras*, pp. 73–101.

Hill, W. Douglas, *The Holy Lake of the Acts of Rama: A Translation of Tulasī Dās's Rāmcaritmānas*, Calcutta: Oxford University Press, 1952.

Hopkins, Edward Washburn, 'Allusions to the Rama Story in the Mahābhārata', *Journal of the American Oriental Society*, vol. 50, no. 2, 1930, pp. 85–103.

Horstmann, Monika, ed., Bhakti in Current Research, 2001–2003 (Proceedings of the Ninth International Conference on Early Devotional Literature in New Indo-Aryan Languages, Heidelberg, 23–26 July 2003), Delhi: Manohar, 2006.

Iyengar, K.R. Srinivasa, Asian Variations in Ramayana, Delhi: Sahitya Akademi, 2003 (1st published 1983).

Jacobi, Hermann, *Das Rāmāyaṇa*, Bonn: Verlag von Friedrich Cohen, 1893.

Janārdan, 'Prajñapuruṣ Rām ke antarjagat kī dvandva-kathā "Saṁśay kī ek rāt"', *Hindustānī*, vol. 41, no. 2, 1980, pp. 46–51.

Jordens, J.T.F., *Dayānanda Sarasvatī: His Life and Ideas*, Delhi: Oxford University Press, 1978.

Joshi, Devdatta, 'Contemporary Rāmāyaṇa Tradition in Gujarat', *Journal of the Oriental Institute* (Baroda), vol. 37, nos 3–4, 1988, pp. 231–51.

Kabīr, *Bījak*, ed. Śukdev Siṁh, Ilāhābād: Nīlābh Prakāśan, 1972.

Kakar, Sudhir, *The Inner World: A Psycho-analytic Study of Childhood and Society in India*, 2nd edn, Delhi: Oxford University Press, 1988.

Kamba–Rāmāyaṇa, tr. Shanti Lal Nagar, Delhi: Parimal Publications, 2008.

Kapur, Anuradha, *Actors, Pilgrims, Kings and Gods: The Ramlila at Ramnagar*, Calcutta: Seagull Books, 1990.

——, 'Deity to Crusader: The Changing Iconography of Ram', in Pandey, *Hindus and Others*, pp. 74–107.

Kāsalīvāl, Kastūrcand, *Mahākavi Daulatrām Kāsalīvāl: vyaktitva aur kṛtitva*, Jaypur: Sāhitya Śodh Vibhāg, 1974.

Kauśik, Ṛṣi Jaiminī 'Baruā', ed., *Rāṣṭrakavi Maithilīśaraṇ Gupta abhinandangranth*, Kalkattā: M.G. Abhinandan Samiti, 1959 (A).

——, *Rāṣṭrakavi Maithilīśaraṇ Gupta abhinandangranth*, Kalkattā: Jaiminī Prakāśan, 1959 (B).

Keislar, Allan M., 'The *Rasik* Concept of Transcendental Sexuality', in Entwistle, *Studies in Early Modern Indo-Aryan Languages*, pp. 179–98.

Kellogg, S.H., *A Grammar of the Hindi Language*, London: Routledge & Kegan Paul, 1965 (1st edn in 1875).

Kesavan, B.S. and Y.M. Mulay, *The National Bibliography of Indian Literature 1903–1953 (comprising Hindi, Kannada, Kashmiri, Malayalam)*, Delhi: Sahitya Akademi, 1966.

King, Christopher, *One Language, Two Scripts: The Hindi Movement in Nineteenth Century North India*, Bombay: Oxford University Press, 1994.

Kohlī, Narendra, *Abhijñān*, Dillī: Rājpāl eṇḍ Sanz, 1981.

——, *Mahāsamar – 1 (Bandhan)*, Dillī: Vāṇī Prakāśan, 1988.

——, *Mahāsamar – 2 (Adhikār)*, Dillī: Vāṇī Prakāśan, 1990.

——, *Mahāsamar – 3 (Karm)*, Dillī: Vāṇī Prakāśan, 1991

——, *Mahāsamar – 4 (Dharm)*, Dillī: Vāṇī Prakāśan, 1993.

——, *Mahāsamar – 5 (Antarāl)*, Dillī: Vāṇī Prakāśan, 1995.

——, *Mahāsamar – 6 (Pracchanna)*, Dillī: Vāṇī Prakāśan, 1997.

——, *Mahāsamar – 7 (Pratyakṣ)*, Dillī: Vāṇī Prakāśan, 1998.

——, *Mahāsamar – 8 (Nirbandh)*, Dillī: Vāṇī Prakāśan, 2000.

Kulkarni, V.M., *The Story of Rāma in Jain Literature as Presented by the Śvetāmbara and Digambara Poets in the Prakrit, Sanskrit and Apabhraṁśa Languages*, Ahmedabad: Saraswati Pustak Bhandar, 1990.

——, 'Jain Rāmāyaṇas and Their Source', in Raghavan, *The Ramayana Tradition*, pp. 226–41.

Kumār, Vinod, *Govind Rāmāyaṇ: Guru Govind Siṁh praṇit Rāmāvatār kathā*, Delhi: Sanmārg Prakāśan, 1969.

Kumāradāsa, *Jānakīharaṇa: Study, Critical Text and English Translation of Cantos XVI–XX*, ed. & tr. C.R. Swaminathan, Delhi: Motilal Banarsidass, 1977.

Lienhard, Siegfried, *A History of Classical Poetry: Sanskrit-Pali-Prakrit*, Wiesbaden: Otto Harrassowitz, 1984.

Lönne, Dirk W., ed., *Toḥfa-e-dil: Festschrift Helmut Nespital*, Reinbek: Dr. Inge Wezler Verlag für Orientalistische Fachpublikationen, 2001.

Lorenzen, David N., *Kabir Legends and Anantadas's Kabir Parachai*, Albany: State University of New York Press, 1991.

——, *Praises to a Formless God*, New York: State University of New York, 1996.

——, ed., *Bhakti Religion in North India: Community Identity and Political Action*, Albany: State University of New York, 1995.

——, 'Introduction: The Historical Vicissitudes of Bhakti Religion', in idem, *Bhakti Religion in North India*, pp. 1–32.

Lutgendorf, Philip, *The Life of a Text: Performing the* Rāmcaritmānas *of Tulsidas*, 1st Indian edn, Delhi: Oxford University Press, 1994.

——, *Hanuman's Tale: The Message of a Divine Monkey*, New York: Oxford University Press, 2007.

——, 'The View from the Ghats: Traditional Exegesis of a Hindu Epic', *Journal of Asian Studies*, vol. 48, no. 2, 1989, pp. 272–88.

——, 'The Secret Life of Rāmcandra of Ayodhya', in Richman, *Many Rāmāyaṇas*, pp. 217–34.

——, 'The Quest for the Legendary Tulsīdās', in Callewaert and Snell, *According to Tradition*, pp. 65–85.

——, 'Interpreting Rāmrāj: Reflections on the *Rāmāyaṇa*: Bhakti, and Hindu Nationalism', in Lorenzen, *Bhakti Religion in North India*, pp. 253–87.

Macfie, J.M., *The Ramayan of Tulsidas or the Bible of Northern India*, Edinburgh: T. & T. Clark, 1930.

Madān, Indranāth, *Samkālīn sāhitya: ek naī dṛṣṭi*, Dillī: Lipi Prakāśan, 1977.

Mādhava Kandalī Rāmāyaṇa, tr. Shanti Lal Nagar, 2 vols, Delhi: Munshiram Manoharlal, 2000.

Mahendra, Rāmcaraṇ, *Seṭh Govinddās: nāṭya, kalā tathā kṛtiyā̃*, Dillī: Bhāratī Sāhitya Mandir, n.d. [1956?].

Mainkar, G., *The Vāsiṣṭha Rāmāyaṇa: A Study*, Delhi: Meharchand Lachhmandas: 1977.

Māthur, Harsvarūp, *Bhāratīy sādhanā aur Sant Tulsī*, Kānpur: Sāhitya Niketan, 1965.

McGregor, Ronald Stuart, *Hindi Literature of the Nineteenth and Early Twentieth Centuries*, Wiesbaden: Otto Harrassowitz, 1974.

——, *Hindi Literature from Its Beginnings*, Wiesbaden: Otto Harrassowitz, 1984.

——, 'The *Dhyān-mañjarī* of Agradās', in Thiel-Horstmann, *Bhakti in Current Research*, pp. 237–44.

——, 'An Early Hindi (Braj-bhāṣā) Version of the Rāma Story: The Rāmāyaṇkathā (A.D. 1442) of Viṣṇudās', in Eck and Mallison, *Devotion Divine*, pp. 181–90.

——, 'Viṣṇudās and His Rāmāyan-kathā', in Entwistle, *Studies in Early Modern Indo-Aryan Languages*, pp. 239–47.

——, 'The Rama Story and Rama Devotion in North India', Vyas, *Ramayana: Its Universal Appeal and Global Role*, pp. 16–21.

——, 'The Progress of Hindi, part 1: The Development of a Transregional Idiom', Pollock, *Literary Cultures in History*, pp. 912–57.

McLeod, W.H., *Historical Dictionary of Sikhism*, Delhi: Oxford University Press, 2002 (1st published 1995).

Meletinsky, Eleazar M., *Poėtika mifa*, Moskva: Nauka, 1976.

——, *The Poetics of Myth* (Series 'Theorists of Myth', ed. Robert A. Segal), tr. Guy Lanoue and Alexandre Sadetsky, New York and London: Garland Publishing, 1998.

Menon, A.G. and G.H. Schokker, 'The Conception of Rāma-rājya in South and North Indian Literature', in van den Hoek, *Ritual, State and History in South Asia*, pp. 610–36.

Millis, John, 'Mallik Muhammad Jāyasī: Allegory and Religious Symbolism in His Padmāvat', Ph.D. dissertation, Chicago: University of Chicago, 1984.

Miśra, Baldevprasād, *Tulsīdarśaṇ*, Prayāg: Hindī Sāhitya Sammelan, 1948.

Miśra, Bhagīrath, 'Aiśvaryarūpopāsak maryāda Rāmbhakta kavi', in Śarmā and Snātak, *Hindī sāhitya kā bṛhat itihās*, pp. 270–313.

Miśra, Bhuvaneśvarnāth 'Mādhav', *Rāmbhakti mẽ madhur upāsanā*, Paṭnā: Bihār Rāṣṭrabhāṣā Pariṣad, 1957.

Miśra, Rāmdīn, '"Rāmcandrikā" prabandhakāvya nahī̃ apitu ek nāṭya-prabandha', *Hindustānī*, vol. 26, nos 1–2, 1965, pp. 30–9.

Miśra, Rameścandra, 'Keśav kā vyaktitva aur racnā', in Siṁh, *Keśavdās*, pp. 18–33.

Misra, Vidya Nivas, 'The Ramayana Story in Indian Folklore: Some Significant Innovations', in Iyengar, *Asian Variations in Ramayana*, pp. 100–7.

Monier-Williams, Monier, *A Sanskrit-English Dictionary*, new enl. and improved edn, Delhi: Motilal Banarsidass, 2002 (1st published 1899).

Nagendra, *Sāket: ek adhyayan*, Āgrā: Sāhityaratna Bhaṇḍār, 1960.

——, ed., *Hindī sāhitya kā itihās*, Dillī: Neśanal Pabliśing Hāus, 1986.

Nair, C.N. Sreekantan and Sarah Joseph, *Retelling the Ramayana: Voices from Kerala*, Delhi: Oxford University Press, 2005.

Nandy, Ashis, *The Intimate Enemy: Loss and Recovery of Self Under Colonialism*, Delhi: Oxford University Press, 1993.

Nārāyaṇ, Pītāmbar, Bhāskaran Nāyar, ed., *Hindī-sāhitya-sāriṇī*, Hośyārpur: Viśveśvarānand Saṁsthan, 1971.

'Nirālā' *see* Tripāṭhī, Sūryakant 'Nirālā'

Nowakowska, Monika and Jacek Woźniak, ed., *Theatrum Mirabiliorum Indiae Orientalis: A Volume to Celebrate the 70th Birthday of Professor Maria Krzysztof Byrski* (*Rocznik Orientalistyczny*, vol. 60, no. 2), Warszawa: Dom Wydawniczy Elipsa, 2007.

Ojhā, Daśarath, *Hindī nāṭak-koś*, Dillī: Neśanal Pabliśiṅg Hāus, 1975

Pandey, Gyanendra, ed., *Hindus and Others: The Question of Identity in India Today*, Delhi: Viking, 1993.

Pandey, Raj Bali, *Hindu Saṁskāras: Socio-religious Study of the Hindu Sacraments*, Delhi: Motilal Banarsidass, 1969.

Pāṇḍey, Rāmlakhan, *Tulsīdāsottar hindī rāmsāhitya*, Ilāhābād: Vibhā Prakāśan, 2003 (1st published 1972).

Pāṭhak, Kamlākānt, *Maithilīśaraṇ Gupta: vyakti aur kāvya*, Dillī: Raṇjīt Priṇṭars & Pabliśars, 1960.

Pattanaik, Devdutt, *The Book of Ram*, Delhi: Penguin Books, 2008.

Peterson, Indira V., 'The Rāmāyaṇa of Vālmīki: An Epic of Ancient India', *Religious Studies Review*, vol. 12, no. 2, 1986, pp. 97–102.

Pollock, Sheldon I., 'The Divine King in the Indian Epic', *Journal of the American Oriental Society*, vol. 104, no. 3, 1984, pp. 505–28.

——, 'The Rāmāyaṇa Text and the Critical Edition', in Goldman, *The Rāmāyaṇa of Vālmīki*, vol. 1, pp. 82–93.

——, 'Introduction', in Goldman, *The Rāmāyaṇa of Vālmīki*, vol. 3, pp. 15–54.

——, ed., *Literary Cultures in History: Reconstructions from South Asia*, 1st Indian edn, Delhi: Oxford University Press, 2004.

Prasād, Tapeśvar Nāth, *Madhyakālīn rāmkāvya dhārā par kṛṣṇabhāvnā kā prabhāv*, Vārāṇasī: Caukhambha, 1981.

Premśaṅkar, *Rāmkāvya aur Tulsī: sāṁskṛtik sandarbh mẽ*, Dillī: Neśanal Pabliśiṅg Hāus, 1977.

Pṛthvīrāj rāsau, ed. Mātā Prasād Gupta, Cirgā̃v (Jhā̃sī): Sāhitya-Sādan, 1963.

Raghavan, V., *The Rāmāyaṇa: In Classical Sanskrit and Prākṛt Mahākāvya Literature*, Chennai: Dr. V. Raghavan Centre for Performing Arts (Regd.), 2004.

——, 'The Ramayana in Sanskrit Literature', in Raghavan, *The Ramayana Tradition in Asia*, pp. 1–19.

——, ed., *The Ramayana Tradition in Asia*, Delhi: Sahitya Akademi, 1980.

Rai, Alok, *Hindi Nationalism*, Delhi: Orient Longman, 2001.

Rai, Amrit, *A House Divided: The Origin and Development of Hindi/Hindavi*, Delhi: Oxford University Press, 1984.

Rājūrkar, B.H., *Rāmkathā ke patr (Vālmīki, Tulsī evam Maithilīśaraṇ Gupta ke sandarbh mẽ)*, Kānpur: Grantham, 1972.

Rāma the Steadfast: An Early Form of the Rāmāyaṇa, tr. John Brockington and Mary Brockington, London: Penguin, 2006.

Ramakrishnan, *The Epic Muse: The Ramayana and the Paradise Lost*, Delhi: People's Publishing House, 1977.

Ramanujan, A.K., 'Three Hundred *Rāmāyaṇas*: Five Examples and Three Thoughts on Translation', in Richman, *Many Rāmāyaṇas*, pp. 22–49.

Rāmāvatāracarita, tr. Shanti Lal Nagar, Delhi: Munshiram Manoharlal, 2001.

Rastogī, Śiv Avatār, 'Tulsī aur *Vinaypatrikā*', in Ārya and Agravāl, *Tulsī mānas sandarbh*, pp. 405–11.

Rāy, Gopāl, 'Sāhitya mẽ lālūvād', *Samīkṣā*, January–March 1992, pp. 2–4.

Reynolds, Frank E., 'Rāmāyaṇa, Rāma Jātaka, and Ramakien: A Comparative Study of Hindu and Buddhist Traditions', in Richman, *Many Rāmāyaṇas*, pp. 50–63.

Richards, J.F., ed., *Kingship and Authority in South Asia*, Delhi: Oxford University Press, 1998 (1st published 1978).

Richman, Paula, 'E.V. Ramasami's Reading of the Rāmāyaṇa', in idem, *Many Rāmāyaṇas*, pp. 175–201.

——, ed., *Many Rāmāyaṇas: The Diversity of a Narrative Tradition in South Asia*, Delhi: Oxford University Press, 1991.

——, ed., *Questioning Rāmāyaṇas: A South Asian Tradition*, Delhi: Oxford University Press, 2003.

Richmond, Farley P., 'Characteristics of the Modern Theatre', in idem, *Indian Theatre: Traditions of Performance*, pp. 387–406.

—— et al., eds, *Indian Theatre: Traditions of Performance*, 1st Indian edn, Delhi: Motilal Banarsidass, 1993.

Rocher, Ludo, *The Purāṇas*, Wiesbaden: Otto Harrassowitz, 1986.

Ruben, Walter, *Studien zur Textgeschichte des Rāmāyaṇa*, Stutgart: W. Kohlhammer, 1936.

Rūpkalā, Sītārāmśaraṇ Bhagvānprasād, *Śrībhaktamāl*, 8th edn, Tejkumār Bukḍipo–Navalkiśor Bukḍipo: Lakhnaū 2005.

Śāh, Umākānt Premānand, 'Ma. Viśvanāth Siṁh praṇīt "Saṅgīt Raghunandan"', in Kauśik, *Rāṣṭrakavi Maithilīśaraṇ Gupta abhinandan-granth*, pp. 734–41.

Sahāy, Śivnandan, *Gosvāmī Tulsīdās*, 2nd edn (1st published in 1916), Paṭnā: Bihār Rāṣṭrabhāṣā Pariṣad, 2000.

Saklani, D.P., ed., *Rāmāyaṇa Tradition in Historical Perspective*, Delhi: Pratibha Prakashan, 2006.

Sanāḍhya, Devaṛṣi, *Hindī paurāṇik nāṭak*, Vārāṇasī: Caukhambā Vidyā-bhavan, 1961.

Saṅkṣipt pṛthvīrāj rāso, ed. Hazārīprasād Dvivedī and Nāmvar Siṁh, 8th revd edn, Ilāhābād: Sāhitya Bhavan, 1990.

Sarasvatī, Divyānand, *Mānasvarṇānukramaṇikā*, Ṛṣikeś: Svāmī Divyānand Sarasvatī, 1993.

Śarmā, Ānandnārāyaṇ, 'Kavi Keśavdās', in Siṁh, *Keśavdās*, pp. 41–50.

Śarmā, Ātmārām 'Aruṇ', *Śrī rāmcandroday kāvya: ek satyānveṣaṇparak ākalan*, Dillī: Bhāgyavanti Prakāśan, 2002.

——, 'Śrīrāmcandroday kāvya: samīkṣātmak viśleṣaṇ', *Hindustānī*, vol. 43, no. 3, 1982, pp. 3–10.

——, 'Aruṇ', 'Śrīrāmcandroday kāvya: samīkṣātmak viśleṣaṇ', *Hindustānī*, vol. 48, no. 4, 1987, pp. 29–36.

Śarmā, Devendra and Vijayendra Snātak, eds, *Hindī sāhitya kā bṛhat itihās*, vol. 5, Vārāṇasī: NPS, 1974.

Śarmā, Haricaraṇ, *Nirālā aur Rām kī śakti-pūjā*, Jaypur: The Students' Book Company, 1965.

Śarmā, Rajendra, 'Vāh! Rām – āh! Rām', *Haṁs*, no. 8, 1992, pp. 71–2.

Śarmā, Rāmvilās, *Nirālā kī sāhitya sādhanā*, 3 vols, Dillī: Rājkamal Prakāśan, 1969–72.

Sarma, Satyendra Nath, 'Folk Versions of Rama-katha in Early Assamese', in Singh and Datta, *Rama-katha*, pp. 110–19.

Śarmā, Vinaymohan, ed., *Hindī sāhitya kā bṛhat itihās*, vol. 8, Vārāṇasī: NPS, 1972.

Śāstrī, Rajnīkānt, *Mānas mīmāṁsā*, Ilāhābād: Kitāb Mahal, 1949.

Śāstrī, Vedvrat, 'Tulsī kā jīvanvṛtt', in Ārya and Agravāl, *Tulsī mānas sandarbh*, pp. 1–11.

Saxena, Rajeev, 'Hero Rama and Villain Vasishta', *Indian Literature*, vol. 155, 1993, pp. 193–6.

Sazanova, N.M., *'Okean poėzii' Sur Dasa*, Moskva: Izdatel'stvo Moskovskogo Universiteta, 1973.

Schomer, Karine, *Mahadevi Varma and the Chhayavad Age of Modern Hindi Poetry*, Delhi: Oxford University Press, 1998 (1st published 1983).

Seely Clinton, 'Homeric Similes, Occidental and Oriental: Tasso, Milton, and Bengal's Michael Madhusudan Dutt', *Comparative Literature Studies*, vol. 25, no. 1, 1988, pp. 35–56.

——, 'The Raja's New Clothes: Redressing Rāvaṇa in Meghanādavadha Kāvya', in Richman, *Many Rāmāyaṇas*, pp. 137–55.

Sehgal, N.C., 'Maithilīśaraṇa's Works: A Chronological Survey' in Nagendra, *Maithilīśaraṇa Gupta*, pp. 44–61.

Sekhon, Sant Sikh and Kartar Singh Duggal, *A History of Punjabi Literature*, Delhi: Sahitya Akademi, 1992.

Shackle, Christopher and Rupert Snell, *Hindi and Urdu since 1800: A Common Reader*, London: School of Otriental and African Studies, 1990.

Shah, Umakant P., 'Rāmāyaṇa in Jaina Tradition' in Iyengar, *Asian Variations in Ramayana*, pp. 57–76.

Sharma, Arvind, *Viśiṣṭādvaita Vedānta: A Study*, Delhi: Heritage, 1978.

Shivaramamurti, C., *Rāmo Vigrahavān Dharma: Rāma Embodiment of Righteousness*, Delhi: Kanak Publications, 1980.

Shulman, David, 'Divine Order and Divine Evil in the Tamil Tale of Rama', *Journal of Asian Studies*, vol. 38, no. 4, 1979, pp. 651–69.

——, 'The Fire and Flood: The Testing of Sītā in Kampaṉ's Irāmāvatāram', in Richman, *Many Rāmāyaṇas*, pp. 89–113.

Siṁh, Aniruddh, 'Mahātmā Banādās', in Siṁh, *Rām bhakti sāhitya*, pp. 319–21.

Siṁh, Bhagavatīprasād, *Rāmbhakti mẽ rasik sampradāy*, Avadh Sāhitya Mandir: Balrāmpur, 1957.

——, *Mahātmā Banādās: jīvan aur sāhitya*, Vārāṇāsī: Viśvavidyālay Prakāśan, 1976.

——, *Rāmkāvyadhārā: anusandhān evam anucintan*, Ilāhābād: Lokbhāratī Prakāśan, 1976.

——, 'Rāmlalā nahachū: punarvicār', in Siṁh, *Tulsī: sandarbh aur samīkṣā*, pp. 126–44.

——, 'Bhuśuṇḍi Rāmāyaṇa and Its Influence on the Medieval Rāmāyaṇa Literature', in Raghavan, *The Ramayana Tradition*, pp. 475–504.

——, ed., *Śrī Rām viśvakoś*, vol. 1, Vārāṇasī: Siddhārtha Prakāśan, 1992.

Siṁh, Naṁvar, 'Rāmkathā kī udheṛ-bun', *Haṁs*, no. 8, 1992, pp. 67–71.

Siṁh, Tribhuvan, ed., *Tulsī: sandarbh aur samīkṣā*, Vārāṇasī: Tulsī Śodh Saṁsthān, 1976.

Siṁh, Uday Pratāp, ed., *Rām bhakti sāhitya: anveṣak aur rāhī (Pro. Bhagavatī Siṁh jīvan aur darśan)*, Mahātmā Banādās Sevā Samiti: Ayodhyā, 1999.

Siṁh, Vijaynārāyaṇ, *Tulsī ke rāmkathā kāvya*, Dillī: Granthalok, 2007.

Siṁh, Vijaypāl, *Keśav aur unkā sāhitya*, Dillī: Rājpāl eṇḍ Sanz, 1961.

——, ed., *Keśavdās*, Dillī: Rādhākṛṣṇa Prakāśan, 1970.

Singer, M., ed., *Krishna: Myths. Rites and Attitudes*, Chicago: University of Chicago Press, 1968, pp. 47–63.

Singh, Avadhesh Kumar, 'Rāma, His Carita, Mānasa and Kathā', in idem, *Rāmāyaṇa Through the Ages*, pp. 1–46.

——, ed., *Rāmāyaṇa Through the Ages – Rāma-Gathā in Different Versions*, Delhi: D.K. Printworld, 2007.

Singh, B.P. *see* Siṁh, Bhagavatīprasād

Singh, K.S. and Birendranath Datta, eds, *Rama-katha in Tribal and Folk Traditions of India*, Calcutta: Seagull Books, 1993.

Singh, Rāma Dhārī 'Dinkara', 'Maithilīśaraṇa Gupta as a Poet of the Renaissance', in Nagendra, ed., *Maithilīśaraṇa Gupta: An Anthology*, Delhi: Bansal & Co., 1981, pp. 91–112.

Sītārām, 'Satyavatī kathā', *Hindustānī*, vol. 6, no. 4, Aktūbar 1936, pp. 464–5.

Słuszkiewicz, Eugeniusz, *Przyczynki do badań nad dziejami redakcyj Rāmāyaṇy*, Kraków: Polska Akademia Umiejętności, 1938.

Smith, W.L., *Rāmāyaṇa Traditions in Eastern India: Assam, Bengal, Orissa*, Delhi: Munshiram Manoharlal, 1994 (1st published 1988).

——, 'Mahiravana and the Womb Demon', *Indologica Taurinensia*, vol. 10, 1982, pp. 215–22.

Snātak, Vijayendra, *Hindī sāhitya kā itihās*, Dillī: Sāhitya Akādemī, 1996.

Snell, R., *The Hindi Classical Tradition: A Braj Bhāṣā Reader*, London: School of Oriental and African Languages, 1991.

——, '"*Barvai*" Metre in Tulsīdās and Rahīm', in Entwistle and Mallison, ed., *Studies in South Asian Devotional Literature*, pp. 373–405.

Śrīvāstav, Devakīnandan, *Tulsīdās kī bhāṣā*, Lakhnaū: Lakhnaū Viśvavidyālay, 1957.

Stasik, Danuta, *Opowieść o prawym królu. Tradycja Ramajany w literaturze hindi*, Warszawa: Wydawnictwo Akademickie Dialog, 2000.

——, 'The Divine Marriage: the Nuptials of Rām and Sītā as Seen by Tulsī', *Cracow Indological Studies*, vol. 1, 1994, pp. 245–51.

——, 'On Modern Retellings of Rām-kathā in Hindi Literature: Bhagvān Siṁh's Novel "Apne apne Rām"', *Berliner Indologische Studien*, nos 11/12, 1998, pp. 259–68.

——, 'Text and Context: Two Versions of *Rāmlalānahachū*', in Entwistle, *Studies in Early Modern Indo-Aryan Languages*, pp. 379–92.

——, 'Tulsidas' Vision of the Nuptials of Ram and Sita', *Hindi: Language, Discourse, Writing*, vol. 1, nos 3–4, October 2000 – March 2001, pp. 295–306.

——, 'On the Nature of Rāma in Tulsīdās's Rāmcaritmānas', in Lönne, *Toḥfa-e-dil*, pp. 487–500.

——, 'Modernising the Rāmāyaṇa Tradition: M. Gupta's *Sāket*', in idem and John Brockington, eds, *Indian Epic Traditions: Past and Present*, Warszawa: Wydawnictwo Naukowe PWN, 2002 (*Rocznik Orientalistyczny*, vol. 54, no. 1), pp. 159–72.

——, 'Before Tulsīdās: The Beginnings of the Rāmāyaṇa Tradition in Hindi Literature', *Rocznik Orientalistyczny*, vol. 55, no. 2, 2003, pp. 87–95.

——, 'Gniew boży w hinduizmie – na przykładzie poematu Ramćaritmanas' (in Polish), in Duszak and Pawlak, *Anatomia gniewu*, pp. 75–83.

——, 'Sāket: Maithilīśaraṇ Gupta's Version of Rām-kathā', in Balcerowicz and Mejor, *Essays in Indian Philosophy, Religion and Literature*, pp. 51–7.

——, 'Crow Bhuśuṇḍi and His Story of the Deeds of Rām', Stasik and Trynkowska, *India in Warsaw*, pp. 293–9.

——, 'God's Anger: Notes on the Nature of Tulsīdās's Rām', in Horstmann, *Bhakti in Current Research*, pp. 295–304.

——, 'In the World of Tulsīdās's *rām-kathās*', *Rocznik Orientalistyczny*, vol. 58, no. 2, 2006, pp. 114–31.

——, 'On the Threshold of Modern Hindi Drama? A Few Remarks on *Ānand Raghunandan*', in Nowakowska and Woźniak, *Theatrum Mirabiliorum Indiae Orientalis*, pp. 362–7.

——, 'He Who Dwells in the Hearts of All: Notes on the Nature of Rām in Hindi Literature', *Archiv orientální/Oriental Archive*, vol. 75, no. 3, 2007, pp. 305–27.

—— and John Brockington, eds, *Indian Epic Traditions – Past and Present* (*Rocznik Orientalistyczny*, vol. 54, no. 1, 2002).

—— and Anna Trynkowska, eds, *India in Warsaw: A Volume to Commemorate the 50th Anniversary of the Post-War History of Indological Studies at Warsaw University (2003/2004)*, Warszawa: Dom Wydawniczy Elipsa, 2006.

Śukla Śrī Lalit, 'Śabarī āj bhī sārthak hai', *Hindustānī,* vol. 50, no. 1, 1989, pp. 77–9.

Śukla, Rāmcandra, *Hindī sāhitya kā itihās,* 13th edn, Kāśī: NPS, 1961.

———, *Gosvāmī Tulsīdās,* 2nd edn, Vārāṇasī: NPS, 1983.

Suryakant, *Index Verborum to Tulasī-dāsa's Rāmāyaṇa,* Delhi: Meharchand Lachhmandas, 1973 (1st published in 1937).

Tagare, G.V., 'Introduction', in *The Yogavāsiṣṭha of Vālmīki,* ed. Vasudeva Laxmaṇa Sharma Pansikar, Delhi: Motilal Banarsidass, 1984 (1st published 1918).

Taṅkamaṇi Ammā, 'Keral mẽ rāmsaṁskṛti', in Siṁh, *Śrī Rām viśvakoś,* pp. 543–51.

Thapar, Romila, 'A Historical Perspective on the Story of Rama', in Sarvepalli Gopal, ed., *Anatomy of Confrontation: The Babri Masjid–Ram Janmabhumi Issue,* 2nd edn, Delhi: Penguin Books, 1993, pp. 141–63.

The Adhyatma Ramayana, tr. Rai Bahadur Baij Nath, Delhi: Oriental Reprint, 1979 (1st published 1913).

The Jātaka or Stories of the Buddha Former Births, ed. E.B. Cowell, Oxford: The Pali Text Society, 1990 (rpt), vol. 4.

The Rámáyana of Tulsi Dás, tr. F.S. Growse, 6th edn, Allahabad: Ram Narain Lal, 1914.

Thiel-Horstmann, Monika, ed., *Bhakti in Current Research, 1979–1982,* Berlin: Dietrich Reimer Verlag, 1983.

Tivārī, Balbhadra, *Kavivar Viṣṇudās aur unkī rāmāyan kathā,* Ilāhābād: Sāhitya Bhavan, 1976.

Tivārī, Gopīnāth, *Bhāratendu kālīn nāṭak sāhitya (1850–1900 ī.),* Jālandhar–Ilāhābād: Hindī Bhavan, 1959.

Tiwari, B.D., 'Hindi Versions of the Ramayana', in Iyengar, *Asian Variations in Ramayana,* pp. 83–99.

Tokarz, Franciszek, *Z filozofii indyjskiej. Kwestie wybrane,* 2nd edn, part 1, Lublin: Towarzystwo Naukowe KUL, 1990.

Tomar, Mohansiṁh, *Hindī rāmkāvya aur Viṣṇudās kī rāmāyan kathā,* Dillī: Takṣaśilā Prakāśan, 1979.

Torvey Rāmāyaṇa, tr. Shantilal Nagar, Delhi: B.R. Publishing Corporation, 2004.

Trīpāṭhī, Rāmnareś, *Tulsī aur unkā kāvya,* rev. edn, Dillī: Rājpāl eṇḍ Sanz, 1953.

Tripāṭhī, Vyāsmaṇi, *Rāmcandrikā mẽ nāṭya tatva,* Dillī: Sākṣī Prakāśan, 2003.

Tripathi, Surya Kant Nirala, *A Season on the Earth: Selected Poems of Nirala,* trans. David Rubin, New York: Columbia University Press, 1976.

Trivedī, Śivāśaṅkar, *Ācārya Śrī Tulsī kṛt 'Agniparīkṣā' kī agniparīkṣā*, Sardāśahar: Śivāśaṅkar Trivedī, Sṛjancetnā, 1970.

Tulpule, Shankar Gopal, *Classical Marāṭhī Literature: From the Beginning to A.D. 1818*, Wiesbaden: Otto Harrassowitz, 1979.

Tulsi Baljit, 'Rāmāvatār (Rāmāyaṇa) by Guru Gobind Singh', in Raghavan, *The Ramayana Tradition*, pp. 517–32.

Tulsī Dās, *Kavitāvalī*, tr. F.R. Allchin, London: George Allen & Unwin, 1964.

——, *The Petition to Rām: Hindi Devotional Hymns of the Seventeenth Century*, tr. F.R. Allchin, London: George Allen & Unwin, 1966.

Uddīn, Nizām, 'Tulsī aur Keśav', in Ārya and Agravāl, *Tulsī mānas sandarbh*, pp. 383–92.

van Daalen, Leendert A., 'Remarks on the Princeton Translation of Vālmīki Rāmāyaṇa, esp. on vol. III by Sh.I. Pollock', *Indologica Taurinensia*, vols 19–20, 1993–4, pp. 79–92.

van den Hoek, A.W. et al., eds, *Ritual, State and History in South Asia: Essays in Honour of J.C. Heesterman*, Leiden: E.J. Brill, 1992.

van der Veer, Peter, *Gods on Earth: The Management of Religious Experience and Identity in a North Indian Pilgrimage Centre*, London–Atlantic Highlands, NJ: Athlone Press, 1988.

——, 'The Politics of Devotion to Rāma', in Lorenzen, *Bhakti Religion in North India*, pp. 288–305.

Varmā, Dhīrendra et al. eds, *Hindī sāhitya*, 3 vols, Prayāg: Bhāratīy Hindī Pariṣad, 1959–69.

——, *Hindī sāhitya koś*, 2 vols, Vārāṇasī: Jñān Maṇḍal, 1985–6.

Varmā, Rāmkumār, *Hindī sāhitya kā ālocnātmak itihās (saṁvat 750–1750)*, 5th edn, Ilāhābād: Rāmnārāyaṇ Lāl Benī Mādhav, 1964.

Varmā, Vimal, 'Khoe hue kāl kī khoj', *Sāmayik paridṛśya*, nos 4–5, 1995, pp. 175–85.

Vaudeville, Charlotte, *Étude sur les sources et la composition du Rāmāyaṇa de Tulsī-dās*, Paris: Adrien-Maisonneuve, 1955.

——, *Kabīr*, vol. 1, Oxford: Oxford University Press, 1974.

Vedalankar, Shardadevi, *The Development of Hindi Prose Literature in the Early Nineteenth Century (1800–1856 A.D.)*, Allahabad: Lokbharati Publications, 1969.

Venugopal, Saraswathi, 'Ramayana Episodes in South Indian Folk Literature', in Singh and Datta, *Rama-katha*, pp. 100–10.

Vijayendra Snātak, *Hindī sāhitya kā itihās*, Dillī: Sāhitya Akādemī, 1996.

Vijayśrī, *Adhyātma rāmāyaṇa: ek vivecanātmak adhayan*, Dillī: Alaṅkār Prakāśan, 1979.

Viśvanāth, ed., *Hindu samāj ke pathbhraṣṭak Tulsīdās*, Dillī: Viśvavijay Prakāśan, n.d.

von Glasenapp, Helmuth, 'Zwei philosophische Rāmāyaṇas', *Abhandlungen der Geistes- und Sozialwissenschaftlichen Klasse* (Akademie der Wissenschaften und der Literatur in Mainz), 1951, pp. 5–98.

Vyas, Lallan Prasad, ed., *Ramayana: Its Universal Appeal and Global Role*, Delhi: Har-Anand Publications, 1992.

Warder, A.K., *Indian Kāvya Literature*, 2nd edn, vols 2–4, Delhi: Motilal Banarsidass, 1990–4.

Weber, Albrecht, *Über das Rāmāyaṇa*, Berlin: F.R. Dümmler, 1870.

Weimann, Robert, *Literaturgeschichte und Mythologie: methodologische und historische Studien*, Berlin: Aufbau-Verlag, 1971.

Whaling, Frank, *The Rise of the Religious Significance of Rama*, Delhi: Motilal Banarsidass, 1980.

White, John J., *Mythology in the Modern Novel: A Study of Prefigurative Techniques*, Princeton: Princeton University Press, 1971.

Winternitz, M., *A History of Indian Literature*, vol. 1, Calcutta: University of Calcutta, 1927.

Wirtz, Hans, *Die westliche Rezension des Rāmāyaṇa*, Bonn: Universitäts-Buchdruckerei von Carl Georgi, 1894.

Yajnik, Hasu, 'The Oral Tradition of Rāmkathā in Gujarātī Folk Songs', in Entwistle, *Studies in Early Modern Indo-Aryan Languages, Literature and Culture*, pp. 411–16.

Zbavitel, Dušan, *Bengali Literature*, Wiesbaden: Otto Harrassowitz, 1976.

Zograf, G.A., *Chindustani na rubeže XVIII i XIX vv.*, Moskva: Izdatel'stvo vostočnoj literatury, 1961.

Zvelebil, Kamil Veith, *Tamil Literature*, Wiesbaden: Otto Harrassowitz, 1974.

INDEX